HOW
THE COLD WAR
BEGAN

HOW
THE COLD WAR
BEGAN

THE IGOR GOUZENKO AFFAIR AND THE
HUNT FOR SOVIET SPIES

With an Author's Note for U.S. Readers

AMY KNIGHT

CARROLL & GRAF PUBLISHERS
NEW YORK

HOW THE COLD WAR BEGAN
The Igor Gouzenko Affair and the Hunt for Soviet Spies

Carroll & Graf Publishers
An Imprint of Avalon Publishing Group, Inc.
245 West 17th Street, 11th Floor
New York, NY 10011

AVALON
publishing group incorporated

Copyright © 2005 by Amy Knight

Published by arrangement with McClelland & Stewart Ltd., Toronto, Ontario, Canada
First Carroll & Graf edition 2006

Library of Congress Cataloging-in-Publication Data is available.

ISBN-10: 0-78671-816-1
ISBN-13: 978-0-78671-816-0

9 8 7 6 5 4 3 2 1

Printed in the United States of America
Distributed by Publishers Group West

To Molly Knight Raskin

CONTENTS

CHRONOLOGY OF MAIN EVENTS
IN THE GOUZENKO AFFAIR

June 1943	Igor Gouzenko arrives in Ottawa with GRU team.
October 1943	Anna Gouzenko joins her husband.
September 1944	Gouzenko hears he is being called back to Moscow. His boss Zabotin manages a postponement.
August 6, 1945	United States detonates atomic bomb on Hiroshima.
September 5, 1945	Gouzenko leaves the Soviet Embassy for the last time, with the intention of defecting.
September 6, 1945	Canadian prime minister William Lyon Mackenzie King learns of the defection.
September 7, 1945	Gouzenko arrives at RCMP headquarters for debriefing.
September 29, 1945	Mackenzie King travels to Washington to meet President Harry Truman.
November 8, 1945	Elizabeth Bentley signs her first statement, revealing an espionage network in Washington and New York.
February 3, 1946	Drew Pearson breaks the Canadian spy story.
February 13, 1946	Royal Commission on Espionage begins taking testimony from Gouzenko.
February 15, 1946	Canadian spy suspects arrested and interrogation by the RCMP begins.
March 2, 1946	The first of the spy suspects is formally charged.
March 4, 1946	First Interim Report of Royal Commission appears.
March 5, 1946	Alan Nunn May arrested in London; Winston Churchill gives his "Iron Curtain" speech in Fulton, Missouri.

June 1946	Fred Rose trial and conviction.
July 1946	Final Report of Royal Commission on Espionage appears; last of Soviet diplomats suspected of spying leave Canada.
March 1946–1947	Trials of Canadian spy suspects.
January 1947–July 1948	U.S. Federal Grand Jury hears testimony from Bentley and Whittaker Chambers.
August 1948	Harry Dexter White testifies before HUAC; dies.
November 1948	Chambers produces documents to back up his charges against Hiss.
December 1948	Alger Hiss indicted for perjury before a Grand Jury.
January 1949	FBI arrests Sam Carr.
May 1949	Senator Pat McCarran's Subcommittee on Immigration interviews Gouzenko in Ottawa.
May–July 1949	First Hiss perjury trial, ending in a hung jury.
January 1950	Hiss found guilty and sentenced to five years in prison; Klaus Fuchs confesses to espionage.
September 1950	FBI requests report on Herbert Norman from RCMP.
May 1951	Donald Maclean and Guy Burgess defect to Soviet Union.
August 1951	Herbert Norman mentioned in Senate Internal Security Subcommittee (SISS) hearings.
March 1953	Stalin dies.
January 1954	SISS takes testimony from Gouzenko in Ottawa.
March 1957	Norman's name again brought up at SISS hearings.
April 4, 1957	Norman commits suicide.
January 1963	Kim Philby defects to Moscow.
June 1982	Gouzenko dies.

NOTE: I have used the Library of Congress system of transliteration from the Russian Cyrillic. Exceptions are well-known names, such as Gouzenko, which appear in the more familiar Anglicized forms.

AUTHOR'S NOTE

When I first started my research on the Gouzenko affair, I did not expect that it would involve rethinking the sensational Alger Hiss case, which polarized American public opinion during the McCarthy era and aroused heated debate among historians in the United States in the past five decades. Ever since new documentation emerged in the 1990s, said to prove conclusively that Hiss was a spy, many historians have considered the Hiss case closed.

But a close scrutiny of this new evidence—prompted by my suspicion that the FBI distorted statements made by Gouzenko to help make their case against Hiss—led me to join the small minority of Cold War scholars who remained unconvinced that Hiss was a Soviet agent. The first supposedly definitive proof against Hiss was the now famous March 30, 1945 telegram from the Soviet intelligence chief in Washington, Anatolii Gorsky, to Moscow headquarters. Gorsky's message, deciphered by the U.S. National Security Agency (as part of a secret program called Venona) and made public in 1995, contained references to a spy code-named "Ales," who was said to be Alger Hiss. As I explain in this book, there were actually far too many uncertainties of meaning in that fragmented message to come to any conclusions about the identity of Ales.

Since my book was published in Canada last year, the NSA has released the original Russian version of the decryption. Far from resolving the ambiguities, as many had hoped, the original makes it even more doubtful that "Ales" was Alger Hiss. To mention one example: the Russian text makes it clear that the group of spies run by Ales consisted of his family members. They had for many years provided such valuable military secrets to the Soviets that they were awarded decorations. It is highly improbable that Hiss's family could have had any military information worth sharing with the Soviets. Hiss's wife, Priscilla, was a stay-at-home mother, and his brother Donald a lawyer for the State Department.

The other much-cited evidence against Hiss appeared in a book called *The Haunted Wood* by Allen Weinstein (currently the archivist of the United States) and Alexander Vassiliev (a former KGB officer), published in 1999 and based on documents that Vassiliev consulted in the KGB archives. The fact that several of the messages from Soviet intelligence operatives reproduced in The *Haunted Wood* contained references to Alger Hiss led readers to the conclusion that he was a spy. But it turned out that the original Soviet messages did not mention Hiss by name. Weinstein inserted the name Hiss in place of the Russian code-name Ales. His co-author later observed that he had warned Weinstein against doing this: "I never saw a document where Hiss would be called Ales or Ales may be called Hiss. I made a point of that to Allen [Weinstein]." In addition, Weinstein omitted from the book two important pieces of documentation, written by the above-mentioned Gorsky, that Vassiliev copied and handed over to him. Gorsky's messages (which came to light only recently) seriously undermine the theory that Hiss was the spy codenamed Ales.

Although these new Russian materials do not prove that Hiss was innocent of charges of spying, they make it clear that his case, one of many touched upon in this book, is far from settled. For those who disdain historical ambiguities, this may come as unwelcome news. But the historian's job is not to come up with absolute truths. As Arthur Schlesinger Jr. recently observed, "history is never a closed book or a final verdict. It is always in the making."[*]

April 2006
Basel, Switzerland

---

*Arthur Schlesinger Jr., "History and National Stupidity," *The New York Review of Books*, April 27, 2006, p. 16. For a discussion among scholars on the Hiss- "Ales" issue, including the recent new evidence, see the postings on the Humanities and Social Sciences Net at www.h-net.org/~hoac, January-February 2004, March 2005, and November 2005. Also see David Lowenthal, "Did Allen Weinstein Get the Alger Hiss Story Wrong?" posted on History News Network at www.hnn.us/articles, May 2, 2005.

INTRODUCTION

The great enemy of the truth is very often not the lie . . . but the myth.

John F. Kennedy

On September 12, 1945, FBI director J. Edgar Hoover sent an urgent letter by special messenger to Matthew Connelly, secretary to U.S. president Harry Truman at the White House.[1] Hoover had some alarming news: The Royal Canadian Mounted Police (RCMP) had informed the FBI that they had learned of an extensive Soviet espionage network in Canada. Their source, a "former employee" of the military attaché's office at the Soviet Embassy in Ottawa, claimed that Stalin's government had made "the obtaining of complete information regarding the atomic bomb the Number One project of Soviet espionage." The source also reported that a British atomic scientist working in Canada, who had spent time at a research laboratory at the University of Chicago and was well acquainted with the process for separating uranium, had been a Soviet spy of long-standing. The scientist had furnished the Soviets with a sample of U233, which was immediately flown to Moscow, and also passed on top secret information about U.S. naval technology.

There was more to this disturbing story. The Soviet source had told the RCMP "an assistant to an Assistant Secretary of State under Mr. Stettinius [Edward Stettinius, U.S. Secretary of State until June 1945]" was "a paid Soviet spy." The spy's name was unknown at the

1

present, but the RCMP was making further inquiries. Hoover told Connelly that "The Canadian situation is being followed closely and any additional information will be brought to the attention of the President and you."

Hoover's letter must have caused considerable consternation at the White House. The bombing of Hiroshima and Nagasaki just a month earlier had demonstrated the terrible destructive power of the atomic bomb. The thought that the Soviets might gain access to the secrets of its production was frightening. On top of that, America's closest ally and neighbor to the north, with whom it shared many secrets, was penetrated by Stalin's spies, and the Kremlin was very possibly getting information about what was going on at the highest levels of decision-making at the State Department. Six days later, Hoover, who had dispatched an FBI agent to Ottawa immediately upon hearing about the case, had enough information to transmit a formal FBI report, "Soviet Espionage Activity," to Frederick Lyon, chief of the Foreign Activity Division at the State Department.[2]

The top secret report, dated September 18, 1945, described the source in Canada. His name was Igor Gouzenko. He was a cipher clerk at the Soviet Embassy, who had "severed all his relations with his employers" on September 5 and was now in hiding with his wife and fifteen-month-old child. Gouzenko had "furnished considerable information regarding Soviet espionage activity directed against the United States and Canada." In addition to the British nuclear expert, there were spies in Canadian government offices and agents in the United States, and an American scientist currently working for the U.S. Navy was being developed as "a possible Soviet agent." Moreover, although Gouzenko had worked for Red Army Intelligence (known as the GRU), he had learned that the other Soviet intelligence branch under the notorious security police, the NKVD, had also "penetrated departments of the various governments."

As for the traitor in the State Department, the FBI report repeated what Hoover had said in his earlier letter to the White House: "an individual identified to date only as *an assistant* to an Assistant Secretary of State under Stettinius is a paid Soviet spy" [italics added]. Up to this point, the RCMP had been debriefing

Gouzenko. But shortly thereafter, the FBI conducted its own interview with the defector. The results were provided in a second FBI report on Soviet espionage, dated September 24, and sent again to the State Department.[3] Anyone who saw both reports would have noticed immediately that the description of the spy in the State Department had changed: "Guzenko [sic] was questioned carefully regarding the possible identity of the individual in the Department of State under Stettinius who is a Soviet spy. Guzenko stated he did not know the man's name but that he had been told that *an Assistant to Stettinius* was a Soviet spy" [italics added].

This change was highly significant, as it narrowed down the list of possible State Department spies considerably. There were many assistants to the six Assistant Secretaries of State, but only a handful of assistants to Stettinius himself. One of them was Alger Hiss, a brilliant Harvard-educated lawyer who had played a key role in the founding of the United Nations. Hiss had been appointed director of the State Department's Office of Special Political Affairs the previous March and had worked directly under Stettinius. A "New Dealer" from the Roosevelt era, Hiss was already on the FBI's radar screen. A former Soviet agent named Whittaker Chambers, an American, had told the FBI that Hiss had been a member of a communist group in the mid-1930s. The statements of the defector in Ottawa gave the Chambers allegations new weight.[4]

But Gouzenko had told the RCMP initially that the spy was an "assistant to an Assistant Secretary of State." This was cited specifically in Hoover's letter to the White House and in the first FBI report, so the FBI must have thought that the RCMP had recorded Gouzenko's statements accurately. Given that the change came after the FBI questioned Gouzenko directly (through a translator), is it possible that the interviewer already had Hiss in mind and suggested to Gouzenko that he might in fact be talking about an assistant to Stettinius? Whatever the truth (and we will probably never know), this seemingly minor alteration in Gouzenko's description would acquire huge significance. The charges that Hiss was a Soviet agent took hold, and his case eventually became a *cause célèbre* for both sides of the American political spectrum in the turbulent McCarthy era.

The spy in the U.S. State Department, however much it preoccupied Hoover, was just one element of a case that would involve Canada, Britain, and the United States in a concerted and protracted effort to respond to the threat of Soviet spying. For the Canadians, the immediate problem was what to do about their over twenty civil servants and scientists implicated by Gouzenko. And the British, of course, had to deal with Gouzenko's allegation that one of their top atomic experts was engaged in espionage. In short, the Gouzenko defection, which remained a closely guarded secret, quickly assumed enormous proportions for those in the upper echelons of the three allied governments. Indeed, Canadian prime minister William Lyon Mackenzie King was so alarmed by Gouzenko's revelations that he traveled to Washington to see President Truman personally at the end of September and then continued to London to discuss the problem with newly elected British prime minister Clement Attlee. For the next several months, in the corridors of the White House, Whitehall, and the Canadian Parliament Buildings, the revelations of Igor Gouzenko would be a source of deep concern.

Gouzenko was not the first Soviet defector to emerge from Stalin's intelligence apparatus with claims about Soviet espionage. Before him was Walter Krivitsky, a rather shadowy figure who had worked for Soviet military intelligence in the Netherlands as an "illegal," or an agent under deep cover, in the 1930s. Krivitsky sought political asylum in France in 1937 and showed up in the United States late in 1938. The FBI was not particularly interested in him, perhaps because what he said was marred by exaggerations and inconsistencies and because his first step was to sell his sensational story to the *Saturday Evening Post*. But when he mentioned that the Soviets had a spy in the British government, he was invited to England for a debriefing. Krivitsky's claim that a young British aristocrat was a Soviet mole in the Foreign Office turned out to be true (he was talking about Donald Maclean, one of the notorious "Cambridge Five" spies). But at the time MI5 (Britain's counterintelligence service, similar to the FBI) was also skeptical about the defector. Sir

Dick White, who would later become MI5's director, observed, "I did not wholly trust Krivitsky. He wasn't using his real name and he wasn't a general. He hadn't mastered enough to give us a proper lead."[5] In 1939, Krivitsky published a book, *In Stalin's Secret Service*, about his life as a spy. But once the Soviet Union entered the war against the Nazis, there was less interest in what Krivitsky had to say. As his currency declined in value, Krivitsky became increasingly despondent. In 1941, he committed suicide.[6]

Another high-profile defector was Viktor Kravchenko, an employee of the Soviet Purchasing Agency in New York. Kravchenko announced his defection publicly in April 1944, but in fact he had been in touch with the State Department and the FBI beforehand, offering to furnish information about Soviet espionage. The FBI listened but was standoffish, which was apparently why Kravchenko went to the press. The State Department actually wanted to send Kravchenko back to the Soviet Union so as not to offend the Russians, America's war ally. But the FBI, which was not worried about diplomacy, managed to keep this from happening. Like Krivitsky, Kravchenko aroused skepticism. The British, for example, were dubious about his claim of being a political dissident. He might have been sincere, they posited, but on the other hand, "he may have been recalled and just decided it was nicer here . . . he may have been caught with his wrists in the till and decided to take the breeze . . . he may have a girlfriend here of whom his superiors disapprove"[7]

The allied counterintelligence agencies had long known that the Soviets were engaged in espionage against their countries. Although they were distracted by the fascist threat, they had conducted surveillance against the Soviets and their communist contacts throughout the war years. But the diplomatic requirements of the wartime alliance had prevented them from being much more than observers of Soviet spying. Now it was different. The war was over and the alliance was crumbling. Moreover, unlike the others, Gouzenko had concrete evidence to back up his claims about Soviet espionage – a dazzling cache of stolen GRU documents. The intelligence chiefs were not inclined to sweep this defection under the carpet for diplomatic reasons.

This was especially true of Hoover. The FBI chief had been convinced for some time that his country faced a serious threat from Soviet attempts to infiltrate the U.S. government and scientific community. But Hoover felt himself at odds with Truman on the issue. In Hoover's view, Truman and his advisers, especially his new secretary of state, James Byrnes, were soft on communism and more concerned about protecting civil liberties than about unmasking spies in the government. Gouzenko's defection offered Hoover the perfect chance to draw attention to the communist danger. The case, if exposed, would discredit the liberals who surrounded Truman and enable Hoover to play center stage in Washington. In mid-October 1945, Hoover wrote a memorandum to his top aides. The Gouzenko case, he told them, was their "no. 1 project and every resource should be used to run down *all* angles very promptly."[8]

Britain's MI5 and MI6, the agency responsible for intelligence-gathering abroad, also responded urgently to the Gouzenko case.[9] MI6 chief Sir Stewart Menzies (who signed himself as "C") had never stopped fearing Soviet spies during the war. "We have been penetrated by the Communists," he observed in 1944, "and they're on the inside but we don't know exactly how."[10] MI6's British representative in North America, Sir William Stephenson (later immortalized as the "Man Called Intrepid"), rushed to Ottawa when he heard the news of the defection. Stephenson, like Hoover, had an agenda. His intelligence liaison body in New York, the British Security Coordination (BSC), was about to be dismantled because it was a wartime agency, and Stephenson would soon be out of a job. According to one historian, "The cipher clerk's defection provided him with a golden opportunity to keep the BSC alive until its post-war existence could be guaranteed. For the next months, therefore, he did his best to ensure that the BSC played an active role in the Gouzenko affair."[11]

❧

The defection came at a time when the West was struggling with a post-war world fraught with uncertainties, especially regarding the Soviet Union. The Soviets had fought valiantly against the Nazis (suffering staggering losses of close to 20 million soldiers and civilians). No one doubted that had it not been for the Soviet Union, which battled the Wehrmacht on the ground in Europe single-handedly until June 1944, the Allies would never have defeated Hitler's army. Admiration for "heroic Russia" and its people was widespread in the West. A grateful Churchill said of Stalin at the Yalta Conference in February 1945, "I walk through this world with greater courage and hope, when I find myself in a relation of friendship and intimacy with this great man, whose fame has gone out not only over all Russia, but the world."[12]

Even the intense Western antagonism toward communism had become more muted during World War II. Although most people still considered communism a threat to democracy, its adherents in the West were officially tolerated. And the appeal of communism among left-wing groups, after plummeting when the Soviets signed the Molotov-Ribbentrop non-aggression pact with Hitler's regime in 1939, regained its strength once the Soviets were seen battling the Fascists on the Eastern Front. Communists in the United States restored their earlier coalition with the liberals. In Canada, the Communist Party, which had been banned in 1940 and renamed the Labour Progressive Party, gained a new legitimacy. Fred Rose, who represented the LPP from the Montreal-Cartier riding, had been elected a member of Parliament in 1943 and was returned in 1945, when the LPP received more than one hundred thousand votes in the federal election. The picture was similar in Britain, where there were several communists, or communist sympathizers, among the Labour members of Parliament.[13]

Nonetheless, for the governments of the United States, Britain, and Canada, their alliance with the Soviets lost much of its raison d'être once Hitler was defeated. Indeed, the friendship had become strained soon after the Yalta Conference, when it became clear that Stalin's government was intent on extending the hold of communism throughout Eastern Europe. Just weeks later, a gravely ill President Roosevelt privately expressed his misgivings about relations with the Soviet Union: "We can't do business with Stalin. He has broken every one of the promises made at Yalta."[14] It was one thing for the West to find common cause with the Soviets against the Fascist enemy, quite another to reach a modus vivendi with them in solving the problems of a war-torn world afterward.

The bombing of Hiroshima and Nagasaki in August 1945 had raised the level of tension with the Soviets further, in large part because it changed the balance of international power. The United States now had a weapon of mass destruction at its disposal and had shown its willingness to use it. Meanwhile, the Soviets, who were working furiously to develop their own atomic bomb, were still several years behind. As one historian put it, the bombing of Japan "destroyed Stalin's expectations of being second to none among the great powers."[15]

Unbeknownst to the Western allies, Stalin had in fact initiated a program to develop the bomb in late 1942, while his country was still deep in the struggle against Hitler. As part of this program, the Soviets had begun an ambitious effort, coordinated by NKVD chief Lavrentii Beria, to steal Western atomic secrets. Thanks to their recruitment of Klaus Fuchs, a German-born British scientist, the Soviets had even managed to learn some details about the American atomic program at Los Alamos (the so-called Manhattan Project), where Fuchs had been employed since 1944.[16] But they still had a long way to go to produce an atomic bomb.

❧

During the autumn of 1945, the three allied governments and their intelligence agencies tried to determine what course of action to take with regard to Gouzenko. Few doubted the truth of Gouzenko's claims, especially since he had documents to back them up. Indeed, within a short time investigators had compiled a list of more than twenty probable spies, including Canadian civil servants and scientists, four possible Soviet agents in America (one of whom was thought to be Alger Hiss), and the British atomic scientist Dr. Alan Nunn May. Gouzenko also mentioned hearing of a spy in Britain code-named "Elli," but his description was considered too vague to follow up on at the time.

The problem for the three allies was to decide when to move against the suspects and thereby let it be known publicly that Gouzenko had defected. All parties agreed they should coordinate their actions and make arrests simultaneously, but they all had different agendas. MI5 officials worried that May, who returned to London in mid-September, might escape to the Soviet Union, so they were anxious to take action. The White House and the State Department, along with the King government, realized that the Gouzenko case was inextricably involved with their efforts to come to terms with the Soviets on a host of other issues, including control of the atomic bomb. They were concerned that premature action on the spy scandal could influence public opinion against the Soviets and destroy any effort to reach an accord with them in the newly established United Nations.

Through a constant stream of telegrams and numerous high-level secret meetings, the intelligence chiefs, diplomats, and politicians of Britain, Canada, and the United States negotiated over the Gouzenko problem for months, assuming, as they planned their strategy, that the Soviets knew nothing other than that Gouzenko had disappeared. Unfortunately, this was not the case. The NKVD had a mole at the highest level of the intelligence community in Britain who was reporting to Moscow every development in the Gouzenko case. Kim Philby, who years later would defect to the Soviet Union after falling under suspicion in Britain, was at the time chief of counterintelligence for MI6. As such, he learned immediately of Gouzenko's defection and not only saw all correspondence on the case, but also sat in on meetings with MI5 to devise strategies. Philby enabled Moscow to limit the damage done by the defection and prepare in advance its responses as the situation unfolded. Despite the risks he took for his Soviet controllers, Philby was clever enough to keep ahead of his colleagues and their counterparts in the allied services.[17]

The months of discussion about what to do with the spy suspects came to an abrupt halt on February 3, 1946, when veteran American journalist Drew Pearson broke the story on his Sunday evening radio program. The next day Prime Minister Mackenzie King informed his cabinet about the top secret case and cleared the way for arrests of fifteen Canadians – a process which would lead to a public outcry over violations of civil liberties. The story of the Canadian arrests, and that of Nunn May in early March, made front-page news in the West for the next several weeks, with wild speculation about the defector, the spies, and the extent of the espionage. The already fragile post-war peace had now been destroyed by a new threat – the Allies' erstwhile friend in the fight against Germany and Japan had been stealing their atom-bomb secrets. A chill descended over Western-Soviet relations, a chill that would descend inexorably into the Cold War.

~

Although tensions between the Soviet Union and the West had been simmering for months, it was the Canadian spy case that brought them out in the open, confirming once and for all that the Soviets were enemies rather than friends. The defection set in motion a search for communist spies that reached epidemic proportions in North America. And it abruptly put an end to movements in the United States, Canada, and Britain for international, civilian control of the bomb. The news that the Soviet Union was trying to steal atomic secrets completely discredited the idea of atomic cooperation with the Soviets. Western scientists who continued to advocate such cooperation were labeled "reds" and fell under the scrutiny of the FBI and its Canadian and British counterparts.

The defection, after it was confirmed in messages from Philby, also sent shock waves throughout the Kremlin. Soviet intelligence officers were recalled to face interrogations by their bosses in Moscow, who were under instructions from Stalin to get to the bottom of the affair. What had gone wrong? How could it be that a cipher clerk managed to circumvent tight security and escape for good, wife and child by his side, with stolen documents in hand? Was it the fault of the NKVD, which was responsible for security at the embassy, or the GRU, which employed the defector? For the Russians the defection was nothing short of a disaster, calling for a thorough reexamination of their intelligence operations.

The Gouzenko affair did not end with the resulting spy trials in Canada and Britain, or with the publication of a lengthy report on the case by a special Canadian Royal Commission. Indeed, for some, such as the brilliant Canadian diplomat Herbert Norman, whose name was drawn into the web of espionage allegations that grew around Gouzenko, a terrible ordeal was then just beginning. There were others as well whose careers and reputations would be destroyed as a result of Gouzenko's claims, including a leading American geneticist named Arthur Steinberg, who had the misfortune to befriend a Canadian scientist later charged with spying. The Canadians, who had initially seen the Gouzenko defection simply as an opportunity to draw attention to the communist danger and participate on an equal footing with their American and British allies, would increasingly find themselves drawn into an unrelenting witch-hunt for spies, with even their future prime minister Lester B. Pearson on the Americans' list of suspects.

~

Igor Gouzenko was presented to the West as a man of courage who did a great service in opening up the eyes of the world to Soviet treachery. But like most defectors, Gouzenko is more complicated than that. The popularly accepted account of his defection and the subsequent investigation leaves many unanswered questions. Was Gouzenko really a hero? Those who were accused unjustly of spying, and who had their names and reputations tarnished for life as a result, viewed Gouzenko as an opportunist whose word should never have been trusted. But was it really his fault that his allegations were used for the purposes of *realpolitik*? Once he made his pact with Western intelligence services, much of what Gouzenko did or said was out of his control.

To understand Gouzenko's historical legacy, we must go back to the beginning, to that fateful day in September 1945 when he walked out of the Soviet Embassy in Ottawa with a sheaf of secret documents. What motivated this obscure young cipher clerk to betray his country and embark on what would become a life of fear, acclaim, and, eventually, frustration and poverty? What evidence did he actually produce to show that there was such a massive Soviet spy ring in North America? And what were the driving forces that led Western government officials and politicians to seize on Gouzenko's allegations and engage in an unprecedented struggle against the communist menace?

For decades, much of the official documentation on the Gouzenko affair in Canada, Britain, and the United States was kept under wraps as part of long-standing secrecy regulations. But government files in all three countries have opened up, and recently the intelligence services of Canada and Britain have released an impressive amount of exciting new evidence. In 2003, the Canadian Security Intelligence Service (CSIS), at this author's request, declassified hundreds of RCMP Gouzenko documents, and at the end of that year the British made a large portion of their MI5 Gouzenko file publicly available. It is now possible to document, for the first time, the details of the defection and the response of the allied governments, and to examine the impact of the case in the years that followed. And thanks to "glasnost," we now can learn about the impact of the Gouzenko affair in the Soviet Union, the turmoil it created in the Kremlin, and the repercussions it had for the Soviet intelligence apparatus.[18]

In chronicling Gouzenko's story, this book renews a debate that began in the McCarthy era and divides historians to this day. To what extent were the people accused of passing secrets to the Soviets during the 1940s really spies, and to what extent were they merely individuals sympathetic to the communist cause and unwittingly drawn into the Soviet espionage network? Another important question, one that resonates particularly strongly in today's post-September 11 world, is whether the harm that was done to Western interests by those who did spy justified the widespread abuse of individual rights, the vast expenditures of public resources, and the shattering of so many innocent lives. Was the Gouzenko affair necessary to open up our eyes to the evils of the Soviet empire, or did the defection produce an overreaction that polarized Western society and diverted Western governments from a more reasoned and productive response to Soviet espionage as we gradually came to understand its capabilities and aims? Can we say today, with over fifty years of hindsight and a vast amount of new archival documentation, that the Cold War, as fought by the West against Soviet espionage in the early post-war years, was worth fighting? This book aims to answer these questions.

Chapter 1

THE DEFECTION

If Gouzenko hadn't fallen into the Western intelligence services' lap, they would have had to invent somebody like him.

Ian Adams, Canadian journalist

There was nothing ordinary about Igor Gouzenko. But then spies – especially those who decide to defect – are by definition a unique species. Exceptionally ambitious and highly intelligent, Gouzenko had never been destined for the life of an average Soviet citizen in the grim and stifling Stalin era. Born in 1919 in the village of Rogachev, not far from Moscow, he never knew his father, who disappeared during the civil war that followed the Bolshevik Revolution. His mother was a schoolteacher, with a higher degree in mathematics, and she struggled to raise her three children on her own. At one point, she had to send Igor, the youngest, to his grandmother to live because she could not make ends meet. Eventually, however, Igor's mother got a job in Moscow, where Igor was able to join the family.[1]

Because of his strong academic record, Igor was accepted to study at the prestigious Moscow Architectural Institute. There he met Svetlana Gouseva, called Anna by Igor, an honor student and a beautiful brunette. At five feet seven inches, Anna was one inch taller than the sturdily built Igor, and four years younger. She had also lived a more privileged life than he had. Her father was a noted engineer, who participated in building the Moscow subway, and his family lived well, albeit by Soviet standards. Anna and Igor, who was brown-haired, with an oval face and deep-set, penetrating eyes, were attracted to each other instantly. After a quick courtship, they were married, and by all accounts they remained a passionately devoted couple throughout their eventful, often stormy, forty-year union. Both were strong-willed, intense and purposeful, and both were artistically talented. Their daughter Evelyn remarked years later, "My earliest recollections of my parents were at the easel." In addition to painting, Igor would also produce an award-winning novel.[2]

The war put an end to Gouzenko's studies, but he was lucky enough not to be sent to the front. Instead, the NKVD, the Soviets' secret police agency, singled him out – after a careful screening to ensure his political reliability – from among a group of Young Communist League members for a special assignment. Following courses at the Military Engineering Academy in Moscow and rigorous examinations in mathematics and sciences, Gouzenko was sent to the Higher Intelligence School of the Red Army, where he began training as a cipher clerk with Soviet military intelligence, known as the GRU. Because cipher clerks were the linchpin of the Soviet espionage effort, the year-long course was exacting, but Gouzenko passed with flying colors.[3]

In June 1943, Gouzenko arrived in Ottawa on his first (and, as it would turn out, his last) mission abroad, accompanied by his new boss, Col. Nikolai Zabotin, and Zabotin's assistant, Major Alexander Romanov. Anna, who was pregnant, would follow in a few months. Ottawa at that time was bustling. Formerly a rough-and-tumble lumber town on the majestic and sprawling Ottawa River, a major route for lumber and fur traders, Ottawa had in 1857 been designated Canada's capital. It retained its unsophisticated frontier character well into the next century, but with the advent of the Second World War, Ottawa, while still a "small town" compared to other world capitals, came into its own. The rapidly expanding civil service brought so many new inhabitants to the city that temporary buildings were erected along its perimeters. At lunchtime, the cafeteria of the elegant and grand Château Laurier Hotel, which stood on the Rideau Canal next to the imposing Houses of Parliament, was filled with government officials, diplomats, politicians, and journalists trading wartime news. In the evening, remnants of the same crowd, those not attending a gathering at one of the embassies, filled the bar.

From the moment they arrived, Gouzenko and his fellow GRU officers, who stayed at the Château Laurier while awaiting permanent living quarters, were in the thick of Ottawa life, a life infinitely more attractive and comfortable than the drab and difficult one they had left behind in Stalin's Russia.

Col. Zabotin was officially the new Soviet military attaché to Canada, but unbeknownst to his Canadian hosts, he was also the *rezident*, code-named "Grant," in charge of GRU operations in Canada. With the intense fight against the Nazis turning in their favor, the Soviets had begun in earnest to launch an atomic-bomb project, and they wanted to speed up their progress by taking advantage of Western research. Canada, which had invited the Soviet Union to establish a legation in Ottawa in 1942 (it was elevated to an embassy in 1944), was assisting the United States and Britain in work on the atomic bomb. So the newly arrived GRU officers were instructed to recruit Canadians who could provide information about this research, as well as about other military-related issues. Their reports, and the responses from Moscow, were sent back and forth by telegraphed messages, which Gouzenko was responsible for ciphering and deciphering.[4]

Zabotin's group was not the first to carry out espionage for the GRU in Canada. In 1942, as part of a Canadian Mutual Aid program, Major Vsevolod Sokolov had arrived as the official Soviet inspector of Canadian war production plants that were supplying weapons to the Soviets. In a classic example of biting the hand that feeds you, Sokolov set up an Ottawa-based GRU spy ring using Canadian Communist Party officials Fred Rose and Sam Carr, who participated in the day-to-day running of the network. (Both Rose and Carr would eventually be arrested because of Gouzenko.) And for more than two decades before that, Canada had been used as an entrée for Soviet spies heading for the United States. According to one Soviet intelligence report, "A false Canadian identity document and passport enabled spies to cross from Canada to the United States without much difficulty and to remain indefinitely in the United States without molestation. . . . Canadian passports were also used by Soviet spies in Europe during the 1930s." Officials from the Canadian Communist Party participated actively in this process, providing assistance to the Russians whenever required and also working with their comrades in the American Communist Party.[5]

As accredited diplomats from an Allied power, Zabotin and his staff, which was soon augmented with additional GRU officers, found a welcoming environment in Ottawa and indeed wherever they went in Canada. Canadians felt a special affinity for their Russian neighbors. Both countries had vast and undeveloped territories, including an Arctic North. They had in common the long, frigid winters of their lands. And of course there was Russia's heroic role at the Eastern Front. As one source described it, "Wartime differences were allowed because there was a common enemy. Even the left-wing theatre was acceptable enough for the New Theatre Group to go to Ottawa to do *We Beg to Differ* for the troops. Eaton's, the largest department store in Montreal and owned by a long-established English-Canadian dynasty, flew the hammer and sickle. Stalin was on the cover of *Time*. Across Canada, Soviet-Canadian friendship societies were formed, as were many organizations sending aid to the USSR. . . . The National Film Board of Canada made a pro-Russian film called *Our Northern Neighbour*."[6]

Colonel Zabotin was highly popular with Canadians, particularly with ladies. There were rumors he had seduced one or two married women in the Ottawa diplomatic set.[7] And no wonder. The son of a Tsarist military officer and a graduate of the prestigious Frunze Military Academy, thirty-four-year-old Zabotin was a decorated veteran of the ferocious 1942 Battle of Stalingrad, the first major victory for the Soviets against the Germans. Over six feet tall, he was strikingly handsome, with a broad smile and thick, prematurely gray hair. And he had a magnetic personality. As Gouzenko described Zabotin, "He must have been well educated because the polish of his Russian speech was a treat to hear. His bright, gay conversation sparkled with references to his place in the Ural Mountains, to his dogs and horses. We assumed that he belonged to a privileged family, a fact borne out by his sudden shifting of the conversation whenever we tried to learn more about his family." Zabotin, Gouzenko added, was an obvious choice for the job of GRU *rezident*: "Zabotin looked every inch a soldier, and Red Army soldiers were then at the peak of their popularity with the democratic world."[8]

Soviet diplomats in Ottawa, including those secretly working for the GRU, earned high marks for their hospitality, and their receptions were always well attended. According to one Canadian, the Soviets were "the toast of the town. They were sought after for their boisterous energy, their entertaining stories, their generosity with unrationed liquor, their mammoth parties."[9] The hospitality was reciprocated. Zabotin and his crew even received a rare invitation to an exclusive Canadian lodge owned by a wealthy Ottawa manufacturer for duck hunting.[10]

Zabotin operated differently from his predecessors in Ottawa. They had cautiously refrained from contacting agents directly, using men like Rose and Carr as go-betweens. Under the more daring Zabotin, GRU officers often contacted recruits or potential recruits themselves. With the atmosphere toward the Russians so cordial, the GRU apparently thought the risks involved had diminished.[11] Within a short time the GRU had managed to establish itself within Ottawa's government and diplomatic circles and to enlist a small group of civil servants and scientists to pass it information.

What drew the recruits into the GRU's net? Most of them were well-educated young intellectuals who had been attracted to communism in the late 1930s with the rise of the popular front. They had participated in societies like the Spanish Relief Committee, the League Against Fascism, and the Civil Liberties Union. The spread of fascism abroad and the desire for social change at home drew these people from a philosophy of liberalism toward communism. Most attended Marxist study groups organized by the Canadian Communist Party, where they were spotted by the Soviets as likely candidates for their growing network of agents. In the words of Gordon Lunan, a captain in the Canadian Armed Forces, who would spend five years in prison for acting as a middleman for Zabotin's team, "I admired the Soviet Union for what I believed then to be its enlightened world view. I wished it well, but like most of my comrades, I suspect, I would not have wanted to live there or to make Canada over in its likeness. RCMP claims to the contrary notwithstanding, the real glue that bound me to my comrades and them to me was the shared desire for a more humane society, a fairer distribution of wealth."[12] The feeling of wartime comradeship with the Russians seems to have justified, for some of these communist sympathizers, actual collaboration with them. As one source put it, "In the context of World War II, it was possible for well-meaning, politically naive citizens to pass information to the Soviet Union, Canada's ally in the battle against the Nazis, without considering themselves traitors."[13]

∾

In addition to the GRU, the Soviets had a second espionage ring, run by the Ottawa NKVD *rezident*, Vitalii Pavlov. Born and raised in Siberia, where his father was an accountant and his mother a village teacher, Pavlov studied automobile mechanics at a technical institute before being singled out to join the NKVD. The Stalinist purges that began in 1936 had decimated the ranks of the secret police, and Pavlov was part of a cohort brought in to fill the vacuum. In 1938, after graduating from the NKVD Higher School in Moscow, where he gained fluency in English, Pavlov joined the Foreign Department of the NKVD and spent a short time in the United States before the war broke out. Accompanied by his wife, Klavdia, and young son, he arrived in Ottawa in 1942 as the Soviet consul when the Soviet legation was established. Like Zabotin, Pavlov was exceptionally good-looking, with typically Russian high cheekbones, a thick head of curly hair, and slightly slanted large eyes. This was his first official posting abroad, and Pavlov was young, in his late twenties, and inexperienced. But he was determined to succeed at his job.[14]

Judging from Pavlov's memoirs, the new consul's responsibilities as a diplomat, especially before Georgii Zarubin arrived as Soviet ambassador to Ottawa in 1944, prevented him from devoting as much time as he needed to his espionage operations for the NKVD. He was charting new territory, and the GRU already had a more established and extensive network. Also, the NKVD's responsibilities included security at the embassy, so Pavlov had to keep a close watch on what his colleagues were up to, a difficult task in Ottawa's open society. Pavlov was nonetheless able to cultivate wide connections in Canada's political and diplomatic circles, where Russian hospitality was so greatly appreciated. Few suspected that the young consul was from the NKVD – and after a few drinks, Pavlov's interlocutors often said things worth passing on to Moscow headquarters.[15]

But it was not as if the Canadian security services had their eyes closed. Or as if they and their allies in the British and American intelligence communities were uninterested in knowing what the Soviets were up to. Gouzenko had been warned in Moscow that as a cipher clerk he would be prey for Western counterespionage agencies. He was always to be on his guard against foreigners who might try to recruit him. He also had to carefully observe the rigorous and cumbersome embassy security regulations, lest he come under criticism from Pavlov or Zabotin.[16]

According to Gouzenko, Pavlov had his hands full at the Soviet Embassy, which, under the impact of the oppressive Stalinist bureaucracy, was seething with intrigue, backstabbing, and petty corruption. Morale was bad and there was constant bickering. With alcohol flowing freely, drinking episodes occasionally got out of hand; fights over women resulted in broken dishes, and hangovers lasted well into the afternoon. Ottawa landlords started complaining that their Russian tenants were keeping their apartments in deplorably filthy conditions; they were allowing their residences to deteriorate into pigsties. Pavlov, the minder of all these ill-behaved Russians, reported back to Moscow that when inspecting one of his compatriots' apartments, the "stench and dirt made my hair stand on end."[17]

Despite all the unpleasantness at the embassy, Gouzenko was blissfully happy with Anna, who had arrived in October 1943 and given birth to their first child, a son named Andrei, a few months later. The Gouzenkos were struck by how pleasant life was in Canada compared to the dreary existence back home. Canada was not a shining example of economic prosperity, but it was far better off than the Gouzenkos' own country, which was staggering under the devastation wrought by its struggles against Germany. As Gouzenko observed, "The unbelievable supplies of food, the restaurants, the movies, the wide open stores, the absolute freedom of the people, combined to create the impression of a dream from which I must surely awaken."[18]

Winters in Ottawa were even colder than those in Moscow, but the sun shone a lot, the snow was uniquely clean and white, and there were never the interminable queues for groceries. Anna and Igor bought their first dining set, on time, and settled into a pleasant existence. The couple was, in Gouzenko's words, "supremely content" in their home, a small and rather drab apartment at 511 Somerset Street. Gouzenko later said, "I heard Zabotin remark more than once that living abroad spoiled some Russians. It had certainly spoiled Anna and me. In Ottawa we had a comfortable apartment of our own. In Moscow a place that size would have been shared by four or five families."[19] Gouzenko also found Canadians easygoing and approachable. Amazingly, he recalled some years after his defection that "he even enjoyed talking to the police because they were friendly and warm."[20]

Then, "like a bolt from the blue," came terrible news. In September 1944, Gouzenko was called into Zabotin's office. Sitting at his desk and staring numbly at a letter that had just arrived from Moscow, Zabotin informed Gouzenko, "For reasons unstated, the immediate recall of you and your family has been ordered by the Director."[21] Gouzenko was paralyzed with fear. It had been only fourteen months since he had first arrived, for a tour of duty that was to last three years. Why was his stay being cut short? He must be in some sort of trouble, and under Stalin's repressive regime, trouble meant a labor camp or, even worse, a firing squad.

Gouzenko knew how the Soviet secret police had dealt with intelligence officers in the past. In 1939, newly appointed NKVD chief Lavrentii Beria recalled scores of Soviet operatives from abroad and had them imprisoned or executed as part of a vendetta against his predecessor, the notorious instigator of the purges,

Nikolai Yezhov. The war years had brought a respite, but the same vindictive and ruthless men were running the security and intelligence services, and the same rules applied: mistakes, if discovered, were unforgivable.[22]

Gouzenko's colleague Alexander Romanov had been sent ignominiously back to Moscow from Ottawa a few weeks earlier, because of episodes of drunken and disorderly conduct, including inappropriate advances to the wife of a general in the Canadian Army. But something much more innocent than that, such as an indiscreet remark in front of an informer, might also get a GRU officer blacklisted and sent back to headquarters.[23] Pavlov or one of his assistants seemed always to be within earshot. And Gouzenko knew he had made some mistakes. He had arrived late to work, and been reprimanded, on several occasions. He had once left scraps of secret documents on the floor in his cipher room, where they were discovered by a cleaning lady and turned over to one of the embassy officials.[24] Also, of course, he should not have been talking to Ottawa policemen.

Unknown to Gouzenko, however, he had not fallen into disfavor with the NKVD, but with a Moscow-based GRU colonel named Mikhail Mil'shtein (alias "Milsky"), who had made an inspection tour of GRU "residencies" in North America in the summer of 1944. Mil'shtein, who published his memoirs shortly before his death in 1993, recalled that Zabotin spoke highly of Gouzenko and asked Mil'shtein to meet with the cipher clerk, even though Mil'shtein was not supposed to interview members of the technical staff, who had no diplomatic status. Mil'shtein claimed he was suspicious of Gouzenko from the start, especially when he found out that Gouzenko had unauthorized access to a safe in one of the cipher rooms. He was also taken aback by a request from Gouzenko to participate in operational work, as an intelligence agent – a request that Mil'shtein turned down.[25]

The final straw for Mil'shtein was when he found out that Gouzenko and his family were on their own at 511 Somerset Street, although the embassy rules dictated that they reside in buildings where other staff were living, so they could keep an eye on one

another. When Mil'shtein brought this violation to Zabotin's attention and suggested that the Gouzenkos move into his building,
Zabotin did nothing about it. It seems that Mrs. Zabotin did not
want to be disturbed by the Gouzenkos' baby and thus persuaded
her husband to keep the family away. (For their part, this suited the
Gouzenkos well, because, according to Igor, the Zabotins quarreled
frequently and loudly late into the night.) Upon his return to
Moscow at the end of July 1944, Mil'shtein had reported his concerns about Gouzenko. Although they were not entirely convinced
that Mil'shtein's suspicions warranted any action, GRU leaders
decided nonetheless to order the young cipher clerk back home.
They did not want to take chances with an employee who had access
to all their secret communications.[26]

Luckily for Gouzenko, the generous-spirited Zabotin liked him
and, uncharacteristic as this may seem for a Soviet intelligence officer,
was willing to go to bat for him. (Zabotin had also lobbied hard for
the disgraced Romanov, a fellow veteran of the Battle of Stalingrad,
but to no avail.) So, in a move that would have disastrous consequences for his own future, Zabotin persuaded Moscow headquarters
to postpone the departure on the grounds that Gouzenko's cipher
skills were indispensable to the GRU's work (which they probably
were).[27] Gouzenko was relieved when he heard the news, but he knew
that this was only a reprieve. That night, sometime in September
1944, he broached the idea of defecting with Anna, whose advice he
always respected. She concurred with the plan. Gouzenko wrote later,
"I felt a great load lifted from me. The die had finally been cast. And,
best of all, Anna agreed on the course. There was no use pointing out
the dangers – she knew them full well. There was no necessity of
stressing absolute secrecy. She knew certain death lay ahead if the least
hint of my intended desertion got about."[28] Dramatic as these words
may sound, they were true. Gouzenko had embarked on a plan of
action that was fraught with peril. Not only for him, Anna, and their
little boy, but also for their families in Russia, who stood to suffer the
unfettered wrath of the Stalinist system of justice.

It is not clear exactly what Gouzenko's plans were as the next year went by. He heard in the spring of 1945 that his replacement would be arriving in Ottawa within a few months, but he took no action for some months after that. He apparently used the time to learn more about the various agents his embassy colleagues had recruited, and to gather evidence that would arouse the interest of the Canadian counterintelligence services. He had heard about Viktor Kravchenko's defection to the United States a year earlier and was inspired by his example. But Gouzenko did not intend to defect empty-handed, as Kravchenko reportedly had. He wanted to have something tangible to offer his potential hosts, something that would give credence to what he planned to tell them about Soviet espionage. The Cold War was still a long way off, and the Canadian government would be reluctant to offend Moscow by protecting a Soviet citizen who had committed treason. He had to produce something impressive if he was going to be received with open arms in Canada.

The problem for Gouzenko was that the GRU recruits in Canada had not managed to steal any earth-shaking secrets, especially regarding atomic research, which was the Kremlin's top priority. Contrary to what the Soviets apparently assumed, Canada's participation in the American atomic-bomb project was limited. Although Canada was an important supplier of uranium to the Americans, Canadian scientists, and all but a few British ones, were excluded from the highly secret research conducted as part of the Manhattan Project. Canadian work on an experimental heavy-water reactor in Montreal, which would be used for a full-scale reactor at Chalk River, Ontario, after the war, was peripheral to the atomic research being carried out in the United States.[29] In comparison with Klaus Fuchs, who was passing valuable information about the American bomb project to the Soviets, the Canadian recruits had much less to offer.

Also, as Gouzenko's memoirs reveal, the GRU station in Ottawa during the 1943–45 period was not exactly a model of efficiency-driven productivity. GRU employees wanted to make the most of their stay in the West and enjoy the "good life" while they could. But at the same time they were anxious to please their bosses back home.

Intelligence output was often exaggerated as a result and low-grade information was presented as being much more significant than it actually was. According to Gouzenko, "Everybody on the Military Attaché staff began to find reasons for remaining after hours so that their check-out signature would appear frequently in the 'overtime' section of the time journal which was always mailed to Moscow. This developed into something of a competition typical of most Soviet institutions. We faked our work to see who could stay longest." Even Zabotin, constantly prodded by his bosses to produce information, was "eager as a schoolboy to be praised for good work."[30]

But Zabotin was distracted by other matters. According to a subsequent British MI6 report, Zabotin began an affair in early 1944 with a Russian émigré, Nina Farmer, who was separated from her American husband and living in Montreal. The "buoyant and attractive" Mrs. Farmer first glimpsed Colonel Zabotin sitting in full uniform with other Soviet officers at a gala performance of the symphony in Montreal. After seeing Zabotin again, this time at a ballet, in early January 1944, she returned with him and his retinue of officers to the lavish Prince of Wales Suite at Montreal's Ritz Hotel, where the group was staying while in town. They danced and feasted until 4 a.m., whereupon Zabotin accompanied Mrs. Farmer to her apartment. According to the report, based on a long interview with Mrs. Farmer in 1946, several months after the spy scandal broke,

> A month later, at the hour of midnight, Mrs. FARMER was rung up by Colonel ZABOTIN apparently in a mood of gay irresponsibility – he was at that time paying a visit of inspection to the ORVIDA war plant and was in good spirits as he had roistered with some Russian engineers whom he had found on the spot. After that, the ice was thoroughly broken and Colonel ZABOTIN would quite often ring her when visiting war plants in the vicinity. He also got in touch with her in Montreal whenever he passed through, and used to take her out, dine and dance with her, and entertain her.[31]

The MI6 report, commissioned when Nina Farmer gained employment in Berlin after the war at the Allied Control Commission for Germany, noted that other witnesses confirmed that Mrs. Farmer was probably Zabotin's mistress. But the report went on to point out that Farmer had no idea her lover was engaged in espionage. The only hint he gave her was when he asked, in a moment of frivolity, what she thought of the name "Grant," his code name for communications with Moscow. Of course, Nina Farmer had no idea what Zabotin was talking about.[32]

Why should Zabotin's infidelity be particularly noteworthy? For someone in his position, his behavior was highly reckless. Not only was his wife just two hours away in Ottawa, Zabotin was cavorting in Montreal with Mrs. Farmer with little attempt at secrecy, even from his colleagues at the embassy, several of whom Mrs. Farmer met. As a Russian who had fled her homeland, she would have been considered an enemy to the Soviets. If the NKVD had learned of Zabotin's liaison (not to mention the money he squandered on her entertainment), he would have been sent back to the Soviet Union on the next boat.

With the distractions of an extramarital affair, and continuous discord at the embassy between the GRU and the NKVD, it is no wonder that the reports Zabotin sent through Gouzenko to Moscow were not all that revelatory. Zabotin and his colleagues provided a lot of information, but judging from the documents Gouzenko brought out, much of it was already published, or too general to be considered valuable. As military attaché in a country that was a war ally, Zabotin was entitled to a certain amount of information *pro forma* from the Canadian government. Shortly before he had arrived in 1943, the Canadian Department of National Defence had set up an organization to liaise with foreign military attachés and supply them with technical information that they might request. Through this arrangement, Zabotin had visited several Canadian military training centers, installations, and munitions plants, and received publications on military weapons. He regularly informed Moscow of what he and his subordinates had learned. But this information came from Zabotin in his role as military attaché. He was also required to send Moscow secret military intelligence obtained in his capacity as GRU *rezident*.

Although the most urgent interest of the GRU was Western atomic research, as late as the summer of 1945 its Ottawa branch was still producing only rudimentary information on the subject. Thus, for example, one of Zabotin's assistants, Major Vasilii Rogov, drafted a telegram for Moscow based on supposedly secret information from Raymond Boyer, a prominent young professor of chemistry at McGill University: "As a result of experiments carried out with uranium, it has been found that uranium may be used for filling bombs, which is already in fact being done. The Americans have undertaken wide research work, having invested $660 million in this business."[33] And in March 1945, Gordon Lunan, recently recruited by Fred Rose, passed on information he had obtained from an electrical engineer, Durnford Smith (code-named "Badeau"): "Badeau informs me that most secret work at present is on nuclear physics (bombardment of radio-active substances to produce energy). This is more hush-hush than radar. . . . In general, he claims to know of no new developments in radar, except in minor improvements in its application."[34]

Neither of these reports would have impressed the GRU leadership in Moscow, let alone Soviet scientists. (In fact the report citing Raymond Boyer stated wrongly that a new Canadian plant to produce uranium was under construction at Grand Mère, Quebec, when the plant was actually at Chalk River.) The Soviets had long been aware that the Americans were working on an atomic bomb, and, thanks to Klaus Fuchs, their scientists knew all about the fissionable material – uranium-235 or plutonium – used in making the bomb.

Another of Lunan's "informers" was Israel Halperin, a young professor of mathematics on leave from Queen's University in Kingston, Ontario, in order to serve in the Canadian Artillery. The GRU in Ottawa wanted Halperin, whose assigned code name was "Bacon," to give them information about explosives plants and "if possible to pass on the [formulas] of explosives and its samples."[35] They also sought to get uranium samples from him. But after several meetings with Halperin, all Lunan was able to produce was a report on the organization and capacity of Canadian explosives plants, which contained nothing that was not a matter of public record.

Halperin, who according to Lunan "made no secret of his liberal views," was happy to help out the Russians by providing open-source information. But when pressed to go further, and when it became clear the Soviets were interested in atomic secrets, Halperin backed off. Thus, Lunan reported to his GRU controller, "It has become very difficult to work with him, especially after my request for Ur-235 (Uran 235). He said that as far as he knows, it is absolutely impossible to get it . . . Bacon explained to me the theory of nuclear energy which is probably known to you. He refuses to put down in writing anything and does not want to give a photograph or information on himself. I think that at present he has a fuller understanding of the essence of my requests and he has a particular dislike for them. . . . He says that he does not know anything about matters that are not already known to you."[36] By early July 1945, Lunan was forced to explain to his controllers that "this fellow is a mathematician, and not a chemist or physicist, which may account for his remoteness from the details of explosive research."[37]

The third individual assigned to Lunan was Edward Mazerall (alias "Bagley"), an engineer at the Canadian National Research Council. By all accounts, Mazerall was also a very reluctant player in the espionage game. It took weeks for Lunan to arrange a meeting with him and he continually begged off the tasks the GRU had set for him. "He lives in the country," Lunan reported, "and his wife is antagonistic to his political participation." Eventually, at the end of July 1945, Mazerall produced two rather innocuous Canadian research reports on air navigation, one of which was a research proposal and the other something that was to be presented at a forthcoming conference on civil aviation, which the Soviets would be attending.[38]

At this point, Lunan, whose wife was expecting a baby, decided to cease his work for the Soviets: "My judgment eventually led me to abdicate my role as intermediary. Rogov [Lunan's GRU controller] was not interested in my assessment of Canadian or international affairs and I was not qualified to appraise information of a scientific nature, or to discuss or evaluate any reciprocal information coming from Rogov. Nor, for that matter, was I prepared to pressure or influence the others to do anything against their own judgment."[39]

As far as can be gleaned from the documents Gouzenko brought out, Durnford Smith was the most "productive" of Lunan's sources. But his information was so technical that the GRU decided to have Rogov deal with him directly. For the brief period of July and August 1945, Smith, an employee of the Canadian National Research Council, passed on a considerable amount of material on radar systems, radio tubes, and microwaves, the bulk of which was in secret scientific journals for the year 1945. But this was far from the secrets of American atomic research that the GRU was so anxious to obtain.

Of all the Canadian scientists the GRU had cultivated, Professor Boyer was the most valuable. Boyer, who came from a wealthy and prominent Montreal family, was a committed communist. He had in fact been recruited by Canadian Communist Party organizer Fred Rose well before Zabotin arrived in Ottawa, and throughout 1943 and 1944 he passed on secret information about Canadian work on chemical explosives, in particular RDX. But he had nothing to offer on the atomic bomb.

The only GRU recruit in Canada in a position to provide information about atomic research was Alan Nunn May, a nuclear scientist from Britain who had been working at the National Research Council in Montreal since early 1943. Born in 1912 in Birmingham, England, May studied at Trinity Hall, Cambridge, in the mid-1930s, earning his doctorate in physics and going on to teach at King's College, London. Cambridge transformed May, as it did Kim Philby and others, into a radical. He joined the Communist Party and in 1935 even spent a few weeks in Leningrad with a group of Cambridge graduates.[40]

May, who had joined Britain's atomic-bomb research team, the so-called Tube Alloys project, in 1942, had already begun passing information about his work on uranium to the GRU when he was still in Britain. But for some reason GRU headquarters did not tell Zabotin about May until early 1945, almost two years after May had arrived in Canada. According to Gouzenko, after Zabotin was told about May, he "remained in a vile mood for some time. He had been working hard to contact somebody immediately involved with the atomic project, yet Moscow had kept quiet about an agent of Dr. May's qualifications who had been practically under Zabotin's nose all the time."[41]

In May 1945, Zabotin sent GRU Lt. Pavel Angelov to contact May in Montreal. Angelov went straight to the scientist's home, catching him by surprise. May was unreceptive. He told Angelov that he did not want to resume contact with the GRU because he feared he was under RCMP surveillance. Angelov persisted, arguing that May was obliged to follow orders from Moscow, and the latter reluctantly agreed to cooperate.[42]

May eventually provided Zabotin's group with a report about atomic research, and, as the FBI pointed out in its initial message to the White House, he even produced a small quantity of radioactive uranium-233, which the Soviets eagerly sent off to Moscow with Zabotin's assistant, Lt.-Colonel Petr Motinov. Motinov, who, like Zabotin, had graduated from the Frunze Military Academy, was trusted with this highly sensitive – and physically harmful – job because he was an experienced GRU officer, having already served in China. As Motinov recalled much later, he was met at the airport by the GRU's chief director: "With great care I pulled the valuable ampoule out from under my waist-band and handed it to the director. He walked slowly to a black car, which stood on the tarmac and put the ampoule inside. I then asked the director 'Who was in there?' 'That's Beria,' whispered the director. Up to this day I still have from that uranium an agonizingly painful wound, and must get my blood changed several times a year."[43]

Zabotin's bosses were not satisfied, probably because most of the information from May had already been published. After receiving May's reports and the uranium sample, the GRU director in Moscow cabled Zabotin in late-August 1945: "Take measures to organize acquisition of documentary materials on the atomic bomb! The technical process, drawings, calculations."[44] By this time May was scheduled to go back to Britain, and there appeared to be no other recruits of his stature on the Canadian horizon. Zabotin and his colleagues had fallen far short of the goal assigned to them two years earlier, to produce new facts about the American bomb that would speed up the Soviet research effort.

Although Moscow was under no illusion it was getting valuable atomic secrets from Canada, the Soviets were nevertheless conducting espionage operations against an ally. Gouzenko planned to show Canadian authorities evidence of an active espionage network: the secret meetings that took place; the code names assigned to new or prospective recruits; the military information being passed to Moscow. Gouzenko was not entirely confident, however, that the materials he had would be enough to persuade the Canadians to grant him asylum. As Anna later recalled, he kept putting off his defection in the expectation that new materials would arrive from the Montreal group of GRU contacts, particularly documents on atomic research from Nunn May. Also, Gouzenko was hoping that something might happen to damage the image of the Soviet Union as an ally of Canada and cause friction between the governments of the two countries. He feared that otherwise Canadians might find it difficult to accept that the "heroic Soviets" were in fact enemies.[45] As it turns out, Gouzenko's concerns were justified. He would have a terrible time convincing the Canadian authorities to take him seriously.

∽

Even today, with many archival materials on the Gouzenko affair now declassified, it is difficult to separate fact from legend in the dramatic story of Igor Gouzenko's flight from the Soviet Embassy in September 1945 and his two-day effort to gain asylum. Once Gouzenko was safely in the hands of the RCMP, he worked with them in preparing an account of those events that was not entirely truthful. It was carefully geared to present him in the best possible light and to avoid controversy when the defection was later made public. Gouzenko embellished the story further in a 1947 article for *Cosmopolitan* magazine, which served as the basis for an autobiography published in 1948. Although his (and the RCMP's) version of the defection became accepted as truth, it contains obvious inconsistencies, as does the official story of what occurred behind the scenes in the Canadian government. As with many important events in history, the real story of Gouzenko's defection became blurred by popular myth.

Gouzenko arrived at his sudden decision to leave the Soviet Embassy for good on the night of Wednesday, September 5, 1945, when he learned he was to hand over his job to a new cipher clerk, Lt. Kulakov, the next day. Gouzenko was not scheduled to leave for Moscow until October, but he would no longer have access to the cipher section's secret documents after the sixth. He claimed initially that he had been earmarking certain documents to take out with him, by folding over the upper right corners. (In later testimony, he talked about stashing papers in a wooden box in his office.) On the night of the fifth, he said, while his colleagues were at the movies, he stuffed the documents under his shirt and walked out of the Soviet Embassy.[46]

His account is implausible for several reasons. Zabotin and Kulakov both had access to Gouzenko's office and files. Had they noticed the folds at the top of certain documents (or come across papers stashed in a box), Gouzenko's plan to defect would have been discovered. Gouzenko, who had already been reprimanded for a security violation, was too intelligent to behave so recklessly. In addition, September 5 was a hot and sultry night in Ottawa and Gouzenko had come to work in his shirtsleeves. In the *Cosmopolitan* article, Gouzenko stated that "There were almost a hundred documents, some of them small scraps of paper and others covering several large sheets of stationery. . . . The documents felt like they weighed a ton and I imagined that they were bulging out from under my shirt."[47] So how did Gouzenko walk out of the embassy unnoticed?

Part of the Gouzenko legend is that he took 109 documents from the GRU. In fact that number refers to the sum of items on a mailing list Colonel Zabotin sent to Moscow in early 1945. Zabotin's list was *one* of the documents Gouzenko stole. The actual number of separate sheets of paper that ended up in the hands of the RCMP, including telegrams, letters, reports, dossiers on agents, and handwritten notes, was around 250, because, as Gouzenko said, some of the documents contained several pages.[48] It would have been physically impossible for Gouzenko to contain all these papers underneath his shirt. Gouzenko later admitted, under questioning by a lawyer, that he had been taking documents home with him for some weeks. This was confirmed by a former RCMP deputy commissioner who worked on the Gouzenko case: "He was preparing for this for a long time and bringing papers home. . . . As soon as he thought there was a chance of returning [to Russia] he probably started collecting material."[49] Why did Gouzenko say otherwise? In order to be credible, he couldn't appear devious. That he had been stealing documents for some time conveyed an impression of calculation and dishonesty, so it had to be covered up.[50]

When he finally left the Soviet Embassy on Charlotte Street for the last time, Gouzenko was nearly overcome with fear. One slight hitch, one unforeseen circumstance, and he would have been thrown into the clutches of the NKVD. This may explain why his behavior that night was not entirely rational. After he left the embassy, Gouzenko did not go to the RCMP with his documents. Instead he headed for the offices of a local paper, the *Ottawa Journal*, intending to spill out his story just as Viktor Kravchenko had done a year earlier at the *New York Times*. He lost his nerve, however, when he reached the top floor of the building, where the editor's office was located, and fled home to Somerset Street, shaken and sweating. Anna urged him to go back. His colleagues at the embassy would not realize the documents were missing until the next day, she reassured him. He still had time.

But when Gouzenko arrived at the offices of the *Ottawa Journal* at nine o'clock in the evening and started to explain himself in what was at best broken English, the response was not what he had imagined. The night editor on duty recalled that Gouzenko was unable to answer any of his questions, that he just stood there and repeated, "It's war. It's war. It's Russia." As one eyewitness later remarked, "Nobody could figure out what the hell the guy wanted."[51] Finally the editor suggested to Gouzenko that he go to the RCMP offices, which were in the building of the ministry of justice, not far from the *Journal*. Gouzenko went to the Justice Building, but he did not try to contact the RCMP. Instead he asked the policeman on duty if he could see the minister of justice. He was told to come back the next morning.[52] Gouzenko cannot have been thinking straight. He had been living in Ottawa for over two years; surely he must have known that government offices were closed in the evenings and that the justice minister was unlikely to be there.

Gouzenko returned home to a frantic Anna. Somehow they got through the night and the next morning the two of them, Anna heavily pregnant with their second child, trudged back to the Justice Building with little Andrei in tow. Gouzenko asked again to see Mr. Louis St. Laurent, the minister of justice, but after waiting two hours he was turned away. Another visit to the *Ottawa Journal*, where Gouzenko was understandably "utterly agitated and almost incoherent," produced no better results. The editors decided that since the story was unsubstantiated and might cause a problem with Canada's ally the Soviet Union, they could not run it. They advised Gouzenko to go to the RCMP's Bureau of Naturalization, where Gouzenko asked for protection and was refused.

By this time Andrei was tired and hungry, so Igor and Anna deposited him at the home of an English neighbor, a Mrs. Bourke, who lived in a house nearby. The couple then took a streetcar to the offices of the Canadian Crown Attorney, where a secretary named Fernande Coulson was receptive to their plight. Interviewed some years later, Coulson recalled that she telephoned the RCMP and a Mountie came over to talk to Gouzenko but told him in the end there was nothing he could do. A desperate telephone call to John Leopold, assistant chief for intelligence at the RCMP, produced mixed results. According to Coulson, Leopold at first said "we can't touch him," but he finally agreed to see Gouzenko the next morning.[53]

Igor and Anna were beside themselves. Time had just about run out. Gouzenko's colleagues at the embassy would have noted his absence by now, and once documents were seen to be missing, their lives would be in danger. After they retrieved Andrei from their neighbor and were back in their own apartment, a driver from the Soviet Embassy arrived and began pounding at their door and shouting. Several minutes went by before he left. A terrified Gouzenko went out on his balcony and pleaded with his neighbor on the adjoining balcony, Harold Main, for help. Main decided he should contact the police and went off on his bicycle to the station. Meanwhile, another neighbor, Mrs. Frances Elliott, heard all the commotion and offered her apartment as a refuge for the pitiful family.[54]

The city police were just as unhelpful as the RCMP. Main said later that the police "seemed to know about it. . . . The Ottawa police were working with the RCMP. I think they already made contact with the RCMP."[55] They agreed to cruise by 511 Somerset, but said they could not do anything more because Gouzenko's apartment was Russian property.

It was not until a group from the Soviet Embassy, led by NKVD *rezident* Pavlov, broke into the Gouzenkos' apartment around midnight and began ransacking it, apparently looking for the stolen documents, that the police intervened. It was like a game of cops and robbers, with the hapless Ottawa police confronting belligerent Russians desperate to find their missing cipher clerk and his documents. The Gouzenkos peered out at the scene through their neighbor's keyhole across the hall. Eventually the Russians gave in to the police and grudgingly departed. One policeman then remained at the Elliott apartment until the next morning, September 7, when Gouzenko was escorted to the RCMP. No one had much sleep at 511 Somerset Street that night.[56]

⟳

The RCMP hesitated to give Gouzenko asylum in large part because Prime Minister King did not want Canada to become embroiled in an unpleasant diplomatic incident with the Soviets. King first learned about the defection on the morning of Thursday, September 6, while Gouzenko was waiting desperately for an audience with the Canadian justice minister, Mr. St. Laurent. The prime minister arrived at his office in Ottawa's Parliament Buildings shortly before the House of Commons was scheduled to convene its new session. Judging from what he wrote in his meticulously kept private diary, King was not in a good mood on this particular morning. Although he had been prime minister and leader of the Liberal Party on and off for almost twenty years, he was nervous about meeting the new members of Parliament, which had a considerably larger number from opposition parties than in previous sessions. And he was weary from the long, painstaking hours spent preparing the government's Speech from the Throne, to be delivered that day by Canada's governor general.

King was not keen to tackle his country's problems as a "middle-power" in the post-war world. Despite its small population (eleven and a half million, less than that of New York state), Canada had contributed in a major way to the war effort and sacrificed over forty-two thousand lives. At the war's end, it had one of the largest armies of United Nations countries. As one source observed, "Canada had fought abroad and produced at home as it had never fought and worked before – and her war record, at home and abroad, had gained her new stature in the world. Canada could no longer be classified simply as a promising young country; she had come of age."[57]

But since the bombing of Hiroshima and Nagasaki a month earlier, the world had become much more complex. How the new weapon would be controlled, and how it would affect the foreign policy of the Western allies, were questions that now dominated Canada's agenda, an agenda complicated by the constant challenge of asserting Canada's role in its alliance with the far more powerful United States and Britain. Because King had chosen to retain the portfolio of minister of external affairs along with that of prime minister, he was deeply involved in Canada's foreign policy and, at seventy years old, beginning to feel the strain. "I really need a complete rest and a change," King had written in his diary two weeks earlier.[58]

Unfortunately for the world-weary prime minister, he was about to be thrust into a political and diplomatic crisis that would test his mettle as never before. King found his close adviser Norman Robertson, undersecretary for external affairs, and Robertson's assistant, Hume Wrong, waiting for him in his office. Both men were looking grave. As King wrote in his diary that night, Robertson told him that a "terrible thing" had happened. "It was like a bomb on top of everything and one could not say how serious it might be or to what it might lead."[59] Just a half an hour or so earlier, Robertson said, a man from the Soviet Embassy had appeared with his wife at the office of Minister of Justice St. Laurent. The man had said that he worked with ciphers and that he had in his possession a number of documents showing that the Soviets had spies in Canada and the U.S., and that "some of these men were around Stettinius [the U.S. Secretary of State] in the States, and that one was in our own Research laboratories here (assumedly seeking to get secret information with regard to the atomic bomb)." King observed further that "Robertson seemed to feel that the information might be so important both to the States . . . and to Britain that it would be in their interests to seize it no matter how it was obtained."[60]

Robertson said the defector was threatening suicide and suggested that the RCMP offer him protection. But King was hesitant: "I said to both Robertson and Wrong that I thought we should be extremely careful in becoming a party to any course of action which would link the govt. of Canada up with this matter in a manner which might cause Russia to feel that we had performed an unfriendly act. That to seek to gather information in any underhanded way would make clear that we did not trust the Embassy." After a talk with St. Laurent, King was adamant that his government not get involved, even if the man was apprehended by Soviet authorities or committed suicide: "My own feeling is that the individual has incurred the displeasure of the Embassy and is really seeking to shield himself."[61]

King would later be criticized for not immediately grasping the importance of what the defector had to offer and for his naïveté in trusting the Soviets. But his reaction was understandable. Apart from wishing to avoid a diplomatic debacle, King also questioned the motives of the potential defector. The man was quite possibly lying to save his own skin, or because he wanted to live in Canada and needed a means to gain asylum. Whatever the case, King was not about to allow a Soviet code clerk to disrupt the cordial diplomacy that had characterized Ottawa's relations with Moscow.

One question that arises from King's diary entry for September 6 is how Robertson was able to give King details about Gouzenko's allegations as early as that morning. At that point Gouzenko had supposedly only mumbled incoherently to the night editor at the *Ottawa Journal*, "it's war, it's war," and spoken briefly to a secretary of St. Laurent, requesting a meeting with the minister. Had someone perhaps been in contact with Gouzenko before he actually defected and been apprised of what he had to say about espionage? A number of other strange circumstances suggest that there was more to the defection story than what was eventually presented to the public.

Though Prime Minister King did not know it, the RCMP had been monitoring the movements of Gouzenko closely since the night before, when he had gone to the *Ottawa Journal* in his unsuccessful attempt to tell the world his story. On September 6 – the day King first learned about the cipher clerk – the chief of the RCMP intelligence branch, Charles Rivett-Carnac, had a secret meeting with Norman Robertson. By that night, as King slept at his Ottawa residence, RCMP officers were stationed outside Gouzenko's apartment building and Robertson was conferring at his home with an "eminent officer of the British Secret Service."[62]

Who was this eminent British intelligence officer? The widely accepted theory, reinforced by what appears in the published (and edited) version of King's diary, is that it was British Security Coordination Chief William Stephenson, who had by some great coincidence (one historian calls it "miraculous") made a rare visit from New York to Canada exactly at the time Gouzenko defected. Stephenson, according to this theory, was staying at Montebello, a luxurious rustic lodge about an hour's drive from Ottawa, just as the incident erupted. Once in Ottawa, he "argued strongly against King's view that Gouzenko should be ignored. The Russian, he said, would certainly have information valuable not merely to Canada but also to Britain, the United States, and other Allies. Furthermore, Gouzenko's life was almost certainly in danger. They should act, and do so immediately, by taking Gouzenko in."[63] Stephenson's arguments were reportedly what persuaded Robertson not to follow

King's decision and instead to allow the RCMP to intervene officially in the Gouzenko case.

But if we consult the unedited text of King's diary in the archives, it becomes clear that the above-mentioned intelligence officer could not have been Stephenson. On September 6, King wrote in his diary, "*The head* of the British Secret Service arrived at the Seigniory Club [Montebello] today. Robertson was going down to see him tonight. I told him he should stay and make this individual come to Ottawa to talk with him" [italics added]. On September 7, King noted that he had authorized Robertson to telephone Stephenson in New York. And on September 8, King records, "Robertson said that Stephenson and the FBI representatives would be here tonight."

King's account in his diary was confirmed many years later by one of Robertson's deputies, who in an interview let it slip that in fact Stephenson was not in Ottawa when the defection occurred: "We wanted to get Stephenson [here] quickly and he was coming by commercial air. I was told to ask the Air Force to bring him up specially but it didn't work – because I couldn't tell them why. You had to pretend that anything you did was perfectly normal. Otherwise it suggested some kind of crisis, which is the last thing they [the government] wanted to do. So I remember talking to the Air Force and they weren't a bit convinced. But he [Stephenson] did turn up."[64]

Some sources have hypothesized that the British intelligence officer referred to by King was none other than MI6 director Sir Stewart Menzies, "C."[65] But a more probable candidate is Peter Dwyer, the MI6 representative in Washington who had worked for William Stephenson during the war. Dwyer was, apart from Stephenson, the top British intelligence officer in North America, and he would play a leading role in the Gouzenko case. In a telegram to London on September 10, British High Commissioner to Canada Malcolm MacDonald referred to one of Stephenson's men "who has been here for the last three days and who knows all the facts."[66] But why would Dwyer have suddenly showed up at Montebello on September 6? Was it just a coincidence that Gouzenko defected the night before?

There are other puzzles about the defection story that remain unsolved. Whatever happened to the Gouzenkos' English friend, Mrs. Bourke, who took care of Andrei and, according to Gouzenko, gave them tea when they went to retrieve him? Although the Royal Commission investigating the case later interviewed all of the other neighbors extensively, Mrs. Bourke was never heard from (or mentioned) after Gouzenko spoke about her in his initial statement to the RCMP.[67] And why did Mr. Edwin Elliott, whose wife, Frances, allowed the Gouzenkos to spend the night in her apartment hiding from the NKVD, write to Mackenzie King months later (after the case was made public) asking for money in exchange for silence about certain aspects of the Gouzenko case? Did Mrs. Elliott know something that she did not reveal in her testimony before the Royal Commission? As it turned out, the RCMP ordered all the neighbors to keep quiet about the Gouzenkos, even after the story became public.[68]

It is also puzzling that as his first step in defecting, Gouzenko, who spoke only broken English and carried a bunch of documents in Russian (which no one at the *Journal* could read), approached a small city newspaper instead of going to the RCMP. He had, after all, placed himself and his family in a situation of real physical danger, which required police protection. Gouzenko later told the RCMP that he did not want to go directly to them, because he thought that someone there might be a Soviet agent: "I knew that the system of military intelligence [the GRU] had not its own agent on the staff of the R.C.M. Police in Ottawa, but I did not know whether or not the system of the NKVD had its own agent there. Therefor [*sic*] I considered that it was dangerous for the whole undertaking to turn to the R.C.M. Police at first as, under the worst circumstances, if there were a Soviet agent there and all this subject were turned over to him, he would be able to direct it into a channel favourable to the Soviet intelligence and to the benefit of the agent himself."[69] What apparently did not occur to Gouzenko was that, even if the *Ottawa Journal* had publicized his story immediately, he would still have had to seek protection from the RCMP and hand over his documents.

Of course, Gouzenko was in a state of high anxiety, so he may not have thought things out clearly. Also, he was mindful of the story of Kravchenko. He was unaware, however, that Kravchenko had been talking to the FBI prior to his defection and, in exchange for providing information about Soviet espionage, had set forth a number of demands, including physical protection, a change of identity, and monetary support.[70] Apparently such a course of action did not occur to Gouzenko. Or did it? Is it possible, as some have suggested, that he had made contact with someone in the Canadian or British intelligence services before he defected but went to a newspaper in order to ensure that he would get asylum?

There is nothing to indicate such prior contact in the RCMP files that have been released, and two former RCMP officers have emphatically stated that Gouzenko was a complete unknown to their agency before September 5, 1945.[71] As for prior communication with British intelligence, again, there is no indication in the MI5 files that have recently been declassified. Nonetheless, the possibility of such an encounter cannot be dismissed out of hand. The British were actively engaged in attempts to recruit Soviet spies, and they considered Canada legitimate territory for such attempts. It might be added that in a September 2001 interview in Moscow, NKVD *rezident* Vitalii Pavlov, although offering no evidence, said that Gouzenko had been induced to defect by a Western counterintelligence service.[72]

If Gouzenko had had some contact with a member of the British intelligence services before September 5 and perhaps had already passed on some documents, this might explain why Norman Robertson knew details about Gouzenko's evidence as early as the morning of September 6. It might also explain how Anna Gouzenko, on the night of September 6, was able to fit all the GRU documents they had at their apartment into her purse before going across the hall to spend the night. Remember that in total, Gouzenko had stolen about 250 sheets of paper. One of the Ottawa policemen later recalled that Anna was carrying a "ladies' handbag": "She showed me her bag with everything they had taken from the Russians. . . . She held onto it all the time, Not him. Her."[73] Because the RCMP hushed up the witnesses and kept all their testimony under wraps for years, we cannot be sure of what exactly Gouzenko said and what he did during this twenty-four-hour period. One thing can be said with certainty: Gouzenko's decision to defect on September 5, 1945, threw everyone, including the RCMP and British intelligence, into a tailspin.

⌇

When King awoke on the morning of Friday the seventh, he called Norman Robertson, who told him that "last night's events had not given him much rest." By now Gouzenko was at RCMP headquarters making a statement. Robertson apparently justified his decision to let the RCMP intervene by the fact that the defector's life was in danger. He appears not to have told King that the RCMP had been well informed of the Russian's movements for almost two days and had already, on the previous afternoon, agreed to meet with him.

The situation became more complicated that evening, after King returned from a garden party at the British High Commission, Earnscliffe. ("It is always that way," King lamented in his diary entry of September 7, "the moment I take an hour or two off for social events, most important events come up.") Robertson told him he had received the particulars of what the defector said to the police and what his documents revealed. "They disclose an espionage system on a large scale," wrote King in his diary. "He [Robertson] said that it went to lengths we could not have believed." Robertson also said Gouzenko's information showed that the former American secretary of state Stettinius had been "surrounded by spies," who had informed the Russian government of everything that was going on. There was currently a spy in the Canadian Department of External Affairs who had access to ciphers, and in a Canadian research laboratory where they were working on the atomic bomb. There was a British scientist in Montreal who was a Russian agent, and also a spy at the British High Commission in Ottawa who saw all the ingoing and outgoing telegrams.[74]

Gouzenko's interview at RCMP headquarters that morning had been with Intelligence Chief Rivett-Carnac and his deputy John Leopold, who knew a little Russian. According to a top secret RCMP report, "Gouzenko was in a highly agitated and emotionally disturbed state. In fact, he appeared close to a nervous collapse. Because of this condition his speech was rather incoherent and his train of thought and expression were confused to the point of being extremely difficult to comprehend . . . these Headquarters were convinced from Gouzenko's actions and temporary mental instability that the weight of his precarious position would have driven him to the murder of his wife and final suicide."[75] In subsequent testimony before the Canadian Royal Commission, another RCMP officer who was present during this first interview had a similar, although less dramatic, impression: "Due to Mr. Gouzenko's highly nervous condition it was difficult to gather a coherent story. It was therefore arranged that Mr. Gouzenko would be interviewed later in the afternoon by Inspector Leopold."[76]

After one more interview with Leopold the same day, Gouzenko and his family were whisked off to a secret hiding place near Ottawa. Amazingly, despite Gouzenko's confusion, and although many of Gouzenko's documents were in handwritten Russian (and thus difficult to decipher), the RCMP was convinced that Gouzenko's revelations were of such significance that they notified British and American intelligence officials immediately. And, only three days later, on the morning of September 10, the Canadian government felt sufficiently confident of the defector's information to issue a secret Order-in-Council authorizing the detention (if necessary) of British scientist Alan Nunn May under the provisions of the War Measures Act.[77] May, who was about to return to Britain, was identified in the documents only by his Russian code name, Alek.

The rapidity with which the RCMP acted might again suggest that someone from the intelligence services had seen Gouzenko or his documents before September 5. But it is equally possible that a cursory look at some roughly translated items from Gouzenko was enough to spur the RCMP into swift action. The defection of a cipher clerk from a foreign embassy was, after all, a momentous occurrence. Gouzenko's desperation, to the point of threatening suicide, made it likely that he was telling the truth about who he was and where his documents came from. With a scientist passing atomic secrets to the Soviets, a Soviet agent operating at the British High Commission, and spies surrounding the American secretary of state, the RCMP had to act quickly.

Chapter 2

A MAN CALLED CORBY

They were the ones who "chose freedom," like Kravchenko, who, following Krivitsky's example, ended up a disillusioned suicide. But was it freedom they sought, or the flesh-pots? It is remarkable that not one of them volunteered to stay in position, and risk his neck for "freedom." One and all, they cut and ran for safety.

Kim Philby, *My Silent War*

While Gouzenko was wandering desperately around Ottawa with Anna and Andrei on the morning of September 6, intelligence officers at the Soviet Embassy were also in a state of panic. As the NKVD's Pavlov recalled, "In the morning our military attaché Zabotin comes to me totally at a loss and he tells me, 'Here we have documents that have disappeared, and our code clerk has also disappeared.' And I say, 'How could they disappear?'" According to Pavlov, "It was stunning news, since although in intelligence betrayal and disappearance is always an option, it is still rather rare."[1] Pavlov immediately notified the NKVD in Moscow about Gouzenko's disappearance, and the news was passed to the GRU. GRU colonel Mil'shtein claimed that his headquarters knew about Gouzenko "before he fell into the hands of the Royal Mounted Police [RCMP]."[2]

Pavlov's options were limited. He needed to get Gouzenko back, but he had to be careful not to cause a scandal in tranquil Ottawa, one that could result in a major diplomatic incident. As his first move, Pavlov sent a driver to 511 Somerset, but the Gouzenkos' door was locked and there was no response to the driver's pounding. A few hours later he took the more decisive step of going to Gouzenko's apartment with a group of his men, one of whom carried a revolver. But the Gouzenkos were not there, and before they could finish their search for the missing documents they were confronted by the Ottawa police and forced to leave.

The final resort was diplomatic pressure. The next day, by which time Gouzenko and his family were in RCMP custody, the Soviet Embassy sent a letter to the Canadian Department of External Affairs, claiming that Gouzenko had stolen money and requesting that Canadian authorities "take urgent measures to seek and arrest I. Gouzenko and to hand him over for deportation as a capital criminal." The letter also complained about the "rude treatment" the Soviets had received from the police at Gouzenko's apartment the evening before.[3]

Norman Robertson, ever the diplomat, wrote back to the Soviet ambassador, Mr. Georgii Zarubin, saying that every effort would be made to find Gouzenko and his family and requesting their physical descriptions. He also apologized for the lack of courtesy shown by the Ottawa police.[4] As undersecretary for Canadian external affairs, Robertson would find himself responsible for handling most aspects of the Gouzenko case. Tall, with a "curious loping gait," Robertson was raised in Vancouver, where his father was a professor of classics at Vancouver College. As was typical for well-bred Canadians of his generation, Robertson had gone to England for graduate work, where, on a Rhodes scholarship, he studied economics at Oxford. He went on to pursue a Ph.D. but gave it up to become a diplomat. Robertson was not an admirer of Mackenzie King. When posted to the Prime Minister's Office briefly in 1937, he had "moved heaven and earth" to get another position. But King liked Robertson, appointing him to the key foreign affairs post in 1941.[5]

The Gouzenko affair was a tremendous challenge for Robertson. As an MI5 official, Guy Liddell, observed sardonically, Robertson "would do anything rather than risk any diplomatic unpleasantness."[6] Yet here he was, on the brink of a showdown with the Soviets.

Robertson was shocked to learn there were spies in the Canadian civil service and also that the Russians could have behaved in such an underhanded way toward their allies. According to his biographer, "For Robertson, worn down as he was by his responsibilities, the Gouzenko case was an unwelcome added burden of incalculable weight, and he became very secretive at this stage. . . . It was a difficult period, and his wife attributed the loss of his good humour and the increase in the number of his deep sighs to Gouzenko and related security questions. Dealing with people's lives troubled him greatly."[7] What would make things even harder for Robertson was that he knew personally several of those named as spy suspects.

Robertson forwarded a copy of the Soviet letter to RCMP commissioner Stuart Wood, asking (as a formality, since Robertson knew Gouzenko was in RCMP hands) for any information Wood might have about Gouzenko. Wood's reply to Robertson on September 10 seems to have been written on the assumption his words would be passed on to the Soviets. Wood admitted that Gouzenko had appeared at RCMP offices on the morning of the seventh in a state of panic. But he then embellished the story considerably: "Mr. Gusenko [*sic*] was in a very excited condition and by reason of this fact was incoherent and exceedingly difficult to understand. He appeared to be on the verge of a nervous breakdown. . . . It was thought in the best interests that if Mr. Gusenko's wife was to be brought to exercise her influence over him, Mr. Gusenko's condition of mind might be improved and that he would then leave the office of his own accord and return to his apartment." Wood went on to report that Mrs. Gouzenko came to RCMP headquarters to calm her husband down, and then the couple were driven in the direction of their apartment. But halfway there, after a heated discussion, they jumped out of the car and disappeared.[8]

To give substance to this story, RCMP headquarters then sent out an all-points "confidential" bulletin to its offices across Canada. The bulletin reported that Gouzenko, his wife, and his child had disappeared with a quantity of stolen money and stated that the Soviet Embassy was trying to ascertain his whereabouts. A physical description of the couple was provided, along with a request that every effort be made to find them. Commissioner Wood even went so far as to send FBI chief Hoover a similar letter, but Hoover of course knew that the whole thing was an elaborate ruse to appease the Soviets and keep them off Gouzenko's trail. The provincial RCMP offices, by contrast, had no inkling that Gouzenko had in fact been given asylum. They engaged in extensive searches for the Gouzenkos, reporting back to Ottawa that the missing persons were not to be found.[9]

Soviet ambassador Zarubin had hoped at first that the Canadians could be persuaded to hand over Gouzenko, but after a conversation with King on September 10 he realized this was probably not going to happen. Zarubin, who, like King, kept a secret diary, recorded that King complained to him about "fatigue and over-work, because in addition to all foreign affairs, he was very busy with significant domestic problems, which the newly-convened parliament would be examining." The fact that King did not mention the subject of Gouzenko made it clear to Zarubin that a behind-the-scenes deal to get him back was unrealistic.[10]

The ambitious subterfuge devised by Norman Robertson and the RCMP was of course pointless. The Soviets were able to confirm early on that Gouzenko was in the hands of Canadian intelligence after Kim Philby tipped them off. Philby would have learned about the defection almost immediately. On September 17, Pavel Fitin, head of the NKVD's foreign department in Moscow, sent the following message to the NKVD's London residency: "The chiefs gave their consent to the checking of the accuracy of your telegram concerning Stanley's [Philby's code name] data about the events in Canada in the 'neighbors' [GRU] sphere of activity. Stanley's information does correspond to the facts."[11]

Another message, from the NKVD London *rezident* sometime in September, read, "Stanley [Philby] reports that he managed to learn details of the information turned over to Canada by the traitor Guzenko. . . . As a result of these affairs the British intelligence and counterintelligence organs are undoubtedly going to take effective measures soon against illegal activity by fraternal and Soviet intelligence. Stanley was a bit agitated himself. I tried to calm him down. Stanley said that in connection with this he may have information of extreme urgency to pass to us."[12] In a follow-up report to the NKVD, Philby analyzed the evidence against Nunn May and gave the opinion that it was inconclusive.[13]

Ironically, in just a couple of days Philby would be reporting to Moscow on another defection – that of NKVD Lt.-Col. Konstantin Volkov, who was the Soviet vice-consul in Istanbul. Volkov had shown up at the British Embassy there on September 4, just a day before Gouzenko made his break with the Soviets. In exchange for asylum, he offered to name 250 Soviet agents operating in Britain, including one who headed a section in British counterintelligence. Fortunately for Philby, who was probably the spy Volkov was referring to, the British were slow in acting on Volkov's offer and it did not even reach the Foreign Office and MI6 until September 19. Philby had an emergency meeting with his Soviet handler that night, and within a few days, before the arrangements for asylum were finalized, Volkov and his wife had been drugged by the Soviets, carried on stretchers onto a plane, and flown out of Istanbul to the Soviet Union.[14]

NKVD *rezident* Pavlov had no such opportunity to get to Gouzenko, and he was deeply concerned. The defection, after all, had occurred right under his nose. It was bad enough that for the past two years Gouzenko had access to all GRU communications to and from Moscow. Pavlov assumed that the traitor had probably told the Canadians and their allies about NKVD operations as well. As a GRU employee, Gouzenko did not have anything to do with the NKVD, but he nonetheless knew how things worked in a general way, and he might have heard some specifics from others at the embassy. Pavlov had no choice but to warn Vasilii Zarubin, head of NKVD operations in New York, "about possible unpleasant consequences for our intelligence operations in North America."[15]

Fred Rose, the Canadian member of Parliament who had been a middleman for the Soviets, received word about Gouzenko's disappearance the day after it happened. Concerned about causing panic, he told his contacts, "Lie low. Don't talk. Nothing will happen."[16] Upon hearing from Rose, Gordon Lunan was stunned: "When Fred Rose gave me the news in September that 'one of the

Russkies has flown the coop,' I realized at once that life would never be the same again . . . I clearly saw prison bars in the future."[17]

Rose told Lunan that nothing was likely to come of the defection because Mackenzie King would be reluctant to trigger an international scandal. And as time went on, with no reaction from Canadian authorities, Lunan began to feel more comfortable. He and Rose even went to the Soviet Embassy on November 7 to celebrate the anniversary of the Bolshevik Revolution. There, Lunan spotted his controller, Col. Rogov, who had cut off contact with him after the defection. Rogov was caught completely off guard when he glimpsed Lunan: "Seeing me, if not cheerfully at least normally at large and taking part in a social event, must have puzzled his programmed mind and suggested God knows what horrible possibilities."[18] Rogov and his comrades had dropped all their Canadian contacts and ceased attempting to gather secret intelligence. Now they were in the awkward position of feigning business as usual while awaiting instructions from headquarters, where their fate and the future course of GRU operations in Canada were being decided. A Damoclean sword hung over all of them, especially GRU station chief Zabotin.

The man at the center of these events, Gouzenko, had been escorted with his family from Ottawa by two armed RCMP officers late in the afternoon of September 7. Their orders were to get the Gouzenkos out of town as fast as possible. Was Gouzenko in real danger? Considering what the NKVD was about to do with Volkov in Istanbul, perhaps yes, although Ottawa was not in easy reach of an experienced Soviet hit team, and it would have been awkward (to say the least) for anyone from the Soviet Embassy to be involved with capturing or killing Gouzenko now that he was in the hands of the RCMP.

However much she worried about her husband's safety, Anna Gouzenko was not worried for herself. While Gouzenko had spent the day at the RCMP, she remained at the apartment with Andrei washing diapers. A Mountie was there to protect them, but she nonetheless had no qualms about going out on the balcony alone.

Igor chastised her afterward for being careless. She might have been shot, he said. Years later she laughed about this episode: "So the Soviets would shoot me, what's the use of me? I know nothing . . . [Canadians] would be horrified that [a] pregnant woman was shot there on the balcony, on her back porch. . . . Even Soviets understand that it would be very bad publicity."[19]

The Gouzenkos and their escorts ended up spending a few weeks in small and rather primitive vacation cabins on a lake about an hour from Ottawa. Anna, having become accustomed to the luxury of her own bath on Somerset Street, did not like it that the only place to bathe was the lake. They were also inadequately supplied with clothes, especially when the weather turned colder. In her haste and confusion when the RCMP driver came to pick her and Andrei up at the apartment, Anna had left almost everything behind, not realizing they would never be able to return.[20] (The Soviets apparently went back to 511 Somerset at some point and confiscated everything in the apartment.) Making matters worse, Gouzenko was so terrified, he could not sleep. At one point, according to the Mounties looking after him, he appeared outside his cabin in the middle of the night, completely nude, screaming for help. He had heard a noise that frightened him.[21]

RCMP officer John Leopold came out regularly to interrogate the defector. Born in Bohemia to Jewish parents, Leopold had emigrated to Canada in 1913 and joined the RCMP five years later, at age twenty-eight. Only five feet four inches tall, Leopold was below the required height to be a Mountie. Being Jewish would also have been a drawback for entering the predominately Anglo-Canadian RCMP, but he seems to have passed himself off as a Christian, and his knowledge of several languages was a much-needed asset. He spent the next decade as a secret RCMP agent, posing as a house painter and working his way up the hierarchy of the radical Canadian labor movement.[22]

Leopold earned a name for himself as a single-minded anticommunist and was a star witness in a trial of members of the Canadian Communist Party in 1931. But he also had a history of personal problems. During the thirties he was almost booted out of the RCMP for alcoholism and insubordination. After the Soviet Union joined the Allies in the Second World War, Leopold was criticized for his obsession with fighting communism. His RCMP job, one Canadian civil servant complained in a 1942 memorandum to the prime minister, seemed "to depend on continuing to uncover Bolshevik plots." But the Gouzenko case would mute Leopold's critics and further his career. In October 1945, he was appointed chief of the RCMP's Special Section (intelligence branch), and other promotions followed.[23]

Ironically, given his intense anti-communism, Leopold's relations with Gouzenko were difficult. Part of the problem was the language barrier. According to one Mountie guarding the family, "Gouzenko's English wasn't too good and Leopold's Russian wasn't very good, so they had a time getting things straight." In the end, the RCMP called in a Russian-speaker, a former RCMP secret agent named Mervyn Black, to act as interpreter. Leopold continued to question Gouzenko with Black's assistance, but there was tension. Gouzenko's daughter would later claim that her father was threatened repeatedly with being handed over to the Soviets, apparently because Leopold did not find him sufficiently cooperative. This both terrified Gouzenko and antagonized him, and he soon made up his mind that Leopold was a Russian agent. On one occasion Gouzenko even refused to ride in the same car with him. "Don't ever have that man around me again," Gouzenko reportedly told another Mountie.[24] It may seem that Gouzenko was paranoid, but he knew from his experience in the GRU that the Soviets had double agents in Western governments. And, of course, Leopold was not exactly a typical Mountie.

At the beginning of October, the Gouzenkos were moved to a larger, heated three-bedroom cottage on Otter Lake, near Smiths Falls, Ontario. This was slightly more comfortable but with the baby coming it would not do for the long term. So after a couple of weeks they were transferred yet again, to a farmhouse located not far from Toronto in a place called Camp X. Situated on the shores of Lake Ontario, Camp X, or Special Training School 103, had been established by William Stephenson in 1941 for the purpose of training

Americans (mainly from the Office of Strategic Services – OSS – or the FBI), Canadians, and personnel from the British Security Coordination in the art of sabotage and counterintelligence. Those trained at the camp entered the so-called Special Operations Executive (SOE) for dangerous missions behind enemy lines. The camp had been closed the year before but was still surrounded by wire fences and thus was ideal from the point of view of security.[25]

Anna Gouzenko, finally able to take a proper bath, looked on their new living quarters favorably, at least compared to what they were used to in Russia. According to one of the Mounties who lived there with them (and slept with a gun under his pillow), "It was a typical old farmhouse . . . not very comfortable. Not very imposing. She [Anna] was pleased as punch with it because she thought it was real nice. It wasn't. It was very awful. She was thinking in terms of one room and three people in a room. Here she had three bedrooms upstairs."[26] Anna, by this time seven months pregnant, was in "nesting" mode, content to keep busy knitting babies' clothes, sewing on a machine provided by the RCMP, and looking after the rambunctious two-year-old Andrei.

Her husband, not surprisingly, remained highly apprehensive. RCMP officer George Mackay, who was Gouzenko's personal guard at Camp X, noted that the defector was "thoroughly frightened as to what his fate might be. . . . He wanted somebody with him all the time."[27] But he felt comfortable enough to begin painting landscapes, including one of the beach on Lake Ontario. (Presumably, his artist's supplies were courtesy of the RCMP.) The man in charge at Camp X, RCMP inspector George McClellan, reported back to Rivett-Carnac on October 8, "Black and I had a long talk with Corby today, and I think for the first time he is relaxing. He was very nervous, but on looking over the situation he feels he is safe."[28]

Corby was Gouzenko's code name, given to him by Canadian authorities to ensure his security and to keep his defection a secret. The idea for the name came from Norman Robertson, who, so the story goes, had been putting all the documents related to the Gouzenko case in an empty box that bore the name of Corby Distillers on the outside. (Founded in the mid-nineteenth century by Henry Corby, the company was, and still is, well known to Canadians who consume spirits.)

Robertson was working closely with the RCMP's Charles Rivett-Carnac on the Corby case. Rivett-Carnac fit the RCMP mould far better than did John Leopold. He was educated in England and had spent several years in India – where his father, an English baronet, had served as a high-ranking police official – before immigrating to Canada and joining the RCMP, in 1920, at age twenty-one. He would eventually rise to become RCMP commissioner.

Long aware that the Soviet Embassy in Ottawa had been trying to recruit agents for espionage, Rivett-Carnac was not completely surprised by Gouzenko's revelations.[29] But this was the first time the RCMP had anything like concrete evidence of Soviet spying. As Rivett-Carnac put it, "So far it had not been possible to gain any positive proof of Russian activities which could be publicly laid on the table, for quite apart from the fact that the war had immersed us in an all-out effort in other directions, the Communist undercover network was of so secret a nature that there was not enough evidence to point this out definitely. If Gouzenko had anything in his possession of value it might close the gap!"[30]

For all his enthusiasm, Rivett-Carnac was out of his depth. Neither he nor anyone else in the RCMP, including Leopold, had experience with defectors. In the words of one observer, the Mounties "didn't know what the hell to do." Another source confirmed that "this was too big for the Canadians to handle on their own. The RCMP was simply too ill-equipped to deal with a major espionage case alone."[31] So they needed help from the Americans and the British, who were more than willing to become involved.

∾

The FBI in Washington heard about Gouzenko on September 8, when their representative in Ottawa, Glen Bethel (stationed there as part of a secret exchange arrangement with the RCMP) telephoned headquarters to say, "a matter had come up in connection with Communist cases which appeared to be of vital importance." There was to be a conference in Ottawa on the matter on September 10,

Bethel said, and he wanted someone from the bureau with a background in communism to attend. The FBI sent Lish Whitson, its top communist expert, "a quiet, studious researcher" who was deeply involved in the FBI's ongoing investigation of atomic espionage and the Comintern, the international organization uniting communist groups. As soon as Whitson arrived in Ottawa he called Hoover's deputy, Mickey Ladd, to say excitedly that they had "hit the jackpot." They had quite a few documents and were "turning up material there all the time."[32] Hoover was delighted. On September 13, he wrote a letter to RCMP commissioner Stuart Wood, thanking him for drawing the Gouzenko case to his attention: "The details of the organized effort and the viciousness of its implications clearly demonstrate the necessity for the emphasis which has been placed by both our organizations on investigations of this type. Please accept my assurances of complete cooperation in this matter." Somewhat later, in November 1945, the FBI sent an agent from its Buffalo, New York, office, as an additional liaison officer on the case in Ottawa.[33]

MI6's Peter Dwyer, who may have arrived in Ottawa as early as September 6, was joined by John-Paul Evans, a colleague from the British Security Coordination in New York. Described by an FBI acquaintance as "a clever, witty and charming Briton," Dwyer was ideally suited for the job of coordinating allied efforts in the Gouzenko case. As William Stephenson's second-in-command at the BSC during the war, Dwyer had been a frequent guest of the RCMP in Ottawa and so was on familiar ground. Moreover, as Kim Philby observed in *My Silent War*, Dwyer "had a great deal more to him than just wit. During the war, he had succeeded in the prickly task of establishing close personal relations with many leading figures in the FBI." According to a former boss, Dwyer's abundant charm did not prevent him from being "tough in a quiet way."[34] Dwyer and Evans began working at RCMP headquarters, sending daily reports to the British Security Coordination in New York, where – due to concerns about the security of communications from Ottawa – Sir William Stephenson had set up a special encoding system. The messages were then forwarded to MI6 in London, where Philby was the first to read them. Not surprisingly, MI5 officials were not keen about this arrangement, because they could not be sure that they saw everything received by MI6. But Malcolm MacDonald and William Stephenson insisted that it was necessary for security reasons.

Although he worked for MI6, the small and dynamic Stephenson, whose "restless attitude toward his place in history" would make him a legend, was in fact a Canadian. A former amateur lightweight boxing champion, Stephenson had grown up near Winnipeg, Manitoba. He became a fighter pilot in World War I and then a highly successful entrepreneur and financial speculator. His extensive business interests and private intelligence contacts attracted the attention of Winston Churchill, who asked him to take charge of coordinating the exchange of intelligence between Britain and the United States during the Second World War. In 1941, the BSC was established for this purpose, with headquarters at 3603 Rockefeller Center. The BSC also was to operate covertly on behalf of the British government and to gain "assurance of American participation in secret activities throughout the world." According to some sources, Churchill had such confidence in Stephenson that he authorized him to view the transcripts from Britain's top secret decoding of German Enigma ciphers at Bletchley Park and then to decide what information to pass to the Americans and Canadians.[36] But given Stephenson's proclivity for self-promotion, this might have been only lore.

Neither J. Edgar Hoover nor MI6 chief Stewart Menzies trusted Stephenson. Hoover and Stephenson had a falling out back in 1942, when Hoover, resentful of Stephenson's prerogatives in wartime intelligence, participated in an effort to curtail the BSC's operations in the United States. In response, "Stephenson told Hoover exactly what he thought of him," accusing him of intrigue and refusing to have any dealings with him. The situation later improved because of Hoover's efforts at reconciliation, but the two remained deeply suspicious of each other. As for Menzies, who gave Churchill daily briefings on the decrypts coming from Bletchley Park, he had reportedly opposed Stephenson's appointment as the representative of British intelligence in the Western hemisphere. Thus it is ironic that Stephenson was able to take charge of the communications network in the Gouzenko case.[37]

Interestingly, Stephenson seems to have decided to steer the FBI and MI6 away from matters concerning the Soviets' cryptology. The British and Americans sent cryptology experts from their military security branches to Ottawa through Stephenson and independent of the regular intelligence services. Although the GRU would have immediately changed all its codes, Gouzenko at least was able to explain to his debriefers how the GRU's cipher system operated.[38]

For security reasons, and perhaps also because of Gouzenko's precarious mental state, the number of interviewers was kept to a minimum. Although the FBI's Lish Whitson interviewed Gouzenko (using Mervyn Black as the interpreter) shortly after the defection, neither Dwyer nor John-Paul Evans talked directly to him. Instead, they passed questions through John Leopold, who would provide written translations, presumably done by Black, of Gouzenko's responses.[39] But one British representative did meet directly with Gouzenko – Roger Hollis, the MI5 officer responsible for monitoring communist subversion in the British dominion. As such, Hollis was MI5's point man for the Gouzenko case.

A tall, stooping man of forty, Hollis had been educated at Oxford, but failed to pass his final examinations. According to Sir Dick White, his boss at MI5, who had been a contemporary at Oxford, Hollis might have been a successful classical scholar, "but he chose instead an Oxford interlude of wine and roses." White thought well of Hollis: "Roger was hard-working, calm and fair-minded. What I liked was his competence and his dry and witty manner." But others recalled "his irksome nasal tone and his predilection for pinching women's bottoms, characteristics redeemed by his fund of 'good, dirty jokes which he told well.'"[40]

Whereas the view toward communism within MI5 had been much more benign since Germany invaded the Soviet Union in 1941, Hollis himself, like Menzies at MI6, was never persuaded that Soviet subversion had ceased to be a dangerous threat. Although Churchill had directed the intelligence services to treat the Soviet Union as an ally and relax pressure on the communists, Hollis ignored the order. MI5 continued to conduct counterintelligence operations, albeit discreetly, against communists in Britain throughout the war.[41]

Unfortunately for Hollis, MI5 had overlooked Alan Nunn May, an outspoken communist when he was studying at Cambridge – reportedly even "protesting against Britain's 'imperialist war' with Germany." Although May was privy to atomic secrets after he was recruited to the Tube Alloys project, MI5 had never conducted a security screening on him. His alleged espionage now created an embarrassment for the British government, which had been anxious to become more involved in the American atomic weapons project. On September 10, British High Commissioner Malcolm MacDonald sent the following message to Sir Alexander Cadogan, British undersecretary for foreign affairs: "Robertson draws my attention to the fact that vetting of United Kingdom scientists sent to Canada on [atomic] project was responsibility of British Government and if these leakages on further investigation prove as serious as they appear at moment then H.M.G. [her Majesty's government] will be liable to criticism by United States Government."[42]

Philby was partly responsible for the decision to send Hollis to Canada on September 16. He did not want to go himself, but it was not because of the Volkov affair. At that point, contrary to most accounts, Philby had not yet learned of Volkov's effort to defect in Istanbul, so he had no idea that he was in danger of being exposed. Philby wanted to avoid going to Canada because, as one source puts it, "this would remove him from the London center, from where every Western move in the [Gouzenko] crisis could be monitored by him and passed on to his Soviet contacts."[43]

The RCMP was preparing to present Gouzenko to the world as a hero, but Hollis considered him differently. As a British historian explained, "Defectors, he reasoned, were deserters or, worse, traitors, distastefully different from captured Abwehr agents." Hollis was not receptive to what Gouzenko had to say: "Instead of tickling Gouzenko's vanity and absorbing lessons about Soviet intelligence techniques, Hollis abruptly left the defector after just one hour and flew back across the Atlantic to chase Nunn May, now living in

London."[44] Hollis returned to Canada for a second interview with Gouzenko, on November 21, 1945, and he considered Gouzenko important enough to raise the idea of taking him to London for debriefing. But Gouzenko later claimed that Hollis misrepresented what he said in the interviews and even went so far as to accuse Hollis of being a Soviet spy.[45]

Mackenzie King shared Hollis's reservations about Gouzenko's motives, but he nonetheless took the defector's revelations seriously and was shocked that the Soviets had been conducting espionage against his country. He confided to his diary on September 11, "This revelation gives one a new and more appalling outlook on the world than one has ever had before . . . I cannot believe that this information has come to me as a matter of chance. I can only pray for God's guidance that I may be able to be an instrument in the control of powers beyond me to help save a desperate situation."

King was extremely pious, but his spirituality was not confined to God. His main inspiration came from talking to his deceased mother through mediums. A lifelong bachelor, King preferred above all the solitude of his country residence, Kingsmere. His greatest pleasure was going for walks with his little Irish terrier, Pat, whom each evening he would kiss goodnight. A descendant of a Scotch-English family, King was not a man of great political vision or intellectual depth, despite his impressive academic credentials, which included post-graduate work at Harvard and the University of Chicago. Yet he had managed repeatedly to win the support of his Liberal Party and the Canadian electorate. One of King's biographers wondered, "Did he stay in office by Machiavellian cunning? Or was the man so ordinary that he was the average Canadian writ large – unconsciously embodying the aspirations of most of his countrymen? Or did he succeed by default, surviving only because his rivals were so tragically incompetent? There was no agreement, no consensus, because somehow this rather pudgy little man, best remembered for his indecision and procrastination or his uninspiring platitudes, could never be reconciled with the political leader who had a talent for winning elections."[46]

Time magazine explained King's persistent success as a politician more precisely, if not condescendingly: Canada was "a country deeply endowed with moral sense. Its feelings about 'decency' stem from deep roots in both its Anglo-Saxon and French traditions." As a result, Canadians, who valued respectability and could even be puritanical, appreciated a leader like King: "A steady, colorless man with too much honor and intellect to be a demagogue, too little fire to be an orator, too little hair and too few mannerisms to be spectacular, King fits his country's mood and pattern."[47]

With his usual self-absorption, King saw himself at the center of the crisis over Gouzenko, and he could not hide his satisfaction that Canada, for once, was getting some attention from its more powerful allies. On September 23, he remarked at a dinner with the small group of intelligence officers and diplomats involved in the case "that it was strange the discovery of all this business should have come to our little country but that perhaps after all, it was true that it was the weak things of the earth that were chosen to confound the strong."[48] King assumed that his government would be in charge of the case, but once the British and the Americans were called in, Canada was not making decisions on its own. Too much was at stake.

❧

The daily telegrams that passed back and forth from Ottawa to MI6, MI5, and the FBI (filtered through the BSC in New York) attest to the sense of urgency with which Canada's allies viewed the Gouzenko affair. Although he probably resented the fact that he was getting its messages through Stephenson (code-named 48000) in New York, MI6 director Menzies, "C," was following developments closely, along with his subordinate Kim Philby. Menzies was a quintessential British spymaster – upper-class and slightly eccentric. He wore the bowler hat of a civil servant and a brush moustache that protruded over "an occasional tight smile." Described as "reclusive, methodical and athletically fit," Menzies was said to be "an avid pursuer of foxes," but the scent of Philby, the cleverest fox of all, eluded him.[49]

J. Edgar Hoover, too, was keeping his eyes on the Gouzenko case, through a constant stream of memoranda from his aides. One of these he sent back with a note on the bottom: "Be certain to give *all angles* of this case preferred attention."[50] He was anxious to make an impression on the Truman White House, whose interest was not easy to attract when it came to alleged communist infiltration of the government. Earlier, when the letter to the White House about the Gouzenko case reached his desk for his signature on September 12, he had written an angry memorandum to his aides. The letter should have come to him sooner, he complained, because the War Department had heard about the defection and undoubtedly was able to inform the president before his letter arrived. Secondly, Hoover said, the form of the letter was "quite unsatisfactory. It doesn't indicate in any sense of the word that the FBI was playing any part in this situation. As I understand it, we sent a man to Canada to confer about it and we did do a considerable amount of work in the way of translation, et cetera, upon it."[51]

Meanwhile, the British had put together a comprehensive report on behalf of the BSC, entitled "Intelligence Department of the Red Army in Moscow and Ottawa, 1945."[52] Like the much briefer FBI document, Evans's and Dwyer's report was based on interviews with "Corby" (Gouzenko) and an analysis of his documents. The report listed twenty-seven individuals who were connected with Zabotin's GRU operation in Canada, including an American scientist named Arthur Steinberg. Steinberg, who was mentioned in the FBI's first report on the Gouzenko case, had come to Canada in 1940 to assume a lectureship in genetics at McGill University and had become friendly with spy suspect Raymond Boyer in Montreal. He returned to the United States in June 1944 to take up employment with the Office of Scientific Research and Development of the U.S. Navy before returning to academia after the war. According to Evans and Dwyer, "Several months ago Freda [a GRU agent] gave this man's name to Grant [Zabotin] and his headquarters expressed considerable interest . . . Steinberg *was to be asked* [italics added] to work either for Soviet Intelligence or for the Communist Party . . . Corby states that the man assigned to contact Steinberg in the

U.S.A. was Zervin (phonetic) of Amtorg [the Soviet Trading Corporation]." (The report did not explain why, if Steinberg had already been living in the U.S. since June 1944, Freda would bother giving his name to Zabotin. But it made clear that, although headquarters "expressed considerable interest" in Steinberg, he did not yet have any association with the GRU. He was merely on the GRU's wish list.)

Evans and Dwyer also mentioned the agent in the U.S. State Department: "Corby asserts that one of the *assistants to-?* [the part in italics was inserted in handwriting] Assistant Secretaries of State, when Stettinius was head of the State Department, was a Soviet agent. He can give no further details and it has so far been impossible to identify this alleged agent."

Hoover was intent on finding out more about the State Department official, who he already suspected was Alger Hiss. In a message to Mickey Ladd on October 23, Hoover again stressed that the case should be given "preferred attention" and asked, "Has anyone from here ever personally interviewed Gouzenko as to matters of special interest to us such as the Soviet agent in the State Department, etc.? Wouldn't it be a good idea to do so, as interrogations through an intermediary are always unsatisfactory?" Ladd responded that "the results of the interview of Guzenko by the Bureau's representative have been furnished to you in detail most recently in the memorandum to you of October 19, 1945."[53]

The memorandum Ladd was referring to was a twenty-two-page report, the most detailed yet on the Gouzenko case, which was also sent to the White House. The report provided a long description of how the Soviet GRU conducted its espionage activities abroad and who the most important recruits were in Canada. And more was said about the suspect in the State Department: Lt. Kulakov, the officer who replaced Gouzenko, had told Gouzenko that while he was still in Moscow he had learned "that an assistant of Stettinius, then the United States Secretary of State was a Soviet spy."[54] In a subsequent, undated report, the FBI observed, "Efforts are presently being made to identify this individual. A review of the Bureau files discloses that Alger Hiss and Donald Hiss, two brothers, who are employed by the State Department, were named by Whittaker

Chambers, a former Soviet agent . . . as members of the government Communist underground. Alger Hiss was the individual in charge of security arrangements for the United Nations Conference in San Francisco. The information available to the Bureau relative to Hiss is being carefully reviewed."[55]

As for Dr. Steinberg, between the first FBI report to the State Department on September 18 and the memorandum of October 19, he had been transformed by the FBI from a possible GRU recruit into an active agent. In the first report, Steinberg was "being developed as a possible agent." The October memorandum reads, "In the event a spy removes from Canada as in the case of Arthur Steinberg whose cover name is 'Berger,' arrangements are made to turn the spy over to the appropriate Soviet representative in the new country." And later, Steinberg "has been identified as the Arthur Steinberg, whose cover name is 'Berger' who was recruited into the spy organization in Canada and later transferred to the United States." Why had the status of Dr. Steinberg changed so significantly? Had Gouzenko been prodded by the FBI to provide additional allegations?

The British were also said by Gouzenko to be harboring a spy in the upper reaches of their government. But, as with Hiss and Steinberg, the information about the spy attributed to Gouzenko (there were no documents) was vague. According to the BSC report by Evans and Dwyer, while Gouzenko was still in Moscow he heard about a Soviet agent in England who worked for the British Intelligence Service. The code name of that agent, "Elli," was noted for the first time in a November 1945 RCMP report on the Gouzenko case. (Coincidentally, "Elli" was also the code name of another suspected spy, a woman who was working as a secretary in the office of the British High Commissioner in Ottawa.) Despite the potentially devastating implications of Gouzenko's allegations, neither MI5 nor MI6 paid them much attention. It was only later that the search for "Elli" would lead to a prolonged and tortuous mole hunt in the British security services, a mole hunt that would cast a deep shadow over Roger Hollis.

The RCMP was continuing to follow up on Gouzenko's information and collect additional evidence against the Canadians who had allegedly been recruited as spies in Zabotin's ring. In Charles Rivett-Carnac's words, "Slowly but surely, we were weaving our net round the agents, gathering up information which had been given us and fitting the odds and ends of details which would later establish without doubt that what Gouzenko had told us was correct. While we ourselves were entirely satisfied in regard to his story, we knew that when prosecutions were entered [into], even with the documents in our possession we would have a fight on our hands."[56]

The documents, often difficult to decipher because some were handwritten and in shorthand, included: three GRU dossiers on alleged spies; thirty-three telegrams between Ottawa and Moscow; one of Zabotin's mailing lists for early 1945; and numerous notes written by Zabotin and his assistant, Col. Rogov, about their recruits and meetings with them. Taken together, the documents confirmed that the Soviets were running an extensive program of espionage in the West. There was even a spy ring in Switzerland, an agent of which was working for the International Labor Office in Montreal. But the documents revealed little about what information had actually been passed to the Soviets, and in most cases they were not sufficient to justify prosecutions.

So RCMP investigators attempted to gather additional evidence that could be used in court. Much of this information was shared among all three allied governments and also sent to the Canadian Royal Commission established in early February 1946 to investigate Gouzenko's allegations. By the time the commission published its final, 733-page report in July 1946, it had accumulated more than six thousand pages of witness testimony and exhibits (classified as secret until the early 1980s). Whereas the Gouzenko documents accounted for thirty separate exhibits, the commission had altogether over six hundred exhibits presented in evidence. So Gouzenko's papers and testimony served as building blocks for what would become an enormous edifice of spy cases, with hundreds of new names brought in.

Early on in the case, Rivett-Carnac and John Leopold enlisted two RCMP officers to maintain surveillance on eleven suspects in the

Ottawa area, to see if they made contact with the GRU or incriminated themselves in any other way. They continued with the surveillance (with no results) throughout the winter.

The RCMP also added two experienced and tough investigators from Western Canada to the Gouzenko team – Clifford "Slim" Harvison and M.E. Anthony. Their job was to verify the authenticity of Gouzenko's documents and to gather more evidence. They had also been designated to interrogate the suspects once they were arrested, so they spent much of their time familiarizing themselves with the case and also getting information, indirectly, from Gouzenko. Harvison, who would eventually become RCMP commissioner, met Gouzenko personally some months later and came to admire him greatly: "In addition to having a remarkable memory, he was obviously a highly intelligent and gifted man. This early appraisal was borne out by the calm, cool manner in which he withstood the attacks of the many defence counsels during the subsequent trials." But Harvison did allow that Gouzenko was far from humble. Indeed, "one got the impression that his considerable talent was somewhat outstripped by his estimation of that talent."[57]

In those early days at Camp X, Gouzenko was easily distracted and had difficulty concentrating, partly of course because his wife and two-year-old son were with him constantly. RCMP Intelligence chief Rivett-Carnac wanted a complete statement from Gouzenko that incorporated all his knowledge of GRU operations in Canada, including names and code names, but it took a long time. In a letter to Rivett-Carnac in mid-October, Inspector George McClellan at Camp X explained why: "I would like to point out that under the living conditions at Rexall [Camp X] at the moment, Black [the interpreter] laboured under much difficulty in obtaining the statement already submitted herewith, and it will take some days to get a complete statement in the manner in which you want it. This is due to the fact that Corby has somewhat of a dreamer mentality and it is extremely difficult to pin him down to the business at hand."[58] On November 2, McClellan explained to Rivett-Carnac why the statement still was not ready: "This, as has been previously mentioned, is a painstaking task and cannot be rushed. Corby's mind is most difficult to pin down to matters at hand, but the statement is being completed and will be forwarded at the earliest possible moment."[59]

Gouzenko eventually complied, providing a detailed picture of Soviet espionage agencies, how they were organized, what their connections were with the Communist Party leadership, and how they went about recruiting spies. He told his interlocutors about so-called illegal agents, who entered Western countries on fake passports and lived under false identities. He discussed spy arrangements in the embassies and how they communicated with Moscow. He talked about the attitudes and motivations of Soviet intelligence officers abroad, and how they might be persuaded to provide information or to defect. The most vulnerable time for Soviet intelligence officers was just before they were to be sent back, when they did not know what to expect upon their return – promotion or arrest.

Gouzenko, clearly with a view to what he hoped his future would be, emphasized the example that would be set by the way he was treated, suggesting that if he was treated well, he could be used to recruit others. Gouzenko told his investigators, "It would be desirable to let word get out in a year or so in the press of Canada, the U.K. and U.S.A. etc. that Gusenko [sic] had settled down to a decent comfortable Canadian life – to prepare the ground psychologically for others. Perhaps a press photograph could appear, he suggested, showing him skiing somewhere."[60]

According to Gouzenko, the weak point in the Soviet espionage ring was the morale of the Soviet staff. "The idea of escaping or 'going over' crosses many minds," he asserted. Gouzenko told the RCMP that "many members of the Soviet mission in Ottawa, and hundreds in their missions in the United States, the U.K., Australia, etc. will be studying the press reports of Gouzenko's case with intense personal interest. Will we use him, extract the last drop of information from him perhaps finally by torture to make sure of all," Gouzenko wanted to know, "and then discard him, shoot him or maybe send him to a labour gang?" That Gouzenko even considered this a possibility shows how little he trusted or understood the motives of his Canadian hosts. He even suggested that, if they did cast him aside or shoot him, they should do it secretly and arrange to have the press cover it up. As his interlocutor observed, Gouzenko "still is apt to attribute to us the technique and controls of the Soviet system which he is accustomed to."[61]

When the RCMP produced its report in November, the debriefing of Gouzenko was completed. As the report noted, "Gouzenko has been thoroughly and extensively interrogated. He has been questioned and cross-questioned in an effort to extract every last particle of information possible."[62]

But the RCMP had another problem – Anna's pregnancy. Gouzenko's former colleagues at the Soviet Embassy, including Vitalii Pavlov, probably knew that she was expecting (although Gouzenko insisted they did not). The Mounties worried that the Russians would be checking at hospitals around the time of the birth and might be able to figure out where the Gouzenkos were located. Their fear was likely unwarranted, given that the Russians had limited resources and were lying low as a result of the defection. But the RCMP wasn't taking any chances.

McClellan devised an elaborate plan. A former doctor at Camp X described for George Mackay, "to his considerable consternation," the symptoms that would necessitate going to the hospital. The doctor himself would deliver the baby and facilitate Anna's entry into the hospital without attracting attention. Igor would not be there for the birth; instead, Mervyn Black would pose as the father. Anna was coached so that she could use only her very broken English, which she had apparently learned in the months since the defection. According to McClellan, "She impresses me as an intelligent woman with a very strong personality and should be able to carry this thing through quite successfully."[63]

In early November, McClellan reported that they had purchased all the supplies necessary for the arrival of the baby: "This was done with some difficulty as all purchasing had to be done by either D/Sgt Spanton [a Mountie at Camp X] or myself, whose knowledge of the necessary requirements is, to say the least, meager. The new baby will now be completely equipped and clothed, and I might say that this fact has done more than any thing to put Mrs. Corby's mind completely at rest." These supplies were soon supplemented by a layette from Saks Fifth Avenue in New York, sent by William Stephenson. Anna Gouzenko gave birth to a healthy baby girl, Evelyn, in early December 1945.[64]

Back at RCMP headquarters, Rivett-Carnac was greatly relieved that the Gouzenkos' presence had not been discovered. But this had been only one of a great many complications that for months had caused him to work fourteen-hour days and suffer sleepless nights. To follow up on Gouzenko's leads and keep track of what the spy suspects in Canada were doing without arousing suspicion required a tight balancing act. In his words, "I had to correlate all the different angles of the case, giving direction for the safety measures of Gouzenko, maintaining contact with the government and keeping in touch with those who were engaged, each within his own separate sphere, in all their different tasks. It was like trying to lead a group of mountaineers roped together along the side of a precipice – a single mistake could mean that all might be swept down."[65]

~

A high priority for Rivett-Carnac, and all those working on the Corby case during its early stages, was to keep the suspects from finding out they were being investigated. Before any of them could be arrested, however, the three allied countries involved had to agree on how to proceed. As Dwyer and Evans expressed it, "Whilst [the RCMP] are of course following up whatever leads they can which do not involve any risk of prematurely 'blowing' the case, vigorous prosecution of the matter is now impossible until high level decisions of policy are taken, since the magnitude of the disclosures places the matter squarely in the diplomatic and political sphere as much as in that of intelligence and security."[66]

At the center of these policy decisions was Nunn May, referred to by the allied intelligence services as "Primrose." Of all the suspected agents, he was the most important because he was said to have passed atomic secrets to the GRU. The strategic value of the information that May actually produced was later thrown into question. But at the time the allied intelligence services were convinced, after seeing Gouzenko's documents and hearing what he had to say, that May was dangerous. On September 10, Norman Robertson and British High Commissioner Malcolm MacDonald convinced Prime Minister King that he needed to agree to a secret Order-in-Council authorizing May's police surveillance and arrest, if necessary. As King observed, "Robertson and Malcolm [MacDonald] represented that if he [May] got away to Moscow he would be able to inform the authorities there of everything within his knowledge."[67]

Nunn May was scheduled to depart Canada by plane for London on September 15 to take up a position at King's College, London. There was much worry, however, that he might have heard about Gouzenko's defection and decided to flee, perhaps to the Soviet Union. One of the RCMP officers in charge of keeping the suspects in the case under surveillance, Sergeant Cecil Bayfield, was therefore given the brief assignment of shadowing May on his journey. Posing as a courier for the British High Commission, Bayfield sat where he could keep an eye on May, but it was an uneventful flight, and when they deplaned, Bayfield spotted two officers from the British Special Branch waiting to take over the surveillance.[68]

It is not known whether May was warned about the defection by the GRU while he was still in Canada. Philby's information sent out first through NKVD stations may have come too late to reach May before he left. In any case, May proceeded with his plans as if nothing were the matter. As allied intelligence knew from Gouzenko's documents, the GRU had originally planned to continue their association with May, and so before May left Canada they had arranged for him to rendezvous with a new Soviet contact at 8 p.m. on October 7 in front of the British Museum in London. May was instructed to carry a copy of the *Times* under his left arm and to say "Best regards from Mikel" when he saw his contact, who would first ask him street directions. The GRU stipulated that, if the meeting for some reason did not occur, then the alternative dates were October 17 and 27 respectively.[69]

British authorities realized they could not arrest May solely on the evidence they had from Gouzenko. As they noted in a top secret report, "It is considered that the evidence at present available is not sufficient to justify the arrest of PRIMROSE or, if he is arrested, to afford a reasonable probability that he would be convicted in a court of law." So they hoped to entrap May in the act of espionage that was to take place when he met with his designated contact on October 7, or on one of two successive dates thereafter. In order for this to happen, however, nothing should be done that could make May suspect they were on to him: "It is not possible to supervise all the movements and activities of PRIMROSE as to ensure against his passing information to the Russians or even making a successful escape from this country to Russia without at any rate gravely imperilling the chances of uncovering a Soviet organisation here and of providing confirmatory evidence of PRIMROSE's guilt. In practical terms this means that if there is to be any chance of successfully covering the expected rendezvous, PRIMROSE cannot be subjected to continuous surveillance until the first meeting."[70]

MI5 officers clearly wanted nothing to come in the way of the meeting between May and his Soviet contact. In a telegram to the RCMP, Captain Guy Liddell observed that May was working every day at King's College and arranging for lodging in London. "His behaviour gives no ground for supposing that he is at all apprehensive." The report went on to note that May's luggage would be arriving by ship in two days, but that it would not be searched because they doubted they would find anything of interest and did not want to "prejudice chance of his keeping rendezvous."[71] Of course, Philby in MI6 had doubtless managed by then to make sure that May was warned. There never would be any rendezvous.

❧

RCMP officials were gathering evidence with plans to ultimately make arrests. But Prime Minister King was about to throw a monkey wrench into the plans. On September 23, when King met for dinner at Laurier House with intelligence advisers, including William Stephenson, to decide on a course of action, he dismayed those present by saying he wanted to talk with the Russians privately "with a view to discovering from them whether they intended to really try to be friends and work for a peaceful world." One can imagine the eyes rolling when King blurted out this new "diplomatic" strategy.

But he was prime minister, and as such had the ultimate say, so he had to be persuaded otherwise. Making the effort, Rivett-Carnac "spoke of what was to be gained by making the whole business public in the way of stopping the communist movement on the continent. That to expose the whole thing might cause our people to cut away from the Russian influence altogether."[72] But King was obstinate, and Rivett-Carnac's words did not sway him.

The next day the RCMP sent King the BSC report on the Gouzenko case, which he spent two hours reading. With his usual naïveté, he was appalled by the perfidy of the Russians: "As I dictate this note, I think of the Russian Embassy being only a few doors away and of there being there a centre of intrigue." Nonetheless, King still was not convinced it was a good idea to arrest the spy suspects. At the very least, he wanted to confer personally with the Americans and British before any decisions were made, which meant a trip to Washington and then London as soon as possible.[73]

Anxious to prevent King from arguing for a quiet diplomatic solution to the Gouzenko case, RCMP commissioner Stuart Wood wrote to Minister of Justice Louis St. Laurent, explaining why the RCMP believed it was important to carry through with arrests and make the affair public: "While we have a most acute realization of the very important diplomatic and political aspects of this case which, of course, have to be given precedence . . . from a purely police and intelligence standpoint I must say that I am very much in favour of arrests and consider that prosecutions should be entered in every instance where the evidence is available and that the whole matter should be brought to the attention of the public." Wood went on to request Mr. Laurent make his opinion known to the prime minister before the latter left Ottawa.[74] Although Wood was eventually able to carry out arrests – and see the Gouzenko case attract a level of public attention he had never imagined – he would have to wait several long and frustrating months for it to happen.

Chapter 3

"PRIMROSE," MISS CORBY, AND THE POLITICS OF ESPIONAGE

Soviet Espionage was Siberia time: the enemy just went on and on; when you got rid of one spy, another would take his place. How would you get satisfaction?

Robert Lamphere, *The FBI-KGB War*

On Saturday, September 29, 1945, Mackenzie King flew to Washington, D.C., with his able lieutenant Norman Robertson to visit U.S. president Truman. Once that was done, he would leave from New York for London. Characteristically, King had dithered about the trip to Washington from the beginning, and had it not been for the prodding of Robertson, he would not have gone at all. King could be a prima donna. Told that President Truman would be leaving for Missouri on the day he planned to arrive in Washington, King churlishly refused the White House's suggestion that he come a day early. Truman had to postpone his trip to accommodate him. Still, King balked at the idea of flying, apparently because it depended on the weather, but also considered it too expensive to go by train. In the end, he did fly, but he was miffed at the Americans. He complained to his diary, "In conversation with Atherton [Ray Atherton, the American ambassador to Canada] toward the last, in his way of speaking, one might have thought that the going to Washington was rather something for which I was asking rather than something which I felt was in part acceptance of the President's invitation and in part obligation which Canada owed to an ally."[1]

In preparation for the visit, Truman had received a background report from the State Department, which included a biographical sketch of King, national leader of the Liberal Party since 1919 and prime minister of Canada, on and off, since 1921: "As a speaker and writer he is lacking the essential gifts of clarity, force or ease. On the floor of the House he is a past master at evasion in answering questions but in rough and tumble debate he scores many more points than he loses. He is primarily a student. He is a bachelor and devotes a large part of his leisure to reading and abstract thinking." The sketch went on to note that King's three main goals were to ensure Canada's recognition as an independent nation, bound to the Commonwealth only by loyalty to the Crown, to support Great Britain, because this was in Canada's best interests, and to promote a closer relationship between Canada and the United States. As for the agenda of discussion between the prime minister and the U.S. president, the State Department made no mention of Soviet espionage. Rather, the focus of the talks was to be a proposal for Canada to start a program of military integration with the United States.[2]

King's agenda was different. During the three-hour plane trip he spent the time rereading the contents of a green folder containing, according to King, "a copy of the statement prepared by our police of the statements of information secured from an examination of CORBY and other sources."[3] This was probably the report he had studied a few days earlier, written by the British Security Coordination.

King and Robertson were met at the airport by the Canadian ambassador to Washington, Lester (or "Mike") Pearson, who later reported (tongue-in-cheek) back to Ottawa: "We went to particular pains to see that the Prime Minister's visit was a pleasant one and for that purpose kept off a storm until ten minutes after their arrival; arranged to have the temperature drop from 92 to 68 within three hours of their arrival, and had the clocks put back that night one hour so that Mr. King would be able to get some additional sleep. I don't really see how hospitality could go further!"[4]

Pearson, an Oxford graduate and a former history professor at the University of Toronto, had a bright future in front of him. In three years, after being elected a member of the Canadian Parliament, he would become minister of external affairs, in 1958 he would become leader of the Liberal Party, and in 1963 prime minister of Canada. Pearson would also achieve international prominence when he was awarded the Nobel Peace Prize in 1956 for his role in resolving the Suez crisis. What led to this success? In the words of his biographer, "He saw his opportunity and devoted himself wholly to grasping it. He was, in fact, extraordinarily ambitious, able to work twelve-hour days year after year, to deny himself pleasures he savoured, to mingle with and even flatter those he loathed." Pearson was exceptionally witty and had a powerful charm, but he was also shrewd and decisive. These qualities would be put to a severe test later, when the Gouzenko case had some unpleasant and difficult repercussions for him.[5]

After King had gone to bed, Pearson and Robertson paid a visit to U.S. undersecretary of state Dean Acheson and "went over the whole ground with him far into the night," including the impact that the Gouzenko case would have on efforts at international, civilian control of the bomb, which was of special interest to Acheson and Truman.[6] Pearson had faced an uphill struggle since coming to Washington in 1943. His job, first as assistant Canadian ambassador and then as ambassador, was to "educate the Americans about the sovereignty of Canada" and disabuse them of the idea that Canada was still part of the British Empire. According to Pearson's biographer, Acheson, whose mother was a Canadian and the heiress to a whiskey fortune, tended, ironically, to look down on Canadians, or at least on the idea of Canadian statesmanship, and "he suffered Canadian fools badly." A graduate of Yale and Harvard law schools, Acheson, "with his beautiful, chalk-stripe English flannel suits, his striking carriage, his bristling guardsman's mustache," cut a formidable figure. Someone wondered how he and Truman, a humble product of Missouri, could possibly get along, but they got along famously. After Truman named Acheson secretary of state in 1949, he said Acheson was "doing a whale of a job" and was his "top brain man" in the cabinet. Pearson evidently had his reservations about Acheson, but as an adept and convivial diplomat, Pearson managed to get on well with him, as did the more retiring Robertson. In fact, Pearson and Acheson had something in common. Both would eventually be called upon to publicly defend protégés who were accused of spying in connection with the Gouzenko case.[7]

Acheson conveyed the information about the spy case to Truman the next morning before King arrived to see him. King, who studied the contents of the green folder again before going to the White House, was seemingly unaware of his subordinates' meeting with Acheson the night before and thought that what he had to say would surprise Truman.[8]

According to King's diary, the president "extended a cordial welcome." After they had covered the rather mundane complications of King's plans for his visit, King launched into a discussion of the espionage case. He apparently went into considerable detail, starting his narration with the story of Gouzenko's defection. Truman then pressed for information on American spies: "He said 2 or 3 times that he was particularly interested in anything I could tell him of what had happened in the U.S. or would give evidence of espionage there. I then said perhaps it would be best were I to read from the report I had with me."

King read aloud from the green folder about the Russian espionage system, about "Primrose" (Alan Nunn May), and others. Then, as he wrote in his diary, "also the statement that an assistant secretary of the Secretary of State's Department was supposed to be implicated." Truman did not seem surprised. (He not only had been briefed by Acheson, but had also received the two FBI reports, the second of which had similarly "promoted" the spy to an assistant secretary.) As King recalled, "Acheson then said that they had thought the report [in the green folder] had reference to an assistant to an asst. secretary. I said of course I knew nothing but what was in the statement as recorded there."[9] As noted earlier, someone had inserted the words "assistant to" followed by a question mark in the BSC report. If King was in fact reading from this document he may have left these words out.

Whatever the case, Acheson realized that the wording was no minor nuance. Getting right the question of whether the spy was an assistant to an Assistant Secretary or an assistant to Stettinius was essential both to knowing where to begin a search and determining how deeply compromised the American policy-making apparatus might be.

The claims emanating from Canada about a State Department spy so bothered Acheson that he requested a conference on "developments in the Canadian case" with FBI chief Hoover, who came to Acheson's office on October 9. Acheson asked Hoover if he had any information on the Soviet agent "who was one of the assistants in the State Department," thus avoiding specific terminology. According to an FBI memorandum, "The Director told Acheson we had not been able to definitely establish the identity of this man. He [Acheson] inquired as to whether the Director had any suspects. The Director said we had one party in mind as a possible suspect, though there was no direct evidence to sustain this suspicion. He [Acheson] inquired as to who this was and the Director told him Alger Hiss, but the Director did not feel it was the time to make any accusation in this matter as there was no direct proof of the same. . . . Acheson stated the Secretary of State was greatly concerned about the matter and it was desired that every effort be made to ascertain definitely the identity of the person referred to."[10] This was troubling news for Acheson. Alger Hiss was a friend and a protégé, whom he admired and trusted. Alger shared with him the same deep commitment to internationalism and the United Nations. Alger's brother Donald had worked directly under Acheson at the State Department a few years earlier and was now a member of Acheson's former law firm. If Alger Hiss really was a spy, it would have immense repercussions for the State Department and for Acheson personally.

The focus of attention in the Gouzenko case, however, remained Alan Nunn May and his possible arrest. Before King had left Ottawa, Alexander Cadogan, British undersecretary of state for foreign affairs, sent telegrams to both Ottawa and Washington saying that British authorities expected to arrest May soon and proposing that the Canadians and the Americans make arrests in the spy case as well. The British were clearly nervous about acting on their own. King and Robertson considered immediate arrests a bad idea, in part because they had been told there was not sufficient evidence in many of the Canadian cases. Even the RCMP now agreed that more time was needed. And King was still leaning toward simply discussing the matter quietly with the Soviets. In Washington, Robertson had conveyed their views to Acheson, who was in complete agreement. And in his meeting with King, Truman repeated the view more than once "that nothing should be done without agreement between the 3 [allies] and above all nothing should be done which might result in premature action in any direction." So anxious was Truman that the Gouzenko case not come out in the open that he had Acheson give a message to the British ambassador to the United States, Lord Halifax, in which he urged the British not to arrest May unless it was absolutely necessary for the sake of security.[11]

A key reason for Truman's and Acheson's concern about publicizing the case was their belief that it would interfere with efforts to reach an international agreement on the atomic bomb. Truman was trying to get Congress to agree to the transfer of authority over the bomb from the War Department to a civilian commission under the president. He and Acheson were convinced that, since the secret of the bomb could not and should not be indefinitely maintained, it was important to have all nations, including the Soviet Union, participate in a treaty that would ensure open exchanges of atomic information and peaceful use of scientific knowledge. These views were expressed forcefully by Walter Lippmann in the *Washington Post* just a few days after King and Robertson's visit. Lester Pearson, for one, noticed the similarity of Lippmann's views with what Acheson had said to him and Robertson. He sent the Lippmann article to a colleague in Ottawa, noting, "Dean [Acheson] discussed this matter with Norman and me last Saturday night in almost exactly the same terms as this article. I suppose that he and others are using Walter Lippmann's column as a trial balloon in this matter."[12]

◁▷

After his meeting with Truman, Mackenzie King went to the British Embassy to pay a call on Lord Halifax, who, in reference to his political cunning, Churchill called the "Holy Fox." Although he had been an admirer of Hitler and a strong advocate of Neville Chamberlain's policy of appeasement toward the Nazis, Halifax was retained in the government when Churchill took power in 1940 because Churchill wanted continuity. Halifax, who wore a prosthesis as he had been born with a withered left arm with no hand, managed to offend King by seating him in such a way that the sun shone directly into his eyes: "It seemed to me to be a poor type of practice for a man like Halifax to adopt. It is I know a way that some people of the Mussolini type and others take. They must watch the countenance of the men they are talking to and have their own in the dark." To make matters worse, Halifax suggested, apropos the Gouzenko case, that Truman and British prime minister Clement Attlee "should work out the matter between them." King was incensed: "I at once interjected I thought it should be worked out with Canada as well. That the 3 of us were equally interested and added that perhaps we were in the most serious position of all as information was coming from Canada."[13]

King and Norman Robertson traveled that same afternoon in a private railway car to New York, where they would board the *Queen Mary* for England the next day. They stayed at the Harvard Club, which not only had cachet, but was also less expensive than a hotel. King was always pinching pennies. (In Ottawa, he reportedly treated Robertson more as an assistant than as the man in charge of Canada's foreign affairs, causing him to spend much of his valuable time "worrying about such items as the cost of linen or the newest stenographer's salary.") Much to the disappointment of a group of men King invited to the Harvard Club that night, he brought them into the bar and then suggested that they all have a lemonade. As his private secretary observed, "It was not just King's wartime teetotalism that dictated his choice of drinks that night: it was also his parsimony. He was a shameless miser and would resort to almost any device to avoid any charge, however minor, to his expense account, or worst of all, to him personally."[14]

⌦

While King and Robertson were en route to England, a heated debate was taking place via top secret telegrams between London and Ottawa. British High Commissioner MacDonald, under pressure from the Canadians, cabled the Foreign Office voicing reservations about May's arrest on or after October 7: "On what grounds and with what purpose would you expect to be able to take action against him? If provisional legal advice referred to above is correct there would be no evidence in Canada on which he could be prosecuted and convicted under Canadian law. Do your legal advisers take a different view as regards English law? . . . So far as your end is concerned, action against PRIMROSE would presumably not . . . involve immediate complications with staff of Soviet Embassy in London. But here the situation is different."[15]

After consulting with the Foreign Office, Roger Hollis wrote a response, which was approved by "C" (Menzies). In essence, the reply was that the Russians would interpret any action less than arrest "as weakness and the effect of this would be to worsen and not to improve relations." As for the legal issues, Hollis threw the ball back in the Canadians' court, giving them reasons why they should make arrests in their country: "Even if you have at present no evidence on which the agents in Canada could be brought into the Court, have you considered whether the products of the questioning of the agents in Canada will not produce material which will allow you to bring the agents to trial possibly in part as a result of some of the agents turning King's evidence?"[16]

As Hollis and his colleagues in MI5 knew, short of catching May red-handed in an act of espionage when he met his Soviet contact, they had no grounds to justify an arrest. The documents produced by Gouzenko referred to him by his Soviet code name Alek, and the only evidence that Alek was May was Gouzenko's testimony, which would not hold up in a court of law. The Canadians, on the other hand, could detain the suspects in their country under a special Order-in-Council issued secretly in early October under the War Measures Act, which remained in force although the war was over. This order allowed police to arrest suspects and hold them for questioning without the normal legal evidence required. Moreover, the suspects did not have a legal right to counsel, which provided an excellent opportunity for skilled interrogators to elicit confessions. Hollis and his colleagues probably hoped that some of the Canadian suspects would incriminate May under questioning. May, having been a member of the Canadian Association of Scientific Workers (CASCW), indeed knew some of the suspects. Raymond Boyer was president of CASCW, and two others, Edward Mazerall and David Shugar, were active in the association. But, unbeknownst to Hollis, May's secret contacts with the GRU were a separate matter. He had been approached by Zabotin's team just months before the defection and solely on the basis of his previous associations with the Russians while in England.

The British were particularly anxious to arrest May because they feared he might defect to the Soviet Union, thereby presenting them with a humiliating counterintelligence failure and discrediting them in American eyes. Prime Minister Attlee wanted to persuade the Americans to give the British a larger share of their atomic secrets, as access to commercial atomic energy would help boost Britain's economic recovery. But if the British were allowing their scientists to get away with passing secrets to the Soviet Union, their membership in the club of nuclear powers would be short-lived.[17]

The Canadians had fewer concerns in this regard because their suspected agents were not high-profile atomic spies and were much less likely to seek haven (or be accepted) in the Soviet Union. They wanted more time to carry out surveillance and gather sufficient evidence before the Gouzenko case was blown publicly. And despite the powers of the Order-in-Council, the Canadians were worried about the legal aspects of prosecution. On October 6 (the day the order was issued in Canada, apparently in anticipation of May's arrest),

Hume Wrong, acting head of External Affairs, sent a telegram to Norman Robertson, who was due to arrive in England on the *Queen Mary* the next day. Wrong noted that the Canadian Department of Justice took the view that, except in three or four cases, "there are grave doubts as to whether prosecution would result in convictions by reason of necessity for complying with the strict rules of evidence."[18] Indeed, RCMP commissioner Wood (whose agency was under the Justice Department) conveyed his hesitation about immediate arrests to both Hollis and Hoover.[19]

∽

On October 7, 1945, King and Robertson were met at Southampton by Roger Hollis, who, as MI5's officer responsible for communist subversion, was under a lot of pressure. The first thing Hollis did was to show King a copy of an October 1 telegram to Alexander Cadogan from Lord Halifax in Washington. The telegram read as follows, "Acheson has now spoken to the President who said that if immediate and imperative reasons of security required an arrest [of May] he would naturally not stand in the way. But if, as he hoped, these imperative reasons were not present he would greatly prefer that action should be deferred pending further consideration and discussion. Acheson told me that the President felt this very strongly." According to King's diary, Hollis said, "the Foreign Office wished to know if I would give approval to an arrest being made tonight." King replied that he agreed with Truman and would not stand in the way of an arrest if the conditions Truman mentioned existed. Hollis hurried off to London with the message.[20] Little did Hollis know, however, that Kim Philby had already reported to Moscow that MI5 planned to set a trap for May. Late that night a disappointed Hollis sent a telegram to Ottawa: "Rendezvous October 7th not . . . attended by either PRIMROSE or contact. No repeat no immediate action therefore called for on your part."[21]

May's failure to appear at the rendezvous did not stop the British, both intelligence officers and politicians, from hoping he would meet his Soviet contact on one of the next alternative dates, October 17 or 27. Contingency plans continued to be discussed in daily telegrams between London and Ottawa. And the topic of arrests in the Gouzenko case came up repeatedly while King and Robertson were in London during the month of October. Attlee and his foreign minister Ernest Bevin went back and forth on the issue. At Chequers, where King visited Clement Attlee on the evening of the seventh, Attlee "said he was in entire agreement, namely, that as much information should be secured both in the U.S. and here before the case would be opened up to the public. Attlee also agreed that an approach should be made in the first instance to the Russians themselves."[22]

But "C" was pressuring Attlee and Bevin, arguing that all the suspects in the Gouzenko case should be arrested without delay, or "the scent will get very cold." "C" and his colleagues were astounded by King's idea of persuading the Soviet government to "turn over a new leaf" and give up espionage. When King and Attlee met on October 11, Attlee had done a complete flip-flop regarding the May case. He said he thought May should be detained immediately and tried to convince King that inquiries should begin at once in Canada. King persuaded him otherwise. The next day Attlee reversed himself yet again, sending Bevin a message that he agreed with King and that "it would be inadvisable to break it [the case] prematurely."[23]

In the end, when it was clear that May was not going to be caught in the act of meeting a Soviet agent, the leaders decided to postpone the entire Gouzenko matter until the upcoming mid-November conference among Attlee, King, and Truman in Washington. But Bevin had reservations: "This will of course mean that PRIMROSE will remain free for the present. We know that he has contact with one top scientist working for the Government on atomic research . . . I feel myself that we are dealing too tenderly with these people and I would prefer that a term should be put to their activities as soon as possible."[24]

∽

King was clearly enjoying his new role as a leading statesman, on a par with the likes of Attlee and Truman. Troubling as it was for Canada, the Gouzenko case had made him the center of attention. He even received an invitation to lunch with Winston and Clementine

Churchill at their new home at Hyde Park Gate. He was delighted. Mrs. Churchill he found particularly charming, and recorded every detail of the visit in his diary.[25] After lunch Churchill, who had been voted out of office in July 1945, revealed how much his attitude toward the Soviet Union had changed since the heady days of Yalta. As King noted, Churchill spoke forcefully of his distrust of the Russians: "He stressed very strongly what realists they were. He called them 'realist lizards,' all belonging to the crocodile family. He said they would be as pleasant with you as they could be, although prepared to destroy you." Then King took the liberty of telling Churchill about the Gouzenko case, after getting Churchill's assurances that he would keep what was said in strict confidence. Like Truman, Churchill did not seem surprised and was ready with advice: "He thought it would be as well to delay action until a careful plan had been worked out but that it should not be allowed to go by default. He felt it was right to talk to the [Soviet] ambassador but to leave it there would be a mistake. The world ought to know where there was espionage and that the Russians would not mind that; they had been exposed time and again." This seemed like an all-out effort to dissuade King from trying to settle the Gouzenko case with quiet diplomacy.

As King was leaving, Churchill added flattery: "He said to me, in reference to the [recent Canadian] elections, other men are as children in the leadership of the party as compared to yourself. You have shown understanding and capacity to lead that other men have not got, or words to this effect. He used the expression that he hoped that God would bless me. No words could have been kinder than his as we parted. It was the sweetest side of his nature throughout – a really beautiful side."

His meeting with Churchill was like a tonic. The rejuvenated King vowed to himself that he would return from England "ready to enter on a larger sphere of work than ever – a sphere of work which will identify me with this new age of atomic energy and world peace." But despite Churchill's efforts, King continued doggedly to follow his own stubborn instincts regarding the espionage case.

Back home, there were worries about what the Soviets were up to in Canada. In mid-October a message from Ottawa to London, presumably from MI6's Peter Dwyer, reported that a waiter known as "Nick the Greek" at Ottawa's Connaught Restaurant, passing himself off as a British intelligence agent, had asked an RCMP plainclothesman if he knew anything about a Russian Embassy employee who disappeared with papers. According to Dwyer, "this is probably an NKVD fishing expedition." Dwyer, who was surely fed up with the endless debate over what to do with the spy suspects, voiced his approval for the strategy of MI5: "I endorse the views set out by Hollis . . . namely that delay will increase chances of Russians getting in first with a trumped up charge and of agents over here perfecting their cover stories and destroying any incriminating evidence which they may still have in their possession. Corby, in conversation a few days ago, also mentioned that Russians might take initiative and would already have started to take steps to cover up over here."[26]

Dwyer also reported that the Soviet agent Ignacy Witczak, who was identified in the Gouzenko case and had been residing in California on a false Canadian passport, was on the run. "A study of Witczak's correspondence with his wife during past month leaves no doubt that a general warning was issued to Canadian and United States networks shortly after Corby's disappearance. . . . He shook F.B.I. surveillance in a Turkish Bath in New York and has now, by lucky chance, been picked up again in Chicago where he is still making every effort to shake surveillance. For all we know he may be making for Seattle where there are Russian ships." Under ordinary circumstances, the report noted, the FBI might arrest Witczak on criminal charges, but "they feel unable to take any action involving a member of GRANT's [Zabotin's] network since instructions are that no action be taken which might precipitate matters."[27]

For the FBI, the Witczak case had been a tremendous exercise in frustration. Witczak was quite a "big fish" in counterintelligence terms. He was a bona fide GRU agent with a fake Canadian identity, and was, the FBI assumed, setting up GRU networks on the West Coast not far from the Manhattan Project. Scores of FBI agents were detailed to follow the movements of Witczak, who traveled from

Los Angeles to New York with the FBI hot on his trail. FBI agent Robert Lamphere, stationed with the New York espionage squad at the time, recalled spending a "long and uncomfortable night" outside Pennsylvania Station looking for Witczak, but it was his colleagues at the coach terminal who spotted the GRU agent as he was getting on a bus: "He was a smallish man with glasses, and immediately panicked and started to run away. While the other agents kept up with him, one man got a message to the field office, and then to headquarters, describing the situation and asking for permission to bring in 'Witczak' for questioning. Headquarters notified the RCMP, which asked that we not bring him in, lest we somehow jeopardize the cases that were just then being developed for prosecution out of the Gouzenko defection."[28] In fact, Lamphere was misinformed: it was Hoover who told the RCMP that the FBI did not have enough evidence to arrest Witczak. But the end result was the same. After a few months of continued FBI surveillance Witczak disappeared completely.

The story of Witczak strengthened the argument of those favoring immediate and simultaneous arrests of suspects in the Corby case in all three countries. Hollis, of course, was the leading exponent of this view. But once he left for North America in the third week of October, MI5 did a bizarre about-face with regard to Alan Nunn May. On October 31, MI5 sent Hollis a telegram in Ottawa stating that "we are inclining toward the view that whatever type of action is eventually decided upon we here ought not to take simultaneous action against PRIMROSE but ought to leave him alone." The reasons MI5 gave for this sudden change of heart were that, first, they did not have enough material to offer interrogators a chance of breaking "Primrose." Second, since he doubtless had been warned by the Russians, this meant that they might have to wait before getting more useful evidence against him. And, finally, "an abortive interrogation of PRIMROSE serves no useful purpose and indeed may induce him to do the very thing we most fear, namely to escape to Russia."[29]

Was Philby, who was responsible for the transmission of the telegram, behind this reversal? As chief of counterintelligence for MI6, he was being consulted on the Corby case and receiving all the reports. It is not far-fetched to suggest that, in Hollis's absence, he was able to impress his views upon others more convincingly.

Hollis, not surprisingly, was far from happy. He telegraphed immediately back to MI5, pointing out that the chances of a successful interrogation of "Primrose" would only grow smaller if he were to be alerted by detentions in Canada before his questioning. It was best to interrogate "Primrose" simultaneously with the Canadian suspects. Hollis concluded that "If policy decision is for prosecution I feel that every effort should be made to prosecute PRIMROSE who is the worst traitor in network . . . RCMP, while not wishing to influence your decision, would undoubtedly be disappointed if you did not interrogate."[30]

The response from MI5 was that they appreciated the force of Hollis's argument but that the risk of an abortive interrogation of "Primrose," possibly driving him to defect, was so great that the final decision would have to be taken by the prime ministers of Britain and Canada, along with President Truman, at their forthcoming November meeting in Washington.[31]

Hollis traveled to Washington for that occasion, and there was great hope on the part of the British and the Canadians that finally a course of action in the Gouzenko case would be decided upon. Malcolm MacDonald chaired three meetings on the subject, and on November 14 a tentative agreement was produced whereby simultaneous actions in the three countries against the Gouzenko suspects would occur in the week beginning November 26. Agents against whom there was a legal case would be prosecuted, and the Canadians would set up a Royal Commission to report on the full facts of the matter. They would also make a diplomatic protest to the Soviet ambassador in Ottawa and demand the recall of military attaché Zabotin and his colleagues.[32]

In fact, although this was purported to be a collective agreement, it appeared that it would be the Canadians who were sticking their necks out. The precise meaning of "action" by the Americans and the British was vague, giving the impression that the Canadians might be the only ones actually carrying out arrests. An annex relating to British action was attached to the draft, pointing out that, unlike the Canadians, the British did not have the emergency powers of the Canadian Order-in-Council, and "Primrose" would have to be questioned without being arrested. He could only be arrested if he confessed to spying. Furthermore, "PRIMROSE gives the impression of being a strong and determined character who will not be likely to lose his head and confess to the authorities unless he is confronted with evidence of his activities of a much stronger nature than is at present available. For the above reasons, the authorities are not very sanguine of obtaining a confession from PRIMROSE on which it will be possible to bring a charge against him."[33] This annex was doubtless attached at the request of Hollis's colleagues in MI5, who did not want to take responsibility for a failed outcome with Alan Nunn May.

For their parts, the Americans were not in any position to arrest the spy in the State Department, whose identity, although thought to be Hiss, had yet to be verified. And Hoover had made it clear that the FBI, constrained by a lack of evidence, would be making no arrests of the other individuals (Steinberg, Witczak, and a woman named Freda Linton) connected with the Gouzenko case.[34] Furthermore, the FBI was now up to its neck in a new espionage case, that of Elizabeth Bentley, a former Soviet agent who had recently approached the FBI with a story of an extensive spy ring in the United States government. Hoover requested that no action be taken by any of the parties in the Gouzenko case for the next two weeks, pending the FBI's investigation into the Bentley affair. The request infuriated MI5 and the British Foreign Office, which could not understand why action in the Gouzenko case would have any effect on the new FBI case. As the Foreign Office noted, "Meanwhile CORBY scents are growing rapidly colder since it is already well over two months since first alarm was given."[35]

A crucial and more public topic of discussion among the three allied leaders at their meetings on November 11–15 was the related issue of international control of atomic energy. Here, too, there were disappointments, especially for the British and the Canadians and the moderates in the Truman administration, like James Byrnes and Dean Acheson, who wanted to share control of the bomb with the United Nations. Far from a significant step forward, the final accord was a vague and tenuous document that called for the creation of a UN Atomic Energy Commission that would study the question of how to control the bomb. According to the document, "specialised information regarding the practical application of atomic energy" would not be shared until effective safeguards against its military use were established.[36] As Truman later recalled, he explained to Attlee and Mackenzie King "that scientists of all countries should be allowed to visit freely with one another and that free inspection of the plans for atomic energy's use in peacetime pursuits should be the policy of every country. But I stressed that this would not necessarily mean that the engineering and production know-how should be made freely available, any more than we would make freely available any of our trade secrets."[37]

If King was disappointed, he certainly did not show it to Truman. In contrast to his previous visit, King had this time been invited to stay at the White House. He was evidently thrilled and wrote an effusive thank-you letter to the president:

I cannot begin to express my appreciation of all that this present visit to Washington has meant to my countrymen and myself; and, in particular what I feel about the honour and privilege of being your guest at the White House, and in this most charming of all official residences, for so many days and at so momentous a time. . . . I believe a real service has been rendered mankind by the declaration of the agreement respecting atomic energy announced yesterday; and which, I am sure, is being received with approval in all parts of the world today. Your own many personal expressions of friendship toward myself have touched me deeply. They will ever be gratefully remembered. . . . The hospitality extended, in so many ways and so generously, from the moment of the arrival of members of my staff and myself,

has been such as to make impossible any adequate acknowledgement of it. I can only thank you for it, and for all that
your friendship means to me, but this I do from the bottom
of my heart.[38]

As a token of his appreciation, King continued, he was enclos-
ing "this somewhat intimate photograph of myself and my old dog
Pat." Truman's reply, a few days later, was much shorter and more
muted. He appreciated the chance to become better acquainted, he
told the Canadian prime minister, and King's picture would "occupy
a place of honor" in his study.[39]

~

Although Truman probably considered the Bentley case an unwelcome distraction, it was an unexpected bonanza for the FBI.
Elizabeth Bentley, like Gouzenko, was a "walk-in," a Soviet spy who
defected on her own initiative and offered information to the other
side. Since 1941, she had acted as a courier between an NKVD agent
named Jacob Golos in New York City and his recruits, who were
mainly employees of the U.S. government in Washington, D.C.
A single woman in her late thirties, Bentley was high-strung, self-
obsessed, and had a weakness for alcohol. She approached FBI agents
on two occasions (August and October 1945) and hinted at her
involvement in espionage. But she had not made a great impression.
The FBI agent who spoke with Bentley in mid-October thought that
she might be a "psychopath rambling on." But he wrote up the interview and routed it to an agent in the espionage section of the New
York office, who eventually reached Bentley and persuaded her to
come in again.[40]

On November 7, 1945, Elizabeth Bentley was interviewed for a
third time at FBI offices in New York City. Bentley's thirty-page
statement, signed the next day, was vague and disorganized (and
betrayed her intense anti-Semitism), but she did mention enough
names of possible espionage suspects to motivate her interrogators
to send an urgent telegram to FBI headquarters. Hoover, in turn,
took Bentley's information so seriously that he contacted William

Stephenson in New York on November 9 to inform him that Bentley had said a former member of his staff at the British Security Coordination, a Mr. Cedric Belfrage, was a spy.[41] Given Hoover's dislike for Stephenson, he must have taken some pleasure in passing on this information.

Philby was keeping the Soviets apprised of developments in Washington. On November 18, he sent a message to the NKVD about the Gouzenko case, giving extensive details of the discussions the allies were having and the alternatives they were considering, but he made no mention of Bentley.[42] The next day MI5 and MI6 received the news that the FBI was requesting a delay in action because of the new Bentley case. Philby duly reported the Bentley defection to the NKVD's London station on November 20.[43]

Although Hoover would insist that the Bentley case was entirely separate from the Gouzenko affair, in fact there were several threads that tied them together. In her initial statement on November 8, Bentley had this to say about Fred Rose, the communist member of Parliament in Canada who had been implicated by Gouzenko in spying for the GRU: "Also during this period he [Golos, her lover and NKVD agent] used to get letters from Canada. I think I know now who they were from. Just before Golos died, Fred Rose, who became an MP in Canada, came down and then went back again. He kept sending messages to me asking me to come to see him. [Bentley seems to have fantasized a great deal about men making advances, but Rose was a known womanizer, so her impression might have been correct in this instance.] As I figure it out, I think what Golos was trying to do was to get material from Canada into this country via Fred Rose because the Russians told me they had no organization in Canada. I think this was in 1939."[44]

Bentley was interviewed almost continuously for the next two and a half weeks, and on November 30, she signed a second, considerably longer, more coherent statement. In her later statement, Bentley altered her recollections about Rose slightly. There was no mention of Rose's visit to New York or messages to her. As for the letters received by Golos, "I subsequently learned that some of the letters that were sent from Canada that I delivered to Golos came from either Tim Buck [head of the Canadian Communist Party] or Fred Rose. I am not certain which one."[45]

In this same statement Bentley brought up the name of another Canadian who would figure in the Gouzenko case as it unraveled – that of Mr. Hazen Sise, a wealthy and prominent Montreal architect with communist leanings. Sise was not among those mentioned by Gouzenko or in his documents, but in investigating one of the suspects, Israel Halperin, the RCMP found Sise's name in Halperin's address book (which also, incidentally, contained the name of Klaus Fuchs). Bentley recalled that Rose sent one of his contacts, a Royal Canadian Air Force pilot, to see Golos in New York and suggest that Golos contact Sise, who was residing in Washington while on assignment with the National Film Board. Golos then assigned Bentley to meet with Sise on her periodic visits to the American capital. Sise furnished her with information that was "primarily gossip he had overheard" in the Canadian and British embassies. In early 1944, Bentley was told by her Soviet controller to cut her contacts with Sise, who "was suffering from nervous indigestion" and "consulting a psychiatrist."[46] Although the only connection between Sise and the Gouzenko case was an address book, the FBI would later inform its field agents that Sise "has been implicated in both the [Bentley and Corby] cases but most deeply implicated in the Corby Case."[47]

The other individual linked with both the Bentley and Gouzenko investigations was Alger Hiss. In her initial statement on November 8, Bentley did not even mention Hiss. But during numerous interviews later in the month, the FBI repeatedly asked her about him. She finally came up with something in her November 30 statement about a man called "Eugene" Hiss who worked at the State Department as an assistant to Dean Acheson. (Hiss never worked as an assistant to Acheson, although they knew each other well.)[48]

According to Bentley, "Eugene" Hiss had allegedly recruited two or three communists in the U.S. government to work for the Russians. But she seemed not entirely sure of what she was saying. A telegram sent from New York to FBI headquarters on November 16 read as follows: Bentley "was questioned at length concerning this information but admitted that the information concerning Hiss was vague, and because of this was reluctant to make any definitive statements as far as Eugene Hiss's activities were concerned."[49]

In addition to the Gouzenko and Bentley statements, the FBI, we know, had heard about Hiss from another defector from the Soviet camp, Whittaker Chambers, in two previous interviews (May 1942 and May 1945). All Chambers said in those interviews was that in the mid-thirties Alger Hiss had been a member of an underground group organized by a communist named Harold Ware. These three FBI sources of information on Hiss – Chambers, Gouzenko, and Bentley – were all decidedly vague. Neither Bentley nor Gouzenko was even able to provide his exact name. Yet Hoover, on November 28, requested permission from the U.S. attorney general to conduct technical surveillance on Hiss: "In connection with this Bureau's investigation of Soviet espionage activity, it has been reported that Alger Hiss . . . has been engaged in espionage for the Soviet Secret Intelligence (NKVD). I recommend authorization of a technical surveillance on Hiss to determine the extent of his activities on behalf of the Soviets and for the additional purpose of identifying espionage agents."[50]

Attorney General Tom Clark sent back a note asking, "Is this man employed at the State Dept. If so, what do we have on him?" Hoover replied with a memorandum citing his evidence briefly. The first section is blacked out in the declassified copies, but it presumably referred to what Gouzenko said, and the next two sections discuss the Chambers and Bentley claims. Chambers was reported as saying Hiss had been a member of an underground espionage group, when in fact Chambers had not even mentioned espionage at this point. And he never brought up the NKVD in regard to Hiss. In fact, all of Hiss's later accusers claimed that Hiss worked not for the NKVD but the GRU, the military intelligence agency to which Gouzenko had belonged. As for Bentley, Hoover neglected to tell the attorney general that her memory on Hiss was so fuzzy she thought his first name was Eugene and that she had told the FBI just days before she could not make any definitive statements about Hiss's activities.[51]

When asked to elaborate on Hiss in a third interview in March 1946, Chambers insisted he had lost all contact with him after 1937 and could provide no further details. According to the FBI, Chambers stated that "as a matter of fact he has absolutely no information that would conclusively prove that HISS held a membership card in the Communist Party or that he was an actual dues paying member of the Communist Party even while he [Chambers] was active *prior to 1937* [italics added]. He volunteered that he knew that in 1937 HISS was favorably impressed with the Communist movement. . . ."[52] Hoover did not report this to the attorney general, and the FBI kept up its surveillance of Hiss.

By the time Bentley signed her November 30 statement, after being prodded for days on end by the FBI, she had implicated close to 150 individuals in spying for the Russians, and Hoover had got approval from the attorney general to have several of them put under physical, wiretap, and mail surveillance.[53] Aside from Hiss, there were two others singled out for surveillance who had, or would have, a connection to the Gouzenko case. One was Harry Dexter White, a top official in the U.S. Treasury, whose case would eventually make headlines when he was accused publicly of spying. Bentley had much more to say about White than she did about Hiss. Specifically, she alleged that White was part of a Washington, D.C., group led by Nathan Silvermaster that passed government documents through her to the Soviets.

Bentley made it clear, however, in her first statement that she had never seen or met White. As one historian put it, "her direct knowledge of White's alleged role in espionage was, at best, sketchy," and "most of her allegations and knowledge of personal information about Harry and Anne Terry White [his wife] were based on informal conversations she 'overheard' in the Silvermaster household . . . or from secondhand gossip."[54] Chambers had never mentioned White in his own interviews with the FBI up to this point, although he would have more to say, and show, later. Secret Soviet telegrams sent in the 1940s that were later decrypted and released by the U.S. National Security Agency in the 1990s – the Venona decrypts – strongly suggest that White was at least an unwitting informant to the Soviets. But at this point the suspicions against White were based solely on flimsy hearsay testimony from Bentley.

The question then arises, how was the FBI able to justify, as early as November 20 (before Bentley had even signed her expanded statement), a round-the-clock surveillance of White that included phone-tapping, mail interception, monitoring of his physical movements, and, by December, recording of his private conversations at home?[55] Without doubt the attorney general and others who were informed of the Bentley case were strongly influenced by Gouzenko's claims about Soviet espionage in the United States.

Another suspect put under technical surveillance by the FBI in December was Dr. Arthur Steinberg, the American scientist implicated by Gouzenko, who was now living in Alexandria, Virginia.[56] Hoover had known about Steinberg since September but had told RCMP commissioner Wood in mid-October that the FBI did not have any evidence on which to make an arrest. Why did the FBI not start its surveillance of Steinberg earlier, so as to gather evidence? Presumably they had nothing to offer the attorney general to justify such an intrusive violation of individual privacy. Had anything come up since then? Or had the FBI somehow squeezed in Steinberg's name as part of the group implicated by Bentley, thus giving them an opportunity to go on a fishing expedition?

⌒

The FBI's trawling yielded nothing, which was hardly surprising. The Soviets knew all about Bentley's defection and told their agents in the United States to cease their activities.[57] Two weeks later, on November 27, 1945, Hoover gave the go-ahead for Ottawa to proceed with arrests in the Gouzenko case. The message was passed to Canadian ambassador Lester Pearson by Acheson, who told him that the United States would not be in a position to take action on the "Miss Corby" (Bentley) case in the near future, because the woman's accusations were unsupported by documents.[58]

What Hoover did not realize was that in requesting a brief postponement in the Gouzenko case he had given Mackenzie King cause to rethink the Canadian strategy and revert to his original idea of handling the matter with quiet diplomacy. King became more inclined toward this plan when he learned that no overt action (that is, arrests) would be taken by the Americans in the Bentley case. This meant that, with the British still dithering about what to do with Alan Nunn May, the Canadians would be acting on their own if they arrested spy suspects. King was well aware of the possible pitfalls for the Canadian government alone if they went ahead with arrests.

In early December, just as the Soviet ambassador to Canada, Georgii Zarubin, of whom King was very fond, was about to leave on holiday for Moscow (in fact Zarubin never returned), King made up his mind to have a talk with him. King wanted to send a message to Stalin through the ambassador about the espionage revealed by Gouzenko and request an end to the Soviets' illegal activities (accompanied by the expulsion of the Soviets in the Ottawa embassy who were spying). The Canadian individuals involved would not be arrested, but instead would be questioned by means of "departmental enquiries."[59]

RCMP commissioner Stuart Wood was beside himself when he learned of King's new plan and immediately sent a letter to Minister of Justice St. Laurent expressing his concerns. First, Wood noted, since it would be impossible to conduct departmental inquiries on such short notice, the suspects, warned as a result of King's meeting with Zarubin, could not be taken by surprise. Second, there was no guarantee of success in terms of obtaining additional evidence or confessions. And finally, the inquiries might bring about uncontrollable publicity. Wood concluded that "I cannot state too strongly that the present suggested method of procedure by means of departmental enquiry is fraught with possibilities of the gravest danger to Canadian interests from a variety of angles."[60]

The British (who had learned of the plan through Malcolm MacDonald) were no less dismayed. MI5 telegraphed the RCMP immediately: "We feel that from a strictly security angle action proposed will yield small results in Canada and will give minimum assistance to security authorities elsewhere. . . . We believe diplomatic protest unaccompanied by prosecution . . . will be taken by Russians as indicative of weakness of evidence on which protest is based."[61]

King's diaries for the crucial period of November to December 1945 have unfortunately disappeared. Given that these are the only months missing out of the many years the diaries cover (1893–1950), the disappearance is perhaps not a coincidence. The keepers of King's diaries after his death were also close aides to the prime minister, and the entries for November to December may have revealed too much information about the espionage case and also reflected badly on King's judgment.[62] But the course of events is nonetheless clear from other papers in the Canadian archives.

An eleventh-hour scheme was hatched among King's advisers, with a hurried meeting to discuss King's new plan on December 3, the day before King's scheduled meeting with the Soviet ambassador. Wood, St. Laurent, Norman Robertson, and Hume Wrong were in attendance. At this meeting, according to a report from Wrong, Wood told King that the Americans had just learned grave information about the "Miss Corby" case, involving Soviet penetration among senior officials in the Treasury, the United States Intelligence Services, and the White House. Wood noted that "if the accusations are true, there are most impelling reasons, from the point of view of security, for as prompt United States counter-action as possible" and added that "the revelation to Soviet authorities of our knowledge of the information brought by Corby would hamper the United States investigation and that Mr. Hoover, he was sure, would prefer postponement." After hearing this, King, who would naturally be reluctant to displease the head of the FBI, decided to await the outcome of the United States' investigation and not mention anything to the Soviet ambassador.[63]

Desperate to prevent King's heart-to-heart with the Soviet ambassador, Wood had lied to the prime minister by exaggerating the "Miss Corby" revelations, which did not include (at that point) espionage among senior officials at the White House. And he completely misrepresented the views of the FBI, which had given the

Canadians permission to pursue the Gouzenko case just a few days earlier. Wood failed to anticipate that King would in fact stretch out the delay indefinitely, and much later he complained to the U.S. military attaché in Ottawa, "We very nearly missed the boat in the early days of the spy case. The Prime Minister kept it in his desk for 4 months, and when I needled him about it, he wanted to turn it over to the courts. That would have been fatal, as legal procedure would have rendered inadmissible most of the essential evidence." But, as one Canadian historian pointed out, Wood himself was partly responsible for this dilemma: "The Commissioner's suggestion that King was in charge of the spy case and 'kept it in his desk' was misleading. The Gouzenko case was seized upon, manipulated and controlled by turns by diplomats and intelligence agencies in Ottawa, Washington and London."[64] At this point, the plans of both Hoover and Wood for the Gouzenko case, namely that the RCMP would round up the Canadian suspects and interrogate them under the emergency law, had backfired.

Although not only diplomats and intelligence officials, but also political leaders from all three countries were preoccupied with what to do about the Gouzenko case for the last three months of 1945, by the end of the year nothing was resolved. The defection remained unpublicized, nothing had been said to the Soviets, and the suspects were still at large. More important, efforts to establish international control over atomic research, under the shadow of the revelations about Soviet espionage, had achieved few results. Liberals in the Truman administration might have seen the espionage case as an additional argument for ending the U.S. nuclear monopoly, on the grounds that the Soviets spied only because they had been excluded from the West's atomic research. But members of the military, including Manhattan Project director General Leslie Groves, who was informed of Gouzenko's allegations within days of his defection (before U.S. secretary of state James Byrnes was informed), doubtless felt differently. Why should the United States share its atomic research with a country that engaged in such deception? The whole idea of international cooperation was based on trust, and the Soviets were clearly untrustworthy. As for the Soviets, they had made it increasingly clear that they were not going to be intimidated by America's nuclear monopoly into making concessions to the West. The fact that they had been caught red-handed in atomic espionage and that, as the NKVD learned from Philby, the allies might try to use this as a bargaining chip while the case was still secret, inclined them even more in this direction. As Byrnes put it, the Russians were "stubborn, obstinate, and they don't scare."[65]

Chapter 4

RED STORM CLOUDS

We are now up against an ideological conflict without parallel since Elizabethan times. The communists today are the papists of the last half of the seventeenth-century.

Escott Reid, Canadian diplomat

The Gouzenkos celebrated their first Christmas in Canada at Camp X in the company of Mountie George Mackay and his wife. Mackay recalled that "we had a turkey and did the whole thing up in a traditional Canadian Christmas. Presents were bought by the police and we had a Christmas tree with lights. Behind it all was to assimilate them into the Canadian way of life." Anna, always resourceful, made the decorations for the tree out of papier-mâché.[1] It cannot have been much of a celebration for any of them, despite the fact that it was also Anna's twenty-second birthday. The Mackays were eager to get away to spend New Year's with family and friends. And Anna and Igor were probably trying hard not to wonder about their families, or about their own uncertain fate.

Anna was also tied up with her new baby daughter. According to Mackay, "when the second baby came, she almost cut herself off from the whole works. She devoted her entire time to the little girl. . . . He [Andrei] didn't come in for the same attention. She would spend hours with the little girl upstairs in her room. So it became an impossible thing to do anything with her in teaching her [English]. She wasn't interested."[2] Igor was still being questioned occasionally, but the RCMP had obtained about as much as they could get from him, and he had a lot of time on his hands. One can only imagine what it must have been like for them, cooped up with a restless toddler and an infant in a small house in the middle of a cold and snowy nowhere, terrified that the Soviets would find them. Anna still barely spoke a word of English, and they were totally dependent on the RCMP for all their needs. The authorities in Ottawa had been told that Gouzenko's mental state was still fragile. A report on the legal aspects of the case, written in early December, observed, "There is always the question of what Corby might do and the possibility that, if this matter dragged on indefinitely, he would commit suicide or suffer a mental breakdown."[3]

Gouzenko repeatedly expressed concern about what the Canadians would do with his GRU colleagues. Would they try to recruit some of them and persuade them to defect, or would they simply expel them as spies? As it turned out, the GRU ordered most of its officers in Ottawa, including Nikolai Zabotin, back home in December. Colonel and Mrs. Zabotin had departed on the S.S. *Alexander Suvarov* bound for Murmansk, a dismal frigid city in the far north of Russia. It was a nonstop trip; there would be no opportunity for those aboard to change their minds about returning to their home country. The Zabotins' fellow passengers included the Soviet vice-consul in New York and the GRU chief *rezident* in the United States, Pavel Mikhailov, who had been recalled because Gouzenko's evidence compromised him.[4] Mikhailov, code-named "Molière," had been in the United States since 1941, actively engaged both in his diplomatic role and in coordinating the Soviet espionage effort in North America. He had maintained close contact with the Ottawa-based GRU staff, furnishing them with a radio transmitter to communicate with New York and arranging their occasional visits to the United States. The Gouzenko defection was a huge blow for Mikhailov, just as it was for NKVD *rezident* Pavlov, who remained in Ottawa, awaiting a decision from Moscow about his fate. Soviet intelligence officers and their agents in North America were all lying low.[5]

However much damage Gouzenko had caused the Soviets, he was not in the danger that he and the RCMP assumed he was, at least not immediately. According to the memoirs of former GRU officer Col. Mil'shtein, GRU headquarters in Moscow had a special, top secret section called *Isk* (meaning, "reprisal"), which carried out punishments, presumably murder, of so-called traitors. But any such acts required the permission of Stalin. After being informed of Gouzenko's defection, Stalin had requested a detailed report and a plan for responding. He then forbade the GRU to kill him. "The war has ended successfully," Stalin is reported as saying. "Everyone is admiring the Soviet Union. What would they say about us if we did that? It is necessary to investigate everything and to designate a special authoritative commission, which Malenkov [the deputy prime minister] should chair."[6]

Georgii Malenkov's commission, which included NKVD chief Lavrentii Beria, GRU chief Fedor Kuznetsov, and several others, began meeting almost daily, from noon until late in the evening, in Beria's headquarters at Lubianka prison in Moscow. For the Soviets, the Gouzenko defection was a crisis that called into question the quality of their intelligence services, and heads were going to roll. Although Malenkov was the nominal head of the commission, Beria, who had several NKVD cronies on the committee, ran the show. Mil'shtein himself was called in for questioning repeatedly and grilled – without being permitted to take a seat – about his 1944 trip to North America and his suspicions of Gouzenko. In the end, Mil'shtein escaped punishment, presumably because he was on record as having warned his superiors about the young cipher clerk.[7]

As for Zabotin, he was rumored in the West to have either received a death sentence or committed suicide. In fact, his life was spared, but only barely. He was sent to a labor camp in Siberia, along with his wife and much-adored son, who had been attending the Soviet Embassy school in Washington, D.C., and was about to enrol in Zabotin's prestigious alma mater, the Frunze Military Academy. The Zabotins were not released until after Stalin died in 1953. Not surprisingly, Zabotin and his wife, who had a stormy marriage from early on, divorced. Zabotin got remarried to a simple country girl and left Moscow for the provinces. But he died just a few years later, his health ruined by his years in Stalin's brutal Gulag.[8]

As a decorated war hero with a promising career ahead of him, Zabotin paid a heavy price for his failure to suspect that Gouzenko was planning to defect and for the lax security that prevailed under his leadership of the GRU residency in Ottawa. But his subordinates in Ottawa were not punished, and continued with successful careers in military intelligence. Indeed, Col. Motinov, who carried the uranium to Moscow, was awarded the plum position of military attaché and chief of the GRU residency in Washington, D.C. Either the Americans did not realize that he had been part of the Ottawa spy ring, or they turned a blind eye.[9]

In keeping with Stalin's diplomatic ploy of not ordering Gouzenko's murder (he could be whimsically merciful at times), the Soviet Embassy in Ottawa issued a statement about Gouzenko, in April 1946, that avoided calling him a traitor. He had stolen money from the embassy, they claimed, and was "indictable for the committed crime *in case of his return to the USSR* [italics added]." But the Soviets had a long-standing policy of murdering defectors as a way of deterring others, and they would not let Gouzenko off the hook permanently. After Stalin died, the Soviet Supreme Court sentenced him, *in absentia*, to "the highest form of punishment," namely death.[10]

Meanwhile, the NKVD had visited its wrath upon the families of both Gouzenko and his wife. Gouzenko's mother died under interrogation at the NKVD's Lubianka prison. He always assumed that his sister Irina, who had been working as an architectural designer the last time he saw her, also perished as a result of his defection. But Gouzenko's criminal file, dating from sometime after 1956, listed his sister as married and living at that time in the district of Cheliabinsk. Curiously, although Gouzenko thought his brother Vsevolod had died during the Second World War, the file also notes that he was living in the same town as Irina. As for Anna's family, her mother, father, and sister Alia were imprisoned for five years, while Alia's daughter Tatiana was sent to an orphanage.[11]

Gouzenko recalled that one of his RCMP interrogators said he thought him "extraordinarily callous" when he knew his family would suffer dreadful consequences. In his 1948 book, Gouzenko rationalized his defection thus: "My decision was a harsh one but, believe me, it was the only way to break the vicious 'hostage circle' used by the Soviet to hold and muzzle those persons sent to foreign embassies. . . . Somebody had to break that circle, and I made the sacrifice in the hope that if I got away with it, others may be prompted to take the gamble, for the ultimate good of a new Russia. There is still another factor to be considered. Mother was getting old and in Russia today, people aren't permitted to grow very old."[12]

Did Gouzenko really believe there were many others who would be similarly willing to sacrifice the lives of their parents (no matter how old) and siblings in that way? Enough to help create a "new Russia"? He told his interrogators on more than one occasion that he hoped some of his colleagues in Ottawa, Zabotin in particular, would follow his lead and defect. Zabotin, who had both his wife and son with him in North America, knew he faced serious punishment on his return. The three of them could have defected during the three months following Gouzenko's disappearance. But to destroy the lives of family back home was for Zabotin or any of the other GRU staff probably inconceivable. Things would change after Stalin died, and defections would increase as the draconian measures against family members gradually ended. But in 1945 the situation was very different: to defect meant death or severe reprisals for family remaining in Russia. It is no small wonder that Gouzenko was so agitated during these early months after he sought asylum. He had not only fear to contend with, but also guilt.

~

While the Soviets were doing what they could to limit the damage of Gouzenko's defection, the British and the Americans were voicing concern about what was happening, or not happening, in Canada. As long as King was firm in his decision not to permit arrests in Canada without simultaneous American arrests, little could be done to force the issue, short of, as the British pointed out, a leak to the press. King was biding his time waiting for the Americans, but after a month, the FBI had come up with nothing against the suspects in the Bentley case. As time wore on, the likelihood of obtaining hard evidence against those actually involved in spying would become even smaller. Hoover clearly realized this and was frustrated that the Canadians were taking no further action against their spies in anticipation of FBI arrests. In early December 1945, he scribbled at the bottom of an internal FBI memorandum on the Gouzenko case (the contents of which are blacked out in the declassified copies): "They [the Canadians] should 'expect' no startling developments from here. It is their *own* decision & responsibility." Two days later, at the bottom of another message about Gouzenko, Hoover observed, "Same spineless policy as pursued here."[13]

During the month of January 1946, the Gouzenko case fell off King's radar screen. He did not mention it once in his January 1946 daily diary entries, although he met with Malcolm MacDonald on more than one occasion. King was preoccupied with domestic politics, as well as by the visit to Ottawa in mid-January of General Dwight Eisenhower and his wife. And his subordinates, including Justice Minister St. Laurent, Norman Robertson, Hume Wrong, and Lester Pearson, spent much of January in Moscow for discussions about the creation of a UN Atomic Energy Commission.

It was a visit to Ottawa on February 1 by another prominent American, President Truman's personal adviser Admiral William Leahy, that forced King to return to the vexed Gouzenko problem. Leahy, a career navy officer in his seventies who had been Roosevelt's White House chief of staff, had apparently come with the specific purpose of finding out Canadian plans for the case. But King did not have the matter on his agenda for conversation. According to King's diary, he and Leahy discussed several other issues before they "talked a little of the Corby case. He [Leahy] felt that we ought to go on with our enquiry if it involved our own civil servants." If Leahy's purpose was to persuade King to take action on the Gouzenko case, he made a crucial error. According to King, Leahy "agreed that it might have far-reaching repercussions. . . . He also felt that another world war would be between Russia and other parts, particularly the U.S. and the U.K., but that Canada would in all probability be the battlefield."[14]

Leahy's observation doubtless put the fear of God into King, who might have delayed acting on the Gouzenko case even further had it not been for the revelations of American journalist Drew Pearson.

On February 3, 1946, Pearson stunned his nationwide radio audience by announcing that a Soviet spy had surrendered himself to the Canadian government and confessed to a "gigantic Russian espionage network inside the United States and Canada." According to Pearson, "this Russian told Canadian authorities about a series of agents planted inside the American and Canadian governments who were working with the Soviets." Pearson seemed unaware that the defection had occurred more than five months earlier, but he did tell his audience that Prime Minister Mackenzie King had made a special trip to Washington to inform President Truman of the details.[15]

King had no choice but to take action. On February 5, he reluctantly told his cabinet about the Gouzenko case and appointed a special commission, led by Supreme Court judges Robert Taschereau and R.L. Kellock, to investigate Gouzenko's accusations. Arrests, he told the cabinet, would follow shortly.[16] King suspected the leak to Pearson was "inspired" by the Americans. "I may be wrong," he wrote in his diary, "but I have a feeling there is a desire at [sic] Washington that this information should get out; that Canada should start the enquiry and that we should have the responsibility for beginning it and that the way should be paved for it being continued in the U.S. This may be all wrong, but I have that intuition very strongly. It is the way in which a certain kind of politics is played by a certain type of men."[17]

Admiral Leahy may not have been far from King's mind when he wrote this entry. As a military man with strongly anti-Soviet views, Leahy, after witnessing King's reluctance to move ahead on the Gouzenko case, had good reason to leak information about the defection.[18] Both he and Truman were unhappy with Secretary of State James Byrnes, who they thought was too conciliatory with the Soviets, and they felt the State Department was lagging on the Gouzenko issue. Truman himself had changed his attitude toward the Russians over the past months, as it became obvious that the Soviets were untrustworthy and unwilling to go along with any

American proposals. In a January 6, 1946, message to Byrnes, Truman had made his views clear: "Unless Russia is faced with an iron fist and strong language another war is in the making . . . I am tired of babying the Russians."[19] But it is unlikely that Truman would have authorized a leak of top secret information to a journalist, and doubtful that Leahy would have done this on his own. Moreover, Pearson's subsequent articles on the Canadian case would cast the White House in a bad light.

Hoover is the more likely suspect. The FBI and Hoover himself, a seasoned behind-the-scenes operator with a constant eye on the press, had a long history of cultivating journalists. Hoover corresponded frequently with Drew Pearson during the war years, mainly about persons in the United States who were sympathetic to the Nazis and about whom Pearson would inform Hoover directly. And in the post-war period, the FBI would make a habit of leaking information about communists to trusted journalists, including Pearson.[20]

Another clue to Hoover's involvement was in a top secret telegram apparently from either Dwyer or William Stephenson, to MI6 on January 10, 1946. It included the following: "From information received from one of our representatives it appears to me that Drew Pearson is aware to some degree of both Corby and Speed [Bentley] cases. . . . Our representative was naturally unable and did not attempt to draw Pearson out on subject but is of opinion that information may have been obtained confidentially from Hoover himself in some general terms in hope of enlisting Pearson's support for dominant position both at home and abroad under present American Intelligence reshuffle."[21]

According to an internal FBI memorandum, Hoover spoke with Drew Pearson by telephone on the morning of February 3, the day of Pearson's evening broadcast. Later that morning, Pearson called FBI public relations chief Lou Nichols, who noted in a memorandum that Pearson "appeared to have complete knowledge of the case."[22]

As one of Hoover's deputies, Robert Lamphere, recalled, the FBI had been frustrated with the way its spy cases were going: "We were near and yet so far. Igor Gouzenko and Bentley had shown that Russians were operating all around us, but we were unable to counter their efforts."[23] Bentley's testimony had to be kept secret, so that she could be a witness before subsequent grand juries. But a public announcement of Gouzenko's revelations was just what Hoover and the FBI needed to create a climate in which to launch their spy hunt more aggressively. The Canadian intelligence attaché in Washington came to the same conclusion. After hearing from a journalist at *Time* magazine that Drew Pearson's source of information was almost certainly J. Edgar Hoover, his assessment in a message to Norman Robertson was that "Hoover wanted to force the issue."[24]

The pro-communist press, not surprisingly, also took the view that Hoover was behind the leak. A piece appearing some months later in the communist magazine *New Masses* claimed that one of Drew Pearson's employees had gone around Washington explaining why his boss broke the story: "It was like this, the Pearson scribe explained to many of his news sources in labor and progressive circles: J. Edgar Hoover asked Drew to use the story, and how could he turn him down? After all, the business works both ways." This piece aroused such intense concern at the U.S. Embassy in London that an official there fired off a letter to Roger Hollis (with a copy to Philby) instructing him "to immediately call the . . . article to the attention of MI-5 and MI-6, at which time it should be unequivocally pointed out to these agencies that the above allegations are, of course, absolutely false and completely without any foundation."[25] The tone of the letter suggested that the Americans were protesting too much.

❧

For the next several days, there was remarkably little public reaction to the broadcast in either the United States or Canada. It was as if North America, still recovering from the trauma of war and struggling to come to terms with the atom bomb, was not ready for news of another crisis.

But this was the quiet before the storm. In his next weekly broadcast, on February 10, Pearson again brought up the Canadian espionage case. Sensational public trials of Canadian government officials for spying would soon take place, he predicted. This prompted a decisive reaction from Ottawa. According to a message from Peter Dwyer to MI6 on February 13, "Royal Commissioners suddenly decided today to prevent any further damage by leaks from Drew Pearson by taking action before his next Sunday broadcast."[26] Two days later, during raids carried out in the early morning of February 15, 1946, the RCMP detained eleven individuals. That afternoon, Mackenzie King made his first public statement on the Gouzenko affair. Information had reached the Canadian government, he announced, that disclosures of secret information to a foreign country had occurred (he did not name the country in question) and that several persons had been detained. The next day, the RCMP detained two more suspects.

The detentions created a sensation. Almost immediately, the press reported that the unnamed country was the Soviet Union and that the spying involved atomic secrets. The story made the front pages in the West for the next several weeks, with wild speculation about the defector, the spies, and the extent of the espionage. The already fragile post-war peace had now been destroyed by a new threat: the Allies' erstwhile friend had been stealing their atom-bomb secrets. Both the White House and the State Department insisted that the Canadian case had nothing to do with Americans in the U.S. government, but it was inevitable that the trail would lead the press in that direction.

And it was inevitable that Drew Pearson, the recipient of inside information on the case, would be among the first to make the connection between espionage in Canada and in the United States. The day after the arrests, Pearson, in his nationally syndicated newspaper column, claimed that "the Russian agent taken by the Canadians has given the names and locations of about 1,700 other Soviet agents operating not only in Canada, but also in the United States. He has put the finger on certain officials inside both the American and Canadian governments," and "photostats showing payments made to United States and Canadian officials have even come to light." Most significant of all, Pearson made a point of noting that the White House and the State Department (considered widely to be bastions of liberal sentiment) had opposed going after these spies in

America, but that the Justice Department (that is, the FBI) was "anxious to arrest and prosecute."[27]

Pearson's story must have pleased Hoover and his colleagues. Of course, the number of Soviet agents cited by Pearson was outlandish, and of course Gouzenko had not produced photostats showing Soviet payments to *U.S. officials*. But such exaggerations didn't hurt. Far from it. The suggestion that the Truman administration was preventing the FBI from fighting espionage effectively gave Hoover a clear advantage in the court of public opinion. He at last had the momentum he needed to pursue his anti-communist agenda more rigorously, an agenda that included forcing both Harry Dexter White and Alger Hiss out of the U.S. administration.

Significantly, the day after Drew Pearson initially broke the story, Hoover had sent a letter (dated three days earlier) to the White House warning President Truman against confirming Harry White's nomination as a member of the governing board of the International Monetary Fund (IMF) and reiterating Bentley's claims about him.[28] As part of the argument against White, Hoover cited a source "high placed in the Canadian government" who pointed out the danger of appointing someone like White, whose loyalty could not be assured. Moreover, Hoover claimed, his Canadian source expressed fear that "facts might come to light in the future throwing some sinister accusations at White and thereby jeopardize the successful operation of these important international financial institutions."

Contrary to what has long been assumed, Igor Gouzenko, in the words of one scholar, "did not possess a shred of evidence, documentary or otherwise, that implicated Harry Dexter White in the Soviet conspiracy."[29] Indeed, Gouzenko never mentioned White in his initial debriefings and would later, under intense grilling by American interrogators, persistently deny that he had any information on him. Hoover of course knew this, so he did not specifically mention Gouzenko as a source. But by citing a high-level Canadian official as saying that sinister accusations about White might be made in the future, he seemed to imply that evidence against White would emerge in the Canadian case. In fact the unnamed source from Canada was not a Canadian. As a top secret file from the Canadian archives reveals, the warning about White came from MI6's Peter Dwyer, who had been based in Washington to liaise with the FBI before being seconded to Ottawa to work on the Gouzenko case.

On January 28, 1946, Dwyer sent the following telegram to his office in Washington with the request that it be shown personally to Lish Whitson of the FBI (who had been in Ottawa for the Gouzenko case earlier):

> For your most private information only we have learned from an informed diplomatic source something which would seem of grave concern. . . . [T]he two British and two Canadian delegates [to the IMF] will nominate and support White. . . . With this backing we gather that White's nomination to this important post would be a more or less forgone conclusion. . . . If we allow Canadian and British delegates to carry out their present plan, we allow them to place a Soviet agent in a position of utmost importance in international relations. On the other hand we should not wish to warn our delegates without your complete agreement. . . . We would appreciate your earliest advice in this as our delegates arrive on Friday.[30]

This telegram makes clear that not only was Hoover misleading about the source of his information against White (it was not a Canadian official), he also misrepresented what this source said. Dwyer's message was simple: he had heard that the British and Canadian delegates would support White's nomination and he wondered if these delegates should be told the information (gleaned from Bentley and transmitted in secret FBI reports which Dwyer would have seen) that White was a Soviet agent. Dwyer did not say anything about "sinister accusations" against White coming to light in the future.

In 1953, when the whole matter of Hoover's warnings to Truman about White became public, Canadian officials would confront Dwyer (who by this time had left MI6 and joined the Canadian government) with the telegram he had sent to the FBI seven years earlier. Dwyer claimed that William Stephenson inspired it, which would not be surprising given that Stephenson was a quintessential behind-the-scenes operator. But Dwyer himself had intimate ties with the FBI. According to Robert Lamphere, Dwyer had such a close relation with Assistant Director Mickey Ladd that "Ladd gave Peter Dwyer permission to drop in at the various offices of the FBI's Domestic Intelligence Division and to talk freely with supervisors such as me. No other intelligence man, even from a U.S. agency, could do so; Dwyer's privilege was unique."[31] Lamphere goes on to say that he personally did not trust Dwyer, who was always engaging in "horse trading" with the FBI – giving out insignificant information while touting it as highly important in order to get a lot in return. Was Dwyer's letter to the FBI about White as straightforward as it seemed, or was it part of this "horse trading" game?

With the help of Dwyer's letter, it soon became "common knowledge" in Washington circles that Gouzenko had implicated White, a rumor that Hoover did not attempt to quell. In a memorandum to his subordinates, written in February 1946, Hoover observed, "I told the Attorney General that I saw Drew Pearson the other day and he mentioned that he understood White was mixed up in the Canadian case. I told Pearson that I could make no comment."[32]

For all Hoover's efforts, Truman was not impressed, and the appointment of White to the IMF went through as planned. Truman's decision not to prevent White's appointment would become the source of a bitter public controversy between him and Hoover in 1953, a controversy in which the Gouzenko case was again dragged up. Although Truman would later be widely criticized for his decision, at the time it was by no means unreasonable. In the report on White sent to Truman along with Hoover's letter on February 4, the FBI admitted that "it should be realized that to prove these charges at this time when they relate to activities occurring in 1942 and 1943 is practically impossible." The report was based solely on what Bentley had said about White. Not only were the charges over three years old, Bentley had stated all along that she had never even met him.

Mackenzie King's diary offers another example of how accusations against alleged spies were distorted and recycled. On February 5, right after Drew Pearson's exposé of the Canadian spy case, King wrote in his diary that he had had a "very confidential" talk with Norman Robertson about espionage: "He [Robertson] tells me that suspicions are directed right up to the top of the [U.S.] treasury, naming the person; also that it is directed against another person who was very close to Stettinius at San Francisco and who took a prominent part in matters there. . . . *The lady Corby concerned* had for two years been employed as liaison between the Soviet headquarters in New York and officials in different government departments, from whom she was securing documents." [italics added]

King quite obviously was receiving an update from Robertson on the allegations of Elizabeth Bentley, referred to by the Canadians as Lady Corby, which were reproduced in reports from the FBI. Robertson was not talking about anything Gouzenko, who by this time had finished his debriefing, had come up with. But this entry was changed in the published version of the diary.[33] It reads, "The lady Corby [named] had for two years . . ." This gives the impression that King is referring to some woman Gouzenko named or identified as a spy and that Robertson was relating new information from Gouzenko. Not having consulted the original diary, numerous historians have added King's comments to their list of evidence against both White and Hiss.[34]

~

The accusations of spying against White and other Americans were at this point still a secret. The center of public attention was Canada, where an unprecedented drama was taking place, a drama in which the prime minister was playing a leading role. King was surprised when, upon waking up on the morning of February 15, he heard about the detentions. He had been told that they would take place early that morning, but had forgotten. Although he was relieved to learn that the police had been deterred from rounding the suspects up at 3 a.m. and had waited until the more civilized hour of 7 a.m., he was concerned about criticisms of his government for using "star chamber" methods in handling the case and about being "held up [in] the world as the very opposite of a democrat."[35]

King had planned to give a public statement after the detentions, but he decided that the Russians should hear it privately first, even though the statement made no specific reference to the Soviet Union. So that afternoon King and Robertson met with the Soviet chargé d'affaires, Nikolai Belokhvostikov, and Vitalii Pavlov, who in addition to being the secret NKVD *rezident* was also second secretary at the Soviet Embassy. King read them the statement, pointing out that the unnamed foreign mission referred to was theirs. He also informed them of an unpleasant incident in Toronto. The new Soviet military attaché in Ottawa, Grigorii Popov, had recently been arrested for drunkenness. Then King launched into a self-effacing apology: "The young men were about to rise when I stopped them for a moment to say how sorry Robertson and I were that it was necessary to speak of these matters at all; that we were all close friends, and that nothing should destroy that relationship." Although Belokhvostikov "had his happy smile" when he shook hands, Pavlov, not surprisingly, was "quite indifferent." He doubtless knew what was coming; the Soviets would not take the public announcement of the espionage case lightly.[36]

King saw himself and his country at the center of an earth-shaking crisis. The day after the roundup of spy suspects he wrote in his diary, "I have been somehow singled out as an instrument of the part of unseen forces to bring about the exposure that has now taken place. There has never been anything in the world's history more complete than what we will reveal of the Russian method to control the continent. . . . As Prime Minister I have had to take the responsibility. The world now knows that I went to see the President and that I also went to see [British Foreign Minister] Bevin." And the next diary entry, on February 17, included this observation: "It can be honestly [said] that few more courageous acts have ever been performed by leaders of the government than my own in the Russian intrigue against the Christian world and the manner in which I have fearlessly taken up and have begun to expose the whole of it."

King apparently forgot that he had pushed all along for a quiet diplomatic solution to the Gouzenko affair instead of exposing the case publicly, and also that just two days before he had apologized to a key figure in the "Russian intrigue," Mr. Pavlov. Why did King refer to the intrigue as being against the "Christian world"? As a subsequent diary entry makes clear, King, like Elizabeth Bentley, associated spying with Jews. Wondering to himself why American officials, Byrnes in particular, denied that the Gouzenko case had any connection to their country, King observed, "I am coming to feel that the democratic party [in the United States] have allowed themselves to be too greatly controlled by the Jews and Jewish influence and that Russia has sympathizers in high and influential places . . . I must say that the evidence is strong, not against all Jews, which is quite wrong, as one cannot indict a race any more than one can a nation, but that in a large percentage of the race there are tendencies and trends which are dangerous indeed."[37]

King was stung by the harsh response of his erstwhile friends the Soviets. Thanks to Kim Philby, the Soviets had an advance copy of King's first official statement on the case, along with reports on how the allies planned to respond publicly to the Soviets. So their counterattack, which focused on King, was well prepared. On February 20, Moscow Radio acknowledged, much to the surprise of many in the West, that the Soviets had indeed been spying, but said the information they received was of little value. The Soviet military attaché to Ottawa "received from acquaintances among Canadian citizens certain information of a secret character which, however, did not present a special interest to Soviet authorities. These matters had already been published." Technical expertise had reached such a high level in the Soviet Union, the radio broadcast went on to say, and so much information had already appeared in scientific journals, that "it would be ridiculous to assert that the communication of such insignificant secret data could create any danger whatsoever for the security of Canada." In other words, Canada was making a mountain out of a molehill. The Soviets also said that the Canadian government's position was "not compatible with friendly relations between the two countries" and implied that King was acting as a lackey for the British.[38]

The Soviets did not let up on King. *Pravda* accused him of starting an anti-Soviet campaign to distract attention from British Foreign Minister Bevin's failure to undermine the Soviets in the United Nations. In late February, the Soviet magazine the *New Times* printed a scathing article that accused King of sympathizing with fascism. After King visited Hitler in 1937, the article said, the Canadian prime minister "advertised him [Hitler] as a 'simple peasant who does not desire anything outside of Germany,' an estimate which does not in the least honor the farsightedness of its author."[39]

Had the Soviets known what King was saying about Jews in his diary, they could have made his views on Hitler look considerably worse. As it was, the maligned prime minister noted despondently in his diary, "The dispatches from Russia make clear that my name is now an anathema throughout the whole Russian empire."[40]

King's reputation was also in danger at home, as he predicted it would be, now that his government was sanctioning the abuse of civil rights. Both the RCMP and the new Royal Commission went to extremes in interrogating the thirteen detainees, two of whom, Emma Woikin and Kathleen Willsher, were women. In fact, the entire process by which the spy suspects were detained, questioned, and later tried in court amounted to an egregious and, for Canada, unprecedented violation of civil liberties.

The suspects were held incommunicado at the Rockcliffe Barracks, an RCMP training establishment on the outskirts of Ottawa. Their accommodation was grim – spartan rooms with narrow, thin-mattressed beds. The windows were nailed shut. They were detained, without access to counsel, under a special Order-in-Council, P.C. 6444, which had been secretly passed in October 1945, when the RCMP was contemplating arrests in the case if the British arrested Alan Nunn May. The order was issued under the War Measures Act, which conferred emergency powers of arrest and detention upon the prime minister and the minister of justice. At the end of 1945, with the war over, the government had relinquished its emergency powers and the War Measures Act was no longer in force. However, when Justice Minister St. Laurent was asked at the time in Parliament if there were any orders outstanding under the act, St. Laurent said no. Later he claimed he forgot about P.C. 6444.[41]

The detention of suspects by the RCMP under Order-in-Council P.C. 6444, while not technically illegal, was not in the spirit of the law. Although the order itself had never been formally revoked, it was issued "pursuant to the powers conferred by the War Measures Act," which had expired. Furthermore, P.C. 6444 authorized only preventative detention, justified by the threat that the subject would communicate secret information to a foreign power if he or she was not detained. As the Royal Commission's report subsequently acknowledged, "the exercise of authority conferred by this Order will be seen to be purely *preventative* in its nature and not *punitive* with respect to past conduct. It is not concerned with and leaves untouched the question of accountability for such conduct under the general law."[42]

Soviet espionage activities in Canada had all but ceased since Gouzenko's defection. The suspects who had actually been spying had long since ended contacts with the GRU, and they posed no threat to Canada's security. This was evident to the RCMP, who had been following them for months. They were simply going about their daily lives, unaware of the turmoil in the upper reaches of allied intelligence and governments. Without doubt, the detentions under P.C. 6444 were not preventative; they were carried out as the first stage of a criminal process.[43]

The detentions fueled a sense of danger and urgency among the Canadian public. A telegram from Ottawa to MI6 noted that "owing to lack of further official information, [the] Canadian press throughout [the] country is speculating wildly with every kind of sensationalism. Stress is continually laid on atomic aspect."[44] The spies were so dangerous, Canada's *Globe and Mail* reported on February 19, that "the police feared either an escape attempt on the part of suspects held in the espionage inquiry here or an organized attempt to deliver them from the well-patrolled barracks at Rockcliffe." The barracks were "bathed in the glare of search-lights." Security had been tightened, and the men on duty were issued live ammunition. For tranquil Ottawa, it amounted to a state of siege; the extraordinary guard detail was "not matched at any project involving top security during the war." Inside the barracks, the dazed detainees were held under constant guard, lest they attempt escape or suicide.

Instructions for the guards, who had to take an oath of secrecy, were extensive:

> The security of the persons detained is of the utmost importance and constant supervision by day and night is to be given to each and every one of them; particular care to be given to attempts to escape or possible suicide. There must be no conversation between the guards and the prisoners. The persons detained are not allowed to communicate with anyone outside. Should they write a letter this will be handed to the N.C.O. in charge. . . . The guards on duty on the grounds will be on the lookout for any possible signaling from the barracks' windows or from neighboring houses or parked cars or any other place. . . . Detained persons must under no circumstances be allowed to speak with one another. As far as possible they should be prevented from seeing one another. Individual guards will keep a minute diary of their watch. . . . These reports are of the utmost importance and it will be necessary for the guards to keep their eyes and ears highly attuned and observe everything that goes on.[45]

RCMP criminal investigators Harvison and Anthony, who had by now spent close to three months gathering evidence in the case, handled the interrogations. Harvison, described by one of the accused spies as "a tall, thin, almost cadaverous man with a long bony face," whose "eyebrows and unshaven tufts on his cheekbones gave him somewhat the appearance of a raccoon," rose to the occasion.[46] He was tough and ruthless in the face of what he saw unambiguously as communist enemies. Having chased after Fred Rose for years, Harvison was anxious to finally lay hold of some of Rose's

Norman Robertson and William Mackenzie King, London, England, May 1944 (*LAC [Library and Archives Canada]/C-015134*).

Mackenzie King with his beloved dog "Pat" at Kingsmere, Quebec, 1940s (*LAC/C-024304*).

Churchill, Truman, and Stalin, on outwardly friendly terms at the Potsdam
Conference, July 1945 *(Harry S. Truman Library / no. 63-1457-29)*.

Igor Gouzenko, circa 1945 *(LAC/C-138882)*.

Svetlana Gouzenko, circa 1945 *(LAC/C-138884)*.

The Gouzenkos' apartment building at 511 Somerset St., Ottawa *(LAC/C-128803)*.

U.S. secretary of state Dean Acheson, date unknown *(Harry S. Truman Library/photo no. 85-63).*

Former MI6 official Peter Dwyer, early 1950s *(LAC/PA-192730).*

Cambridge-educated British nuclear physicist and spy Alan Nunn May, circa 1945 *(LAC/C-138883)*.

Notorious British spy Harold "Kim" Philby, August 1955 (*EMPICS*).

MI5's Sir Roger Hollis, date unknown (*EMPICS*).

Clement Attlee, Harry Truman, and William Mackenzie King, concluding talks on atomic energy in Washington, D.C., November 1945 (*LAC/C-023271*).

GRU colonel Nikolai Zabotin, leader of the GRU spy ring in Canada *(TNA [The National Archives] Britain: PRO).*

NKVD officer and second secretary of the Soviet Embassy Vitalii Pavlov, who was on his first foreign mission abroad *(TNA: PRO).*

GRU major Vsevolod Sokolov, who recruited Emma Woikin *(TNA: PRO).*

GRU major Vasilii Rogov, Gordon Lunan's handler *(TNA: PRO).*

agents. (Rose himself was not apprehended at this time, presumably because he was a member of Parliament and the RCMP wanted first to gather evidence against him from his recruits. And Sam Carr, the other Communist Party official who had been running agents, had fled the country.)

Harvison later claimed that he and Anthony carefully explained to the suspects the reasons for their detentions and the authority under which they had been detained. Also, that they told the detainees "it was their right, if they so wished, to refuse to answer questions or provide information."[47] The prisoners' accounts were much different. Gordon Lunan, who had been detained at Montreal's Dorval Airport on his return from a tour of duty in England, recalled Harvison telling him on their first encounter, "Well, we've tangled with you reds before and you scream your heads off but there is no way you're going to wiggle out of this one. You know why you're here. Are you ready to tell us what you know?" (Harvison later fell back on anti-Semitism, apparently unaware that Lunan's wife was Jewish. "Are you going to stand by," he asked Lunan, "and let people with names like Rosenberg, Kogan, Mazerall, Rabinovitch, and Halperin sell Canada down the river?") When Lunan told Harvison he wanted to see his lawyer, Harvison simply told him he had no rights and was obliged to answer all questions.[48]

Lunan, it will be recalled, had for a few months in 1945 acted as a go-between for GRU colonel Rogov and three of the other accused: Edward Mazerall, Durnford Smith, and Israel Halperin. Because Gouzenko had considerable paper evidence linking Lunan to Soviet espionage, Lunan was considered a key figure in the case. Lunan would say later that he was not an enthusiastic (or effective) participant in this spying venture, which is probably true. He had emigrated from Scotland to Montreal in 1938, when he was in his early twenties, and became active in political movements, such as the leftist Quebec Committee for Allied Victory, before joining the communist Labour Progressive Party. The party then was legal, and Fred Rose, the LPP member of Parliament, was popular and influential. Lunan remembered it as "a period of innocent euphoria during which iron curtains or cold wars would have been laughed off as the ravings of the hard-core right." In 1945, after Lunan moved to Ottawa to edit a publication for servicemen called *Canadian Affairs*, Fred Rose invited himself to Lunan's home for dinner one night and asked if he would like to help out the Russians. It had seemed natural to say yes. Shortly thereafter he was introduced to Rogov by Rose's mistress, Freda Linton, who by the time of the commission hearings had left the country and was living in Washington, D.C., under the watchful eye of the FBI (which had not considered the evidence against her sufficient to justify extradition to Canada).[49]

Lunan had been hoping to get to know the Russians and tell them all about Canadian politics. He was not prepared for the abrupt and secretive manner of Colonel Rogov, who sped around with Lunan in a chauffeur-driven car before giving him his instructions in a white envelope and dumping him out in the street. Rogov was no charmer like Zabotin or Pavlov. He was "shabbily and rather oddly dressed," thought Lunan, "he certainly did not look like a military man. His un-Canadian pants, wide enough and long enough to hide his shoes, made me think of a *New Yorker* report that you could easily pick out the Russian secret servicemen in a crowd because they wore their fedoras undented." Lunan was especially taken aback when Rogov (who called himself Jan) offered him money, which he refused. Lunan would later claim, "Fred Rose screwed me in the whole thing." He would have backed out of it, he said, except that it would have meant that he had broken a commitment to the party.[50]

According to Harvison, Lunan readily confessed: "The 'martyr' welcomed the opportunity to give a statement and filled a notebook with details of his work for the Soviets."[51] In fact, Lunan at first denied any involvement in spying. Then Harvison confronted him with documents that seemed to incriminate him and told him that others had implicated him (indeed, Mazerall had). According to a report from Ottawa to MI6, "Unfortunately for him [Lunan] he colours easily under shock. He did so when his cover name was quoted to him and when shown Photostat of his first instruction from Grant [Zabotin]."[52] After a few days Lunan broke down.

On February 20, another message arrived at MI6 from Ottawa: "After long and delicate interrogation, during which was told of overwhelming evidence against him, LUNAN was finally brought to point where he stated he might be prepared to assist Canadian government and that he could be of great help. He has gone far enough to make retraction difficult and with luck he will make statement tomorrow." Lunan wrote his confession in the notebook he had been given. By this time he was terrified that, because he was a serviceman, he might even be shot. He felt he had no choice but to confess, and name his sources, if he wanted to see his wife and a lawyer. The next day Ottawa reported success: "LUNAN has confessed completely . . . and has implicated fully SMITH, MAZERALL and HALPERIN."[53]

The Royal Commission was supposed to inquire into the extent and nature of the espionage and then hand over a report to the government, which would decide whether to prosecute specific individuals. In other words, the commission was to be a fact-finding body, not a court of law or a punitive agency. Yet it was the commission's lawyers who had written to the Minister of Justice on February 14 requesting that the minister activate the orders for detention and interrogation of the suspects.

The final commission report, issued in the summer of 1946, stated that the commission had no jurisdiction over the interrogation carried out by the RCMP. The report also stated that "the transcription of whatever interrogation took place . . . was not made available to us, nor was it referred to by Counsel, except that in a very few instances in connection with certain points which arose, the witness was referred to statements made by the witness during interrogation."[54]

What this meant was that, if suspects denied their guilt before the Royal Commission, they would be reminded of statements they had made to the RCMP, statements supplied in many cases after weeks spent in solitary confinement, with little sleep and no access to lawyers who could advise them on their rights. Thus they frequently broke down and confessed. Confessions, not the prevention of further acts of espionage, were the purpose of the detainment. As one cabinet minister put it, "If we had let them see a lawyer, he would have told them not to talk."[55]

If this strategy worked well with Lunan, it worked even better with twenty-five-year-old Emma Woikin. The young woman was hauled out of bed by the RCMP on the morning of February 15. Code-named "Nora" by the GRU, she was by all accounts a pitiful spy. Sobbing her way through Harvison's interrogations, she confessed to everything she was accused of and never even mentioned a lawyer. A former cipher clerk at the Canadian Department of External Affairs, Woikin had come to Ottawa from Saskatchewan two years earlier, after the suicide of her husband and the subsequent death of her baby. Her parents were Russian Doukhobors, and she herself spoke Russian. Alone in the "big city" of Ottawa, anxious to find friends, and still emotionally overwrought over her personal tragedies, she had gravitated to the Federation of Russian Canadians, where Soviet Embassy employees maintained an active presence. According to an official at the Department of External Affairs who rented a room to Woikin, she was "a highly emotional, maladjusted and unstable person, with a naïve and child-like sense of values and in need of a simple, direct object of admiration and devotion."[56]

Woikin found that object of admiration when she became acquainted with Major Vsevolod Sokolov from the Soviet Embassy, whose charms won her over. Sokolov, described as "an attractive man with an intelligent face, an easy manner, and a look of coiled energy that suggested sexuality," invited Woikin to his house, where he lived with his wife, Lida. With the sanction of Zabotin, they met frequently. Sokolov gave the young woman expensive perfume and made her feel important. He also told her about how wonderful life was in the Soviet Union, where poverty, he said, did not exist. Before long Sokolov asked Woikin if she would like to help the Russians, which she enthusiastically agreed to do. She was enamored with everything Russian (including Major Sokolov) and happy to help.[57]

Woikin memorized the contents of telegrams she was instructed to decipher at External Affairs and then made written summaries. Lida Sokolov, who began meeting Woikin for coffee, passed these on to her husband. On one occasion, however, the arrangements were more elaborate. Woikin was instructed to go to a washroom next to a suite of dentists' offices. She taped her documents to the underside of a porcelain toilet-tank cover, where they were later retrieved by an embassy chauffeur.[58] Canadian authorities refused, on grounds of national security, to release the contents of four of these "top-secret reports" (in Woikin's handwriting), which Gouzenko had stolen from the Soviet Embassy. When Woikin's summaries were finally declassified almost forty years later, it emerged that none of the information she transmitted to the Sokolovs could have been of any value to the Soviets. Based on communications between Canada's Department of External Affairs and the British Secretary of State for Dominion Affairs in London, the four reports summarized brief discussions of political conditions in Austria and Eastern Europe (which could have been read in any newspaper) and a discussion on Spain between the Soviet ambassador to Britain and the British foreign minister. This was hardly the stuff of serious espionage. But the information was secret, and Woikin therefore had violated the law in revealing it to her Russian friends.[59]

Lida Sokolov told Woikin in mid-September 1945 that they could not meet anymore because there was "some trouble." A week or so later Woikin was transferred from the cipher division. Nonetheless, when the RCMP rousted her out of bed on the morning of February 15, it came as a complete shock. Just three days after Woikin's arrest, the RCMP was able to report that she had confessed and dictated a statement. She even admitted to having accepted a present of fifty dollars from Lida Sokolov. The RCMP, in a secret telegram sent to MI6, clearly understood that Woikin was more a victim than a spy: "This is a pathetic case. Canadian of Russian parentage, she lived in considerable poverty. Her newborn child apparently died of lack of medical care and her husband committed suicide. In resultant nervous condition she was therefore fair game to diplomatic representatives of Soviet Union – particularly after she had found employment in cipher room of External Affairs. Conscious of her origins and vaguely believing she might assist political system, under which she was led to believe poverty did not exist, she agreed to work for them."[60] This understanding of

121

Woikin's extenuating circumstances did not prevent the RCMP from giving her a good working-over at the Rockcliffe Barracks. Like Lunan, she was led to believe she might be executed for her crimes.

Woikin was doomed from the start. She was still without legal counsel when she appeared on February 22 before the Royal Commission, which wrung further details out of her with little difficulty. By the time she was brought before the magistrate on March 2 to be formally charged with violating the Official Secrets Act, Woikin's mental state was precarious: "She wore no hat and her hair looked as if it had not been combed for days . . . she was 'in shock.' The first charge against her was read. In a flat, unnatural monotone, Mrs. Woikin said 'I did it.' The magistrate interrupted to ask her if she wished to be represented by counsel. She merely shook her head and repeated over and over, 'I did it.' . . . The clerk asked her to plead guilty or not guilty. She replied: 'I did it.' The magistrate tried to explain that she would have to offer a plea one way or another. She kept on repeating the same three words. Finally he was able to get through to her, and she said, in a voice that [could] scarcely be heard: 'I did it. I'm guilty.'"[61]

Woikin's family in Saskatchewan scraped together money for the fifteen-hundred-dollar bail and hired her a lawyer for her trial. But given her confessions to the RCMP and the Royal Commission, there was little the lawyer could do, except to elicit some sympathy for her from the judge and to emphasize that the secrets she had betrayed were very minor. Woikin, the first of the spy suspects to be tried, was sentenced to two and a half years in prison.[62] Given she had feared she would be executed, she may have considered her punishment mild. And she may well have deserved it. Nonetheless, it was a sad day for the Canadian system of justice.

Chapter 5

COLD WAR JUSTICE

For one brief moment, the communist trials would place Canada at the center of world politics. For the Western public, this was the moment when the Cold War began.
                                        Merrily Weisbord, *The Strangest Dream*

While the RCMP interrogated suspects at the Rockcliffe Barracks, the Royal Commission, whose hearings were held in secret, was questioning Gouzenko. He was filling in the blanks – which were many – that appeared in the evidence he had produced. The commissioners, judges Taschereau and Kellock, were trying to establish the real identities behind the code names in the Russian documents and to explain the many anomalies that had cropped up. This was no easy task. As observed in a top secret message from Ottawa to MI6, "Corby's documents have to be interpreted with the greatest care and reservation."[1] The commissioners were also encouraging Gouzenko to provide additional verbal testimony that might help them establish the guilt of the detainees.

Gouzenko, who testified for several days, was a model witness. Whatever mental torment he had suffered at Camp X, he pulled himself together for his appearances before the commission. He understood what the commissioners were after, and, within certain bounds, was anxious to please them. On February 14, the day before the detentions, a message to MI6 read: "Corby is making [an] excellent impression on the judges."[2] Although an interpreter was present, most of the time Gouzenko answered questions in his still imperfect English. He was methodical and understated, impressing the commissioners with his knowledge and his unhesitating responses. The commissioners and their counsels were full of appreciation. The young man who had been for more than two years the linchpin of the GRU communications network was, now that he had seen the light of democracy, an object of admiration and respect. He was on their side in a struggle against the insidious and dangerous phenomenon of communist sympathizers among their own citizens. They hung on his words, depending on him to help them wade through the morass of espionage language.

The RCMP still feared the Soviets would attempt to abduct or assassinate their charge, so Gouzenko was housed in the Justice building on Wellington Street during the period of his testimony, leaving Anna on her own at Camp X with the children. Confined thus, he was living and breathing the process of the Royal Commission. Given these pressures, it is even more remarkable that he held together so well. But his questioners were disposed in his favor, and he knew that his future in Canada depended on his performance before the commission. His earlier testimonies for the RCMP, which had dragged on laboriously and caused his frustrated interrogators to threaten to send him back to Russia, were far behind him.

The cases against the suspects, based on Gouzenko and his documents, were far from straightforward. A case in point was the evidence against Fred Poland, a young journalist from Montreal who was swept up in the RCMP's net because of some pages from Colonel Zabotin's notebook. The scribbled Russian notes had puzzled investigators. At first the name Zabotin jotted down appeared to be "Holland," but then someone looked at it again and decided it was Polland.

The brief description by Zabotin did not fit Fred Poland.[3] The individual concerned was said to be working in Toronto as part of the intelligence branch of the Royal Canadian Air Force, and in the process of being transferred to Ottawa. Squadron Leader Poland had been stationed with the RCAF in Ottawa since the spring of 1942, over a year before Zabotin arrived in Canada, and was transferred to the Wartime Information Board in early 1944. What was the highly secret information Zabotin recorded as received from "Holland/Polland"? A map of training schools in the area, marked "for official use only." When pressed for more information about Fred Poland, Gouzenko said he remembered seeing a 1943 telegram from Zabotin to the GRU in Moscow suggesting that Poland was such a good worker that he should be handed over to the NKVD. Given the rivalry between the GRU and the NKVD, and the fact that Zabotin's notes indicated only a vague knowledge of this agent, Gouzenko's recollection was probably wrong.[4]

Not surprisingly, there had been considerable hesitation about including Poland in the February 15 roundup. The day before, Commissioner Taschereau had asked Counsel Williams, "As to Poland; the witness mentioned Polland, with two 'l's' but he did not identify that cover name of Polland as being the person mentioned in your application [for arrest]." Williams replied confidently, "The evidence will be placed before you to show that a man named F.W. Poland occupied the position indicated in the note of Colonel Zabotin at the time." "That he works in Toronto in the Intelligence Branch?" Taschereau asked. "Yes," was the response. Commissioner Kellock chimed in: "You say 'at that time.' What time?" Williams assured the commissioners (wrongly) that Poland had worked in Toronto "during the whole period of 1943" and also that he would have further evidence to show his guilt; namely, that Poland shared an Ottawa apartment with Gordon Lunan.[5]

A telegram to London on February 18 (apparently from Dwyer) made a reference to the weak case against Poland: "there is [a] possibility that POLAND, against whom evidence was anyway light, may prove to be only very slightly involved. He is at present writing [a] statement on activities of LUNAN, with whom he shares an apartment. He will be better assessed after serious interrogation." (Presumably, "serious interrogation" meant the RCMP would be employing more extreme forms of pressure.) Yet on February 20, the message about Poland was the same: "Interrogator is not prepared to give any opinion yet, but there must continue to be very considerable doubt as to POLAND'S implication [in spying]."[6]

Despite the RCMP's Gestapo-like tactics, Poland confessed to nothing. He was brought to trial on recommendation of the Royal Commission and acquitted. Edward Mazerall, on the other hand, a twenty-nine-year-old electrical engineer employed by the Canadian National Research Council, confessed early on and implicated Lunan, who had been his contact. On February 18, the following telegram was sent to MI6: "MAZERALL has written guarded confession, admitted to working for LUNAN and quoted his own cover name 'BAGLEY.' He has minimized importance of how much information he gave. He has implicated no one else and only mentioned LUNAN with reluctance. Fred ROSE first approached him. He is an impracticable idealist." Two days later, the RCMP was able to report, "Mazerall's nerves and memory are improving simultaneously. He has recalled considerable details of [the] communist cell to which he belonged . . ."[7]

∽

While the Canadian press was making free use of the word *treason* (an offense which could bring the death penalty), the fact remained that, while the spying had occurred, Russia was a friend, not an enemy. It was difficult to prove that persons passing information to a friendly nation were doing serious harm. Thus it made more sense for the Canadian authorities to charge the suspects under the Official Secrets Act, which was modeled after a similar law in Britain and was open to sweeping interpretation by the courts.

Revised in 1939, the law stipulated that the onus was not on the court to prove guilt, but on the defendant to prove his or her innocence. In addition, the definition of guilt was so broad that any contact with an agent of a foreign state could be interpreted as a crime. Thus, for example, section 3(2) read, "It shall not be necessary to show that the accused person was guilty of any particular act . . . he may be convicted if, from the circumstances of the case, or his conduct or his known character as proved, it appears that his purpose was a purpose prejudicial to the safety or interests of the State." And section 4(a) stipulated that "a person shall, unless he proves to the contrary, be deemed to have been in communication with an agent of a foreign power if he has either within or without Canada visited the address of an agent of a foreign power or consorted or associated with such agent or . . . the name or address of, or any information regarding such an agent, has been found in his possession. . . ."[8]

This law was later to prove embarrassing to Norman Robertson, who had been in contact with MP Fred Rose on numerous occasions over the years and even entertained him at his home in the exclusive Rockcliffe section of Ottawa. Rose furnished Robertson information during the war about Fascist and Nazi activities in Canada, information that Robertson passed on to the RCMP. And Rose also discussed with Robertson government policies toward the Communist Party. In October 1946, during the trial of one of the accused spies, the fact that Rose had been invited to Robertson's house came up and was mentioned in the papers. Robertson, who was by then Canadian High Commissioner to London, was mortified, and sent a long letter explaining his position to Lester Pearson, who had recently been appointed Canadian Minister of External Affairs.[9]

In fact, Robertson was well acquainted with others among the suspects. Fred Poland was associate secretary of the Ottawa branch of the Canadian Institute of International Affairs, to which many of Ottawa's leading civil servants, including Robertson, belonged. Robertson had also had close links with the Wartime Information Board, where both Poland and Gordon Lunan had held senior positions. As Robertson's biographer observed, "The spy net stretched widely, and Ottawa was still a small enough town that Robertson must have felt very uneasy as he contemplated the list of suspects."[10] For Robertson – with his prominence, and his record of loyal service to the Canadian government – his contacts with alleged spies amounted to nothing more than a political embarrassment. But for the thirteen scientists and civil servants languishing at Rockcliffe Barracks, association with the ubiquitous Rose and other communists was crucial evidence of guilt.

In addition to Emma Woikin, three other suspects – Kathleen Willsher, Gordon Lunan, and Edward Mazerall – appeared before the Royal Commission on February 22, 1946. Kathleen Willsher, who had been working in the office of British High Commissioner Malcolm MacDonald, had confessed early on to the RCMP, telling them she had meant only to help the cause of the Canadian Communist Party, not the Soviets. Willsher was a cooperative witness before the commission, in large part because she, too, thought she might be executed if she did not confess. "Yes," she said, "I know I can be shot quite easily, if necessary."[11]

Educated at the London School of Economics and fluent in several languages, Willsher had come to Canada in 1930 and within a few years joined the Canadian Communist Party. Like Woikin, Willsher was attracted to the party because it offered her a useful cause, as well as social contacts. According to her testimony to the Royal Commission, she conveyed general information verbally to the party because she was told that it would help in persuading the Allies to open a second front in the war against Germany. Nothing very specific, she insisted, and no written documents. Although the commissioners claimed that the transcripts of RCMP interrogations were not available to them, their lawyer made free use of them. Thus, while questioning Willsher he consulted the RCMP transcript to correct and clarify her statements.[12]

Remarkably, the only documentary evidence against Willsher provided by Gouzenko turned out to be letters that she never saw and could not have crossed her desk at the British High Commission. When Zabotin received the letters he mistakenly attributed them to Willsher in his long list of Canadian documents sent to Moscow. Although the Royal Commission acknowledged this, they had the admission from Willsher about passing on verbal information, which was enough for them. She pleaded guilty to violating the Official Secrets Act at her subsequent trial and was sentenced to three years in prison. Had Willsher been allowed to have a lawyer after being arrested by the RCMP, she doubtless would never have been convicted.[13]

As Gouzenko reluctantly acknowledged to the commission, the mailing list he stole from the embassy was not typed by Zabotin but by the wife of the embassy driver, who did secretarial work for the

GRU. Also, it was dated January 1944, while the items listed as having been sent to Moscow were from well after that date. Yet for the RCMP and the Royal Commission this document was one of the major pieces of evidence against the spy suspects. Thus, according to the mailing list, an individual code-named "Ernst" passed along a lot of information about the dispatch of munitions to England during the period of November to December 1944. Gouzenko said that Ernst was Eric Adams, an employee of the Bank of Canada, who Willsher acknowledged as a contact. But in late 1944 Adams was working for the Canadian Industrial Development Bank, examining credit applications from Canadian factories. And in some scribbled notes stolen by Gouzenko, Zabotin described Ernst as a Jew who worked as a coordinator in a "united committee of military production of the U.S. and Canada."[14]

Adams was not Jewish and was not involved with any joint military committee either at the Canadian Industrial Development Bank or the Bank of Canada. This did not stop the commission from asking the RCMP to detain Adams. The fact that Adams was flirting with communism and had visited the Soviet Union with his wife some years before clinched it for the Royal Commission, which pronounced him a spy. Adams had withstood the efforts of the RCMP to get him to talk and insisted on his innocence to the Royal Commission, but the commissioners did not believe him. Once Adams got to trial, his lawyer grilled Gouzenko, who persisted in claiming that Ernst was a Jew who worked in coordinating American and Canadian war industries. Gouzenko recalled having seen a GRU dossier on Ernst (which he never mentioned to the Royal Commission) confirming that his name was Eric Adams, but he then said he never opened the file. The court acquitted Adams.[15]

As one legal expert later pointed out, the commission's failure to inform those being questioned that they could refuse to answer on grounds of possible self-incrimination might have been less reprehensible if the commission had stuck to its mandate of merely gathering information. But the commission far overstepped its bounds: "the commissioners felt it their duty not only to report misconduct, but, in effect, either to perform the function of the grand jury or magistrate or to provide briefs for counsel who would conduct the prosecutions for the Crown."[16] The Ottawa Civil Liberties Association came to the same conclusion: "If the Commission was to usurp the functions of a court and bring in findings of guilt, it has no right to depart from the established rules of evidence binding on all courts."[17] The fact that the two commissioners were members of the highest court in the country and their counsel, E.K. Williams, was head of the Canadian Bar Association made their disregard for legal rights especially shocking.

Given that the burden of proof in Official Secrets Act cases was shifted onto the defendant, and that the rules of evidence were so broad, it was almost impossible for the accused to mount an effective defense, especially without a lawyer. Adams, Woikin, Lunan, and several other defendants had lawyers only once their cases came to trial. By this time they had already been pronounced guilty of violating the Official Secrets Act by the Royal Commission, which questioned them on the basis of earlier interrogations by the police (where they had incriminated themselves).

Although Gordon Lunan was highly intelligent, articulate, and assertive, he was naive about legal matters, something that in retrospect he acknowledged: "The Canada Evidence Act extends protection against self-incrimination to witnesses provided they do not perjure themselves. A common thief knows all about this – but not, alas, an educated well-read thirty-year-old whose only brush with the law had been the odd traffic ticket." But, he allowed, "of course, some inner-voice whispered that such protection surely must exist."[18]

For whatever reason (perhaps simply a sense of guilt or resignation in the face of what he saw as overwhelming evidence against him) that "inner-voice" had still not made itself heard when Lunan appeared before the Royal Commission after confessing to the RCMP. Still without counsel, Lunan readily gave the Royal Commission details on his activities as a contact between the Soviet GRU and their Canadian sources. When he appeared before the Royal Commission for a second time, he noticed that RCMP inspectors Harvison and Anthony were working in the same building, on the floor below, available to the commissioners and their lawyers for advice. As Lunan recalled, "The RCMP had played the cue ball by supplying the commissioners with a script in the form of a transcript of the police interrogation. The job was to get it into the Commission record virtually unchanged. . . . When my testimony seemed to diverge from what the commissioners had been led to expect, they would adjourn briefly for the off-the-record consultation with the RCMP and Justice Department officials. What they were in fact doing was preparing a masterly prosecution brief for use in court proceedings to follow, and who better able to do it than two of the most distinguished jurists of the day."[19]

The Order-in-Council authorizing the detentions referred to the "communication of information to agents of a foreign power to the prejudice of the public safety or interests of Canada and friendly powers." And the act creating the Royal Commission stipulated that it was to determine whether the passing of information was "inimical to the safety and interests of Canada."

But in fact the commissioners' criterion for guilt was not whether the passing of such information harmed Canada, nor even whether a suspect had passed information at all. Eric Adams, for example, was not "Ernst," but his library was full of communist books. Fred Poland may or may not have been the individual referred to by Zabotin in his barely legible notes – and in any case all that Polland, or Holland, gave to the Soviets was a 1943 map not even classified as confidential – but Poland had communist leanings and his roommate in Ottawa was none other than Gordon Lunan. In the eyes of the commissioners, both Adams and Poland were guilty.

~

Along with Roger Hollis at MI5 and Kim Philby at MI6, Mackenzie King was following the spy case closely. Daily, he received and read many pages of evidence from the RCMP and the Royal Commission on Espionage, including all of Gouzenko's testimony. As time wore on, with most of the suspects still being held for interrogation without access to lawyers or contact with their families and without having been formally charged, the press became critical of the judicial procedures. The *Ottawa Journal*, for example, commented, "We do not treat murderers that way." In a letter to Secretary of State Byrnes at the end of February, the chargé d'affaires at the American Embassy in Ottawa observed that "if the most serious charges are not subsequently made against at least some of those detained, the Government will be open to severe criticism, parliamentary and otherwise."[20]

King grew increasingly anxious. He knew he would face attacks from the opposition in Parliament. He was particularly upset when he woke up on February 27 and saw on the front page of the *Globe and Mail* a story about the wife of one of the detainees (later identified as David Shugar), who had returned from a trip to discover her husband gone and their home ransacked. "I was amazed," she was quoted as saying in the article, "to find that the letters we had written each other while my husband was away two years in the services, and my childhood diaries had been taken away." She reported that "for three days my husband was refused information as to the authorization under which he was held" and that she still did not know whether he was being held as a witness or a suspect. What particularly upset King was the reference to a letter the woman had sent to him protesting the fact that her husband was being held incommunicado. "I have received no acknowledgement," she said.[21]

King was beside himself, all the more so since he had not slept well and he felt he was coming down with one of his frequent colds: "I was much annoyed and distressed to find that no answer had gone to the woman who had written to me about her husband being confined. I had given it to Robertson four days ago and had asked since if a reply had been sent. I wanted it answered immediately." Robertson, it seems, did not share King's concerns about the legality of the RCMP sweep and the public reaction. When an irate King telephoned him that morning, he merely expressed surprise that the letter had not been answered.

King was uncharacteristically adamant with Robertson: "I said I thought it was wrong that those who are suspected should be detained indefinitely and that some way should be found to shorten the enquiry and give them the full rights of protection which the law allows them. . . . I said at the beginning unless this part was carefully handled we would create a worse situation than the one we were trying to remedy. People will not stand for individual liberty being curtailed or men being detained and denied counsel and fair trial before being kept in prison. The whole proceedings are far too much like those of Russia itself."[22]

That afternoon, King met with Justice Minister St. Laurent and Royal Commission lawyers E.K. Williams and Gerald Fauteux. By this time he had calmed down and was persuaded to be patient. Within two days, Williams and Fauteux assured him, at least five or six would have admitted their guilt. (The point being that lawyers and family should be kept away in the meantime.) King did manage to have the commissioners step up the timing of their public report on the hearings, which he felt was essential to legitimize the detentions in the eyes of the Canadian people. As Stephen Holmes, the second-in-command at the British High Commission, made clear in a March 2 telegram to London, King and his ministers wanted a speedy report to offset the "formidable charges of interference with civil liberties."[23]

On March 4, the commission released its first interim report, timed to coincide with the completion of testimony by Woikin, Lunan, Mazerall, and Willsher and with their immediate arraignment.[24] The brief report focused attention on a long list of demands that Moscow headquarters had given the GRU residency in Ottawa, including requests for information on the atomic bomb. While noting that the four accused had violated the Official Secrets Act, the report avoided the question of how much of that information the GRU actually obtained, and also whether Canada's interests were harmed. The issue of national security was mentioned only in regard to Mazerall. The commission noted that the two confidential reports on radar that Mazerall gave to the Soviets through Lunan were shortly thereafter presented at a conference (where the Russians, incidentally, were present) and that this "should be considered as an extenuating circumstance in Mazerall's favour." (Mazerall would nonetheless be sentenced to four years in prison on charges of conspiracy to violate the Official Secrets Act.) As for the question of lawyers, the report claimed that "an opportunity was given to have counsel, but none desired to be represented by counsel or to adduce any evidence in addition to his or her own testimony." In fact the offer of counsel was not given to any of them until after they had testified before the commission, at which point it was useless.

In Washington, Canadian ambassador Lester Pearson received an advance copy of the report late on March 2, and was so unimpressed, as he said in a letter to Norman Robertson the next day, that he hoped it would be held back and revised: "I must say that several re-readings of it do not weaken my opinion that it is not . . . a very impressive document, combining unevenly the sensational and the inconsequential and leaving the reader without any clear impression whether there is any real connection between the tasks laid down for the Soviet intelligence people in Canada and the information which the four persons mentioned were able to supply."[25]

Pearson went over the report with both Undersecretary of State Dean Acheson and Secretary of State James Byrnes on March 3. Acheson also found the report wanting. And Byrnes suggested to Pearson that they withhold the report entirely, despite the fact that, as Pearson explained, it was being issued to quell criticism in Canada about violations of civil liberties. Byrnes had given what was for him a harsh speech on relations with the Soviet Union a couple of days earlier in New York, and he had seen the draft of a strongly anti-Soviet speech Winston Churchill planned to give in Fulton, Missouri, on March 5. He feared it would appear to the Russians that the three governments had deliberately organized these events to coincide. As Pearson reported, "It almost looked as if the three things were stages in a planned campaign."[26]

Pearson had also seen a copy of Churchill's speech. Before meeting Byrnes, he had paid a visit to Churchill, who was in Washington, about to depart the next day for Missouri with President Truman. Because Churchill would be making several references to Canada in his speech he had asked Mackenzie King to come down to Washington to meet with him. King was unable to make the trip, so he sent Pearson in his place. When Pearson arrived at the British Embassy, "the great man was still in bed, propped up with pillows, looking pink and white, as always, with a big cigar in his mouth, also as always, and reading a book." Pearson went into another room to read what Churchill planned to say – "very strong stuff indeed, with some magnificent passages and others that will arouse very considerable controversy."[27] It was his now famous "Iron Curtain" speech.

Mackenzie King called Churchill later that afternoon to convey Pearson's positive reaction. "When talking with Churchill, I mentioned that we would be having a pretty strong statement coming out from the Commissioners tomorrow. He said to me: 'Oh you are so completely right' or words to that effect. . . . That if a similar course had been adopted when Britain learned that Germany was re-arming this last war might never have taken place. . . . He went on to repeat: 'Do not hold back anything – go ahead. Keep firm to the position you have taken. I am sure that it is the only thing that will save the situation as it has been developing. It is the same tactics all over again.' Churchill could not have been more emphatic or stronger than he was."[28]

Churchill in fact had not yet read the Canadian report, but he knew what was in it and was no doubt pleased that it reinforced what he planned to say in Fulton. Churchill's Fulton speech set the tone for a new era in East-West relations, making it clear that the wartime alliance was no longer viable because the Russians wanted "the indefinite expansion of their power and doctrines." An "iron curtain" had descended across Europe, Churchill said, necessitating a Western alliance to resist the Russians and sustain peace and democracy. He also stressed that it would be "wrong and imprudent" to entrust the secret knowledge of the bomb to a world organization.

Mackenzie King, who seems to have lost interest in the idea of international control of the bomb, thought the speech was wonderful and telephoned Churchill right afterward to say so. He wrote in his diary that "He [Churchill] and the President were together. He was obviously both relieved and greatly pleased that I had rung him up. I told him what I thought about his speech, being all circumstances considered, the most courageous made by any man at any time, having regard to what it signifies at the moment and for the future. . . . He thanked me very warmly, said it was so kind to let him know." Churchill asked King if he would mind letting Prime Minister Attlee know how he felt about the speech, and he readily agreed to do so.[29]

King was ecstatic. That evening, he committed to his diary the words of praise he believed he had heard from Churchill: "What he [Churchill] did say most emphatically was something to this effect: 'I have followed your career over so many years and have been impressed so deeply with it, with your political wisdom and sound judgment that I value very deeply your approval of what I have said.'"[30] King was particularly delighted because President Truman had overheard Churchill's words. What good luck! It likely did not occur to him that Churchill's motives were not entirely pure. Churchill had gone out on a limb by delivering such a strong anti-Soviet message. He probably anticipated some criticism back in England, where Prime Minister Attlee was even urged from the backbenches of the Parliament to dissociate himself from Churchill's harsh words.[31] It might be useful if he could say the speech had some strong supporters.

~

Well before the release of the interim report and Churchill's speech, tensions had been building in London over the Gouzenko issue. Hollis was becoming irritated at Philby's constant interference. In mid-February, Philby sent Hollis a draft of a paper he prepared on the case for "C" and the service directors of intelligence. Hollis returned the draft, pointing out some "small inaccuracies," and then added a note to Philby:

> I feel that the question of circulating this document from your Office to the Directors of Intelligence is a matter of some embarrassment. The case took place in Canada and has ramifications in this country and in both Canada and here the security responsibility rests on our Office and not on yours. The close cooperation which we have had over this case has,

of course, given you just as much information as we have about it and as you know, we have welcomed this. But when it comes to putting out such a paper to the Directors of Intelligence, it may, I am afraid, give the impression that the responsible department is yours and not M.I.5. Would it be possible, in order to avoid this, that you should put out a covering letter when circulating this document, saying that it has been shown to the department responsible for dealing with counter-espionage in the Empire and that M.I.5 agrees that this is an accurate account of the case.[32]

Shortly before Hollis wrote to Philby, the May case had taken a new twist. On February 15 – the day of the RCMP roundup in Ottawa – two "very experienced" MI5 interrogators interviewed May. They had already had several meetings with top MI5 officials to devise the proper strategy and had decided they would tell May at the outset that the interview was in connection with an inquiry being conducted by a Canadian Royal Commission. In order to prevent May from refusing to discuss his activities because they were scientific secrets, they asked May's superior, the head of the British Atomic Council, to arrange the meeting and give May instructions to withhold nothing from the investigators.[33]

According to a report MI5 sent to Ottawa, May was caught completely off guard: "PRIMROSE turned very pale and was clearly greatly distressed. He frequently paused as long as two or three minutes before answering questions and almost always limited his replies to 'yes' or 'no.' The impression given was that the interrogation came as a great shock to him, but that once having pulled himself together and overcome this, he was following the programme of admitting nothing. . . . It will be seen from the statement that PRIMROSE made a blank denial of all connection with the CORBY case. If therefore, your interrogation in Canada produces any information, which implicates PRIMROSE, it will be of great value to us. . . . On the conclusion of the interrogation PRIMROSE dined alone at the Regent Palace Hotel and afterwards went to a cinema. He made no contact."[34]

Philby, of course, knew about the planned arrests in Canada and MI5's intention to interview May at the same time. But he apparently did not see to it that May was warned, as he had done when May was supposed to meet a Soviet contact some months earlier. Philby probably worried that a warning to May might arouse suspicions among his colleagues that there was a spy in their midst. Moreover, he knew that unless May confessed, the evidence against him was insufficient to justify an arrest. As MI5 had come to realize, although May had been acquainted professionally and socially with some of the other spy suspects, he would not have discussed his connections with the GRU with them. Thus the likelihood that any of those interrogated by the RCMP in Ottawa would incriminate May was small.

Less than a week later, however, in a second interview with May, MI5 got a break. May broke down and made a thorough confession. But he was still at large, mainly because the British did not want to complicate the situation in Canada by arresting May before the commission report appeared. On March 1, Hollis and Philby took part in a high-level meeting at the Foreign Office, chaired by Undersecretary for Foreign Affairs Neville Butler. Philby told the group that May's confession had been relayed to the Royal Commission on the condition that it would not be used in the commission's next report (presumably because publication of the confession would prevent it being used as evidence against May). The group agreed that, upon the approval of Prime Minister Attlee, May's arrest would take place on March 6 and that, since the Canadians would publicize their report on the spy case, May's trial would be open to the public.[35]

Another concern was the former employee at the British High Commission in Ottawa, Kathleen Willsher. The British had tried to persuade the Canadians to treat Willsher separately from the others – and to exclude her name from the first interim Royal Commission report altogether. They were afraid that her case would raise embarrassing questions in Britain about the leakage of their top secret information to the Soviets, especially if it was publicized just as May was arrested. In fact, both MI5 and the Foreign Office were caught off guard when they learned that the Canadians' report would come out earlier than expected, on March 4 rather than March 6, the day they planned to arrest May. They urged the Canadians to delay, especially when they learned the report's scope was much wider than they expected. But the Canadians proceeded as planned.

Stephen Holmes at the British High Commission in Ottawa telegraphed London on March 2 to say that Canadian authorities were under considerable pressure to release the report and bring at least some of the detainees before the court as soon as possible. "The arrest and charging of Willsher," Holmes continued, "is of course regarded by Canadian authorities as [the] logical outcome of our request that she be interrogated and detained for that purpose and I am afraid that we are in a very difficult and delicate position for asking for Commission to be pressed to modify their report in any way or alternatively for pressing Canadian government to postpone on her account its publication and intended action against their own first batch."[36] London cabled back to Holmes that, in view of the Canadian attitude, "we withdraw our suggestion that action should be postponed."[37]

The Canadians quite clearly did not want to stand alone before the public in the Gouzenko case, and suffer criticism for violating civil liberties, just because they had been the first to take action against the spy suspects. They wanted it known that the Russians were spying against Britain and the United States as well. This is why the report mentioned specifically that the Russians asked about the movement and placement of American troops and the "particulars as to the materials of which the atomic bomb is composed." The report also said that Willsher "had access to practically all secret documents" in the British High Commissioner's office. The High Commission objected strongly, telegraphing London to say that the "[Royal] Commission's specific reference to Willsher is inaccurate to [the] extent she did not . . . have access to any documents in this office relating to atomic energy."[38]

∽

Mackenzie King anticipated a huge reaction to the Royal Commission's first (interim) report, noting in his diary on March 4, "I imagine telegraph wires all over the world will be alive with the information it contains as they have not been in days since the beginning of the last war." And indeed, the press in North America and Britain gave the report wide play. (This was the first time that the Canadians had openly named the Soviet Union as the country in question.) The commission's report, together with the news of the arrest on March 5 of Dr. Nunn May, whose link with the Canadian story was taken as evident, made banner headlines on the front pages of all the major newspapers. Most press reports sounded a note of extreme alarm about the leakage of secrets to the Russians and sensationalized the story by claiming that the Russians were planning a third world war. But the more cautious *New York Times* – bearing out Lester Pearson's misgivings – ventured the observation that "much of the information asked for . . . could have been obtained by any military attaché by request" and that "there is no indication in the report that any of this secret information was obtained or communicated." A writer for *The Spectator* in London noted, "The righteous horror which was expressed appears to me somewhat exaggerated. It is the duty of service attachés to obtain all the information they can."[39]

Contrary to what King had hoped, the hastily put-together report and the issuance of formal charges against four of the thirteen spy suspects did not stem the tide of domestic criticism against the government for its iron-fisted justice. According to a message to MI6, "In spite of Commission's first interim report, press on question of rights of detainees and civil liberties has not materially decreased, largely as result of agitation of wives and lawyers who have been retained but who are not allowed to see clients who have not been charged."[40]

A *Globe and Mail* editorial on March 6 called the commission's justice "a totalitarian procedure" and expressed the view that "All the rules of freedom, the basic liberties of the individual, must, we all know, be subordinate on occasion to the safety of the state. But there is nothing in the acceptance of this which licenses the Government to suspend all the judicial safeguards in order to facilitate police work or make easier the conduct of an official inquiry."[41] Two days

later, M.J. Coldwell, leader of the socialist Co-operative Commonwealth Federation, protested the illegal detentions of the spy suspects:
"The war was fought to destroy states which made such police
activities a general practice. To say that it is necessary to resort to
totalitarian methods in order to secure evidence is no valid excuse
for abrogating the elementary principles of Canadian justice."[42]

With nine suspects still in RCMP custody, the issue of civil liberties continued to plague King. The Royal Commission was pro-
ceeding too slowly for the political agenda of the King government.
He wrote in his diary on March 12, "St. Laurent and I feel very
indignant at the length of time the commissioners are taking in
detaining men: also we were both astonished that Kellock [one of
the two commissioners] was going to adjourn sittings for some days
to keep some engagement with a YMCA meeting." Parliament was
due to reconvene on March 14, and King knew he would face some
hard questioning by the opposition for allowing the spy suspects to
be held for such a long time without charge. King apparently
relayed his views to the Royal Commission, and the postponement
was canceled.

On March 15, the commission released its second interim
report, giving evidence against four more spy suspects: Raymond
Boyer, Harold Gerson, Matt Nightingale, and David Shugar.
Professor Boyer was not only one of Canada's leading scientists – as
president of the Canadian Association of Scientific Workers, he was
also a political activist. Because CASCW advocated unions for tech-
nicians, the RCMP had already labeled it a subversive group, and
none other than Inspector Harvison had been secretly investigating
its activities for the RCMP's Intelligence Branch. The charges against
some of CASCW's leading members for giving information to the
Soviets was hugely significant to the RCMP. It confirmed the RCMP's
idea that CASCW was an arm of the Soviet Communist Party.[43]

Boyer, who made no secret of his communist leanings (he had
contributed substantial sums to the Labour Progressive Party), took
the strategy of openly acknowledging to the commissioners that he
wanted to help the Russians, apparently assuming that, since his intentions were pure, he would get off easily. He told the commission

that he had given Fred Rose the new formula that he had devised (and received acclaim for) for the chemical explosive RDX. Rose then passed the information to the GRU. Boyer went on to say that "Mr. Howe [the Canadian Minister of Munitions and Supply] was willing to give it to the Russians and was not allowed to do so by the Americans. I felt throughout the work that it was unfortunate that . . . there was not closer scientific liaison in connection with such information between the Russian war effort and ours . . . I felt it was of great importance that the scientific war effort on the two fronts should be coordinated."[44]

Like most of the other defendants, Boyer never accepted payment from the Russians. (Gouzenko added a negative twist to this in his testimony: "The professor was very rich and did not need money.") There could be no doubt his motives were sincere. According to a message to MI6, "His interrogator Inspector Harvison, who would not be deceived and who has dealt so brilliantly with Lunan and Mazerall, is satisfied that Boyer was motivated by what appeared to him at [the] time to be sincere reasons." And a later message noted, "Boyer is a highly intelligent man, makes no effort whatever to cover his own [garbled] nor communist activities of his friends. We are inclined to believe he is telling the whole truth."[45] Whatever his motivation, Boyer had signed a secrecy oath, which he had knowingly violated. He was later sentenced to two years' imprisonment.

Harold Gerson, a geological engineer and the brother-in-law of another suspect, Scott Benning, also knowingly acted as an agent for the GRU. The RCMP had a document from Gouzenko showing that the GRU had proposed to Moscow that they subsidize a geological engineering consulting office in Ottawa for Gerson, apparently to use as a cover for his acting as an agent for the Russians. According to a report to MI6 on February 27, "Gerson has been re-interrogated by [the] RCMP. This time he was shown photostats of his own handwriting from Corby documents and was severely shaken." And on the next day, "RCMP interrogator states Gerson has been enquiring how many years imprisonment he would be liable to receive. This indicates further that he is likely to talk soon."[46] Of those arrested, Gerson and Gordon Lunan received the harshest sentences – five years.

Matt Nightingale and David Shugar, by contrast, were, from a legal standpoint, highly questionable cases. Nightingale, an engineer for the Bell Telephone Company, was accused of spying for the GRU while he was in the Royal Canadian Air Force during the war, working on the installation of landline communications. Asked about the case by the *Toronto Daily Star*, a former fellow officer in the RCAF gave his views of Nightingale: "An extremely fine chap and a gentleman. . . . The idea of a fellow like Matt thinking it out quietly and deciding to make some money out of cutting the throats of his friends and selling his country down the river is simply inconceivable."[47] In fact, Nightingale had been attending communist study groups in Montreal for several years. But according to the lawyer he subsequently retained, Nightingale "was just a big farm boy from a Quebec farm. He was married to a girl with great ambitions to become a socialite and because of her took part in meetings with friends of Russia. He was at those meetings all right, but he didn't tell anyone anything."[48] The RCMP had picked up Nightingale because his name was found in some notes Gouzenko had stolen allegedly written by GRU colonel Rogov. The notes referred to meetings Rogov had had with Nightingale, but the RCMP had no evidence that any documents or information had been passed to the GRU.

Like the others, Nightingale was frightened and intimidated. On February 18, three days after his arrest, a report to MI6 noted, "Nightingale is likely to sing shortly as he came through his interview badly and asked for writing materials later." Nightingale admitted to having met with Rogov, but to nothing more. The view of his interrogators was that "for reasons of their own Russians did not make any serious use of him." Nonetheless, Nightingale was brought before the Royal Commission. "Commission have been hearing Nightingale for the last day and a half and will have to continue tomorrow," read another message to London. "He appears an accomplished liar . . . Commission will make final attempt to extract truth." In the end the commission could only conclude weakly in its second interim report that if Nightingale "did not in fact give to the U.S.S.R. secret and confidential information, he may very well have conspired to furnish such information." Nightingale was nonetheless committed for trial by the magistrate. He was acquitted the following November.[49]

Dr. David Shugar's case was even more of a problem for the commission, not just because of lack of evidence. His wife had launched a press campaign on his behalf and was embarrassing the RCMP and the commission. Shugar, a young and very talented biochemist and an active union organizer with a reputation for political radicalism, was acquainted with Communist Party official and GRU recruiter Sam Carr. He acknowledged to the RCMP that he had had conversations with Carr about military matters when he was in the navy, but he insisted that the talks were very general and that he never came close to discussing secret information.

Gouzenko had produced nothing to suggest that Shugar had ever been an agent for the GRU. Instead, the RCMP and the Royal Commission presented what was essentially a GRU wish list of what might be ascertained from Shugar should he be recruited, and offered the list as proof that he had actually delivered information to Zabotin and his crew. As late as August 1945, despite various assignments proposed for Shugar by Zabotin and Rogov, his assigned handler, Sam Carr, had not even given the GRU Shugar's full name, address, or telephone number – although the GRU had assigned Shugar, like many other prospective agents, a code name, "Prometheus." On August 14, the GRU director wrote to Zabotin, "I have advised that until the receipt from Prometheus of information and the establishment of his possibilities in the Navy Department, the contact with him should be maintained by Frank [Carr]. Should it prove that Prometheus is a truly valuable man to us, direct contact may then be established with him."[50]

Compared with the other detainees at the RCMP barracks, Shugar had been bold and defiant. He declared that the entire proceedings were ridiculous and demanded to see both a lawyer and his wife, to no avail. Eleven days later he went on a hunger strike in protest and abstained from food and water for almost four days. He also wrote a series of appeals to the minister of justice and other officials. Meanwhile his wife had been giving the press details from Shugar's letters to her about his treatment in RCMP custody. Correspondence between Shugar and his wife was cut off, and it was decided to send Shugar before the Royal Commission earlier than planned.[51]

On March 9, the following report, probably from Dwyer, was sent to MI6: "SHUGAR was taken [to the Royal Commission] next, largely because activities of his wife and his own hunger strike are sources of embarrassment. . . . [He] refused to reply to question concerning members of Communist study group to which he belonged while at McGill. He persisted when warned that such refusal must be taken as contempt by Commissioners." The report went on to observe, however, that Shugar would most likely not be committed for contempt, "since this would eliminate any possibility of extracting even partial admission from him which would seem essential to substantiate Corby documents *which do not in themselves constitute legal case.*" [italics added][52]

Shugar confessed to nothing. According to a report from Ottawa on March 11, "He is still sullen and answers have to be dragged out of him. . . ." As a result, the bizarre conclusion of the second interim report was as follows: "Shugar denies having given, or having agreed to give, any secret information, but has no explanation for the existence, in the documents above referred to, of the references to himself. We were not impressed by the demeanour of Shugar, or by his denials, which we do not accept. In our view we think he knows more than he is prepared to disclose. Therefore, there would seem to be no answer on the evidence before us, to a charge of conspiring to communicate secret information to an agent of the U.S.S.R."[53]

Shugar later wrote a letter to a member of the Canadian Parliament about the commission's practice of making decisions based on the demeanors of witnesses: "These men have made, in my opinion, a mockery of our courts of law and have placed in danger all those democratic institutions of ours for the preservation of which this past war has been fought."[54]

At Shugar's preliminary hearing before the court, his lawyer got Gouzenko to admit, under cross-examination, that the GRU never received any information from Shugar and knew nothing about him except that he worked in the navy. The magistrate dropped all charges, but this was not the end of Shugar's nightmarish experience at the hands of the Canadian justice system. Canadian authorities revived the charges on the basis of subsequent testimony from one of Shugar's former bosses that was cited in the Royal Commission's final report. Shugar was charged with conspiracy to violate the Official Secrets Act, tried in December 1946, and acquitted. But he had lost his job with the Canadian government, and when he applied to be reinstated he was refused. Faced with "a solid wall of rejection," he eventually moved back to his native Poland.[55]

Shugar, who would become a professor at the University of Warsaw, gained a reputation as one of Europe's leading biophysicists. He received numerous citations and awards for his publications and contributions to his field, and at age ninety, in 2005, was still actively engaged in his profession. The experience he endured at the hands of the RCMP and Royal Commission, which he compares to the Star Chamber of Charles I, remains vivid in his memory. Nonetheless, after almost sixty years, it is a topic he is still reluctant to discuss.[56]

The commission excused its civil rights violations by claiming that the spies were so dangerous and their crimes so serious that extreme measures were called for. Yet, the most serious offender in terms of possible damage to national security, Alan Nunn May, was not arrested for two and a half weeks after the Canadian group was taken in. After his arrest the Royal commissioners asked the British if May could come over and testify; they wanted to include his statements in their final report and thereby buttress their case. Hollis responded, "Your anxiety to have either Primrose or his statement available to the Commission for the purposes of their final report and the consequent desirability of concluding trial of Primrose as soon as possible is appreciated. Director of P.P. [public prosecutions] advises that there may be serious legal and practical difficulties in securing the attendance of Primrose in Canada but is consulting the Home Office on this matter."[57]

Toward the end of March the British director of public prosecutions flew to Ottawa to discuss how to coordinate the May case with the report. He agreed to allow the commissioners to publish May's statement as long as they waited until his trial was over.[58]

May's trial was a relatively quiet affair, with minimal publicity in the British press. He pled guilty to the charge of violating the British Official Secrets Act but refused to mention any names of those to whom he passed on information. His defense counsel emphasized before the judge that May had passed on information to the Russians at a time when they were allies and that he had acted out of his conviction that the information should be shared with the Russians rather than out of any desire for personal gain. May, in his February 1946 statement to the police, had said that he had given information to the Russians "about a year ago," which would mean February 1945. His counsel made the point that attitudes toward the Russians were different then: "February 1945 was a time at which the then Prime Minister had not made the statements which he is since reported to have made [a reference to Churchill's "Iron Curtain" speech]. At that time the British Army were mostly in Holland, certainly not across the Rhine, and the Russians were in the course of their drive to Berlin. It was customary to refer to them as Allies who were doing at least their fair share in the war."[59]

In fact, May passed the uranium samples and report on atomic research to the GRU not in February, but in August 1945, after the Americans had used the atomic bomb against Japan. Apparently the prosecutor had not seen the Gouzenko documents or read any of his statements, which MI5 and MI6 had in their possession. Otherwise, he surely would have pointed this out. Another discrepancy arose when the prosecutor mentioned the discovery of May's crime: "No suspicion whatever had arisen that he had been betraying the trust which he had voluntarily undertaken, but toward the end of 1945 or at the beginning of this year after he had been back in this country for some little time information came into the hands of the Military

Intelligence authorities of this country which led them to make certain enquiries of him."[60] Either the prosecutor did not know or was covering up the fact that British intelligence authorities had been aware of May's involvement with the Russians since the beginning of September 1945.

May's attorney, not surprisingly, tried to downplay the value of the material May passed on to the Russians, claiming that at most May might have enabled the Russians to speed up their atomic research slightly. In fact, May's contribution to Soviet knowledge of the atomic bomb was minimal, if not completely without value. Shortly after the spy case broke, May's superior in Montreal, John Cockcroft, was asked to assess the possible damage that he caused to the allies' national security, particularly concerning the atomic bomb. In addition to having access to samples of uranium, Cockcroft said, May had knowledge of experiments with isotopes of uranium, which could have helped the Soviets in developing a chemical separation process. May also had knowledge of the design of the experimental plant at Chalk River, but that was not of major importance, and even May's visits to American atomic facilities would not have been all that useful for his reports. Cockcroft also said that May could have given the Russians information of far greater value had he chosen to.[61]

Somewhat later, in September 1946, the Americans asked the Canadians to assess for them the military information disclosed as a result of the Gouzenko case. In response, G.J. Mackenzie, president of the National Research Council, came up with a detailed reply. With regard to atomic energy, nothing was disclosed beyond what was already published in the famous Smyth Report issued by the U.S. government on August 12, 1945, and entitled "Atomic Energy for Military Purposes." Furthermore, noted Mackenzie, "It is possible that a minute quantity of plutonium may have been obtained, but we have no definite knowledge. There has never been at any time any information about the bomb in Canada, and no information could possibly have been obtained from this country."[62]

Alan Nunn May was sentenced on May 1, 1946, to ten years' hard labor. Had he given evidence to MI5 on other Soviet agents, either in Canada or Great Britain, his sentence would probably have been lighter. But May, like Raymond Boyer, had acted out of political conviction, which he presumably held on to.

May was released from prison in 1952, after six years. During his incarceration, his scientific colleagues continued their association with him and saw to it that his research work was published. After his release, May returned to Cambridge and married Hilde Broda, a young doctor. He was blacklisted from university faculties, but he apparently was able to catch up on the field of theoretical physics and to conduct research in a private scientific laboratory. Form 1961 to 1978, he worked as a researcher in solid-state physics in Ghana, where his wife started a new career in medicine. May then moved with his family back to Cambridge, where he lived a very private life. He died in 2003.

Shortly before his death, May taped an extraordinary confession, which a family member relayed to the British press.[63] He had never spoken out about his spying before and evidently wanted to set the record straight. He revealed that, in 1942, while conducting his military-related research, he had received a U.S. report stating that the Nazis were about to produce radioactive "dirty bombs" (which turned out to be false). Worried about the consequences for Britain's ally, the Soviet Union, which was under heavy attack by the Nazis, he decided to warn the Soviets through his contacts in the British Communist Party. Henceforth, he was considered a Soviet recruit and was later approached for information on the atomic bomb while he was in Canada. In his words, "It seemed to me that [the Soviets] ought to be informed, so I decided to provide information."

A simple enough decision, but a fatal one. May's spying did more than ruin his promising career. It contributed to the deepening rift between the Soviets and the West and to the defeat of the movement to internationalize control of atomic secrets. Had it not been for him, the only atomic scientist among the GRU recruits in Canada, the Gouzenko case might never have caused the sensation it did.

With May's sentencing, and the conviction of Kathleen Willsher, who had been in British employ in Ottawa, the formal involvement of the British in the Gouzenko case was pretty much over. But that did not stop MI5 and MI6 from closely following the hearings and trials in Canada. New information and important revelations continued to flow from the testimony by Gouzenko, the defendants, and other witnesses. And there was still the question of the spy Gouzenko had said was in the British secret service. This issue had been shelved at MI5 and MI6 when all the attention turned to Alan Nunn May and the arrests in Canada. But it would eventually resurface.

Chapter 6

ANTI-COMMUNIST AGENDAS

I had no intention to skip. Whatever the consequences, I meant to go through with it, having enough faith that the good people of Canada will in the days to come get a much better insight into the politics behind the spy trials.

Fred Rose, letter to Canadian justice minister Louis St. Laurent, July 1946

At 11 p.m. on March 14, 1946, just hours after Fred Rose appeared in the Canadian Parliament for the first session of the new year, the RCMP arrived at his Beechwood Avenue apartment in Ottawa. Rose was on the telephone with a correspondent from the *Toronto Daily Star* who had called to ask him about rumors that he was about to be arrested: "Well, I haven't been," said Rose. "Here I am." Then he interrupted himself: "Oh, oh. Two men have just come in." "Police?" asked the reporter. "Of course." According to Rose's wife, Fanny, who had arrived earlier that day from Montreal to watch the Parliament's opening session, there was "never so much as a knock. . . . They just came in and took Fred away."[1]

The *Star* reporter hurried over to the Rose apartment to talk to Fanny. After dabbing her red eyes and accepting a cigarette, she told the reporter, "He was an ideal father to our daughter Laura, who is nine and a half. She was so excited about my trip here to Parliament. She kept asking me what I was going to wear . . . and now look what has happened." There was a bottle of wine sitting on the table; the Roses had been about to open it in celebration of Fanny's visit. "He is a very good man, Fred is," she continued. "I have been married to him for 18 years and I know."[2]

At 4 a.m. the next morning, thirty-eight-year-old Rose was arraigned by a magistrate in a Montreal court and bail was set at ten thousand dollars. The prosecutor claimed that a car bearing a Michigan license plate was parked outside Rose's apartment at the time of the arrest and suggested that a plan was afoot to whisk him across the border. According to the *Star*, "Rose, short and dapper in gray suit and gabardine coat, appeared calm, but not unconscious of the excitement which seemed to pervade the small, crowded courtroom. He looked straight ahead as photographers' flash-bulbs popped on every side, but as the flashes continued from unexpected corners, he broke into an embarrassed laugh and shrugged appealingly to the photographers."[3]

Mackenzie King was relieved when he heard about Rose. He and his advisers had been concerned that Rose would not leave the parliamentary grounds, where, as an MP, he was immune from arrest. Rose (code-named "Debouz" by the GRU) had not been detained in mid-February along with the other spy suspects; if the RCMP, and the King government, were seen to be detaining a member of Parliament without a formal charge in an effort to coerce him into confessing, it would have caused a public uproar. In fact just a couple of weeks earlier, both Norman Robertson and commission counsel Williams had expressed the view to the RCMP's Charles Rivett-Carnac that it would be better if Rose were to disappear altogether. As Williams said, "It would relieve a very embarrassing situation." Rivett-Carnac and his colleagues had been strongly disapproving. Given that Rose was one of the chief instigators of the spying, they felt he should be made to account for his crime.[4]

The RCMP got its way. Without a confession, the initial evidence against Rose from Gouzenko was weak, but once the other GRU recruits incriminated him there seemed to be ample evidence to justify an arrest. The arrest was carefully planned to coincide with the tabling in Parliament of the Royal Commission's second interim report on the espionage case. Raymond Boyer had given testimony before the commission that deeply implicated Rose in the GRU spying effort, although the report itself did not mention Rose by name.

This latest drama in the Canadian spy case aroused tremendous reaction south of the border. The Canadian Embassy in Washington reported that in the United States the "press from every region front-paged the arrest of Fred Rose and charges against the four scientists." The Rose case was an all-time first in the West. Never before had a publicly elected official been charged with spying for the Soviets. And the fact that the official in question was a prominent leader of the Canadian Communist Party made the case even more significant; it confirmed the direct connection between indigenous communist parties and the Soviet intelligence services. As for the four scientists added by the Royal Commission to its public list of spy suspects, although the interim report mentioned only that they had passed military information to the Soviets, the impression conveyed in the American press was that the atomic secret was out.[5]

The American press was quick to draw inferences from the unfolding spy case. The *New York Journal-American*, under a caption "How Many of These Are in the U.S.?" printed a large picture of Fred Rose accompanied by the statement in the interim report that some suspects "holding strategic positions" admitted that "they had a loyalty which took priority over the loyalty owed by them to their own country." According to a message to Ottawa from the Canadian Embassy in Washington, the statement about loyalty "was seized upon" by members of the House Un-American Activities Committee (HUAC) and the Military Affairs Subcommittee of the Senate "to reinforce their demands for a thorough housecleaning of the State Department."[6]

Even before these alarming new developments, the spy scare in the United States – which had begun with the announcement of the Canadian case in mid-February 1946 – had been growing in intensity, giving impetus to a wave of anti-communist measures. HUAC began investigating possible leaks of information at the U.S. military's atomic research complex at Oak Ridge, Tennessee, and the U.S. Army ordered that all officers with "subversive" views be moved out of positions of trust. Most significant of all, especially for the future of East-West relations, the movement for civilian control of the bomb and for international cooperation in atomic research suffered a new and devastating setback. Until early 1946, the so-called McMahon Bill, which placed atomic energy under the control of a civilian Atomic Energy Commission, had enjoyed strong public support and stood a good chance of being passed by the U.S. Senate. Once news of the Canadian espionage case came out, support for the bill plummeted. In March, General Leslie Groves testified before the Senate Committee on Atomic Energy, and "used the spy scandal to cast doubt upon the wisdom of giving sole control over atomic energy to civilians." The committee voted six to one in favor of an amendment giving the military jurisdiction over almost all phases of atomic energy research.[7] The newly formed Federation of Atomic Scientists, which had lobbied strongly for the McMahon Bill, voiced strenuous opposition to the amendment, but to no avail. In the words of one historian, "Despite the scientists' insistence that there were no real atomic secrets to be lost, the news from Canada revived barely submerged beliefs that espionage posed the most serious threat to the U.S. atomic monopoly."[8]

That several of those named by Gouzenko, including Boyer and Nunn May, were prominent scholars who had been active in the left-wing Canadian Association of Scientific Workers (which also advocated international control of the bomb) made a deep impression in official Washington. Henceforth their colleagues in the United States would no longer be trusted. Scientists who advocated an internationalist approach were automatically considered secret friends of the Soviets.[9]

In Canada, the Royal Commission's claim that some of the spy suspects had admitted allegiance to the Soviet Union gave the concern about internal subversion a new urgency. Canadian-based *New York Times* reporter P.J. Philip reported that the "alien loyalty" issue had "profoundly moved this country, in which national consciousness and loyalty are relatively new developments." It was only recently, Philip pointed out, that a single Canadian patriotism had emerged from conflicting allegiances. "Now suddenly and alarmingly there has developed evidence of a loyalty to a political doctrine and foreign national system that has nothing in common with Canadian liberty."[10]

In fact, as the spy case demonstrated, most Canadians did not have a single, undivided allegiance to their country. Canada had not gained independence from Britain until 1867, almost one hundred years after the U.S., and it was still a member of the Commonwealth. The Anglo-Canadians, who predominated in the government, were often far-removed in cultural, economic, and political terms from the mainly Catholic French Canadians of Quebec. Indeed, French Canadians had their own sense of national identity, and many wanted Quebec to have more autonomy. (Significantly, the French-language media paid scant attention to the espionage affair. In one of the rare articles on the subject, a Catholic newspaper drew the conclusion that, since the spies were mainly English-speaking Canadians, it showed that the French were morally superior.)[11] As for the Canadian West, its sense of Canadian patriotism was so weak that successive prime ministers up to the time of Mackenzie King had worried that the region might try to secede and join the United States.

Canada was a huge, sparsely populated, polyglot country composed of different ethnic groups, many of them comprising recent immigrants without strong feelings of patriotism. In Montreal, where several of the spy suspects lived, linguistic, ethnic, and religious divisions were deeply aggravated by rising labor discontent and the growth of urban slums. Widespread anti-Semitism, in a city with a large population of Jews from Eastern Europe, added an additional dimension to the prevailing social disharmony, drawing members of the Jewish intellectual, cultural, and scientific elite, and also working-class Jews, toward radical leftist politics.

Fred Rose, a working-class Jew, was a direct product of this environment of political pluralism and ethnic ferment. Born Fred Rosenberg in Lublin, Poland, Rose had immigrated to Montreal with his Jewish parents in 1920, at age thirteen. He trained as an electrician, but soon was spending most of his time promoting international communism. After joining the Soviet-sponsored Young Communist

League in 1925, Rose became an agitator and propagandist for the party. A 1928 RCMP dossier on twenty-one-year-old Rose (still known then as Rosenberg), described him as five feet four inches tall, with brown hair and dark blue eyes, "very talkative and inclined to speak quickly." According to the dossier, his ability as an agitator was impressive: "Is a good speaker and commands the interest of his audiences. Also [a] good organizer. Has his whole heart in communism."[12]

In 1930, Rose was selected as a representative of the YCL of Canada for training in Moscow, where he spent six months. (He told Canadian authorities he was headed for Germany, along with two other Canadian students. But on the ship bound for Europe, one of them blurted out their secret plan to travel to the Soviet Union and the news got back to the RCMP.)[13] The Soviets were skilled both at training and indoctrinating young foreign recruits, and at shielding them from the grim realities of Stalinist life. Rose doubtless saw little of the long bread lines, and never heard about the millions of peasants who were dying as a result of Moscow's efforts to force them into collective farms. His Soviet trainers would have filled his head with lofty notions about the ultimate goals of communism and convinced him of the evils of the capitalist system, which he was to convey to the proletariat back in Canada.

After Rose's return to Montreal in late 1930, he became a paid party functionary and threw himself into his mission of spreading the communist word. It did not take long before he was arrested on charges of sedition (specifically, he was accused of trying to incite a crowd to revolt against the government) and sentenced to a year in prison. The ordeal did nothing to dampen Rose's commitment to the communist cause, despite the fact that he had a wife and small daughter to take care of. Upon his release in 1932, he resumed his public speaking and wrote and distributed pamphlets glorifying the Soviet Union and castigating the "imperialist" powers of the United States and Britain, along with their "junior partner," Canada. Rose went into hiding when the Canadian Communist Party was outlawed in June 1940 and an order was issued for his arrest. He reemerged in

1942 and that year reportedly approached Zabotin's predecessor in Ottawa, Major Sokolov, with a request to work for the GRU. Sokolov then contacted the GRU *rezident* in New York, Pavel Mikhailov, who oversaw GRU operations in North America. Mikhailov was able to provide Rose's bona fides, and Rose was put in charge of the GRU's Montreal group, which included Raymond Boyer and Harold Gerson. The next year, in August 1943, Rose ran for election to the Canadian Parliament and won. To Mikhailov, this was important news, and immediately he sent a telegram to the director of the GRU in Moscow: "Fred, our man in LESOVIA [code name for Canada], has been elected to the LESOVIAN parliament."[14]

As a recruiter for the Soviets, Rose was one of the GRU's most important Canadian agents. But he was playing a dangerous game. What made him embark on the life of a spy when he was having such success as a leader of the Canadian Communist Party? That Rose was duped by the Soviets into thinking their country was a glorious utopia may not seem surprising if considered in light of his experience in Canada as a working-class Jew from Eastern Europe. But his decision to spy for the GRU is more difficult to fathom. Rose's participation in the GRU's espionage effort was to prove catastrophic for the Canadian Communist Party. When it became known that he and party organizer Sam Carr – two of the party's leaders – had been directly involved in spying, support for the party, not surprisingly, plummeted, and its political agenda was completely discredited. As one historian put it, "With their slavish loyalty to Moscow the Communists not only shot themselves in the foot as a party; they also harmed the entire Canadian Left, non-Communist as well as Communist."[15]

In fact, three years before Rose's arrest for spying for the GRU, Mikhailov sent a word of warning to Moscow that he wanted passed on to the GRU in Ottawa: they should be "increasing caution to the maximum" with regard to Rose. Mikhailov clearly saw the dangers of having a high-profile communist and a politician like Rose participate in the Soviets' espionage operations. If Rose were to be exposed, it would damage not only the Communist Party, but also the GRU, including Mikhailov, who had helped his colleagues in Canada to organize their network.

Rose's espionage was not detected by the RCMP until Gouzenko came along. RCMP officers had been conducting surveillance on Rose for years before his arrest, but their focus was on his domestic political radicalism and his efforts to stir up discontent among urban working classes. The fact that Rose was meeting with officials from the Soviet Embassy in Ottawa on a regular basis from 1942 onward apparently either went unnoticed or gave little cause for concern at RCMP headquarters. After all, the Soviets were allies and Canada was preoccupied with the Nazi threat.

The FBI had also failed to notice Rose, although he maintained close contact with Soviet agents in America, including Mikhailov, and, according to Elizabeth Bentley, made several visits to New York. In March 1946, when the news of the Canadian spy case was dominating the press, Bentley's memory was triggered and she elaborated further about Rose to the FBI: "She distinctly recalls ROSE had seven or eight names of Canadian governmental employees for whom he desired [Jacob] GOLOS to arrange contacts, presumably in Canada. It was learned [that] Informant [Bentley] saw this list of names, but recalled none of them except that the name of ERIC ADAMS, also a subject in the current Canadian case, may have been included."[16]

According to Bentley, Rose had spent ten days in New York, much of the time in private conversations with Golos, who reimbursed Rose for his expenses with money from the Russians. His wife accompanied Rose, but his girlfriend – a young Jewish woman with horn-rimmed glasses who spoke with a Canadian accent – was there at the same time. She wore a Canadian Army uniform. Thinking that this might be Freda Linton, Rose's mistress and courier, the FBI showed Bentley a photograph of Linton, but Bentley could not identify her as being the person she had met. She went on to tell the FBI that in the early part of 1944, "several young Canadians of both sexes in uniform contacted her in New York and simply mentioned [that] FRED ROSE had suggested that they look her up."[17]

Although the FBI had been playing down the relationship between the Gouzenko and Bentley cases, Hoover's deputy, Mickey Ladd, thought Bentley's new testimony suggested strong connections. In a long memorandum to Hoover giving the details of Bentley's testimony, Ladd concluded:

The above-noted contacts between Fred Rose, Jacob Golos and the informant Gregory [Bentley] are believed of considerable significance in view of the light they throw on the apparent organizational connections between the subjects of the Silvermaster case [which arose out of Bentley's accusations against American government officials connected with Nathan Silvermaster] and the subjects of the Guzenko [*sic*] case. . . . This information, of course, raises the definite possibility that at least at one time there was such a direct organizational connection between Fred Rose and Jacob Golos, between the Soviet espionage parallels involved in the Corby case in Canada and the Soviet espionage parallels involved in the Silvermaster case in the United States.[18]

There was another espionage thread leading from Canada to the United States. A Soviet GRU agent named Arthur Adams who had been operating in New York since 1938 had previously lived in Toronto and had obtained a false Canadian passport there through Sam Carr's network. In contrast to the Rose case, the FBI had known about Adams for some time, and he had been under constant surveillance since he was observed in 1944 obtaining material from a physicist at a Chicago research laboratory. It is difficult to say how much information on atomic matters Adams passed on to the GRU before he fled the United States in early 1946. (He died in Moscow in 1970 and was buried with honors in Moscow's Novodevichy Cemetery.) Adams met with at least one or two scientists who were connected with the Manhattan Project, and a Russian source claims that he gave materials on atomic research (along with a sample of pure uranium) to the GRU. According to this source, in early 1944 Adams described in detail to the GRU the destructive powers of the atomic bomb, explaining that it was intended for Japan, but "there is no guarantee that our allies would not try to pressure us, once they have such a weapon at their disposal."[19]

The FBI was eager to arrest Adams, but they lacked evidence. For FBI officer Robert Lamphere this was frustrating: "Our agents followed Adams around the clock. . . . The man knew he was being tailed, and wasn't going to renew his contacts. Wasn't that a waste of man-power?"[20] The FBI was also reportedly told by the State Department to hold off on arresting Adams because they did not want to damage relations with the Soviets, so J. Edgar Hoover again resorted to his tactic of using the media to pressure the Truman administration. In early December 1945, the *New York Journal American* published a sensational story, out of the blue, about a Russian atom spy called "Alfred Adamson" who had entered the U.S. from Canada in 1938. He was "a small, gnome-like man. . . . He has a furtive walk, a pair of deep-set piercing eyes and a nervous habit of always looking over his shoulder." The story, while not entirely accurate, correctly related the basic facts of Adams's efforts to get atomic secrets: "A year ago Adamson is known to have passed information and what is believed to be atomic bomb plans to a member of the Russian Consulate here. The Soviet official, whose name is known to this newspaper, left for Moscow two weeks after his contact with Adamson. His plane flew direct to the Kremlin. The diplomatic pouch he carried, under international law, was immune from search or seizure."[21]

Noting that the spy "has had access to some of the most carefully-watched secrets in American military history," the *Journal* blamed the State Department for the fact that he was still at large: "The arrest of Adamson cannot be made without the sanction of the State Department, which must rule on the seizure of agents working for a foreign power. Proof of the activities of this Kremlin vassal was given to the State Department two years ago, and since that time the FBI has been in constant communication with officials of the State Department regarding his operations. Yet Adamson and his confederates are still not under arrest." As observed in a message to MI6, the piece was inspired by the FBI: "This story comes . . . most opportunely when [the] FBI are preparing Speed [Bentley] case for consideration of State."[22]

❧

Hoover and the FBI were well aware of the power of the press. So too were the RCMP and the Canadian government. They had high stakes in Fred Rose's pre-trial hearing, held in Montreal on March 22. It was the first public hearing in the Gouzenko case, and they pulled out all the stops. A message from Ottawa to MI6 noted, "You may possibly be surprised at the amount of material which will be used, but the reason for this is that the Montreal Courts are unpredictable and Crown [the prosecution] is anxious to ensure that the strongest possible case is made against ROSE immediately while the going is good."[23]

The heavily guarded star witness was Igor Gouzenko, making his first public appearance immaculately dressed in a single-breasted light gray suit. Gouzenko had been alarmed at the possibility of appearing in public, and the RCMP had requested that the court hear his testimony in camera, but to no avail. The prosecution wanted to take full advantage of Gouzenko's debut as a witness.[24] To protect his secret identity, photographers were barred from the courtroom and sketches were not permitted, but a reporter from the *Montreal Star* provided this description:

> Against a background of six alert Mounties in a crowded and dramatically hushed courtroom today, Igor Gouzenko . . . told his story of espionage in Canada. . . . Fair skinned, with dark brown hair, and intelligent but slightly stolid features, he obviously had had a recent haircut. . . . His hair was parted to the side and his hands, with fists half clenched, rested on the top of the witness box.[25]

According to a reporter for *Time* magazine, "The first impression I had of him when he came into the witness stand was his size.

He seemed to me a very short person. . . . The other thing I noticed about him was his cocky manner. . . . He threw his shoulders back and barked out his answers. He also managed to convey a slight contempt for everybody who was quizzing him."[26]

Gouzenko's testimony, in which he named Fred Rose and Sam Carr as recruiters for the GRU, and also discussed the other accused spies, held the courtroom spellbound. The prosecutor, anxious to establish Gouzenko's credibility as a witness, had prepared himself well and asked Gouzenko all the right questions. (He had obviously studied Gouzenko's secret testimony before the Royal Commission, which the counsel for the defense was not able to see.) When asked why he decided to seek asylum in Canada, Gouzenko failed to mention that he had been called back early to Russia because he was in trouble and instead gave his well-rehearsed speech about his love for Canadian democracy. He made his decision, he said, because he wanted to let the Canadian people know the Russians were spying on them in preparation for a future war. According to the Montreal *Gazette*, "Gouzenko spoke for a solid twenty-five minutes detailing the differences between Canadian democracy and Soviet life. No orator, he spoke slowly, picking his phrases . . . the crowd hung on every word. Counsel did not interrupt him, and they were dramatic minutes to everyone in this room."[27]

Rose's attorney, J.L. Cohen, did not cross-examine Gouzenko. Cohen, described by one observer as "a chubby man who smoked cigars and wore his hat square on the top of his head," was a brilliant and flamboyant Toronto lawyer who was known for his sympathy toward underdogs.[28] This was the first time he had seen Gouzenko, and he was unfamiliar with much of the evidence the prosecution produced at the hearing, so he had presumably decided to postpone his cross-examination until Rose's trial. But in his closing remarks, Cohen voiced skepticism about Gouzenko's motives for wanting to stay in Canada: "A telegram comes . . . asking Colonel Zabotin to send him back to Moscow. Gouzenko would not like this, and I don't blame [him]. Here he is living in Ottawa, and living well, certainly very well as compared with the way of life in Russia and in Moscow in 1944. . . . His overwhelming admiration of our way of life and his abhorrence for the way of life he was brought up in came to the front at the time he was to be replaced . . ."[29]

Cohen also observed that, according to documents, Zabotin did not bother to notify Moscow of Rose's reelection to the Canadian Parliament in June 1945 until fully a month after the election: "I would hate to believe that if Debouz [Rose] was so important to the schemes of Soviet Russia, they would not have known prior to the 12th of July that their recruiting agent in Canada was re-elected."[30] Cohen, of course, was unfamiliar with the ways of the GRU's residency in Ottawa, where Zabotin and his staff were not always on the ball.

Carefully rehearsed as Gouzenko was, he and his handlers made blunders. Gouzenko named five detainees who had not yet completed testimony before the Royal Commission and who had not been formerly charged, possibly prejudicing their right to a fair hearing. And he mentioned two other individuals as being agents, when in fact they were not. A telegram to MI6 noted, "this could therefore throw doubt on [the] reliability of [the] rest of Corby's evidence in the hands of [a] good defence lawyer." The Canadian Department of External Affairs, anxious to avoid a deep rift in relations with the Soviet Union, was also unhappy about Gouzenko's hyperbolic prediction that the Soviets were preparing for a third world war.[31] But as one Canadian writer pointed out, part of his job in testifying for the prosecution was to establish a climate of fear: "When you look at the trial transcripts you get an idea of the role of Gouzenko. . . . 'third world war was going to be staged by the Russians against the west.' . . . 'secret cells impregnated by communist agents' – in other words, terrifying rhetoric. And he would always give the whole set-up at the Soviet Embassy with all these scary-sounding foreign names and code names. That was the ritual at both these trials [of Rose and Boyer]."[32]

When asked by the prosecutor about the identities of those mentioned by code name in GRU documents, Gouzenko also named Arthur Steinberg, "a person in the United States," and discussed the telegram that supposedly incriminated him, which was presented in evidence at the hearing. And he mentioned Ignacy Witczak, who had entered the United States from Canada using a false Canadian passport, but by this time had fled abroad. The FBI had Steinberg under intensive surveillance, keeping his case under wraps while they gathered evidence. And the Witczak case was an embarrassment that the bureau did not want publicized. As a message to MI6 observed, "Mention of Arthur STEINBERG and WITCZAK without prior warning to FBI or USA government would again seem most injudicious."[33] Gouzenko's testimony prompted a hasty memorandum to Hoover from his deputy Mickey Ladd: "Gouzenko named by name and cover name practically all of the Soviet agents who have figured in the above case . . . also several of the figures involved in the United States, including Ignacy Witczak and Arthur Gerald Steinberg, both of whom, as you will of course recall, have been the subjects of extensive Bureau investigations." Ladd went on to note hopefully that, although the Canadian press had mentioned Steinberg, thus far the American press had not, although there were several U.S. correspondents covering the trial in Montreal.[34]

In fact, Gouzenko's reference to Steinberg was reported in several American newspapers, which raised speculation in the United States as to why he had not been arrested.[35] The problem, as usual for the FBI, was that they had no evidence against Dr. Steinberg. A garbled telegram from Zabotin to his bosses mentioning Steinberg as a possible recruit and Gouzenko's hearsay statements that he remembered other telegrams about him would never hold up in court. Hoover was well aware of this, and thus would have much preferred that the Canadians had kept both Steinberg and Witczak out of the picture.

Gouzenko was a tireless and effective witness in the Rose hearing, but in the view of one observer the prosecutors let him go too far in their zeal to nail Rose: "The Crown Counsel in Montreal allowed Corby to go much further than was intended or expected. . . . [The] general opinion at the moment seems to be that [the] desirability of establishing [a] strong case against ROSE in Quebec Courts would not justify irrelevant lengths to which Counsel has gone."[36]

It was probably not necessary for the prosecution to bring up the names of Steinberg and Witczak in order to strengthen the case against Rose. But the RCMP, which was guiding the prosecution, may have had other motives for doing so, since they and the Canadian government would have preferred not to go it alone in publicly prosecuting spies. While the British had finally taken the requisite legal action against Alan Nunn May, the Americans were still doing and saying nothing in public. U.S. secretary of state James Byrnes had denied there were any spies in the United States who were connected to the Canadian case, and the FBI, when repeatedly asked by the press about the implications for the United States, had "no comment." It is probably no accident that on March 28 the FBI learned from a member of the American press that, according to a high RCMP official, "the case in Canada is amateurish compared to what exists in the United States and he cannot understand why we do not crack down." Hoover was "very much disturbed."[37]

Had the Canadians understood the complex role that the FBI played in the American political system, and the tensions among the FBI, the White House, the State Department, and Congress, they might not have expected so much. Hoover's cryptic messages to RCMP commissioner Wood in the autumn of 1945, explaining that his agency faced legal constraints the Canadians did not, apparently failed to make clear to the Canadians that the FBI could not, for a very long time, proceed with arrests. On the other hand, Hoover never told the Canadians the truth – that they would have to go it alone. Instead, he had pushed them into it.

Raymond Boyer's testimony at the Rose pre-trial hearing added to the spy fever. His explanation that he had willingly handed over the secret of the RDX explosive to Rose because "he was anxious to do what he could to have the Soviet Union obtain the process offi-cially from Canada" reinforced the image of Communist Party members as clandestine agents of Moscow in North America. This statement coincided with news from Seattle that a Soviet military officer, Lt. Redin, had been arrested on suspicions of spying. Although the FBI refused to comment on any connection that Redin might have with the Canadian case, Congressman John Wood, the chairman of HUAC, gave a different impression. His immediate reaction was that his committee should confer with the Canadians "on any 'interlocking activities' between reported attempts to obtain American bomb secrets and alleged Soviet espionage in Canada." An article in the *Christian Science Monitor* cited the Redin arrest as "the first official acknowledgement here that a Moscow spy ring may have been operating in the United States as well as Canada." The article went on to observe that "new concern has developed among congressmen and government officials over the security of American secrets. President Truman's assurance that the nation's security is airtight against foreign spies is being questioned."[38]

HUAC's decision to intervene in the Canadian case was unwelcome news for both the FBI and the State Department. On March 29, Ladd informed Hoover that their liaison with the RCMP, Glen Bethel, had called asking for instructions as to what to do if members of HUAC showed up in Ottawa. Hoover's response: "He must make *no comment* and of course should not accompany any representative of the Committee."[39] The State Department concurred. American ambassador to Canada Ray Atherton told Bethel he had written to Washington strongly recommending that no one from HUAC be permitted to come to Canada to inquire into the Gouzenko case. Any such trip, Atherton said, "would be neither wise nor proper."[40] HUAC continued to pursue the matter. In June 1946, Congressman Wood asked U.S. secretary of state Byrnes to send a letter to the Canadian government formally requesting an interview with Gouzenko. Apparently Byrnes did not cooperate, because HUAC was never invited to Ottawa.[41]

By March 1946, Hoover was reaping what he had sown. He had wanted the publicity from the Canadian spy case to raise the alarm about espionage in his country and strengthen public support for his anti-Communist agenda. But he did not like the press claiming there was a huge network of spies in the United States busily collecting atomic secrets under the nose of a helpless FBI. And he certainly did not need HUAC racing up to Canada to interfere in the Gouzenko case. Whatever connections the case had with the United States, Hoover did not want them addressed, at least for the moment.

On the evening of March 18, four days before the Rose hearing in Montreal, Mackenzie King had given his long-awaited explanation of the spy case to a hushed House of Commons, its galleries packed with onlookers. Far to the left of King sat Fred Rose, who had been released from custody on bail. He took his place quietly and listened without apparent emotion. King's complicated tale lasted for almost an hour and a half, but his audience hung on his every word. As the *Winnipeg Tribune* described it, "Calm in voice and gesture – he might have been talking academically about a change in the tariff – Mr. King last night told the most dramatic story ever unfolded in the House of Commons."[42]

In fact, King had found the speech, which he gave without notes, a terrible ordeal: "I was horrified to find that I was excessively tired. I could feel the whole weight of my body from my neck down and also the drawing of my throat from fatigue which made it very difficult for me to raise my voice and speak out clearly. . . . What distressed me even more in speaking was that I saw clearly my mind would get just a little clouded at times, from weariness. I was not quite sure I was using the right words and not feeling sure of the points which I wanted to develop."[43]

But King soldiered on, persuading the House of Commons that his government had made the right decisions in what he said was "the most serious situation that has arisen at any time in Canada." The Canadian government had moved so cautiously, King explained, because it realized how far-reaching the repercussions might be. He gave a detailed description of Gouzenko's defection and the steps his government had taken in the following months, revealing that he had even considered visiting Stalin personally to get an explanation of the Soviet spying activities in Canada. King ended with a declaration of faith in the friendship between Russia and Canada. Stalin, he suggested, might not even have known about his country's espionage efforts in Canada: "What I know, or have learned of Mr. Stalin from those who have been closely associated with him in the war, causes me to believe that he would not countenance action of this kind on the part of officials of his country. I believe that when these facts are known to him and to others in positions of full responsibility, we shall find that a change will come that will make a vast difference indeed."[44]

King plainly still indulged in fantasies about Stalin. Had he any inkling of how the Soviet leader operated, he would have realized how unrealistic his image of him was. Stalin, to use a modern term, "micromanaged" everything, trusted no one, and allowed for little, if any, individual initiative in his huge government and party apparatus. Inherently suspicious of the security and intelligence services, he followed closely everything they did (with the help of legions of informers). Indeed, although many Soviet citizens wanted to believe that Stalin had not approved of the purges of 1936–38, when the NKVD murdered millions of innocent citizens, the NKVD had been following Stalin's direct orders. He even went over transcripts of the interrogations of some of his former party colleagues. Although Stalin distrusted his intelligence services and was often reluctant to believe their reports, he kept well abreast of their espionage operations abroad.

Mackenzie King, understandably, knew little of Kremlin politics, which were shrouded in mystery for the West. King's world was one of sensible, well-meaning politicians who felt a duty to work for the public good. Anxious to include Stalin in this vision, King talked himself into the possibilities of personal diplomacy. He believed that if he could only meet with Stalin, somehow he could make him see the light, and the Russians would again become friends with the West. The day after his speech, King noted in his diary that he asked the Czech ambassador to Canada, Frantisek Pavlasek, if he would please give Czech president Eduard Benesh a message for Stalin, "letting Stalin know the kind of man I am and what I stand for in my lifelong efforts to improve conditions of the masses and in the way of international friendship. Pavlasek said he would be delighted to do that and would send word this afternoon. I know Benes [sic] is a great friend of Stalin's and I know what Benes feels about myself. I had in mind that a meeting with Stalin is almost sure to come sooner or later. I had this in mind in what I said Monday night."[45]

Four days later, after Stalin had made a public statement in favor of world peace and the United Nations, King mused, "I am wondering very much if that utterance of his at this time is not the result of what I said in the House on Monday; with what I know of Stalin, I thought he was a man who would not countenance what had been done here. . . . Also I am wondering if Dr. Pavlasek did not cable Benes [sic] on Monday as he said he would, and Benes since cabled Stalin as to the type of man I am . . ."[46]

King did not let matters rest there. He decided to send a personal message through Benesh to Soviet foreign minister Viachislav Molotov, known in Western diplomatic circles as "Mr. No," because of his cold manner and his iron-fisted methods. The message, now in the Russian archives, read as follows:

> The measures taken against spies in Canada were not and are not directed against the Soviet Union and Generalissimo Stalin, as the hostile press has asserted to the Soviet Union. It is necessary to have recourse to the internal considerations of the Canadian government to understand these measures. I would be very obligated to you if you would explain this affair to Generalissimo Stalin, as my friend, who from personal ties knows my character and can confirm that I am very interested in maintaining cordiality and friendship with the Soviet Union. I am also certain that the spying operations were conducted without the authority of Ambassador Zarubin, towards whom I have the greatest respect.[47]

Stalin did not respond to King's gestures of friendship. Quite the opposite. Through diplomatic channels, the Soviets let the Canadians know how much the bad publicity displeased them. And while they had been willing to acknowledge that Zabotin and his GRU group had been gathering information illicitly, they were incensed that Gouzenko had referred to Pavlov and his subordinates as NKVD spies. A note of protest from the Soviets in Ottawa, released to the press on April 4, stated: "The Soviet Embassy deems it its duty to declare that the slanderous statements of the criminal [Gouzenko] as well as the reports in the Canadian newspapers based on these statements regarding the mentioned diplomatic members of the Soviet Embassy in Canada are completely fictitious and deserve no credit." To reinforce its claim that Pavlov and his men were diplomats, not spies, the Soviet Embassy sent a brazen note to the Canadian Department of External Affairs in May 1946 notifying them that Pavlov had been promoted from second to first secretary of the Soviet Embassy in Ottawa.[48]

That Moscow voiced indignation over the claims about Pavlov, while at the same time acknowledged publicly that Zabotin and his GRU officers had been spying, might be explained by the simple fact that Gouzenko's documents had not implicated the NKVD. But there were other factors as well, in particular the rivalry between the two intelligence agencies. Although the GRU's job was to collect military intelligence, there was considerable overlap with the intelligence gathering of the NKVD, so the two services often competed for agents, information, and, of course, influence with the Kremlin. The Gouzenko defection was a black mark on the GRU, and the foreign-intelligence body of the NKVD (renamed the MGB in March 1946) was going to make sure it stayed there.

In early April 1946, a leading MGB official in Moscow sent out a lengthy message to residencies abroad, apparently in response to Gouzenko's references to its agents at the Rose hearing. It was a scathing indictment of the GRU residency in Ottawa.[49] First, the official noted, because the GRU's work in Ottawa was organized so that each operational employee had detailed knowledge of the operations of other staff members, "personal dossiers on the agent network became common knowledge." Another problem was that the agent network made extensive use of members of the Communist Party in Canada, who were well known to the Canadian authorities (Fred Rose being a good example). And Gouzenko, thanks to a "decline in vigilance and a disregard for elementary principles of security," had access to information on the NKVD and to "state secrets of the highest importance."

The message failed to mention yet another black mark against the GRU, the arrest in Toronto of Zabotin's replacement, Grigorii

Popov. In addition to his drunken and disorderly conduct, Popov was discovered to be carrying a concealed weapon. The documents the RCMP found on him convinced them that, like Zabotin, he was a GRU agent. Popov, presumably at Ottawa's request, was recalled to Moscow in March, leaving by ship from Philadelphia. When Popov was en route from Canada to the United States, Dwyer dispatched a top secret cable to London: "I drew FBI's attention to [the] fact that he is almost certainly being recalled in disgrace and they propose to attempt to approach him if occasion offers with view to persuading him to follow in CORBY's footsteps. I believe they may have some reasonable chance of success since his wife and child are traveling with him and he must be well aware of what awaits him if he returns." As it turned out, the opportunity to speak alone to Popov did not present itself. Even if it had, Popov would probably have refused. The rest of his family, and that of his wife, were hostages in the Soviet Union.[50]

As the MGB's message observed, Gouzenko's defection had "caused great damage to our country and has, in particular, very greatly complicated our work in the American countries." But while the author of this message placed the blame for this catastrophe squarely on the GRU, he could not get around the fact that Pavlov and the NKVD shared responsibility for ensuring security at the embassy in Ottawa. In the final paragraph of his coded message he instructed the MGB residencies to heighten their vigilance drastically:

In the instructions which we are sending you by the next post, rules and regulations are given for ensuring security in the work and for fostering in our comrades the qualities of party vigilance and discipline. You are directed to observe these rules and regulations scrupulously, applying them everywhere in actual practice. Without waiting for the receipt of the instructions, ascertain how matters stand in your RESIDENCY. Take all necessary measures to improve the organization of all agent networks and operational work, paying special attention to tightening security. The work must be organized so that each member of the staff and agent can have no knowledge of our work beyond what directly relates to the task which he is carrying out.[51]

Gouzenko's defection was a wake-up call to both Soviet intelligence agencies. Their operations were foundering and serious changes were called for. But Beria himself would not preside over these changes. He relinquished his job as NKVD chief in early 1946 to take charge of the Soviet atomic bomb project. In August 1949, Beria would oversee the successful detonation of the first Soviet plutonium bomb. But by the time the Soviets exploded their first hydrogen bomb in August 1953, Beria had been imprisoned by his rivals in the wake of the power struggle that ensued after Stalin's death in March of that year. He was executed in December 1953, on the orders of the new Soviet leader, Nikita Khrushchev.[52]

❧

Although Mackenzie King was willing to give Stalin, and even the Soviet ambassador to Canada, the benefit of the doubt about their involvement in espionage, he was not so inclined when it came to the Canadian spy suspects. It never occurred to King, if we are to judge from his diary and his public statements, that any of those detained by the RCMP might have been innocent. (And he continued to focus on the Jewish angle, observing, inaccurately, in his diary that "It is a rather extraordinary thing that most of those caught in this present net are Jews, or have Jewish wives or [are] of Jewish descent.") King was certainly concerned about the violations of civil liberties by Canadian authorities, but his concerns centered on the image of his Liberal government rather than on the individuals whose rights were being violated. As he lamented in his diary, "It will always be held against us and the Liberal party that we sanctioned anything that meant so much in the way of deprivation of liberty for a number of people. Moreover, as I saw at the start, it has raised an issue in the minds of people even more important than that of espionage and will probably result in several of the persons being freed altogether when they come before the court, or given trifling sentences."[53]

King wrote this on March 21, after a week in which he and his government had come under strong criticism in Parliament for their treatment of the spy suspects. The leader of the Opposition, John Bracken, compared the methods employed by the police to those of a totalitarian system. Another speaker said that the Canadian people would never live down the fact that the rights and liberties of their fellow citizens were abrogated in those "black days." And a former Liberal cabinet minister named Chubby Power delivered a blistering attack on the government, ending with the following: "I cannot wish to turn back the pages of history seven hundred years and repeal the Magna Charta. I cannot by my silence appear to approve even tacitly what I believe to have been a great mistake on the part of the government. If this is to be the funeral of liberalism I do not desire to be even an honorary pall-bearer."[54]

Despite the criticism, the RCMP still held five people in custody at Rockcliffe Barracks: Eric Adams, Durnford Smith, Scott Benning, Fred Poland, and Israel Halperin. These were the suspects who had wisely refused to confess to the RCMP and would be the "least cooperative" with the Royal Commission. They were not released until March 29, whereupon they were immediately charged and arrested. The Royal Commission's third interim report was issued on the same day. Of the five, all would be acquitted at trial, except Durnford Smith, one of Lunan's recruits, who was sentenced to five years in prison.

Smith, a thirty-four-year-old English Canadian from Montreal, had just submitted his Ph.D. thesis for a doctorate degree in physics at McGill University. As a result of the accusations against him, McGill authorities suspended him from the university, making his thesis ineligible for consideration. Six of the arrested spies were McGill graduates, and the university was getting unfavorable publicity. (In mid-March, a Quebec newspaper observed, "You send your boy to McGill a Canadian democrat and he graduates an international communist.")[55] McGill's scientists had been active in the war research effort, particularly in the areas of chemical warfare and explosives, as well as in atomic science. In order to expand its postwar research program, the university needed more funding, and thus wanted to limit any damage to its reputation.

Smith, married and the father of two small children, had, as noted, refused to cooperate with the RCMP. According to a report sent to MI6 in February, "Durnford Smith flatly denies any knowledge of affair nor will he admit to recognizing Photostat of his own handwriting. He suggested it was probably a forgery. He is however in bad nervous state and his guard reports that he was physically sick after his first interview. He will probably confess later." Two days later, the picture was less optimistic: "DURNFORD SMITH has again been exhaustively interrogated. He is acutely apprehensive but every approach produces only denial. In view [of the] evidence against him, it is most likely he will not be further interrogated as it will almost certainly prove profitless."[56]

Despite Smith's intransigence, his interrogator, Clifford Harvison, could not help but admire him. Harvison's son later recalled, "One thing my dad couldn't get over during the pre-trial detention was that there never was a night that Durnford Smith didn't sit down and write a delightful children's story for his kids. My dad said how a guy with what was on his mind could write really delightful material like that for his kids really got to him. And he said it told him something about the sort of man he was."[57]

Smith was a "difficult witness" when he appeared before the Royal Commission on March 19, demanding that he have a lawyer before testifying. The commissioners tried to insist that, since they were not a court but merely a body of inquiry, there was no need for the "witnesses" to have lawyers. By this time the remaining detainees knew that the others had been arrested following their appearances before the commission, and they realized that their testimony would be used to prosecute them. The following interchange took place between Smith and the commissioners:

> Smith: I feel it is not fair to make me testify until I have seen
> Mr. Aylen [his lawyer].
> Kellock: Mr. Smith, there is not any question of fairness
> involved. You are here as a witness . . .

Smith: But is it not true that all previous witnesses have been subsequently placed under accusation?

Taschereau: There is no accusation against you.

Smith: But all previous witnesses before the Commission, as far as I know, have been subsequently accused. I cannot rid myself of the feeling–

Taschereau: There is no witness that has been accused when he came here as a witness. When the investigation is finished and we have finished our work we will make a report to the government and the government will deal with you as they deem advisable, but for the moment you are just a witness for the purpose of this investigation . . .

Smith: I have the feeling I am not really a witness.

Taschereau: Oh yes, you are a witness.

Kellock: It does not matter what your feeling is . . .[58]

The commission finally relented, and Smith was able to have his lawyer with him. But the lawyer faced an uphill struggle. The commission had papers from Gouzenko to show that Smith, who at the time was working for the National Research Council on matters relating to radar, had had meetings with Gordon Lunan and GRU Colonel Rogov and that he handed over secret or confidential documents, including several from the Library of the National Research Council. Gouzenko also brought out some notes, on radar optics and on the staff of the National Research Council, which were in Smith's handwriting.[59] What clinched the case against Smith, however, was the testimony by Lunan to the RCMP and the Royal Commission that he had recruited Smith and that Smith had indeed given materials to the GRU. According to a message to MI6, "He [Lunan] confirms step by step events shown in Corby papers and his testimony makes findings against still recalcitrant Durnforth [sic] SMITH and HALPERIN [a] foregone conclusion."[60]

Lunan seems to have regretted his statements incriminating Smith, which were elicited at the Rockcliffe Barracks when he was under extreme duress and in fear of being executed for treason.

Indeed, according to one source, he was "sickened" to discover that he had implicated Smith, along with his other two recruits, Mazerall and Halperin. Lunan refused to testify at Smith's trial, but by then it was too late. The prosecution was able to use his earlier statements as evidence.[61]

As before, it was not clear whether the information Smith gave to the Soviets was particularly valuable, despite the fact that much of it was classified as secret. Apparently the GRU photographed it and sent it to Moscow, but this does not necessarily mean it was important. Zabotin and his colleagues were not scientists and would not have been able to evaluate the significance of what they got from Smith. And they seem to have been unclear about what Smith did, asking him at one point to supply them with uranium-235, when his research had nothing to do with uranium or the atomic bomb. But Smith did violate the Official Secrets Act, and for that he paid dearly, spending the next five years in prison. After serving his sentence, he eventually gained his doctorate and taught physics at the University of New Brunswick.

Israel Halperin, described in an MI6 telegram as "shaken but slippery," also refused to talk, thus making it especially difficult for the RCMP and the Royal Commission because they had very little evidence against him. As noted earlier, Halperin had never provided documents to Gordon Lunan and was shocked when he was asked for a sample of uranium-235. (Again, the request was pointless, because Halperin was a professor of mathematics, not a physicist.) The documents from Gouzenko showed that, as was so often the case, the GRU had an extensive shopping list and had earmarked Halperin, whom they code-named "Bacon," as one of the sources of information. But it is clear that there was a huge gap between what the GRU wanted and what it got.

From Halperin, they obtained nothing beyond verbal information about Canadian Army research on explosives, which Halperin furnished to Lunan in April 1945. Lunan wrote up the information in a one-and-a-half-page report.[62] The Royal Commissioners observed "we have been told that this information conveyed to Lunan by Halperin was of a highly secret nature." But Halperin did not consider it secret and even advised Lunan (who edited a magazine for the armed services) to go directly to his chief and ask for the information. Lunan, however, demurred: "I advised him that this was not wise as I do not wish to show any official interest in this field until and unless we decide to do an article on it. He claims there is no particular secrecy about the set-up, but I persuaded him to give me the whole report on the matter."[63]

Lunan continued to press Halperin for written information, but Halperin consistently refused. As Lunan reported to his GRU controllers: "It is impossible to get anything from him except . . . verbal descriptions, and I am not in a position to understand everything fully where it concerns technical details." In his memoirs, Lunan was more explicit about where Halperin stood: "I soon came to realize that he was an unwitting victim who had no intention of becoming involved in what after all could be construed as technically illegal even if he was in general supportive of the Russians as allies and in favor of the sharing of scientific knowledge."[64] In the end, Halperin begged off entirely.

The Royal Commission had ordered Halperin's arrest simply because his name appeared in the Russian documents. Lunan's subsequent admission that he had met with Halperin, though no proof that Halperin had violated the Official Secrets Act, was taken as additional evidence against him. Halperin had returned to teaching at Queen's University in Kingston, Ontario, when the RCMP arrested him at dawn on February 15, 1946. Married and the father of three small children, Halperin, whose parents were Russian Jews, had already achieved considerable prominence in the field of mathematics. Born in Montreal in 1911, he had received his doctorate in 1936 from Princeton, a renowned center for mathematics that attracted scholars from all over the world.

As Halperin later described his years at Princeton: "It seemed to me we were all monks in a monastery, all working with the purest motives to discover mathematics and to share it with others. . . . Those were the days when refugees were coming out of Europe, and those in mathematics seemed to head first for Princeton, because the Institute and the University's math department were both there. It was a tremendous concentration of talent. There was hardly a day that in the common room we wouldn't see a new face and ask who that was, and the answer would be some mathematician we'd heard of, who was a great researcher."[65] In the course of a distinguished teaching career at Queen's and later the University of Toronto, Halperin would publish more than one hundred scientific papers.

Like Smith, Halperin insisted upon having a lawyer present when he was brought before the Royal Commission and refused to be sworn in. When told by the commissioners that they could force him to testify, he asked, "Does that include physical intimidation?" Halperin finally was allowed to have counsel, but he nonetheless refused to answer the commissioners' questions, declaring after six days, "I will not open my mouth here again." According to an MI6 report, he "attempted to leave [the] room and was restrained."[66] The commissioners deemed him guilty, and he was charged in court with conspiracy to violate the Official Secrets Act.

Halperin's arrest shocked the scientific community in North America, which launched a campaign on his behalf. In Canada, theoretical physicist Leopold Infeld, a professor at the University of Toronto and a firm opponent of keeping atomic research secret, spearheaded the movement for the acquittal and release of Halperin, along with that of David Shugar. In the United States, a group of physicists from Princeton and MIT, including Albert Einstein, addressed a petition to Prime Minister King asking for a fair trial for Halperin: "Professor Halperin is known to the undersigned, not only as a mathematician of high standing, but also as a man of the greatest integrity. We find it impossible to believe that he is guilty of any real breach of trust or honor." The petition went on to say that, even if Halperin had given general information to a fellow army officer about a weapon already in wide battle use, it would be only a technical violation of security regulations: "Such 'violations' were common occurrences among civilian scientists and army officers alike, in the normal process of cutting red tape. If such formal matters are considered crimes then almost every Army officer or scientist engaged in war research is guilty of crime."[67]

Although Halperin was acquitted in March 1947, this was not

enough to clear his name. Once he and the others had been deemed guilty by the commission, which published its final report in July 1946, they would always be under a shadow of suspicion. The commission eventually printed an addendum to the published copies of its final report, noting in June 1947 that nine of the people accused of passing secrets had been acquitted by the courts. But the commissioners left the impression that this was because the court was constrained by legal technicalities that excluded valid evidence against the suspects: "It should not be assumed that in any case the evidence before the Royal Commission and that adduced in the criminal proceedings were the same."[68]

The FBI apparently concurred. In March 1947, FBI agents interviewed Halperin's former roommate at Princeton, John Blewett, and his wife, Hilda, both American physicists who had been offered positions at the Brookhaven National Laboratory and were waiting for security clearances. John Blewett recalled that the FBI agents were "vividly" interested in Halperin: "The thing I remember most is they said, 'What do you think of your friend Halperin now' And I said, 'I don't think he's guilty.'" The Blewetts' clearance was held up for months.[69]

Meanwhile, Halperin had had to fight for his job at Queen's University, where members of the board of trustees tried, unsuccessfully, to have him dismissed for "impropriety." After this baptism of fire as one of the first victims of the Red Scare, Halperin not only went on to earn his reputation as one of Canada's most prominent mathematicians, he also became a tireless human rights advocate for scientists, and in 1999 received an award from the New York Academy of Sciences for his decades-long work to achieve freedom for repressed scientists around the world.[70]

Lunan's refusal to testify at Halperin's trial was of course a great help to the defense because it obliged the prosecution to rely on the Royal Commission transcripts, where Halperin had refused to implicate himself. But the incriminating testimonies of others before the commission were used at their trials. The defense lawyers in several of the spy cases tried to have the Royal Commission transcripts disallowed as evidence in court, because the defendants had been without counsel and had not been warned about self-incrimination. In addition, as attorney Joseph Cohen pointed out, the commission had free use of RCMP interrogation transcripts and counseled repeatedly with the RCMP throughout the hearings. No cross-examinations were permitted. While all these factors caused outrage among civil liberties advocates, the courts allowed the transcripts to be used as evidence in all cases.

Why did the courts favor the prosecution on these issues? First, the motions were without precedent, having never before been confronted in a Canadian court, and the judges were reluctant to question the legality of actions of the federal government under the authority of an Order-in-Council. Second, the judges seemed to think that since the nation was in jeopardy and the security of Canada was at stake, the normal judicial process could be ignored. In the words of one scholar, "The judges who presided over the spy trials were unanimous in their belief that an emergency justified circumventing certain aspects of the legal process. While this was consistent with the court's practice during the war, it is significant that they chose to extend the same principle to a commission that had elicited confessions from suspects detained by the government in peacetime."[71]

Thanks to the public debate over civil liberties that arose in Canada in response to the spy trials, the government was challenged in its claim that a threat to national security justified the abrogation of certain fundamental legal rights. And civil liberties advocates launched a broad movement for the creation of a Canadian Bill of Rights to avoid such violations in the future. Canada was forced to face, head-on, the crucial problem of balancing national security with individual rights. Nonetheless, as a result of the whole chain reaction Gouzenko's defection had unleashed, innocent lives had crumbled, brilliant careers were destroyed, and Canada had been thrown into a spy frenzy. While the excesses began with the RCMP roundup and Royal Commission hearings, they would soon take on a more sinister aspect as they spilled over to Canada's southern neighbor.

Chapter 7

THE RIGHT WING UNLEASHED

My loyalties, emotional and intellectual, are for my country, but my training as a scientist and as an American impose upon me the necessity to weigh and to question actions. This I have done and will continue to do.

Dr. Arthur Steinberg, responding to questions by the
International Organizations Loyalty Review Board, 1964

U nlike some defectors, Gouzenko did not disappear into obscurity after he told his secrets. Following Rose's pretrial hearings, he appeared as the key witness in the Canadian spy trials of 1946 and 1947 and later testified twice before U.S. Senate subcommittees. Gouzenko's allegations in 1945 took on a life of their own, implicating many people who were not directly connected with the Ottawa GRU net and arousing suspicions against many more. Every time Gouzenko spoke up, the list of possible spies got longer, especially in the United States. The repercussions would be felt for more than a decade.

Because the documents Gouzenko produced were confusing and complex, as well as being questionable as evidence, the prosecution in the Canadian spy trials needed Gouzenko to explain them and provide background. As he testified, Gouzenko was steady and composed, even when cross-examined for two days by the formidable defense attorney Joseph Cohen in the Fred Rose trial, which took place in June 1946. According to one observer at that trial, where guards were positioned around the courtroom to take on would-be assassins, he "was an exceedingly good witness and stood up very well under cross-examination."[1]

Gouzenko went over yet again the dramatic details of his efforts to defect, and testified at great length about the evils of the Stalinist system and the intention of the Soviet Union to wage war against the West. All this was meant to give credibility to Gouzenko and divert the jury's attention from the awkward fact that he had transmitted information from Rose's recruits to the GRU in Moscow. Gouzenko was, technically speaking, a co-conspirator with those tried for passing secrets, but one who had changed sides and become an ardent foe of the country he had spied for.

Cohen, who had declined to question Gouzenko at Fred Rose's preliminary hearing, had since been able to study all Gouzenko's statements. He set about attacking the star witness's credibility. Cohen made a special effort to trip up Gouzenko on the question of why he did not approach the RCMP after he decided to defect. He began by asking Gouzenko if he had known about the RCMP before he came to Canada. The witness responded that indeed he had been interested in the RCMP since boyhood and had even bought books about them here in Canada. Asked why he had not gone directly to the RCMP for asylum, Gouzenko replied, as Cohen expected, that he thought the RCMP might have been infiltrated by spies. Cohen professed to find this incredible: "You have told us that you knew the high reputation of the Mounted Police. You claim that you were in great fear for your safety and for that of your family. . . . And you expect us to believe that you avoided the police because you thought there might be a spy in their ranks?" While Cohen paused for breath Gouzenko seized the moment: "He nodded toward the accused, Fred Rose, and said in a loud, clear voice, 'Why not? There was one in Parliament.' There were no further questions from the defense."[2]

Fred Rose was found guilty after the jury deliberated only thirty minutes. His sentence was six years in prison. In a bitter letter written the next month to Justice Minister St. Laurent, protesting the fact that he was not allowed bail pending his appeal, Rose claimed that the RCMP's Harvison, a key behind-the-scenes player for the prosecution, had a vendetta against him because he campaigned throughout the war to expose Harvison's "vicious anti-Sovietism." And then there was the fact that Rose was Jewish. According to Rose, although a dozen or so Jews were among the panel of over one hundred persons called for jury service at his trial, "hardly was a Jewish name called when Mr. Brais [the prosecutor] said 'stand aside.'" Rose claimed that "Mr. Brais, in a manner that could hardly add dignity to a Canadian court, played around with the name Rose-Rosenberg. And this hardly a year after the victory over the Nazi barbarians who murdered six million Jews!"[3]

Making matters worse for Rose, the Canadian Communist Party (the LPP), on orders from the Soviets, made it clear he was on his own and was not to implicate the party in his defense. Rose, a loyal communist who believed the party came first, was out in the cold. Not surprisingly, his appeal was rejected at the end of 1946 and he was sent to a penitentiary. In 1951, after serving his term, Rose returned to Montreal and his family. But he was an outcast, unwelcome in the Communist Party and shunned by old friends. His attempt at reviving his former trade as an electrician failed. After two years he left Canada for his native Poland, never to set foot on Canadian soil again.[4]

By the time Gordon Lunan came up for trial in November 1946, Gouzenko was indomitable. Cohen, again, was the defense lawyer, but Lunan thought he did poorly: "J.L. [Cohen] barely cross-examined the key witness, who, of course was Gouzenko. Igor was in better shape physically and emotionally than J.L. and had had ten months of coaching and rehearsal."[5] Cohen put forth several arguments in defense of his client, including that the documents in evidence against Lunan had been stolen and belonged to the Soviets, which made them inadmissible. Also, Lunan was charged with conspiracy to violate the Official Secrets Act, but the individuals he was alleged to have conspired with, Colonels Zabotin and Rogov, were beyond the geographical and legal jurisdiction of the court. Finally, Cohen noted in a pointed reference to Gouzenko, "the Crown [has] no right to proceed with [a] charge of conspiracy against Lunan if some person or persons known to the Crown to have been associated with the conspiracy, are not being proceeded against."[6] But Lunan had confessed early on that he was an agent of the GRU, so he had already sealed his fate – a five-year prison sentence.

As successful as the prosecution was at using Gouzenko, the result in terms of convictions was unimpressive. Only seven of the original thirteen suspects arrested were found guilty in the courts, receiving sentences ranging from two and a half to five years. In addition, a doctor named Samuel Soboloff received a fine for helping to procure a false passport for Ignacy Witczak. But three others – Henry Harris, William Pappin, and Agatha Chapman – who were rounded up after mid-February by the RCMP were acquitted.

An acquittal, of course, did not mean that life was back to normal. As one journalist observed, "They were held and questioned without knowing what the charges were or able to see lawyers. By the time they came to trial their names and pictures and what they had allegedly done were published as truth in Canada and around the world."[7] For many, the trauma and humiliation were difficult to bear. This was particularly true for Chapman, a talented and successful young economist who had received a master's degree from the University of Toronto and was working at the Dominion Bureau of Statistics. Her name did not come up in the Gouzenko documents, but she knew several of the accused spies, who participated in Marxist study groups held at her home on Somerset Street in Ottawa, just a few blocks from where the Gouzenkos lived. In her testimony before the Royal Commission, Kathleen Willsher, who belonged to one of the study groups, claimed Chapman was a secret GRU contact, so the RCMP arrested her. Despite her eventual acquittal, Chapman lost her job, and the publicity was such that she felt compelled to leave Canada for several years. In the early 1960s, she took her own life.[8]

Meanwhile, with much fanfare, the Royal Commission released its final report in July 1946. It was distributed throughout the world. Whatever judicial verdicts were forthcoming, they did not deter the commission from coming to its own conclusions about the guilt of the spy suspects. And the report, which read like a spy thriller, with code names and Russian documents and testimony from Gouzenko, left the impression that the pronouncements of the Royal Commission were definitive.

Writing for the *Saturday Evening Post*, Sidney Shallet called the report "one of the most remarkable documents of its kind ever made public." It "clearly established the methodical intent of the Russians to pry out every bit of private information the western allies possessed, including the facts on the bomb." The widespread conclusion in Washington, according to Shallet, was that the Soviets were similarly spying in the United States, but on a much larger scale. "Canada," pointed out Shallet, "is a country of 12,000,000 whose war secrets were infinitesimal compared with ours. The Russian diplomatic corps and other representatives there numbered about 190. The United States is a country of more than 130,000,000, center of the atomic-bomb development and other of the war's greatest secrets, and the Russians have more than 1,000 diplomatic and other representatives here."[9]

A British diplomat at the High Commission in Ottawa, in an unsigned message to London, was more discerning. He described the report as "a brilliant study . . . a most readable document and misses no point in the drama of the story." Nonetheless, "One cannot avoid the impression that the attempt to give dramatic effect has led at times to unjustifiably extravagant language; the search for brilliance has not necessarily always led to an impartial judicial conclusion. Indeed, on close examination it appears remarkable at times that the document should have been issued over the signatures of two judges of the Supreme Court."[10]

By way of illustration, the diplomat noted that the judges inappropriately used epithets (such as "undeniably," "unhesitatingly," "extremely") throughout the report. Secondly, their personal views came through. They wrote of Gouzenko, "We have been impressed with the sincerity of the man and with the manner in which he gave his evidence which we have no hesitation in accepting." By contrast, David Shugar, for example, was an "evasive witness . . . he exhibited that same concealment and air of furtiveness shown by other witnesses." And thirdly, the British diplomat noted, "the report states as facts what can, on the evidence, only be regarded as inferences drawn from them." The library of Eric Adams, ransacked by the RCMP, was reported to be "literally full of Communist books." Adams also had materials on civil liberties, which led the commissioners to conclude that "Adams was interested in civil liberties, but solely from the Communist point of view."

The British diplomat also had doubts about Gouzenko: "The point still remains that the whole story hangs on the single thread of Gouzenko's evidence and on the documents which he produced. . . . But he was merely a subordinate official who was probably very far from knowing anything like all the story and yet the Commissioners tended to see the whole matter through Gouzenko's eyes. . . . This criticism might perhaps not have been so valid had not the Commissioners themselves fallen into the trap of writing their report in such a manner as to give the appearance that they regarded Gouzenko's evidence as statements of fact."

As for the judicial aspects of the Royal Commission Report, again the diplomat had strong reservations, noting, as had others, that the commission constituted itself as a judicial tribunal, trying people suspected of illegal activities, but without charging them with a crime. The comments that the commissioners made in their report, a public document, would inevitably be prejudicial to the suspects in formal judicial proceedings.

What about the longer term consequences of the Gouzenko affair? The diplomat observed that Canadians felt pride that their country had taken such a strong and independent line in an internationally important matter, but "this feeling was mingled to some extent with an uneasiness that, if this was the price of being a great power, then many Canadians would prefer [Canada] to remain as she was." What was the price? The disquieting abuses of civil liberties in a country that considered itself a democracy. The shock and scare of learning that their erstwhile ally, the Soviets, were plotting against them. And the worry that the deepening rift with the Soviet Union would make Canada a focal point of Soviet aggression – that

Canada, lacking the military resources of a great power and with a huge expanse of open borders, would be in the line of first attack.

〜

Mackenzie King was still trying to handle the whole Gouzenko matter as delicately as possible, but once the Royal Commission's final report came out, his task became especially difficult. When he received the report on July 12, 1946, King confided in his diary, "It is a huge volume. I am sorry for this. I am afraid it will be made use of by Russia as an effort on the part of Canada to destroy Communism and may hinder rather than further the object we have in mind."[11]

Not only did the report discuss Vitalii Pavlov's role as head of the NKVD at the embassy, it also named five others who were still employed there and had allegedly engaged in espionage. Clearly these individuals could not remain in Canada after being publicly identified as spies, but King wanted to avoid a formal request that they leave. Instead, he asked for an interview with the Soviet chargé d'affaires, Nikolai Belokhvostikov, to suggest that the embassy employees return to the Soviet Union before the report was released three days later. According to King's diary, Belokhvostikov "coloured up quite a bit" when King mentioned the additional names. Belokhvostikov said that it would be up to Moscow to decide if they should be recalled.[12]

Pavlov, who was still at his post in Ottawa, was incensed: "It was not enough that the authorities could not accuse me of anything. They also wanted to deprive me of the possibility of packing my things calmly." He says that he insisted to Belokhvostikov that they be given a week and this was conveyed to King.[13] Pavlov and his colleagues then packed their bags and departed for New York, where they boarded a ship bound for Leningrad. The group included GRU colonel Boris Sokolov, who had successfully lured Emma Woikin into the GRU's espionage net, and A.N. Farafontov, who had participated in the midnight raid of Gouzenko's apartment on September 5. Sent ignominiously back to their homeland, the hapless Russian envoys at least had the chance to do some last-minute shopping. A porter in Montreal who helped carry some of their bags onto the train bound for New York mopped his brow and declared they were the "heaviest he had handled in months." One of the Russian wives, laden with the results of a buying spree in Montreal, could not resist a friendly glance at photographers as they boarded the train. But in general they were a grim and nervous bunch, far from the "cheery chaps" they had been before the defection. According to the *Montreal Star*, the Russians answered questions from the press with grunts and glares as they passed through the railway station.[14] It was a sorry end to the warm bond of goodwill that had developed between Canadians and Russians during the war years.

No wonder the Russians were glum. Their future in Stalinist Russia was far from certain. Pavlov, whose fate had been hanging by a thread for months, was especially anxious. "The return trip from Canada to the Soviet Union is deeply entrenched in my memory," he recalled in his memoirs. "I was in a sort of enfeebled state. Evidently, this was a result of the constant strain I had been under since Gouzenko's betrayal. I had borne a heavy burden of responsibility for the security of the diplomatic mission, its employees and their family members. So during the trip I rested emotionally and physically, although thoughts about 'the Gouzenko affair' continued to trouble me: what would be the reaction of the Center to this whole story?"[15]

The "Center" gave him a cool welcome home. As Pavlov expected, when he and his wife, Klavdia, arrived in Moscow with their Canadian-born toddler, they were not assigned an apartment (Pavlov, like all Soviet citizens, was at the mercy of the Communist bureaucracy for his housing). The three of them had to live for the next year with Klavdia's sister and her husband – five people in a single twelve-square-meter room that was part of a communal apartment. At work no one seemed interested in Pavlov's opinions about the Gouzenko affair, although there was a lot of whispering about it. Pavlov knew that the leaders of the foreign intelligence service deliberately shielded themselves from officers who returned after long periods of service abroad. They had their own views of what was going on outside the Soviet Union, and they looked upon the returnees, with all their practical experience, as an unwelcome disruption.[16]

But quite clearly there was more to Pavlov's situation than that. He was under a cloud at the foreign intelligence service. For the next two years he was not given a permanent assignment at headquarters. And his bosses "accidentally" demoted him from major to captain. A few months after Pavlov returned, he was indirectly denounced at a meeting of the Communist Party organizers for "doing nothing" during his time in Canada and allowing serious failures to occur. He weathered the storm, and eventually became head of the Foreign Intelligence "Illegals" Department (for agents abroad under deep cover). Then in 1961 he was appointed deputy chief of Foreign Intelligence in what was now called the KGB. From 1972 to 1984 Pavlov was the KGB's main representative in Poland. A few years after his return from Canada, Pavlov learned that Beria and the NKVD leadership had initially planned on arresting him as a punishment for the Gouzenko defection. Apparently both Pavlov's immediate boss and the head of the NKVD's foreign intelligence service intervened to prevent this from happening. But it was a close call.[17]

~

There were no winners in the Gouzenko affair, except perhaps Gouzenko himself, who seemed to be enjoying the limelight. Mackenzie King and his government became the focal point for the growing antagonism the Soviets felt toward the West as the spy scare took hold. The West would soon become accustomed to vitriolic attacks from Moscow, but this was 1946, and the chill of the Cold War arrived with a shock. In August 1946, after a long lull in public commentary by the Soviets, *Pravda* published an article by Soviet journalist David Zaslavsky entitled "A Sorry Finale to a Shameful Comedy."[18] The article, which would have been inspired and approved by the Kremlin, was a lengthy and scathing attack on the Canadian government and the Royal Commission for "engineering" the spy scandal in order to harm the Soviet Union. Instead of handling the incident through diplomatic channels, the Canadian government, according to *Pravda*, deliberately inflated it into a "major international event." The "unbridled anti-Soviet campaign" that followed was intended to damage the Soviet Union politically.

According to *Pravda*, the Royal Commission Report was "733 pages of cheap gossip, stupid invention and manifest shameless lies. The judges, Taschereau and Kellock, who put their signatures to this bundle of nonsense, will not bequeath happy memories in the history of Canadian justice." The article ridiculed the judges for accepting as authentic the documents of the "scoundrel" Gouzenko and claimed that Gouzenko had been bribed by a "secret organization in Canada" (presumably part of the RCMP) to steal secret documents from the Soviet Embassy and turn against his country. In Zaslavsky's words, "What has been done in Canada is a reproduction of another scale of Hitler's firing of the Reichstag, which was necessary for the fascist conspirators to do away with the German communists. The rounding up of the leaders of the Labour Progressive Party of Canada followed immediately the abduction of secret documents from the Soviet Embassy."

Even for the Soviets this was aggressive language. What were they trying to accomplish? Or rather, what was Stalin trying to accomplish? Most historians agree that Stalin was at this point the sole architect of Soviet foreign policy. Molotov, Beria, and other members of Stalin's circle had only a limited influence on his decision-making. He had initially shown some willingness to cooperate with the West in the aftermath of the war, but Hiroshima changed his attitude irrevocably. As one source put it, "It was the atomic bombardment of Japan and the abrupt end of the war in the Pacific that convinced Stalin that his dream of a postwar partnership was not to be fulfilled. The old demons of insecurity were back. The bomb threw the Kremlin leader off balance – and eventually back into the curse of tyrants: neurotic solitude."[19]

However irrational his thinking was, given that his country had yet to develop the atomic bomb, Stalin became convinced that the only approach to the West was one of confrontation. He had already signaled this change in attitude in February 1946, in an "election" speech at the Bolshoi Theater in Moscow. Now, with this scathing denunciation of the United States' atomic ally Canada, the Soviet counteroffensive went into high gear.

But Zaslavsky's *Pravda* article contained grains of truth. The Canadians had possessed the option of quiet diplomacy rather than publicly exposing the Gouzenko case. The Soviets knew, through Philby and through King's overtures to Stalin, that King had even pushed for such an approach. Secondly, as the Canadian press itself had reported, the Royal Commission had pursued such a heavy-handed approach that some critics made comparisons with Hitler's Gestapo. (Of course, considering more than a million Soviet citizens had perished in Stalin's purges, it was ridiculous for *Pravda* to lash out at another country for violations of legality.) Zaslavsky was also close to the mark in saying Gouzenko had accused people who were innocent and that the significance of the information handed over to the Soviets had been much exaggerated.

It no doubt infuriated the Soviets that the allies were distributing the espionage report in an effort to fight domestic communism. At a conference of foreign ministers in Paris in August 1946 (during which the *Pravda* article appeared), British foreign secretary Bevin told Mackenzie King that he planned to have copies of the report sent to every trade union in England. According to King, "He said he has had to fight that Communist business from the days before he was Minister of Labour in the trade unions. That that report would do more to help to save the situation among the labour element in Britain than anything he can think of."[20]

The Gouzenko case revealed to MI5 something of the Soviet's extensive espionage efforts, but MI5 still was not responding forcefully to the threat. The fact that Alan Nunn May had been recruited by the GRU while he was at Trinity Hall in Cambridge, for example, did not lead MI5 to scrutinize others who had attended Trinity at the same time, such as Guy Burgess and Donald Maclean. Both were spying for the Soviets while working for the British Foreign Office. And MI5 gave scant attention to the fact that Klaus Fuchs, a leading atomic scientist and a British subject, was among the several hundred people listed in their copy of Israel Halperin's address book.[21]

The FBI also received copies of Halperin's address book, but because Fuchs, who had participated in the Manhattan Project at Los Alamos, had returned to Britain, and because the RCMP told the FBI that they had made the Halperin evidence available to the British, FBI officers assumed MI5 would be investigating Fuchs. But this did not happen. When Fuchs returned to England in 1946 to continue atomic research, MI5 gave him only a cursory vetting. Ironically, this was the one instance where "guilt by association" would have actually put the authorities on the trail of a genuine Soviet spy.[22]

In fairness to MI5, the connection between Halperin and Fuchs, who would later confess to passing atomic secrets to the Soviets, turned out to be meaningless as far as possible espionage went. Fuchs, a German-born Jew, had been interned in Quebec as an enemy alien at the beginning of the war, and Halperin, aware of the plight of this fellow scientist and anti-Nazi whom he had never met, had mailed him some magazines.[23] It was not much of a connection, but MI5's failure to investigate Fuchs in 1946 would have enormous consequences and prove to be a huge political embarrassment for the British.

Although the FBI left the Fuchs matter for the British to deal with, the bureau took an active part in helping the Canadians go after one of their alleged spies, Sam Carr, who disappeared at the time the spy scandal broke in early 1946. Carr, a leading Communist Party organizer and propagandist in Canada, was a key figure in the Canadian espionage case. Born Schmil Kogan in Ukraine in 1906, he had little formal education, leaving school when he was twelve because his father was killed in a pogrom. He immigrated to Canada in the 1920s and settled in Toronto, where as a young unskilled worker he was enlisted into the cause of the Canadian Communist Party. Carr, who at some point studied at the Lenin Institute in Moscow and spoke fluent Russian, became, in addition to an organizer, a prolific contributor to Communist Party journals and newspapers in Canada and the U.S. In 1945, he ran for a seat in the Canadian Parliament as a member of the LPP, but was defeated. Like Fred Rose, Carr was well known to the RCMP, which had arrested him twice for subversive activities over the years. Indeed, in the early 1930s, Carr served almost three years in Canada's Kingston Penitentiary. Yet the RCMP had never investigated him for involvement in espionage.[24]

In fact, as early as the 1920s Carr embarked on the same dangerous road taken by Rose. He was recruited by the forerunner of the NKVD, and then, in 1942 or 1943, was passed on to the GRU.[25] According to documents smuggled out by Gouzenko, Carr recruited agents and helped in obtaining the false passport used by the GRU illegal Ignacy Witczak. In July 1946, the Canadian government issued a warrant for his arrest on charges of violating the Official Secrets Act. The RCMP plastered "Wanted" signs all over Canada, but Carr had disappeared. He had gone to Cuba for a Communist Party conference in January 1946 and entered the United States upon his return the next month. As the FBI learned much later, he had been booked on a train from New York to Toronto but heard through his Soviet contacts (doubtless using Philby's information) of the impending arrests in Canada. So he remained in the United States, living in New York City under the alias Jack Lewis while his wife and son remained in Toronto. When they arrested the other suspects, the RCMP asked the FBI to be on the alert for any information about Carr, and the bureau requested its branch offices to do a "discreet spot check" for his possible whereabouts. It took three years for the FBI to track him down.[26]

The FBI finally arrested Carr at his shabby basement apartment on West 74th Street in Manhattan on January 27, 1949, and charged him with entering the United States illegally. Hoover was unhappy with the way the case was handled. When he heard Carr had been located, he noted that "it looks like another three ring circus is being staged." And upon hearing of Carr's arrest: "I am greatly concerned that Carr has been in the U.S. for three years and we never had any inkling of it. There must be some grievous gap in our Communist coverage." Carr was taken immediately to FBI offices, "where every effort was made to question him as to his knowledge of Soviet intelligence matters and participation therein." But he refused to talk. He was then delivered into the custody of U.S. Immigration officials at Ellis Island, who were instructed by the deputy attorney general to "throw the book at him."[27]

A few days later, after another fruitless interview by the FBI, Carr and his wife, Julia, who had been visiting him from Toronto when he was arrested, testified before a Federal Grand Jury in New York. Members of the Grand Jury were interested in a possible connection between the Carrs and the people named by Elizabeth Bentley and Whittaker Chambers in recent testimony before them, including Alger Hiss. Julia Carr had nothing to offer. She politely told the Grand Jury that she did not know any of the people they asked her about, which was probably true. As for her husband, he made it clear that he would not be answering many questions "inasmuch as there is already a rather protracted case [in Canada] which involves many, many things and which I have to face."[28]

Although Carr worked for the GRU and had been living in the United States for three years, he apparently had no knowledge of Hiss, Chambers, and the slew of other names he was presented with. When shown a photograph of one J. Peters, the GRU agent who had allegedly recruited the Chambers-Hiss group, Carr responded, "It looks like an awful criminal, but I never seen him."[29] Carr was handed over to Canadian authorities. In early April 1949, Hoover's deputy reported to his boss that the jury in Ottawa returned a verdict of guilty against Carr on charges of procuring a fraudulent passport. Of a possible maximum sentence of seven years in prison, the judge sentenced Carr to six.[30]

Another Canadian fugitive from the Gouzenko case also eluded the FBI for three years. This was the mysterious Freda Linton, said to have been Fred Rose's mistress. Her name had cropped up several times during the Royal Commission hearings. Linton was a peripheral figure in the Canadian spy affair, and the case against her was flimsy: a brief mention of her in two of the GRU documents, along with some added recollections of Gouzenko. Gouzenko testified to the commission that he had met Linton at the home of Major Sokolov in Ottawa in the fall of 1943, and that Sokolov told Zabotin she had given him "some materials." He described her as a "typical

Jewess, dark, black hair, long nose, about 5'6", thin face, single and anxious to get married."[31]

Linton had worked as a secretary to the head of the Canadian National Film Board, John Grierson, and she was mentioned in reference to Grierson in the notebook of one of the GRU officers. Grierson was hauled before the Royal Commission and asked about her. He vigorously denied any knowledge of her communist activities, but Raymond Boyer acknowledged that she was a communist.[32]

When the RCMP attempted to serve Linton with a subpoena in May 1946, she was nowhere to be found. The Royal Commissioners concluded that Linton's flight was proof of her guilt, and that she had been used by Fred Rose as a conduit between the GRU and the recruits. But there was no evidence that she had passed secret information or had done anything more than contact some of the alleged recruits. Three years later, Linton, married and seven months pregnant, gave herself up in Montreal. She hired Joseph Cohen to defend her and he managed to get the charges dropped. But she had nonetheless been labeled as a spy, and she lived the rest of her life under a false identity.[33]

~

The FBI was particularly interested in Linton because Gouzenko had said she arranged, on behalf of Fred Rose, for "the handing over" of American scientist Dr. Arthur Steinberg to a Soviet agent in Washington, D.C. This allegedly occurred when Linton had made a trip to Washington in August 1945 as part of her work for the National Film Board. The FBI considered Steinberg to be a possible link between the Canadian spy case and suspected espionage in the United States, which is why bureau agents went to great lengths in investigating him, as did the House Un-American Activities Committee (HUAC) and the Senate Internal Security Subcommittee (SISS). The investigations never came close to showing that Steinberg had spied for the GRU, but Steinberg nonetheless endured years of torment.

Steinberg's connection with Canada had begun in 1940, when, with his wife, Edith, and young son, he arrived in Montreal to teach in the Department of Genetics at McGill University. He was still completing work on his Ph.D. in zoology, awarded the following year by Columbia University. Like many Jewish academics and scientists at this time, Steinberg was left-leaning politically. When he was a student during the 1930s, he was interested in the "Russian experiment" and was active in leftist anti-Fascist organizations. At McGill, he became close with Professor Raymond Boyer, whose wife was Jewish and had befriended Edith. Steinberg and his wife soon gravitated to the group of communists centered around Boyer in Montreal. As with others in the group, Steinberg became an active member of the Canadian-Soviet Friendship Society and had even met Fred Rose.

Steinberg later explained his political interests: "I was not anti-Communist nor was I pro-Communist; I was simply interested in learning what the Russians were doing. I lost interest when genetics was outlawed [in the Soviet Union] and when the Nazi-Soviet pact was signed. Despite this, when the Russians were allied with us during World War II, I joined the Canadian-Soviet Friendship Society, along with many others who were interested in Russia, to help an ally who was taking the brunt of the Nazi attack."[34]

However innocently Steinberg might have viewed his associations, the fact remained that the GRU was cultivating this group, through Fred Rose and others, for its espionage operations. Eventually, judging from a document that Gouzenko furnished, Zabotin and his colleagues earmarked Steinberg as a possible recruit. Steinberg's close friendship with Boyer and his own scientific knowledge made him an obvious candidate. Boyer, as noted earlier, had been working on a new method of producing the chemical explosive RDX, and had devised a formula that greatly accelerated its production. The Canadians and the Americans were shipping RDX to the Russians to support their war effort, but they lost much of it, because their convoys to Murmansk were suffering heavy losses to the Germans. With the aim of saving Russian lives, Boyer decided to give his formula directly to the Soviets.[35]

Steinberg had a background in statistics, so he had helped Boyer on RDX by doing a statistical analysis of Boyer's data. But he stressed in an interview with this author that he had "no idea that Boyer was passing information on RDX to the Soviets."[36] Steinberg left Montreal in June 1944, before the rather slow-moving GRU had a chance to make any overtures to him in Canada. He was ineligible for U.S. military service for medical reasons, but until mid-August 1945, he served as a civilian member of its U.S. Navy Operations Research Group, under the Office of Scientific Research and Development, based in Washington D.C. There, he conducted research on various weapons, some of which he designed himself. Steinberg was apparently approached by the Soviets shortly before he left on a trip to Hawaii that summer in connection with his naval research, but he refused to cooperate with them. Understandably, Steinberg would not mention this to the authorities, but his omission soon came back to haunt him.

When Steinberg was first mentioned publicly as a spy suspect at the Fred Rose hearing in March 1946, it did not attract much attention. The Royal Commission Report released in July 1946, however, had more to say about Steinberg. The report reprinted a note written by Zabotin on May 12, 1945, observing that their agent Fred Rose should contact Steinberg [code-named "Berger"] in Washington and propose that he work for them: "Debouz [Rose] is to tie up with Berger and depending on the circumstances is to make a proposal about work for us or the corporation [the Communist Party]. Contact in Washington with Debouz's person. To work out arrangements for a meeting and to telegraph. To give out 600 dollars. If Debouz should be unable to go to U.S.A. then there should be a letter from Debouz to Berger containing a request to assist the person delivering the letter to Berger."[37]

This note was not in itself incriminating because it left open the question of whether the contact had been made, and, if it had been made, whether Steinberg was receptive. But Gouzenko, in his testimony to the Royal Commission, added further details:

Q: Who is Steinberg, do you know?
A: That is a scientist in the United States.
Q: How did you learn that?

A: In previous telegrams. . . .

Q: Did you ever hear him discussed by Zabotin or Motinov or any of the others in the Embassy?

A: There were telegrams which were written by Colonel Zabotin. . . . In the telegram which Colonel Zabotin sent to Moscow he described him as a scientist who was a friend of Debouz [Rose] and was very well acquainted with the development of the atomic bomb. . . . In later telegrams that were sent it was pointed out that Debouz's man had handed over Steinberg to the Military Intelligence in Washington . . .

Q: Do you know the name or the cover name of Debouz's man in Washington?

A: No, but in the telegram that reported the handing over of Berger, it mentioned that it was done through Freda [Linton]. It was not a contact; it was handing over.[38]

In reproducing Gouzenko's testimony for its published report, the Royal Commission left out his statement that Zabotin described Steinberg as "very well acquainted with the atomic bomb," presumably because it was so patently untrue. Either Zabotin was exaggerating to his superiors or Gouzenko's memory was faulty. The commission members also failed to mention a much more important document, perhaps because they never received it from the RCMP. The document in question, which was not included in the list of items from Gouzenko that served as exhibits for the commission's inquiry, was a telegram Zabotin received from Moscow reporting on the results of the attempt to recruit Steinberg in Washington: "SORVIN's [a GRU agent in Washington] man conducted the first meeting with 'BERGER.' The latter assured him that he was an ordinary draughtsman. Besides which he announced that he must soon depart for Java. We consider that he is simply afraid and wants to get rid of us. Find out all the details about 'BERGER' from 'DEBOUZ' [Fred Rose]. What kind of a man is he? During the conversation 'BERGER' expressed himself thus – 'but we are allies.' This is very dangerous talk."[39]

This message shows that Dr. Steinberg, about whom Moscow knew precious little, refused to be recruited. Indeed, he pointed out that he was a mere employee, presumably in order to show that he did not have access to atomic or other military secrets, and that he was going away (to Hawaii, not Indonesia). He also said that his spying would be wrong because the Americans and the Russians were allies. The GRU concluded that Steinberg wanted to get rid of them and that what he said to the Soviet agent was "dangerous." Steinberg clearly never even came close to being a GRU recruit. Did the Canadians, in addition to omitting this evidence from the Royal Commission Report, forget to show the telegram to the FBI? Possibly. But FBI investigators had been in Ottawa, interviewing Gouzenko and sifting through his evidence from the very beginning. Another possible explanation is that the telegram contradicted a theory – that Steinberg was a spy for the Russians – that the FBI was reluctant to discard.

In fact, the FBI had already gone further in its accusations against Steinberg. In a secret security memorandum of November 27, 1945, which was circulated among top U.S. government officials, the FBI reported that Steinberg had been recruited by a woman named Freda and successfully transferred to a GRU agent in Washington. But the report added an additional bit of speculation on Steinberg's activities vis à vis the GRU: "Information developed by the Royal Canadian Mounted Police indicated that it is possible that X [Steinberg] was the individual who furnished information concerning the Navy's radio proximity fuse to Dr. Alan Nunn May, the British scientist stationed in Canada, who was an agent of the Soviets and who passed on a 'garbled' description of the proximity fuse to the Soviets."[40]

The proximity fuse had been developed by the U.S. Naval Research Laboratory, under the Office of Scientific Research and Development. Referred to as the "invention that won World War II," the fuse was a radar device that made anti-aircraft artillery twenty times more effective. (The Americans did not give the Soviets access to the proximity fuse, which was a highly guarded secret. But atomic spy Julius Rosenberg was later accused of assembling a duplicate fuse and smuggling it to the Soviets in December 1944.)

The RCMP, it seems, had determined that Steinberg was an acquaintance of Nunn May, apparently because they were both scientists at McGill and both involved in pro-communist social circles, as well as being members of the Canadian Association of Scientific Workers. Since Nunn May's verbal information on the proximity fuse, as reported in a July 1945 telegram from Zabotin to Moscow, would have come from an American, the RCMP reasoned that it was probably Steinberg.[41]

Steinberg's work in naval air operations could have involved the proximity fuse, used by the navy against Japanese suicide fliers, but it is not clear that Steinberg had the technical knowledge to pass on anything significant to Nunn May or the Russians. Also, of course, he had not been living in Montreal since June of 1944, although he visited there on occasion. Most important, the GRU kept its recruits from knowing who its other spies were, so it is highly unlikely that Zabotin would have requested Nunn May to get secret information from Steinberg.

The FBI apparently took no note of the fact that Steinberg's work for the navy was considered highly valuable for the war effort. In September 1945 he was awarded a certificate of merit for his contribution to the successful prosecution of the Second World War. And in early January 1946, he received a letter of commendation from the chief of Naval Operations, in connection with his work on new tactics in naval air operations. "Your initiative and imagination," the letter read, "your diligence and conscientiousness in the performance of your duties resulted in a distinct contribution to the war effort." A few weeks later, the chief of the Office of Field Service of the Office of Scientific Research and Development, sent Steinberg a letter: "May I express the appreciation of the Office of Field Service and my own personal thanks for your splendid work while you were affiliated with this office . . . you did very important analytical and statistical work for the Air Operations Research Group both here in Washington D.C. and at Pearl Harbor. Your studies on anti-shipping operations are the standard references."[42]

This letter arrived just a couple of weeks before Steinberg's close friend Raymond Boyer was picked up by the RCMP and confessed to

giving the Soviets the secret formula for RDX. In his subsequent testimony to the Royal Commission, Boyer also mentioned his friendship with Steinberg and admitted that Steinberg was "sympathetic
to communism."[43] Arthur Steinberg's life would never be the same.

~

Steinberg was first questioned by the FBI in 1947, then by HUAC in
1948 and the Senate Subcommittee on Internal Security (SISS) in
1953. In all the interviews he categorically denied, under oath, any
involvement in espionage for the Soviets.[44] Because there was no evidence to prove otherwise, Steinberg was never prosecuted. But the
investigations and the publicity about them damaged his career irrevocably. As with Israel Halperin and David Shugar, the spy label stuck,
even though Steinberg had been guilty of nothing more than an
"infatuation with communism" that ceased before the war ended. In
1946, Steinberg joined the faculty at Antioch College in Ohio, where
he was chairman of the Department of Genetics. By 1948, however,
the accusations against him were being widely reported in the press,
which relied on leaks from the FBI and HUAC. HUAC member Karl
Mundt called publicly for an investigation of the Steinberg charges:
"It should be explored fully to clear Steinberg or show why his name
was so prominently mentioned in the Canadian spy case." Antioch
College asked Steinberg to seek employment elsewhere.[45]

He applied for a professorship at Ohio State University. In April
1948, Steinberg received a letter from a member of the faculty there,
saying that the search committee had concluded that he was the man
best qualified to fill the job, especially because of letters from several
outstanding geneticists who recommended him highly, but that
unfortunately the person who made the final decision had heard
about the charges against Steinberg and would not allow the appointment to go ahead: "Frankly, we felt we were getting nowhere when
we advanced arguments in your favor."[46] As Steinberg said much
later in an interview, "The universities were still very anxious and
worried and I was quietly shifted from one place to another. Every
time I was called to testify I lost a job. There were no hearings at
universities. They just said good-by."[47]

Steinberg was finally able to get a position as a consultant at the Mayo Clinic in Rochester, but the quality and significance of his scientific work was obscured by the HUAC investigation and the ensuing widespread publicity. The *Washington Times-Herald* reported on September 30, 1948, that "sensational developments in the House probe of Soviet atomic espionage are expected to explode when a subcommittee calls a new key mystery witness for questioning in Milwaukee tomorrow. The witness is Arthur Steinberg." Steinberg, the article said, was going to be grilled by HUAC in order to establish a positive connection between "spy work of the Commies in the U.S. and the atomic espionage network smashed by the Mounted Police in Canada." In general the press reports repeated the charges against Steinberg put forth by the Royal Commission and the FBI, making it appear as if they were facts, despite a statement by Representative Richard Vail of HUAC – who interviewed Steinberg on October 1, 1948 – that Steinberg was "in no sense a suspect."[48]

HUAC did not close its file on Steinberg. Its investigators were directed to continue searching for evidence against him. With Steinberg devoting all his time to his academic research, there was not much to go on but recycled versions of past episodes. In July 1950, a resourceful researcher for HUAC reported that a "reliable and confidential source" advised that Steinberg was closely connected with the Canadian spy ring: "He worked directly under the deputy chief of Red Army Intelligence in Canada, one Milshstein, alias Milsky."[49] Of course this was not true, because Mil'shtein was stationed in Moscow and had only once made a visit to Canada – in the summer of 1944 (after which he had asked, as we know, for Gouzenko's recall). Presumably HUAC's source was relying on information that had trickled down from some of Gouzenko's published articles, which were appearing with increasing frequency.

The investigator went on to report an even more unlikely claim: "Steinberg is believed to have broken into the Map Room of the Navy Department while employed there, which room was allegedly locked with three keys. Some of the maps contained in this room were stolen at the time of this entry. Later, the Map Room of the

United States Army was broken into in the same manner and, although no one was apprehended, Steinberg was under suspicion."[50]

Not surprisingly, Steinberg's promising career at the Mayo Clinic came to a premature end, in 1952. He was forced to move on, this time to the Children's Hospital in Boston, where he worked at the Children's Cancer Research Foundation, exploring, among other things, the genetic causes of childhood leukemia. By this time, Steinberg had published twenty scholarly articles and was a leading figure in genetic research, a field with crucial implications for human health. But the heat was on from the anti-communists in Washington, where scientists, no matter what their specialties and what their accomplishments, were highly suspect if they had ever inclined left in politics.

In 1953, eight years after the spy case erupted in Canada, there was a new outburst of publicity around Steinberg when the Senate Internal Security Subcommittee (SISS) decided to interview him. Like HUAC, its House of Representatives counterpart, SISS was an infamous inquisitorial body whose sole purpose was to ferret out communist subversives in the United States. It was established in 1949 as a subcommittee of the Committee on the Judiciary by Senator Pat McCarran, at the time head of the Judiciary Committee. McCarran, who has been called "one of the great monsters of American public life," was a democrat from Nevada who deserted from Roosevelt's New Deal and became a vocal opponent of the policies of his own party. A racist, anti-Semite, and rabid anti-communist, McCarran managed to acquire tremendous power in Washington.[51] When the Republicans gained a majority in the Senate in 1952, Senator William Jenner assumed the chairmanship of SISS, but McCarran remained a key figure in its investigations.

SISS first initiated an exhaustive examination of Steinberg's past – which included going back to his stint in naval research in 1944–45 and making inquiries among his superiors at the time – and then interviewed him in October 1953 in New York City.[52] The interview, attended by Senator Jenner, was short and straightforward. The SISS counsel, Jay Sourwine, was not prosecutorial, but politely asked the pro forma questions with which Steinberg was now familiar. Steinberg reasserted that he knew Raymond Boyer well, but had no idea he was passing information to the Soviets. He said that Gouzenko's testimony about him was untrue and that he never knew a woman named Freda Linton. When they got to Fred Rose, the exchange became almost jocular:

> Sourwine: You said you remembered meeting a man named Rose at a cocktail party?
> Steinberg: Yes.
> Sourwine: What was his first name?
> Steinberg: Fred . . . Fred Rose was a very short man who wore a suit, was as wide as he was tall, and was very voluble. He was somewhat of a social lion at the time, being known as a Communist and outstanding personality.
> Sourwine: You mean to imply that you remembered him because he was a sort of Mr. Five by Five?
> Steinberg: That is right. He was short, stocky, he was so different from all the rest of the people there, all the rest of them being academic people and Rose being anything but academic.

In the back of his mind, Steinberg probably realized that this seemingly innocent cocktail party, where words flowed freely with the loosening effects of a couple of drinks, had helped seal his fate.

Steinberg might have felt uneasy when he was asked, "Did anyone ask you to join a Soviet Intelligence ring?" Steinberg was telling the truth when he answered no. "Sorvin's man" from the GRU who had contacted him in Washington did not ask him to join a group of spies. But he had asked Steinberg for secret information, and that was something Steinberg probably preferred to forget.

After the closed hearing, the subcommittee's chief investigator, Robert Morris, pulled a typical SISS trick. He told the press about a "Mr. X," who, he said, may have transmitted details of the proximity fuse to Alan Nunn May. Morris described "Mr. X" in enough detail to make it clear he was referring to Steinberg. On December 1, 1953, more damning news appeared, when SISS released portions of the November 1945 secret FBI memorandum that related to Gouzenko's revelations. They included the complete FBI statements about "X," a "native-born American citizen who has specialized in the field of zoology" and was "turned over" to Red Army Intelligence in the United States after leaving McGill University. Steinberg felt compelled to write a letter to the head of the Children's Cancer Research Center, explaining how he had become the center of spy accusations and proclaiming his innocence.[53]

The publicity brought new troubles for Steinberg. In late 1953, he and his wife were preparing to purchase a home in Belmont, Massachusetts, when their prospective neighbors started making anonymous telephone calls to them, threatening "dire consequences" if they moved in. The Steinbergs gave up the house. Then came a worse blow: the National Institutes of Health, through the Public Health Service, canceled Steinberg's research grants. Steinberg appealed for help to Dr. Charles Mayo, the head of the Mayo Clinic, who had political connections in Washington. "Failure to change this action," Steinberg wrote to Mayo, "may very well mean the end of my career with the stigma of spy and communist attached to my name." Mayo talked to some senators in Washington about the matter, but with no result.[54]

Steinberg was not the only scientist to have his research funding taken away. The decision to cancel Steinberg's grants reflected a new policy of the Department of Health, Education and Welfare that denied funding for medical research to persons who the Department determined had engaged in subversive activities or whose loyalty to the United States was in doubt. Thirty scientists, including the renowned biochemist Linus Pauling, had their grants for medical research revoked.[55] In April 1954 Steinberg wrote to Oveta Hobby, who headed the Department, requesting that she reconsider his case: "The action of your department has in effect convicted me of very serious charges without a hearing and I may add without even notifying me of the charges or conclusions."[56] Mrs. Hobby never responded to Steinberg's letter.

Steinberg also appealed to Senator Jenner, who had traveled to Canada with Senator McCarran to interview Gouzenko in January

1954 with the stated purpose of finding out more information about Steinberg. Noting that the publicity arising from the committee's investigation had caused him to lose his funding for research, Steinberg asked Jenner to release the results of the investigation: "I know that it is not your wish to have innocent, cooperative witnesses suffer because of unfortunate publicity resulting from testifying before your committee. That is why I am writing to you to ask that you issue a report concerning my testimony before your committee and your findings resulting from your interview with Igor Gouzenko and any other investigations you may have made concerning me."[57]

Steinberg never received an answer. That is the way things worked with the congressional committees who were hunting for spies. Gouzenko's lengthy testimony, taken on January 4, 1954, was kept a secret, declassified only many years later.[58] It had been nine years since Gouzenko defected, and despite his intelligence his memory was not perfect. Gouzenko had originally stated that Steinberg was "handed over" to the GRU in Washington by Freda Linton, on behalf of Fred Rose. But when questioned by SISS, Gouzenko was not so sure:

Q: Did you know anything of Freda Linton's contacts in the United States?

A: No, I don't know, but I know about her further that she was in the United States, but this was after I left.

Q: She went to the United States to hand Steinberg over to Saraev's man, didn't she? [in the earlier reports the GRU agent was named Sorvin]

A: It is possible that she was Fred Rose's man. I don't think she was Sam Carr's man. I think she was Fred Rose's contact.

Q: You are saying you have no knowledge of any contacts she may have had in the United States.

A: No, not to my knowledge.

Q: Are you saying also that you don't know whether she was the one who handed over Steinberg to Saraev's apparatus?

A: No, not to my knowledge.

Q: I want to know if there is anything you can add to what you have already told in detail that will help clinch the truth of what you said about Steinberg?

A: Yes. First of all I say what I said was in documents which I took with me. In other words, not just what I said. The second is that he was I would say in the one stage reluctant . . . in other words I would say he was just scared, but the point is he was contacting agents . . . so far as my knowledge I don't know whether he gave that information that they required from him or not because I believe he was transferred to the Soviet agents working in the United States.

Q: Can you tell us whether there was more than one message passed in reference to Steinberg?

A: There were several telegrams and there were references to him going to – I'm not sure, but anyway in his answer to the contact man he was referring . . . to his ability as a scientist and the value of him, yet stressing the point that he was afraid. That is what I remember definitely, that he was afraid and that he was trying to find some kind of excuse. In other words, in the first stage he was not very much pleased at the approach done by Fred Rose's man, yet he was not doing anything in the way of going to the authorities and tell them that he was contacted.

Q: You are talking about a series of messages all at the same time with regard to Steinberg . . .

A: Yes, approximately I would say within two months.

Q: Were there any messages about Steinberg at any other time?

A: No, he came up at one particular time and then more or less disappeared from our telegrams . . .

Q: You don't know whether he agreed to work?

A: I only knew that the telegram stressed the point that he

was afraid, and that he was worked with caution, more caution than with others . . .

Q: Do you have any information concerning who the individual was who furnished information about the United States Navy's proximity fuse to Dr. Alan Nunn May?

A: No. . . .

Q: It has been reported that you have expressed the opinion that that information came to Dr. Alan Nunn May from Steinberg. Do you remember ever expressing that opinion?

A; No, I don't remember that. I think it is wrong. I don't believe I ever mentioned that particularly.

Q: Could it have come to Alan Nunn May from Steinberg? Would he have any contact with Steinberg?

A: No, that I doubt very much because Steinberg was a new agent. Alan May was old and valuable. I don't think they would put them together.

Gouzenko in effect recanted his claims about Steinberg being handed over to the GRU in the United States by Freda Linton. And he told the subcommittee of the telegram from Moscow to Ottawa, the telegram never mentioned by the Royal Commission or the FBI, which said that Steinberg had backed off when approached by the GRU, claiming he was going away and that their request for information was not a good idea. Gouzenko also said that it was highly unlikely that Steinberg would have passed information to Alan Nunn May.

But none of what Gouzenko said about Steinberg in 1954, which came close to exonerating him, was ever mentioned publicly by SISS. Steinberg continued to be plagued by accusations that he was a spy. In 1956, despite his growing prominence in the field of genetics, he was forced to give up his position at the Cancer Research Center. Luckily, he was able to get an academic job, at Case Western Reserve University in Ohio, and by 1958 was receiving research grants again. In 1964 he was elected president of the American Society of Human Genetics, and by the time he retired from teaching, he had close to two hundred scholarly publications to his credit. But the stigma of the spy label never left him. He had continual problems getting his passport renewed and was on several occasions blacklisted by the U.S. government from participating in certain research projects or government-sponsored conferences.

When asked in 2002 whether his political loyalty would have been questioned if Gouzenko had not made his allegations, Steinberg replied, "I don't think I would have been pestered at all. The Canadian government did a damn stupid thing."[59] Of course it was Steinberg's own government, the FBI, and the anti-communist lobby on Capitol Hill, that distorted Gouzenko's allegations about him and kept them alive for years afterward. Indeed, Steinberg's case illustrates in no uncertain terms the extent to which Cold War anti-communism in America was driven by political agendas rather than genuine security concerns. Steinberg was only one of many American scientists and scholars in other fields who were persecuted in this way.

The Gouzenko affair set the climate for persecution on such a broad scale because it led to new procedures for security screening and loyalty review in both Canada and the United States. The Canadians were much more restrained in using these procedures and thus luckily never experienced their own version of the McCarthy era, but their scientific community suffered nonetheless. A number of Canadian scientists were blacklisted and denied the security clearances necessary for government contracts on the basis of past association with left-wing groups, such as the Canadian Association of Scientific Workers. Even more insidious was the way in which American McCarthyism crept across the border, as the practice of guilt by association and naming names began to draw Canadians into the web of spy allegations woven in the committee rooms of Capitol Hill and the FBI offices twelve blocks away. In the case of one prominent Canadian, this would eventually have deadly consequences.

Chapter 8

THE SOUTH AGAINST THE NORTH

In trying to deal with the menace of communism we must be careful we don't throw away the baby freedom with the dirty bath-water, communism.

Lester Pearson

After its initial draconian response to Gouzenko's allegations, the Liberal government in Canada, which would remain in power until 1957, avoided the more extreme anti-communist measures adopted in the United States. In response to the spy case, the Canadian government had established security screening in the civil service and in immigration procedures. It also strengthened laws against treason and sedition. But the Communist Party was not outlawed as it was in the United States, where party leaders were prosecuted under the Alien Registration Act. The view in Ottawa was that such a measure would simply drive the communists underground. And the Liberal government refused to introduce legislation like the American Taft-Hartley law, which not only restricted the ability of trade unions to declare strikes, but also required union leaders to affirm that they were not communists.[1]

The aftermath of the Gouzenko affair was very different in the United States. The espionage case marked the beginning of a red scare in America that by the early fifties would engulf the country and lead to sweeping anti-communist measures that threatened civil liberties as never before. As one Canadian historian expressed it,

"The contrast with south of the border was striking. Canada, under the guidance of its Liberal elite, seemed to be reaffirming faith in free institutions just as the Americans were rushing to enact illiberal measures."[2]

What accounted for these differences in approach to the threat of Soviet espionage and communist subversion? It was basically a matter of politics. In Canada, the Liberal Party, led by Mackenzie King until his retirement in 1948, and then by King's former minister of justice, Louis St. Laurent, was throughout this period still so firmly entrenched in power that it could afford to resist pressures from the Conservative Opposition to employ more repressive policies against the communists. Truman's Democratic administration, lasting until Republican Dwight D. Eisenhower was elected in 1952, had found it much more difficult to ignore the demands for a clampdown on communists. As one of Truman's advisers put it, "The President didn't attach fundamental importance to the so-called Communist scare. He thought it was a lot of baloney. But political pressures were such that he had to recognize it."[3] Even Eisenhower found it difficult to resist the clamoring of red hunters like Pat McCarran and Joseph McCarthy, until finally they went too far and there was a backlash that resulted in McCarthy's censure by his Senate colleagues in June 1954.

However deep his concerns about overreaction to the espionage threat, Truman did little to stem the tide of anti-communism that arose in Washington after the arrests in Canada in February 1946. In July 1946, two days after the Royal Commission issued its sensational report on espionage, U.S. attorney general Tom Clark had urged President Truman to renew and strengthen the authorization for the FBI to conduct electronic surveillance "on persons suspected of subversive activities." Truman agreed, even if reluctantly. In March 1947, he signed Executive Order 9835, establishing a program whereby all federal employees would be subject to loyalty investigations that screened out those who had been members of a broad list of "subversive" organizations. (This screening also affected scholars like Arthur Steinberg whose research depended on funds from government-sponsored programs.) Within the next four years, over three million government employees would be investigated, at huge expense. Although there were a few dismissals, the investigations revealed no evidence of espionage.

Despite its renewed powers of electronic surveillance, the FBI failed to corroborate any of the claims of its star "defector," Elizabeth Bentley. A frustrated Attorney General Clark, against the warnings of J. Edgar Hoover, convened a Federal Grand Jury in early 1947 to conduct secret hearings about possible espionage among government employees, with Bentley as the chief witness. Bentley rehashed her story, and more than a hundred witnesses were hauled in, including Harry Dexter White. But after thirteen months, there were no indictments. Eager for public attention, Bentley leaked her story to the press, and as a result, HUAC began hearings to investigate her allegations in late July 1948. Alger Hiss and Harry Dexter White, symbols of the New Deal intelligentsia, were on the top of their agenda.[4]

Espionage was increasingly a political football in America. Truman faced re-election in November 1948, and the Republicans, including a young, very ambitious congressman named Richard Nixon, who used the HUAC hearings to place himself in the lime-light, were determined to establish that the Democrats were soft on communism. Both Bentley and Whittaker Chambers testified in detail. But Bentley's statements were unconvincing, especially since she had never met either Alger Hiss or Harry Dexter White. And Chambers only went so far as to say that Hiss and White, along with several other Washington civil servants, had been members of an underground communist group during the time he had been a member of the Communist Party. He told HUAC that he left the party in 1937 and did not mention espionage.[5]

Then suddenly, in November 1948, after many private meetings with Richard Nixon, Chambers came up with films of documents and papers allegedly passed to him by White and Hiss in early 1938. The documents purportedly showed that both Hiss and White had engaged in espionage for the Soviets. By this time Harry Dexter White had died of a heart attack, but a Grand Jury indicted Hiss for perjury because of his allegedly false testimony about his relationship with Chambers and his involvement with communists. Hiss's trial in May 1949 resulted in a hung jury. A second trial began on November 17, 1949, and lasted two months, with Hiss being found guilty of perjury in January 1950.[6]

Incredibly, after testifying explicitly to HUAC that he had left the party in 1937, Chambers had contradicted himself and said he defected in 1938, thus accommodating the dates on his newly produced documentary evidence. Unfortunately for Hiss, the jury that convicted him never knew about the interviews the FBI had conducted previously with Chambers in which he stated, over and over again, that he had left the party in 1937, before he could have collected secret material from Hiss and White. The reports of these interviews remained classified until the FBI released them many years later.[7]

Before Chambers belatedly produced the filmed and typed documents in 1948, the FBI was fully aware there was no evidence to show that Hiss had engaged in espionage. This is made clear in an FBI memorandum written five years later, in November 1953, to accompany a summary report on Hiss: "It is strongly recommended that no dissemination of the attached material be given to a Congressional committee for the following reasons: 1. Up to the time Hiss left the Government in January 1947, the Bureau had no evidence to prove a case against Hiss. . . . No espionage allegations were received from Chambers regarding Hiss until November, 1948. . . . The Bentley espionage allegations involving Hiss in 1945 had not been proven, and Gouzenko's allegation in 1945 regarding a Soviet agent in the State Department who was *an assistant to an Assistant Secretary of State* had not been identified as Hiss, although there was a strong possibility this person could have been Hiss."[8]

The author of the memorandum apparently did not realize that this description could not have applied to Hiss, who in 1945 was well above the level of an assistant to an Assistant Secretary of State in the State Department hierarchy. A week later, on November 20, 1953, another FBI in-house memorandum was circulated. It again confirmed that Gouzenko had initially described the State Department spy as *an assistant to an Assistant Secretary of State.*[9] But by 1953 this was water under the bridge. It was already dogma in Washington's governing circles that Igor Gouzenko had named Hiss as a spy in 1945, and no one questioned it.

⁓

Alger Hiss had become for the Republicans the personification of insidious communist subversion, and his conviction for perjury helped catapult young Richard Nixon to the nomination as Republican candidate for the vice-presidency in 1952. But Hiss's imprisonment for three years on perjury charges was hardly a triumph for the FBI or the attorney general, who had expended so much effort investigating the Bentley and Chambers allegations. Aside from Hiss, only one other individual, a former employee of the War Production Board named William Remington, was convicted, out of the more than 150 people who were investigated by the FBI. And like Hiss, Remington (who would be murdered by fellow inmates in prison) was convicted on charges of perjury, not espionage. The standards of proof in the U.S. judicial system were higher than those of the court of public opinion.

The FBI was further hindered before the Grand Jury convened to hear Chambers's and Bentley's testimony because neither of them was a very credible witness. Both had betrayed their country by serving as agents for the Soviets before "coming clean" with American authorities. And both were prone to contradicting earlier testimonies and fabricating certain aspects of their stories. Gouzenko, by contrast, had appeared honest and resolute, his past and his personal life a clear progression toward righteousness. Yes, he had been a member of the Soviet intelligence apparatus, but it was not by choice that he was born a Soviet citizen and enlisted into the NKVD. His claims that he had defected because he loved democracy and wanted to enlighten the people in the West about Soviet evils were widely accepted. He rarely contradicted himself in his testimony. And of course he brought evidence to corroborate his allegations about Soviet espionage. As we know, the evidence in many cases did not hold up in Canadian courts, but it nonetheless looked impressive.

Gouzenko's apparent heroism, his credibility, and his first-hand knowledge of Soviet espionage kept American red hunters interested in him. They continued to assert that the Canadians (with the collusion of the Truman administration) had covered up the American connection in the case. By talking to Gouzenko in person they hoped not only to discover new American spy suspects, but also to find more evidence to confirm the guilt of Alger Hiss and Harry Dexter White.

Although HUAC was thwarted by the U.S. State Department in its efforts to interview Gouzenko in 1946, Senator Pat McCarran had more success three years later. In May 1949, when he was still Chairman of the Committee on the Judiciary, McCarran sent two investigators from the committee's Subcommittee on Immigration up to Ottawa to interview Gouzenko. The stated purpose of the interview was to examine two specific questions related to immigration procedures and security, but the subcommittee clearly had broader goals. The Hiss perjury trial had just begun. Coming up with further evidence from Gouzenko to corroborate Chambers's and Bentley's claims about Hiss and White would have been highly useful for the anti-communist agenda of McCarran and the other red hunters in Washington.

Upon their arrival in Ottawa the American investigators asked the RCMP for a copy of all the evidence taken before the Royal Commission on Espionage in 1946. The request was turned down, on the advice of the American Embassy, which had consulted with the FBI and apparently wanted to prevent McCarran's subcommittee from going on a "fishing expedition." The FBI had most of the documentation from the Royal Commission, but it had not made it available to the congressional committees. (The FBI also had access to Gouzenko when requested and in fact would interview him once more in August 1950, although the details remain secret.)[10]

The 1949 subcommittee interview was short, yielding only eighteen pages of testimony, and Gouzenko had little new to offer beyond what he had already told the FBI shortly after his defection. When asked about possible American spies in the United States, he mentioned that the GRU had discussed "transferring contact with Steinberg," and made reference to an "assistant of Stettinius" in the State Department.[11]

The Canadian government insisted that Gouzenko's testimony not be publicized, but instead should be made available to the sub-committee for internal use. Despite repeated bullying by Senator McCarran, the Canadians stuck to their guns, pointing out finally that "Had the Canadian Government been aware that it would be pressed to have the Gouzenko evidence published, it would not have agreed in the first instance to the testimony being taken by U.S. officials."[12]

∼

When senators Jenner and McCarran interviewed Gouzenko in January 1954, it was Gouzenko himself who inspired them to seek his testimony by giving the idea that he had something new to say. In October 1953, he had granted an interview to a reporter from the *Chicago Tribune* named Eugene Griffin. Gouzenko talked a lot, but had little to offer beyond the claim that there were still lots of spies operating freely in Canada and the United States. After several long hours, Griffin had become frustrated because he had nothing he could use as a lead for a story. Finally, Griffin asked Gouzenko what he thought about the idea of talking to one of the congressional committees in Washington. Gouzenko responded that it would be "worthwhile," thus implying that he had something new and signif-icant to tell the Americans. He was also critical of the Canadian gov-ernment for not following his advice in handling the Soviet Union and espionage after he had defected.[13]

On October 27, 1953, immediately after Gouzenko's comments to Griffin appeared, the RCMP called Gouzenko in and asked him whether the *Tribune* had reported his statements accurately. Gouzenko stated flatly that he had no information that he had not long since conveyed to Canadian authorities and that the reporter had misquoted him. He denied that he had criticized the handling of his case by the Canadian government and said that he would not be willing under any circumstances to go to the United States to be interviewed by a congressional committee.[14]

Senator Jenner's Internal Security Subcommittee, meanwhile, was prompted by the *Tribune* article to request an interview with Gouzenko, which was forwarded to Ottawa on October 29. One purpose of the interview, as we know, would be to determine the guilt or innocence of Arthur Steinberg, but Jenner and McCarran also hoped that Gouzenko could give them something on Hiss. Hiss had already been prosecuted on perjury charges and was in prison, but there were still a lot of people who thought he was innocent of espionage, a crime he was never charged with because of the statute of limitations that required prosecution within ten years of the alleged crime. The more evidence to prove to the American public that Hiss had been a spy the better. Finally, Jenner and McCarran hoped that Gouzenko would come up with entirely new names of Americans who had been spies.[15]

Persuading the Canadians to allow SISS access to Gouzenko was no easy feat. The reply from Canada to Jenner's request was that there could be no interview because Mr. Gouzenko had been misquoted by the *Tribune* and had no further information to give the Americans. Speaking in the House of Commons on November 17, Lester Pearson, now a member of Parliament and serving as secretary of state for external affairs, discussed the American request and reiterated what Gouzenko had said to the RCMP. Much to the embarrassment of the Canadian government, however, Gouzenko promptly contradicted Pearson. On November 21, 1953, he issued a statement to the press in which he now upheld the accuracy of the *Tribune* story and said he would be most happy to be interviewed by the congressional committee, although he stipulated that the interview be held in Canada. He had not told the *Tribune*, Gouzenko asserted, that he had new information he had not disclosed to the Canadian government, but rather that he would be in a position to offer useful advice to the Americans. Gouzenko's statement concluded, "It appears that Mr. Pearson was ill advised and acted in such haste that he even neglected to read the original interview upon which he based his not correct statement in Parliament."[16]

Meanwhile, SISS, in an effort to pressure the Canadian government to allow them an interview with Gouzenko, launched a personal attack on Lester Pearson by leaking testimony against him given by Elizabeth Bentley two years earlier. Pearson had been a potential target of the red hunters in Washington since 1950, when he argued strongly in the Canadian Parliament against proposed legislation to make communist activities punishable under the criminal code. In Pearson's words, "I hope we will refuse to throw overboard our liberty, remembering that communism is declining in the free countries, including Canada. . . . It is being beaten by the good sense, the loyal patriotism, the belief in liberty under law and maintaining of prosperity, and the eradication of social injustices."[17]

Pearson had aroused further suspicion and anger on Capitol Hill when, in August 1951, he came to the defense of Canadian diplomat Herbert Norman, whose name had been dragged into SISS hearings on communist spies. Pearson accused SISS publicly of "irresponsibility" and "witch-hunting."[18] It is no coincidence that, just days later, the chief counsel of the subcommittee, Robert Morris, called Elizabeth Bentley to testify about Canadian communists. As Morris later expressed it, "Lester Pearson vigorously protested and denounced everything the Senate Internal Security Committee ever did. When we uncovered Herbert Norman he [Pearson] was making all kinds of demands and denounced us. . . . So Pearson was a big enemy of the Senate Internal Security Committee."[19]

Elizabeth Bentley had been going downhill fast since she testified before the Grand Jury and HUAC in 1948. Her main problems were alcohol addiction and lack of money, problems that often appear in tandem. Out of the limelight and frequently without employment, Bentley had begun to drink heavily. She was able for a time to live on the income she received from magazine articles and her book, *Out of Bondage*, a somewhat embellished version of her personal story. But by 1951 she was having trouble keeping up with her bills, so she was always happy to help out the red hunters in Washington, in the hope that rewards might come her way in the future.[20]

Despite her liabilities, Bentley was all the FBI and congressional red hunters had, so they continued to rely on her in going after suspected spies. In her August 14, 1951, testimony to the subcommittee, Bentley reiterated what she had told the FBI more than five years earlier about Canadian Hazen Sise, whom she knew in Washington during 1943–44, when he was working for the National Film Board of Canada. But she added some remarkable new details. She had initially said to the FBI that she met Sise for about a year, beginning in the spring of 1943, and that he had furnished her with "gossip" he overheard from Canadian and British diplomats. Now, with Morris encouraging her, she claimed that she met with Sise for two years, beginning in 1942, and that he handed over "super hush-hush" information from none other than Lester Pearson, who was second-in-command at what was still the Canadian Legation at the time:

> Bentley: I understand from Hazen that Pearson knew Hazen was a Communist and was willing to help. Pearson by virtue of his position used to sit in on American functions, particularly British ones re British policies, all of which was super hush-hush . . .
> Morris [committee counsel]: He was giving this information to Hazen Size [sic]?
> Bentley: This is correct.
> Morris: What did you do with it?
> Bentley: That was turned over to Golos during his lifetime and later on to his succeeding agent.
> Morris: And it went on to the Soviets?
> Bentley: This is right.[21]

The FBI, which was privy to this secret testimony in 1951, was surprised by what Bentley said about Pearson. According to an inter-agency memorandum, "A check of Bureau files failed to reflect that Bentley had provided information regarding Pearson to the Bureau on earlier interviews and contained no information indicating espionage or related activity on the part of Pearson."[22] Its interest piqued, the bureau called Bentley in for an interview to discuss Pearson and Sise three days after her subcommittee appearance, and on two subsequent occasions after that. She provided more details. She and Sise often met at the fashionable Mayflower Hotel in Washington and dined at the French restaurant L'Escargot.

She asserted that Pearson had moved in left-wing circles before World War II. He and Sise, also a "left-winger," had been very friendly in Canada.

Nonetheless, Bentley backed away from alleging that Pearson deliberately passed on information to Sise. In her third FBI interview, "Bentley advised that this information [from Sise] was principally gossip that Sise had overheard and that she could not state definitely whether Pearson was conscious that he was supplying information to Sise, who was in turn supplying the information to an unauthorized source."[23] After yet another question period with Bentley in February 1952, the FBI closed the Pearson case because "interviews disclosed Pearson did not consciously supply information for transmittal to unauthorized parties."[24]

Bentley's accusations against Pearson to SISS in 1951 had not been publicized, although the substance of her comments may have been relayed to Prime Minister St. Laurent through the U.S. State Department. If SISS had released her testimony, it would have created a diplomatic crisis with Canada. But the subcommittee kept the testimony on its back burner. Now, two years later, after Pearson had offended SISS by refusing access to Gouzenko, SISS retaliated. Bentley's testimony about him was made available to Victor Lasky, a virulently anti-communist American journalist.

Lasky, in a speech to the Women's National Republican Club in November 1953, launched a scathing attack on the former Canadian ambassador to the United States.[25] He accused Lester Pearson "of consistently sabotaging United States efforts to unravel the skein of Soviet intrigue in Washington and Ottawa" by making a "determined effort to prevent accredited American investigators from following up Canadian angles to Soviet espionage, which might help destroy the many Red spy centers still flourishing in this country." Incredibly, Lasky cited the Harry Dexter White case as the first item on the agenda for SISS in its requested interview of Gouzenko. White had been dead for five years. "In effect," said Lasky, Pearson "rang down an iron curtain on Gouzenko, who, I understand, is not only full of information, but is anxious to spill it."

Lasky went on to discuss the "strange career of Lester Pearson," who had "effectively squelched any investigations into alleged Soviet ties of not only his closest aide [a reference to Herbert Norman, who was *never* Pearson's closest aide], but of himself." Lasky cited Bentley's testimony that Pearson transmitted vital information to her spy ring through "a wealthy Canadian communist." According to Lasky, Bentley, "whose credibility has never been shattered, despite vicious smears . . . stated flatly and unequivocally that he [Pearson] was one of her best sources of information." This was a far cry from what Bentley had told the FBI.

In a press conference a few days later, Pearson called Lasky's comments "false to the point of absurdity." He went on, "Information which has never been made available to Canadian official sources, to my knowledge, apparently has been made available to somebody called Lasky. Find out who the counsel of the committee [on internal security] was at the time and draw your own conclusions. . . ."[26] Pearson was not naive. He had spent a lot of time in Washington and had many contacts. He knew that the man who had become his arch enemy was Robert Morris.

Pearson also must have known that Hazen Sise was the wealthy Canadian communist Lasky was referring to. Sise had been asked to appear before a U.S. federal Grand Jury in 1948, presumably in connection with Bentley's secret remarks to the FBI about him. He refused the Grand Jury's request, apparently on the advice of Pearson, noting in a letter to Pearson that he was "enormously puzzled – though I have at the same time an uneasy feeling that it might be better to remain puzzled if clarification also means a lot of unpleasantness." When Bentley made a public reference to Sise in June 1949 "as one of several who were on the relay team that passed information to the Russians," he immediately denied that he knew her. Clearly, Bentley had met Sise and, judging from some of the details she provided, she had lunched with him on one or more occasions. But the rest of her allegations were more fantasy than fact. Sise was not in a position to offer anything remotely important to Soviet intelligence. Indeed, if the NKVD was as ambitious in intelligence gathering as it was reputed to be, Hazen Sise would not have merited its attention.[27]

siss kept up the pressure on Ottawa. Following the Lasky speech, a persistent Senator Jenner sent another request to the Canadian government for an interview with Gouzenko. Although the State Department transmitted the request to Canada, Assistant Secretary of State Walter Bedell Smith, a close friend of President Eisenhower, made it clear to Arnold Heeney, the Canadian ambassador to Washington, that he disapproved strongly of Jenner's tactics. As Heeney wrote to Pearson, "I explained pretty emphatically to Bedell Smith our dislike of this procedure and the unpleasant repercussions which it was having, not only with the government, but also in Canadian public opinion. He seemed fully to appreciate this, and indeed expressed personal views of Jenner and his cohort which might well have been your own."[28]

However much the Canadians abhorred siss tactics, they realized they had to reach some form of compromise with this powerful and influential Senate committee. On November 24, Heeney sent a note to the U.S. State Department reiterating that Gouzenko had given all the information he had to the FBI and, in 1949, to the Immigration Subcommittee of the Senate Judiciary Committee. Gouzenko was free to go to Washington if he chose to do so, the note said, but "he naturally must consider the effect of his action on the special measures that we have taken in his interest and at his request to protect his security and conceal his identity." (This presumably meant that the RCMP would stop guarding him if he went on his own to be interviewed by Jenner's committee.) If Gouzenko was willing to testify again, Heeney allowed, the Canadian government would make arrangements similar to those made in 1949. The Americans could interview the defector in Canada, but only with the stipulation that, as before, the substance of the interview not be published without permission from the Canadian government.[29]

While the Canadian offer was in the pipeline, the right-wing elements of the American press, fed by tips from the FBI and siss, was having a field day with the accusations against Lester Pearson and the Canadian government. According to the Washington *Times-Herald*, Pearson and his followers in the Canadian "pinko set" were "dangerous and untruthful" in obstructing the proposed siss interview with Gouzenko.[30] On November 27, 1953, a widely distributed anti-communist newsletter for American business executives reiterated Bentley's charges about Pearson and noted that the major reason for Canada's reluctance to allow Gouzenko to testify was "the anti-anti-Communist feeling of top officials such as LESTER B. PEARSON, who believes the U.S. is somewhat hysterical about Communism and taking too intransigent a stand against it both at home and abroad."[31] Americans could still be convinced that Gouzenko, having defected more than eight years earlier, had valuable secrets to tell about Soviet espionage in their country.

∽

Needless to say, Canadian authorities cannot have been happy with their prize defector for starting these unpleasant controversies by talking to the American press. But as the Americans had learned from their involvement with Elizabeth Bentley, it was difficult, if not impossible, to control what defectors did and said. Bentley was a loose cannon for the FBI, and for the Internal Security Subcommittee. She began leaning on the bureau for money and for legal help after some drunk-driving incidents and trouble with the Internal Revenue Service. If the public found out about her legal woes and her alcoholism, it would damage her credibility as a witness and throw into question her testimonies about spies. Bentley was well aware that this was a bargaining chip for her. In 1955, when the IRS "attached" her bank account for failure to pay taxes, Bentley appealed to Robert Morris, the SISS counsel who had elicited her testimony against Pearson, and also to the FBI. Bentley told the bureau that if it did not solve her tax problem she would "blow the lid off the Administration" and "blow up the works." A personal intervention from Hoover with the Treasury Department finally got Bentley out of her scrape with the IRS.[32]

Gouzenko was now demonstrating that he, too, could be a loose cannon. His power to damage the credibility of the Canadian government was nothing like the power that Bentley wielded, and in contrast to Bentley, Gouzenko's life was not falling apart. But by the early 1950s he was causing the Canadian government significant headaches.

Like Bentley and a host of other defectors, Gouzenko had sold his personal story for publication. It was Mackenzie King who first suggested the idea. The day after the Royal Commission's full report on espionage was published, in July 1946, King asked to see Gouzenko, whom he had never met. The meeting went well. Gouzenko, described by King as youthful in appearance, clean cut, with steady eyes and a keen intellect, made a good impression. King told Gouzenko he was very pleased with the way the young man had conducted himself throughout "the period of great anxiety" and congratulated him on "his manliness, his courage and standing for the right." They talked about Stalin and how he would treat King if the latter paid a visit to Moscow. King then asked him if he had read Kravchenko's book *I Chose Freedom*. Gouzenko said he had, and King wondered out loud whether Gouzenko had thought of writing himself. According to King's diary, "He said that he was writing something, bit by bit. I said to him I thought he ought to have in mind not to do it too quickly but to begin with his own life: his ancestors and early bringing up. His ideas; his training; what caused him to change his views, etc. He told me afterwards he was very pleased to know I had thought well of his writing his life."[33]

Thus Gouzenko, inspired by King and by fellow defector Kravchenko, embarked on his memoirs. Gouzenko's English was still far from perfect, and he had little experience in writing, so he needed a lot of help. He told his story to Mervyn Black, who then passed an English translation to two journalists hired to write a manuscript. The venture turned out to be a great success. Gouzenko's memoirs first appeared in February 1947 as a four-part series entitled "I Was Inside Stalin's Spy Ring" in the American magazine *Cosmopolitan*. Gouzenko received $50,000 for the series, a considerable sum. The magazine had originally offered $5,000, but Gouzenko refused, and kept refusing until he got what he wanted.

A different and longer version of his autobiography was published as a book in 1948. Called *This Was My Choice* in Canada and *The Iron Curtain* in the United States, the book did well, yielding about $6,000 in royalties for Gouzenko. More important, he signed a $75,000 movie contract for the book with Twentieth Century Fox.

The movie, *The Iron Curtain*, starring Gene Tierney, playing Anna, and Dana Andrews, playing Igor, portrayed the dramatic story of their escape from the Soviets in 1945. As one reviewer assessed the film, "It is an anti-communist story without going overboard over what could be termed the 'Red Menace,' instead focusing in on Igor and his wife Anna . . . and the love they have for each other and their baby son." Disappointingly for the Gouzenkos, *The Iron Curtain* was not a success at the box office. It lasted only three days at a movie theater in Montreal. Nonetheless, by 1948, Gouzenko had earned a great deal of money, somewhere in the range of $130,000 to $140,000.[34]

Gouzenko also had another source of income. In early 1947, T.F. Ahearn, a wealthy Ottawa businessman, had provided an annuity of one hundred dollars a month for Gouzenko and his family. Ahearn, who was president of the Ottawa Electric Railway Company, gave Gouzenko the annuity in recognition of the great service he had done: "His action has awakened all Canadians of undivided loyalty to a very grave threat to our national security."[35]

The RCMP was, quite naturally, nervous about Gouzenko's publications. They worried he would be prompted to say things that were not true or would reveal something that would cast an unfavorable light on Canadian authorities. (The FBI had similar concerns when Bentley's book appeared, and pored over it anxiously to see if the details corresponded with her public testimonies, which they often did not.) Before Gouzenko's memoirs appeared in *Cosmopolitan*, RCMP commissioner Wood felt obliged to inform MI5 director Sir Percy Sillitoe and J. Edgar Hoover. Wood lamented in his letter to Sillitoe, "Igor Gouzenko is contracting directly with *Cosmopolitan* magazine and is, of course, a completely free agent in connection with any question relative to his private interests. Under the circumstances, we will of course not be in any position to exercise control over the particulars which appear."[36] As in Bentley's book, there were numerous inconsistencies between what Gouzenko initially told Canadian authorities and what appeared in his published memoirs, but no one seemed to notice. Gouzenko carefully avoided mentioning names like those of Alger Hiss, Arthur Steinberg, and the British spy code-named "Elli," which would have made the FBI and MI5 highly uncomfortable.

On a positive note, Wood told Sillitoe that Gouzenko would now have the financial resources to take up residence in Canada on his own, implying that the Canadian government, aside from the costs of RCMP protection, would be relieved of the day-to-day expenses for Gouzenko and his family. What Wood did not anticipate was Gouzenko's inability to handle money.

By 1951, after investing in a farm that turned out to be a disastrous venture, the Gouzenkos, now with three children, were penniless and in debt. Their only source of income was the hundred-dollar-a-month annuity and the money Gouzenko received for press interviews. (Much to the chagrin of journalists, he always insisted on being paid before he would talk. According to one source, "Gouzenko's critics joked that if you wanted an interview with him, all you had to do was run a cheque up the flagpole."[37]) Gouzenko was working on a novel, but it was a long way from being published. He appealed to a friend, who arranged for him to meet with a well-connected, fervently anti-communist Toronto journalist named Gladstone Murray. Accompanied by a Mountie and going by the name George Brown, Gouzenko told Murray he was in serious financial straits that would continue for at least six months, by which time he hoped to have some money from his next book. He needed three thousand dollars to tide him over until then.

Murray, who knew Gouzenko's real identity, was taken aback: "All I could do myself was to give the fellow $50.00," he wrote to Prime Minister St. Laurent a few days later. Murray told St. Laurent that he had agreed to try to find a wealthy individual who might be willing to help, but that the prospects were not good. He continued, "As Mr. Brown is presumably a kind of ward of the Government, I take this liberty of acquainting you with his predicament. I was uncomfortable at his manifestations of despair. The chances are the cause is bad management but the state of mind nevertheless should be noted." St. Laurent wrote back that he had spoken to the minister of justice, who "tells me he is keeping close touch with this problem which all of us find very perplexing."[38]

Apparently Murray was unable to solve Gouzenko's financial problems, because Gouzenko, for the first time since he defected, was forced to seek employment. He started working as a riveter for $1.47 an hour until sometime in 1952, when he managed to get a contract for the novel he was writing and received an advance of two thousand dollars on his royalties.[39]

Since 1947 Igor and Anna had been living in their own house, on two acres of land in Port Credit, Ontario, a small lakeside town west of Toronto. The Canadian government had provided them with a new identity and cover stories that accounted for their thickly accented, halting English. Now they were Czech immigrants, Stanley and Anna Krysac. Amazingly, *krysac* means rat, or mole, in the Czech language. It is not clear who decided on the Gouzenkos' new surname, but it seems to have been a deliberate slur against Igor. It is possible that the idea for the name came from RCMP officer John Leopold, who was a Czech by birth and was accused by Gouzenko early on of being a spy. It is surprising that Gouzenko would not have realized what his new surname meant. The Russian word for rat, *krysa*, is almost identical.[40]

The Gouzenkos still had one RCMP guard living with them. Gouzenko continued to fear being killed by a Soviet hit man. He told a journalist friend that he had a movie camera at the front of the house and turned it on any car he saw passing by for the third or fourth time. Neither he nor Anna went anywhere without an RCMP guard, and they received all their mail through a lawyer in Toronto. But Gouzenko, for all his concerns about safety, could be reckless. The problems began early on, prompting RCMP commissioner Wood to write to the minister of justice in October 1947, complaining that "Gouzenko's disregard for advice and the manner in which he persisted in doing things his own way, regardless of security, were . . . bound to expose him within a short period of time."[41]

By early 1948, the problem had become worse. In yet another letter to the minister of justice, Wood reported that Gouzenko had managed to get three of his paintings displayed in the window of a Montreal department store, against the wishes of the RCMP. Gouzenko had pushed some journalists to help arrange the display, and, as a result, it received wide attention. As Wood pointed out, Gouzenko's neighbors visited him often and could see his canvases spread all over the house. All it would take was for one of them to visit the display in Montreal and the Gouzenkos' cover would be blown.[42]

To make matters worse, Wood reported, "several members of the Press hold a very low view of Gouzenko's business integrity." It seems Gouzenko had become dissatisfied with his arrangement with the two journalists hired to write his autobiography and approached several other newspapermen with the offer to take over the work. When the original two contractors heard of this, they were incensed and discussed the matter at length with many of their colleagues. Wood warned in his letter, "It only would require one enterprising reporter to produce an article which would be most derogatory to Gouzenko." The fact that Gouzenko was no longer submitting his correspondence to the RCMP for mailing added to the security problems.

Taking all these matters into consideration, Wood stated, it was only a matter of time before Gouzenko's whereabouts were exposed, despite the thousands of dollars the RCMP had spent on security measures for him and his family. Wood told the minister that it was time for a "show-down" with Gouzenko; he should be told he must move to a new location selected by the RCMP and observe all their security rules. Otherwise, the government would be relieved entirely of responsibility for his safety. Wood concluded,

> Undoubtedly, we have been too indulgent to this man in the past. This was due, in part, to the great service that he has rendered this country, and to the natural sympathy which existed for a stranger in a new country who had burned all his bridges behind him. Apparently his personality changed with his affluence, and he mistook kindness for weakness. The continuance of the present conditions can only lead to his complete exposure, or, at the very least, a deadlock in our dealings with him.[43]

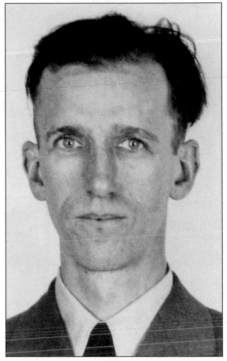

Frederick Poland, former Royal
Canadian Air Force (RCAF) officer,
shared an apartment with defendant
Gordon Lunan *(LAC/e002505783)*.

Matt Nightingale, former squadron
leader in the RCAF, who was approached
by GRU colonel Rogov *(LAC/e002505784)*.

Durnford Smith, engineer with the Canadian National Research Council, recruited by
Gordon Lunan to pass secret information to the GRU, served five years in prison
(LAC/e002505787).

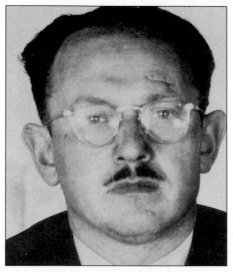

Sam Carr, national organizer of the communist Labour Progressive Party in Canada, provided GRU recruits with false passports, and after being extradited to Canada from the United States in 1949, spent six years in prison *(LAC/e002505788)*.

Scott Benning, former employee of the Canadian Department of Munitions and Supply, accused of passing military production secrets to the GRU and acquitted on appeal *(LAC/e002505789)*.

Gordon Lunan, Scottish-born captain in the Canadian Army, sentenced to five years in prison for acting as a middleman for the GRU *(LAC/e002505790)*.

Edward Mazerall, electrical engineer at the Canadian National Research Council, received four years in prison for violating the Official Secrets Act *(LAC/e002505791)*.

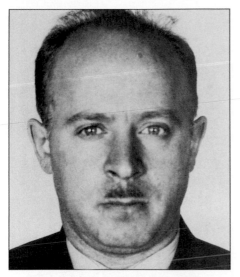

Fred Rose, Canadian member of Parliament and a top official of the Labour Progressive Party, sentenced to six years in prison for recruiting potential GRU spies *(LAC/e002505792)*.

Harold Gerson, brother-in-law of suspect Scott Benning and former employee of the Canadian Department of Munitions and Supply, sentenced to five years in prison for violating the Official Secrets Act *(LAC/e002505793)*.

Kathleen Willsher, who admitted to passing secret documents to the GRU while working at the British High Commission in Ottawa, went to prison for three years *(LAC/e002505794)*.

Emma Woikin, former cipher clerk in the Department of External Affairs, spent two and a half years in prison for passing official documents to GRU major Sokolov *(LAC/e002505795)*.

Dr. David Shugar, a talented young physicist, eventually returned to his native Poland after being acquitted on charges of violating the Official Secrets Act *(LAC/e002505796)*.

Eric Adams, an engineer with a masters degree in business from Harvard, and a former employee of the Bank of Canada *(LAC/e002505797)*.

Dr. Raymond Boyer, assistant professor of chemistry from McGill University and a leading specialist on the explosive known as RDX, served two years in prison *(TNA: PRO)*.

FBI chief J. Edgar Hoover, leaving the White House, 1942 *(Library of Congress/LC-USZ62-123127)*.

American "spy queen" Elizabeth Bentley, 1948 *(Library of Congress/LC-USZ62-109688)*.

Former U.S. State Department official Alger Hiss, testifying at his trial, 1948 *(Library of Congress/LC-USZ62-130365)*.

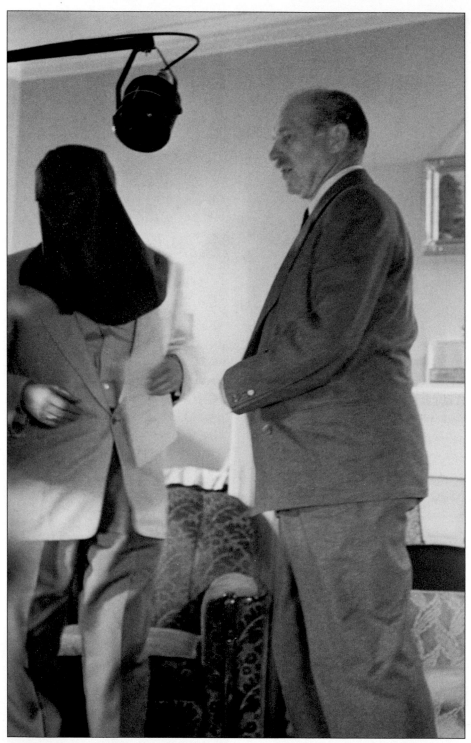

American journalist Drew Pearson, interviewing Gouzenko, January 1954 *(Lyndon B. Johnson Library)*.

"Am I supposed to send my reports to RCMP headquarters or the FBI?"

From *Maclean's* magazine, March 8, 1957.

Canadian diplomat E. Herbert Norman, no date *(LAC/PA-134317)*.

Canadian external affairs minister Lester Pearson, with his wife, receiving the Nobel Peace Prize, Oslo, 1957 *(LAC/C-094168)*.

Wood wanted permission for the RCMP to withdraw its protection completely if Gouzenko refused to cooperate, but St. Laurent's government was not willing to go that far. If Gouzenko or his family were harmed by the Soviet secret police, it would create another international scandal. The Liberals had gone out of their way to present Gouzenko as a hero to the public; they could not now let a hero be thrown to the wolves. He had to be protected, no matter how badly he behaved.

The RCMP tried to persuade Gouzenko to move away from the area. Charles Rivett-Carnac, whom Gouzenko trusted, talked with him for an entire morning about it, but to no avail. Gouzenko refused flat out. By this time there was considerable animosity between the RCMP and Gouzenko. Mountie George Mackay, who had been one of his guards since the days at Camp X, was fed up with him: "He wanted to go against the grain in doing certain things where we felt he was only endangering himself. He was very ready to accuse you of doing something to interfere with his life or his ambitions. Then I left and had nothing more to do with him and said: 'I don't want to hear any more of him.'" Other members of the force felt the same way. One Mountie went so far as to ask for a transfer to another part of the country to get out of guarding Gouzenko.[44]

Relations also broke down completely between Gouzenko and George McClellan. Having replaced Rivett-Carnac as head of the RCMP Special Branch in 1947, McClellan was one of those in the force who was pushing for Gouzenko to be moved out West. He was frustrated with Gouzenko's constant breaches of security and his continued complaints about his guards, whom Gouzenko viewed with intense suspicion. After Gouzenko got wind of McClellan's intentions, he immediately assumed McClellan was, like Leopold, a Soviet spy.[45] Henceforth, he blamed all his troubles with the RCMP on McClellan. As Gouzenko said some years later when asked what caused his relationship with the RCMP to deteriorate, "I don't blame it . . . on the guards, RCMP constable or sergeant, but . . . it was due to [the] influence, due to [the] direct influence from this high-ranking officer."[46]

By late 1953, after Gouzenko gave his famous interview to the *Chicago Tribune*, he was getting a lot of bad press in Canada. On October 30, the *Toronto Daily Star* had a front-page story alleging that Gouzenko had squandered one hundred thousand dollars in "high living" and was "giving his guardians a headache." According to the *Star*, one of his RCMP guardians expressed the view that Gouzenko was anxious to talk to the Americans because he was low on money, and "for money [he] will say just about anything, whether fact or not." For its part, the *Star* went on, the Canadian government was opposed to the Americans' interviewing Gouzenko. They were never sure what he would say. Some of his utterances in interviews were "highly speculative" and "just chatter." (Gouzenko later sued the newspaper for libel and the *Star* agreed to settle, paying him four thousand dollars and printing a front-page apology.)[47] In fact, Gouzenko was not completely penniless; he had by this time received an advance on royalties for his novel, which was about to appear. Although some sources claimed he was paid for the interview with Jenner and McCarran, Gouzenko had more to gain from the boost the publicity would give his book.

No wonder the Canadian government looked upon the visit from senators Jenner and McCarran with apprehension. Gouzenko had become a liability, drawing continued attention to himself by speaking to journalists and asking people for money. And he kept dredging up the espionage issue when the Liberal leadership was attempting to relegate it to the past. No matter what he told the press, Gouzenko had no more secrets to reveal. The Jenner Committee would be grasping at straws, encouraging Gouzenko to come up with any bit of information that would keep the anti-communist campaign going. Unless Gouzenko started to invent facts, the committee's efforts would be for naught.

As we know from what Gouzenko said about Arthur Steinberg, this is pretty much what happened during Gouzenko's testimony to SISS on January 4, 1954, at Montebello, Quebec. The Canadians, with the chief justice of the Supreme Court, J.C. McRuer, presiding, refused to allow the American counsel, Jay Sourwine, to pursue his own line of questioning. McRuer would not allow "hearsay" questions, for example, or questions involving Canadians. The committee was to direct itself solely to issues relating to the internal security of the United States. In addition to Steinberg, Alger Hiss was a key item on the agenda, with Sourwine going over with Gouzenko the familiar ground of the State Department spy in 1945. Gouzenko could add nothing new. In fact, he backtracked on what he had said earlier, in an article for *Coronet Magazine*:

Q: Do you remember also stating that the information which you aided in getting to the politburo included reports of confidential American foreign policy decisions received a matter of hours after they were arrived at?

A: I think not a matter of hours: I don't remember saying that. You mean United States or do you also include Canada? The reference was to United States, no I think that wouldn't be correct . . . this appearance in *Coronet Magazine*; if you remember, it was as told by Gouzenko; it was authorship different from me, and I wouldn't recommend basing anything on this article.[48]

Sourwine led Gouzenko back again and again to Hiss:

Q: Have you ever identified Hiss as the Secretary of Stettinius of whom you spoke?

A: He was later identified as the one of whom Koulakoff [Gouzenko's colleague] spoke . . .

Q: Did you either before or after you broke know anything specific about any other Soviet agents in the American State Department?

A: No, I did not.

Q: Did you have any knowledge of activities on behalf of the Soviet Union of one Harry White or Harry Dexter White of the United States Treasury Department?

A: No.[49]

What a disappointment, especially after Gouzenko had told the *Tribune* just a couple of months earlier that spies were lurking everywhere in North America and that he thought his testimony would be "worthwhile." The committee then listened patiently to Gouzenko as he gave them his advice on how to attract defectors. He had never gotten over the fact that the RCMP had failed to recruit any of his embassy colleagues after he defected. Gouzenko emphasized that it would not be enough just to grant them asylum. They had to be assured of a "good life." Material benefits, he said, should go hand in hand with an offer of citizenship and protection:

Q: By "material" you mean the offer of money, a pension, an annuity or something like that?

A: I would say an annuity at best.

Q: You did not break for the sake of any promise of annuity or pension?

A: No. In fact I didn't know anything of what was ahead of me, but I knew there would be difficulties. In fact my proposal is actually not just jumping to conclusions. It is more or less on the basis of the experience of myself which I lived through all those years, which leads me to understand how another person would feel . . . [an annuity] would make it possible for him to live a much simpler and more normal life, and make it possible for him to really enjoy the life of the society to which he gives service.

Q: Assuming in addition to immunity he was also guaranteed physical protection and security, do you still feel that it would be an added inducement, a necessary added inducement in order to get these people to come, to offer them money as well?

A: I will say he would believe in the sincerity of all the other parts of the proposal . . . a practical man will say they grant you more or less a good life, so he can leave and he knows the difficulties ahead of him. There is nothing wrong with that grant. I do not want to bring up this

case, but suppose you build a monument to some spiri-
tual thing or to an important man. You collect money to
build that monument. What is wrong with that grant?
There is nothing wrong with that. It is good money . . .

Q: I am wondering, and I want your opinion, whether it
might not actually defeat the purpose if there was an
offer of money. Do you think Soviet agents generally can
be lured away from their Soviet allegiance by offers of
money?

A: Yes. . . . If you say "Here is a man. Come on; we will buy
you," of course it hurts him. He will say, "Here, they are
just trying to buy me." But when you say about the citizenship and about protection, and you say an annuity or
a grant passed by parliament in the way of securing his
position, you are helping him adjust himself to society.[50]

This part of Gouzenko's testimony raised awkward questions for
the committee. On the surface, Gouzenko was simply giving them
friendly advice about how to persuade Soviet spies to defect. But he
was also revealing something about his own motivations. Some eight
years earlier, he had claimed that he defected out of ideological and
moral convictions: he had wanted to expose the Soviet Union for
what it was, a tyranny bent on destroying the West. He had not
defected for a better life, he had said, but to serve as an example of
the moral courage of Soviet citizens suffering under the yoke of
Stalinist oppression. Now, in front of the committee, he was claiming that a defector should get money in exchange for his information. Yes, he said, there was the altruistic motivation, but that was
not enough. Defectors, like him, deserved a lifetime payment for
what they did.

Gouzenko's assertion that life in a democracy like Canada or the
United States was not a sufficient enticement for a potential Soviet
defector might have disquieted senators Jenner and McCarran, if
they had been the type of men who were open to reflection. They
had been pursuing former U.S. government officials like Hiss,
White, and many of their leftist and communist associates as if they

were dangerous criminals. White was dead, Hiss was safely tucked away in prison, and most of the others had left government service, but Jenner's committee continued to devote tremendous time and resources to proving their guilt. These men and women had been, for the most part, talented and hard-working civil servants. More important, if they had passed information to the Soviets, they had done so not for money, but because of their ideological convictions. Yet here was Gouzenko saying money was an essential component of an offer to defectors.

Gouzenko reiterated his views a few weeks later in a two-part television interview, his first ever, with journalist Drew Pearson, the man who first broke his story. After the stir he had caused with his *Tribune* interview and his testimony to the Senate Internal Security Subcommittee, Gouzenko was a hot commodity, and Drew Pearson went to a lot of trouble to arrange the interview. There were lawyers involved, so there was doubtless some negotiation over fees. Pearson was impressed by Gouzenko when he met him: "He speaks English quite well, is still young and has a wife with all the vivaciousness of a Russian and some of the beauty of an American. She travels with him wherever he goes." They talked for two and a half hours in preparation for the actual interview, but when the time came for filming Gouzenko insisted on leaving and said he would return early the next day. He did not show up, apparently because the RCMP threatened that they would withdraw all protection if he allowed himself to be filmed. Gouzenko kept Pearson waiting for eight hours before he finally arrived, with a black pillowcase over his head, to appear before television cameras for the first time. As Pearson recalled later, "It was then I came to understand that the young man who had the courage to ransack the code room of the Soviet Embassy in Ottawa was a man who had very definite opinions on almost everything and a stubborn determination to carry them out."[51]

At the beginning of the interview Gouzenko seemed to catch Pearson off guard by asking him an awkward question: "I remember when it was first time I broke the spy ring in Canada, and it was at that time when nobody knew any word about this except you people. You first to know in the American and Canadian press this news.

Now tell me before interviewing, how you did it?" Pearson replied evasively, "Well, now you're putting me on the spot right off the bat, I am supposed to interview you. But I had an awful hard time doing that because that was a very closely held secret . . . but anyway, let me interview you if you don't mind."

After going over the familiar ground of Alger Hiss, Harry Dexter White, and Alan Nunn May, Pearson got Gouzenko on to his favorite topic, luring defectors:

> Pearson: Now should we offer rewards to Russian military men to come our way?
>
> Gouzenko: This is part of my idea of proposals to bring them on our side, but it is a very important part, and I certainly think it helps.
>
> Pearson: Or should we try to find these people jobs?
>
> Gouzenko: Would it be possible for him to find a good job which would use his talent and ability?
>
> Pearson: Well, it's pretty hard to ask a Russian general to take a job as a janitor. If he's going to help the free world, we have to help him.
>
> Gouzenko: I am very glad you brought up this point, because there is a very important human element involved. Sometimes a man makes his decision. The question of dignity is involved, and sometimes, like a general, or colonel, military attaché, he will actually be convinced on our side, and he is our friend. Yet he continues his job only because he is afraid he will be humiliated here; he will be put to work as a janitor.[52]

Gouzenko, of course, was talking about himself. He had not worked as a janitor, but in a similar category of manual labor. And it was demeaning. After risking his life to provide the West with evidence of Soviet spying, he felt he was owed more than this. Despite all the recent publicity, he knew he could not profit financially from his defector status for much longer. He was not willing, like Elizabeth Bentley, to embellish when asked repeatedly about Soviet spies in North America and to cough up new names to please his questioners. But as a result he had lost his star billing as a defector. Indeed, the interview with SISS in January 1954 was pretty much a swan song for Gouzenko as far as the anti-communists in Washington were concerned.

After returning to the United States, senators Jenner and McCarran told the press that their interview with Gouzenko was long and productive and "a great deal was accomplished." But an observant reporter for the *Toronto Daily Star* noted that, whereas the senators had been "jovial and almost talkative" on their arrival in Canada, they looked glum when they emerged from interviewing Gouzenko. No wonder. When the Canadian minister of justice, Stuart Garson, made the transcript public in April 1954, he emphasized again that the evidence disclosed "very little, if indeed there is any information not already available to the public." And the *New York Times* observed, "The testimony consisted mostly of disconnected items of information many of which were given to the Canadian Government in 1945. . . . The eighty-five pages contained no new or startling facts and it did not seem likely that they would contribute to the security situation in the United States."[53] Ironically, the fact that senators Jenner and McCarran had elicited nothing new from their much-publicized meeting with Gouzenko would not stop anti-communists in Washington from claiming that the Canadians were stone-walling and covering up a deeper connection between the Canadian spy case and Americans.

Chapter 9

"ELLI," PHILBY, AND THE

DEATH OF A DIPLOMAT

Whoever fights monsters should see to it that in the process he does not become a monster.
Friedrich Nietzsche

While the Americans back in the autumn of 1945 had seized on Gouzenko's references to a spy in the State Department, no one at MI5 or MI6 had shown much interest in what he had to say about a possible mole in their midst, code-named "Elli." It would be almost twenty years before the British Services would launch an exhaustive investigation to discover who Elli was, an investigation that not only proved fruitless, but also did a great deal of damage to the reputation and morale of MI5 and MI6.

Gouzenko's information about "Elli" was first conveyed during his interview with MI5's Roger Hollis (with the RCMP present), who visited Gouzenko shortly after the defection. According to the report from the British Security Coordination, written in mid-September 1945, presumably after Hollis's visit,

> Corby states that while he was in the Central Code Section [in Moscow] in 1942 or 1943, he heard about a Soviet agent in England, allegedly a member of the British Intelligence Service. This agent, who was of Russian descent, had reported that the British had a very important agent of

their own in the Soviet Union, who was apparently being run by someone in Moscow. The latter refused to disclose his agent's identity even to his headquarters in London. When this message arrived it was received by a Lt. Col. Polakova who, in view of its importance, immediately got in touch with Stalin himself by telephone.[1]

This was a potentially explosive revelation. Gouzenko claimed that a member of the British Intelligence Service (MI6) was secretly working for the Soviets. Moreover, this mole had informed his handlers about an agent in the Soviet Union who was being run by someone from British Intelligence in Moscow. Why did Roger Hollis seem to treat these allegations so lightly? When he heard the information about Elli, Hollis was concentrating on catching British atomic spy Alan Nunn May. The May case was MI5's most urgent priority, and Hollis devoted all his time and energy to it. And, according to MI5 officer Peter Wright, author of the bestselling book *Spycatcher*, Hollis doubted that Elli really existed: "Hollis judged Gouzenko to be confused about the structure of British Intelligence. Gouzenko was wrong, and the matter was buried. This was a mistaken judgment."[2]

Nonetheless, Hollis duly reported Gouzenko's allegations about Elli, which was why they appeared in the BSC report, passed to MI5 and MI6 as well as to the RCMP. He also had a second meeting with Gouzenko in November 1945, of which there is no declassified record beyond its having taken place, and suggested having Gouzenko brought to England for questioning. One of MI5's leading experts on communism, Captain Guy Liddell, looked into the Elli matter and sent a telegram to Ottawa regarding a possible identification that proved negative.[3] But, as with Hollis, Liddell's main preoccupation was Nunn May.

Gouzenko elaborated on the mysterious Elli in an interview with the RCMP in late October 1945. According to handwritten notes summarizing the interview, Gouzenko said it was "possible he or she is identical with the agent with a Russian background who Kulakoff [Kulakov, Gouzenko's successor, who had recently come from Moscow] spoke [of] – there could be 2 agents concerned in this matter. Corby [Gouzenko] handled telegrams submitted by Elli . . . Elli could not give the name of the [British] agent in Moscow because of security reasons. Elli [was] already working as an agent when Corby took up his duties in Moscow in May 1942 and was still working when Kulakoff arrived in Canada in May 1945. Kulakov said agent with a Russian connection held a high position. Corby from decoding messages said Elli had access to exclusive info."[4]

There was, of course, at least one Soviet agent in British intelligence at this time, Kim Philby. Could this have been the individual Gouzenko was referring to? Probably not. Philby worked for the NKVD, not for the GRU, where Gouzenko was employed. It would be highly unusual for an NKVD message to be channeled to the GRU, even during wartime when the two agencies were often gathering the same types of information. Also, Gouzenko said that the agent in question was of Russian descent or background, which did not describe Philby.[5] Nonetheless, although Philby knew that Gouzenko worked for the GRU, it did not stop him from worrying that Gouzenko was referring to him. Indeed, he was so agitated by Gouzenko's defection that his NKVD handler, as we have seen, had to "calm him down."[6]

In speaking to Senator Jenner's subcommittee in January 1954, Gouzenko broached the subject of the British spy again. (The two-word name of the agency to which Gouzenko said Elli belonged is unfortunately blacked out in the released testimony.) Gouzenko explained, "I thought it would be of interest to the American authorities because I understand that sometimes they do their work in cooperation with the British authorities."

Jay Sourwine, the subcommittee's counsel, was snappily dismissive:

Q: Was he in connection with the United States? Was he in a place to dispose of United States secrets? What is the United States connection with him?
A: Like I said in my previous statements, I thought in dealing with your particular case you would be in a better

position to evaluate the importance or non-importance of that matter because you knew better than I if there is any connection whatever.

Q: Can you identify this agent?

A: It was by cover name, and anyway I gave all this information to the Royal Commission and I believe it was probably passed over to the FBI.

Q: Have you any reason to believe the Royal Commission has not made that available to the United States?

A: No, I have not. On the contrary, I think it is in the files of the FBI.

Q: What is the purpose in telling us, then?[7]

This was a rather curious reaction. Sourwine could not have been ignorant of the fact that two important British spies, Guy Burgess and Donald Maclean, had fled to Moscow in 1951, and Philby, who was close to both of them, was under a cloud of suspicion. By 1954 it was well known in the U.S. government that all three had been in a position to compromise American secrets. Burgess had been employed at the Foreign Office and served as first secretary to the embassy in Washington, D.C., before he defected. Maclean had been a diplomat in Washington (with access to information that even Congress did not know) from 1944 to 1948. Before leaving Washington he had been head of the American Department of the Foreign Office. And Philby had been Britain's intelligence liaison officer in Washington from 1949 to 1951. Given the close alliance between the governments of Britain and the United States and the cooperative arrangements between their security services, a Soviet spy in Britain was of potentially enormous importance for the Americans.

This of course must have been Gouzenko's reasoning when he mentioned Elli to the subcommittee. He did not realize that SISS was not involved in the realities of counterespionage; its overriding domestic political agenda focused entirely on finding communists in the United States and exposing potential ones. Even the FBI, which was responsible for counterespionage and had received

Gouzenko's information about Elli several years before, had not given it much attention. This, the FBI seems to have reasoned, was Britain's problem.

Speaking to the Jenner subcommittee, Gouzenko claimed he had written three pages about Elli sometime earlier, but he did not say for whom. Although the cover name was a female one, Gouzenko said, it might have been a man. He went on, "There was identification, a further clue . . . this particular one [referring to Elli] . . . had a Russian background. This may mean that he was on a commission in Moscow previously or maybe it could be that some of his relations had a Russian background, or maybe he was engaged previously on Russian questions. But from the telegram it was clear, and I also described in the detail the circumstances under which this telegram came to my attention."[8]

It was not until 1963, the year Kim Philby defected to Moscow, that the issue of Elli and a possible British mole aroused the interest of the British security and intelligence services. Philby, who had retired from MI6 soon after Burgess and Maclean disappeared and was working in Beirut, had long been assumed to have been a spy, but no one could prove it. His defection was prompted by an interview with an MI6 officer who accused him of spying. The fact that Philby's first comment when he saw the officer at his door was "I rather thought it would be you" led members of MI5 and MI6 to assume he had been warned about the visit ahead of time and that the warning must have come from yet another spy in one of their agencies. As a result, a joint MI5–MI6 committee called Fluency was formed in 1964 to investigate penetrations of British intelligence. It was chaired by Peter Wright, who later would describe the mole hunt in *Spycatcher*.[9]

The Fluency Committee soon turned to Gouzenko's allegations about Elli. But by this time the story had inexplicably changed. Instead of Elli being a spy in British intelligence, MI6, Wright saw information suggesting Gouzenko said that Elli was a spy in "five of MI," which he later changed to MI5. Wright contacted the RCMP to request an interview with Gouzenko, but was told that this was not a good idea. The RCMP claimed that Gouzenko was an alcoholic (which was not true) and was always after money (which was). An interview, the RCMP said, would make these problems worse and inevitably be leaked to the press by Gouzenko.[10]

Wright says he then asked the RCMP for notes of its debriefing of Gouzenko, only to be told they had been destroyed.[11] But the notes, quoted above, were in the records of the RCMP. Was the RCMP being deliberately uncooperative, or did Wright not press very hard? If Wright had seen the notes of Gouzenko's RCMP debriefing he would have known that Gouzenko made no mention of MI5 to the RCMP. Moreover, Gouzenko's statements confirmed that Elli was from MI6 because Elli was privy to information about a British secret agent in Moscow. MI5, a counterintelligence agency, did not recruit agents in the Soviet Union, as MI6 was designated to do.

It also appears that the Fluency Committee did not consult the BSC report of September 1945, which quotes Gouzenko as referring to an agent in British Intelligence. Perhaps they did but were still in doubt about which agency Gouzenko was referring to. The committee decided to interview Peter Dwyer, who, it will be recalled, was one of the authors of the BSC report and had been sending messages to MI6 headquarters from Ottawa after the defection outlining Gouzenko's information. Dwyer had returned to Washington as MI6 liaison there, but in late 1949 relinquished his post (to none other than Philby) and moved to Ottawa to work on security matters for the Canadian government. At some point during the Fluency investigation, Maurice Oldfield, Philby's replacement in MI6, appeared on Dwyer's doorstep in Ottawa with the rest of the "mole-hunters" and interviewed Dwyer for two days. The interviews, which left Dwyer "exhausted and irritated with security intelligence and its bottomless well of suspicion," apparently yielded no firm answers to the question of who Elli was.[12]

With Wright insisting that Elli was from MI5, the suspicions in Britain fell on Roger Hollis, director of MI5 since 1956. Hollis's accusers apparently did not know that Gouzenko had described Elli initially as being of Russian descent or having some connection with Russia, which would have ruled out not only Hollis but also most others in MI5. By the time he retired in 1965, Hollis had faced several grueling interrogations, none of which exonerated him. Even Hollis's former colleague, Sir Dick White, who became head of MI6 when Hollis succeeded him at MI5, considered it entirely possible that Hollis was Elli. When he paid a visit to J. Edgar Hoover in 1966, White felt compelled to tell the FBI chief that "various allegations have been made against Roger Hollis and an investigation is under way."[13]

The FBI's Robert Lamphere wrote in his memoirs that he also thought Hollis was a spy and assumed that Hollis had tipped the Soviets off about the American success in deciphering their coded messages (the Venona project): "To me, there now remains little doubt that it was Hollis who provided the earliest information to the KGB that the FBI was reading their 1944–45 cables. Philby probably added to that knowledge after his arrival in the United States, but the prime culprit in this affair was Hollis." Significantly, Lamphere based his assumptions partly on what he thought Gouzenko had said, that "he told his interviewers that there was a top Russian spy inside MI-5."[14]

Nonetheless, not everyone agreed with this view. The identity, or even existence, of Elli remained a subject of deep controversy in MI5. It hung over the service like a black cloud. Fluency ceased its work after Hollis retired, but in the autumn of 1972, right around the time that Hollis died, the Elli investigation was reopened. MI5 asked again to interview Gouzenko, and this time the RCMP not only acquiesced, it also provided MI5's interviewer, Patrick Stewart, with the notes of the initial debriefing of Gouzenko. Stewart, accompanied by several Mounties, met Gouzenko at the Royal York Hotel in Toronto. He showed Gouzenko a copy of the BSC report and the notes from his interview with the RCMP shortly thereafter, both of which had Gouzenko saying Elli was working in British Intelligence, MI6, not counterintelligence, MI5. Gouzenko went into a fury and threw the papers across the room. He claimed that he had not said what was written in the BSC report, that someone had falsified his statements. As for the notes of the RCMP interview, which were in the handwriting of the translator, Mervyn Black, Gouzenko said they had been forged. He demanded, to no avail, that he be allowed to take the notes home so he could compare them with his copies of Black's handwriting.[15]

Why was Gouzenko so upset? He had been dismayed when the MI5 officer who had interviewed him in September 1945 did not seem interested in Elli. Gouzenko had planned to give him more details, but the man left after just a few minutes. For years afterward, Gouzenko wondered why no one had acted on his information and followed up on the Elli case. Apparently, he convinced himself that it was a cover-up and that Elli worked for MI5. Later, when he realized that the MI5 officer who had interviewed him in 1945 was Roger Hollis, and that Hollis was suspected of being a mole, Gouzenko became certain that Hollis had deliberately misrepresented his statements to hide the fact that he was Elli. But the records spoke for themselves. Unless Gouzenko had given the wrong information in his interviews after his defection, Hollis, as a member of MI5, could not have been Elli.[16]

❧

Robert Lamphere may have been receptive to the theory that Hollis was Elli because MI5 had so many failures in its counterintelligence efforts against the Soviets. Not only did MI5 overlook Alan Nunn May until Gouzenko defected with proof that he was Soviet agent, the service, as noted earlier, also failed to investigate Klaus Fuchs, who had been working at a top secret nuclear facility in Britain since 1946. FBI officials first suspected Fuchs of espionage on behalf of the NKVD in 1949, when as part of the Venona project they deciphered a 1944 telegram to Moscow from the NKVD in New York. The telegram gave details about the Manhattan Project summarized in a top secret paper written by Fuchs for the Americans. Working with MI6 liaison Peter Dwyer, Lamphere soon concluded, after looking at the background of those who had access to the paper, that Fuchs had passed the information to the Soviets. The FBI reported the discovery to MI5, where it was received with great consternation. In late 1949, MI5's William Skardon, who had interviewed Alan Nunn May three years earlier, questioned Fuchs and got him to confess.

Fuchs was arrested on February 2, 1950, and charged with violating the Official Secrets Act.[17]

The FBI and MI5 had an additional shock when they learned of the defection of Maclean and Burgess in 1951, made worse because it was clear that Philby was probably a spy as well. It was bad enough to contemplate the secrets that had been compromised by Maclean and Burgess. The implications of Philby's treachery were even graver. Lamphere and his colleagues had shared highly sensitive information with him. Philby had even learned about the top secret Venona project, which was known to only a select group in the American intelligence community. The realization that such information, especially information concerning deciphered Soviet messages, had been passed on to the Soviets was devastating. In Lamphere's words, "I sat at my desk and tried to recollect precisely how much Philby had been told about the FBI's counterintelligence operations, and how much he might have deduced from conversations with Peter Dwyer. . . . What about the techniques we were perfecting, the direction and training of our agents, our relations with the British, the French and the Canadian intelligence services? Philby had been in a position to know so much!"[18] Peter Dwyer must have been equally disturbed when he heard Philby was probably a spy. It meant the Soviets had had access to all the information in the secret messages about the Gouzenko case that he had sent in 1945 and 1946 to MI6 and MI5.

Philby would also have been in a position to inform the Soviets that Fuchs was under suspicion, because he was in Washington in late 1949, at the very time Dwyer and Lamphere were closing in on Fuchs. But, as was the case earlier when he found out that Nunn May was about to be interrogated by British authorities, Philby apparently thought he would risk exposing himself if he passed on the information to Moscow. In fact, he even helped in the Fuchs investigation. According to a Russian biographer of Philby who interviewed him after he defected, "It is possible that Philby's arrival in Washington and his participation in the search for the leak of secret information from Los Alamos [the Manhattan Project] hastened the discovery of Klaus Fuchs. Kim did not clarify the situation during our conversations."[19]

One additional piece of evidence the FBI had added to their case against Fuchs was the fact that his name appeared in Israel Halperin's address book. Although the information from Fuchs was going to the NKVD, not to the GRU, which was alleged to have recruited Halperin, the FBI still considered the address-book entry significant. On October 21, 1949, Hoover sent a letter to the Atomic Energy Commission, apprising the committee of his agency's findings on Fuchs. To reinforce the FBI's case, Hoover mentioned the entry in Halperin's address book and went on to observe, "With respect to Israel Halperin, documents abstracted from the Soviet Embassy at Ottawa, Canada, by Igor Gouzenko, Soviet Code Clerk who defected to the Canadian authorities on September 5, 1945, supported by the testimony of Gouzenko himself, established that Halperin was a member of the Soviet Military Intelligence espionage network operating in Canada during the period 1942–1943." The charges against Halperin were dismissed, Hoover went on, because the prosecution did not have independent evidence, "a condition precedent to the admissibility of Soviet documents."[20]

Hoover was distorting the facts. It was true that the prosecution required "independent evidence" beyond Gouzenko's documents and statements in order to prosecute the Canadian spy suspects. Such evidence consisted mainly of confessions of the suspects or statements implicating them by others, such as Lunan. In Halperin's case, the evidence showed that, while he flirted with communism and the idea of helping out the Soviets, he had refused to furnish written information or convey secrets to Gordon Lunan. Lunan's testimony had confirmed this. In short, not only was there no independent evidence of Halperin's guilt, the Gouzenko documents themselves did not incriminate him.

Despite the fact that Halperin had been cleared by the courts, the FBI considered his address book (which is still classified as secret) as a key piece of evidence against possible spies. It included the names of 163 individuals living in the United States, all of whom the FBI attempted to identify and investigate. Many of these individuals, such as John Blewett, Halperin's roommate at Princeton, were listed in the address book for obviously personal, not political reasons. But that did not deter the FBI. As one historian observed, "It is as if Halperin's address book was a carrier of a virus, infecting all who came in contact with it."[21]

⌒

One of those who would be "infected" by the Halperin address book was Canadian diplomat E. Herbert Norman. Norman had known Halperin ever since they roomed across the hall from each other as undergraduates at the University of Toronto in the early 1930s. Unfortunately for Norman, the Halperin connection was just one of several circumstances that would make him the object of allegations by spy-hunters in Washington. The allegations would turn out to be false, but they haunted him throughout his career and the damage they caused was very real. The Norman case would become a topic of intense controversy in Canada, arousing the passions of both sides in the debate over the West's response to Soviet espionage, just as the Hiss case polarized Americans for years. But Norman's story was more about the McCarthy era in the United States than it was about Canada, because the source of his torment was the FBI and the Senate Internal Security Subcommittee.

Born in 1909 in Japan, where his parents were Canadian Methodist missionaries, Herbert Norman was strongly influenced by his religious upbringing and his family's belief in the importance of public service. Introspective and intellectually curious, Norman was an excellent student who had the makings of a scholar early on. His innate desire to learn was stimulated by his home environment, where he was surrounded by books, and also by numerous trips abroad. By the time he was a young teenager, Norman had visited several countries in Asia and the Middle East. He learned to speak Japanese, which was no small achievement for a young person raised in an English-speaking family.[22]

Norman left Japan in 1929 to study at the University of Toronto, where he completed his undergraduate degree four years later. In 1933, Norman went on to Trinity College, Cambridge, for two

years of postgraduate studies in history. Like many bright young
men of his generation, Norman was attracted to communism at
Cambridge. It was a natural reaction to the Great Depression and
the rise of fascism, especially for someone who was raised with a
strong social conscience. Norman did more than just discuss
Marxism as a philosophy in small study groups at Cambridge. He
became, by his own acknowledgment, committed to the political
ideology of communism, and, judging from a letter he wrote to his
brother a few years later, may have actually joined the party in 1934.
In Norman's case, however, the activities that party membership
entailed amounted to little more than participation in a hunger
march and attempts to recruit some Indian students to the party. By
all accounts, Norman was on the periphery of the communist movement at Cambridge, not part of the inner group of communists that
included Burgess, Maclean, and Philby.[23]

After returning to Canada in 1935, Norman briefly joined the
communist-dominated Canadian Friends of the Chinese People
before leaving for Harvard with his new bride, Irene, to pursue a
doctorate degree in Japanese history. At Harvard, where he was supported by a fellowship from the Rockefeller Foundation, he continued to take an academic interest in Marxism and was a member of
the left-wing League Against War and Fascism. But his work toward
his doctorate, which included courses in both Japanese and Chinese
languages, took precedence over all else. Norman was sensitive,
earnest, and idealistic, but he was also ambitious.[24]

In 1939, shortly before he was awarded his doctorate, Norman
accepted a position at the Canadian Department of External Affairs.
His knowledge of Japan, his wide-ranging intellectual talents, and
his diligence made him a valuable asset for the Canadian diplomatic
corps. He was posted the next year to Tokyo, where he remained
until after the Japanese attacked Pearl Harbor. By this time he had
grown out of his infatuation with communism, but his political affiliations back in the thirties had nevertheless permanently shaped his
identity. Had he been able to foresee the intense anti-communist
campaign that would emerge in North America after the war,

Norman might have been more circumspect in his activities as a student and more cautious about his relationships with communists and socialists. As he admitted much later, "I talked quite recklessly in those years and in a way I was very carefree and did not weigh my words." A chance encounter in 1936 with a young Canadian named Pat Walsh, an RCMP undercover agent, would come back to haunt him. Four years later, Walsh denounced him secretly to the RCMP as a communist.[25]

Norman's doctoral thesis, "Japan's Emergence as a Modern State," which he defended successfully at Harvard in 1940, became a highly acclaimed book that earned him a reputation as a leading scholar in Japanese history. With the publication of two more books and several articles, Norman came to be regarded as one of the greatest living Western experts on Japanese culture, history, and language. As Norman's biographer pointed out, however, his expertise in Far Eastern affairs and his scholarly reputation would actually become a drawback for him as a diplomat in the post-war years, when anti-intellectuals who were suspicious of Asia specialists came to dominate the political agenda in Washington.[26]

Most conservative Republicans were so-called Asia-Firsters, who, during World War II, had urged the U.S. government to focus more on the threat posed by Japan in the Pacific. They were critical of what they saw as the State Department's bias toward Europe and its failure to make a stronger commitment to shoring up Nationalist China against the communists. And they blamed the policy failures squarely on the Asia specialists. The big question, from this perspective, became "who lost China" to the communists in 1949. This would be a burning issue in Washington during the early part of the 1950s. The fact that Norman was a Canadian diplomat did not shield him from the American red hunters. As his biographer expressed it, "Expertise in Asian affairs became even criminal, sometimes treasonable, in the eyes of McCarthyites who sought to attribute a failed foreign policy to the misdeeds, misperceptions, wrong-headed analyses and seditiously leftist views of the experts . . . Herbert's academic specialization became in itself 'evidence' of possible wrong-doing when linked with his many professional asso-ciations, personal and institutional, that quite naturally followed from expertise in the field."[27]

In terms of guilt by association, Norman appeared highly cul-pable. Not only had he roomed across the hall from Halperin at the University of Toronto, he had later been friendly with him at Harvard, where both were in a Marxist-oriented study group. Furthermore, Norman's thesis had been published by the Institute of Pacific Relations (IPR), a respected think tank in New York that attracted the most prestigious scholars and policy experts on the Far East. Norman had been a research associate at the IPR for a year, and he continued his contacts there well after he received his doctor-ate, attending IPR conferences and contributing to its publications. This was hardly surprising, given Norman's area of expertise. The problem for Norman was that the institute was widely considered to be a communist front organization. His association with the IPR was soon to become a black mark on his career, especially when in 1951–52 Senator McCarran's SISS held eighteen months of hearings into possible communist subversion by the institute.

~

After working in Ottawa during the war years, Norman returned to Japan late in the summer of 1945 as head of the Canadian Liaison Mission in Tokyo. As such, he was seconded to the U.S. Army's Counterintelligence Corps, which was attached to the headquarters of General Douglas MacArthur. Norman's responsibility was to oversee the interrogation of Japanese political prisoners held during the war and to supervise their release from prison. In the process, Norman attracted the attention of the head of American counter-intelligence in Japan, Major General Charles Willoughby, a rabid anti-communist.

On the orders of Willoughby's predecessor, General Elliot Thorpe, Norman and a young State Department officer named John Emmerson had organized the release of a group of political prison-ers that included two communists. They had been in prison for eight-een years. When he heard they were to be released, Willoughby was outraged. He launched an investigation of Norman and Emmerson as part of his campaign against "leftists and fellow-travelers." Willoughby soon came to view Norman as a key figure in the group of Far East experts who influenced policy during the Occupation and who opposed Willoughby's advocacy of a so-called soft peace, which gave free rein to the right-wing elements that had dominated Japan before World War II. What made Norman especially suspect in Willoughby's eyes was his association with the IPR and the American Asian experts connected with it. Willoughby, whose imagination seemingly knew no bounds, would eventually reach the conclusion that Norman was an espionage agent.[28]

Despite Willoughby's suspicions, others at the American Supreme Command thought exceedingly well of Norman. General Thorpe wrote a letter to Prime Minister King in praise of him: "I should like to express to you my personal appreciation of Dr. Norman's services. His profound knowledge of Japan, his brilliant intellectual attainments and his willingness to give of his utmost to our work has made his contribution to the success of the Occupation one of great value. During his tour of duty with us, Dr. Norman has won the respect and admiration of all who have been associated with him."[29]

After returning home in January 1946, Norman served briefly as first secretary of the Canadian legation in Washington. He then went back to Japan in the summer of 1946 again as head of Canada's liaison mission to General Douglas MacArthur's Supreme Command, remaining this time until 1950. MacArthur had a great deal of discretion in making policy decisions about post-war Japan. Washington had not given the Supreme Command specific instructions on negotiating a peace settlement, or determining the fate of former Japanese officials, and MacArthur apparently sought Norman's advice on numerous occasions. He was impressed by him.[30]

But Willoughby's secret investigation of Norman and his allegations that he was a communist spy outweighed all the positive evidence of Norman's accomplishments. Eventually it rekindled the FBI's interest in him, which dated back to the autumn of 1942, when Norman had attempted to retrieve the books and papers of a left-wing Japanese economist, Shigeto Tsuru, whom he had known while studying at Harvard. Tsuru had been repatriated to Japan, leaving his library behind in Cambridge, and the FBI had assumed custody of it. According to the FBI report, Norman approached one of its agents in Boston and said that he was acting on behalf of the Canadian government, which had an interest in obtaining Tsuru's collection of books and papers. He reportedly admitted to FBI agents subsequently that the mission was more a personal one. The incident caused the FBI to open a file on Norman, but then they closed it in 1947.[31]

⮑

The FBI file on Norman remained closed until shortly after Norman's name cropped up enigmatically at hearings, held by Senator Millard Tydings in April 1950, to investigate allegations from Senator Joseph McCarthy about disloyalty among State Department employees who were Far East experts. For those on the right of the American political spectrum, the defeat of the Chinese nationalists, compounded by the outbreak of the war in Korea in 1950, was a result of subversion by communists. McCarthy, who brandished the names of over two hundred State Department employees allegedly working for the communists, and Senator Pat McCarran were the most strident adherents of this theory.

It was inevitable that the search for scapegoats would lead to Herbert Norman. General Thorpe, MacArthur's former chief of intelligence, who had been so complimentary about Norman, was called as a witness at the Tydings hearings. One of the senators asked Thorpe whether he had ever been associated with a "man named E. Herbert Norman" in preparing an intelligence report dealing with Asia. Thorpe cautiously responded that he knew Norman, but could not remember the report, which the senator said was prepared for General Willoughby.[32]

The significance of Norman being mentioned at the hearings was not lost on his colleagues. His name was introduced in a context that questioned the loyalty of those involved in Far East policy, and at least one witness to the proceedings drew the conclusion that the question about Norman "had indicated a desire to establish a link with the Canadian espionage enquiry." External Affairs hurriedly sent a cable to Norman in Tokyo informing him about the testimony and warning him not to comment publicly about it. Norman replied that he was at a loss as to why his name would have been brought up at the hearings.[33]

A month later, in May 1950, the FBI reactivated Norman's file, presumably because he was mentioned during Thorpe's SISS testimony. In the process, FBI agents took another look at Halperin's address book. They immediately noticed that it contained several references to Norman. In early September, the FBI contacted the RCMP, mentioned the address book, as well as the 1942 encounter between Norman and the FBI when Norman tried to obtain the contents of Tsuru's library, and asked the RCMP for their information on Herbert Norman. The news about Halperin's address book was an embarrassment for the RCMP, as it admitted sometime later: "We cannot feel too satisfied over the fact that Norman's name was not picked out of the Halperin notebook earlier. . . . The only thing that can be said in explaining the failure to process the Halperin diary names sooner is the bulk involved. . . . The Halperin notebook was one of the many Royal Commission exhibits, which totaled 601 and filled 12 filing drawers. Index-carding of all the individuals mentioned was not finally completed until November 1951."[34]

∽

The RCMP hastily put together a report, dated October 17, 1950, and sent it off to the FBI.[35] It would seal Norman's fate, because it gave the FBI information that could be used to suggest he was a Soviet spy. In addition to the address book, the RCMP referred to three other pieces of evidence that raised questions about Norman's loyalty. First, that Norman's name had also appeared in the address book of Frank Park, a suspected member of the Canadian Communist Party, the LPP, and a well-known figure in Ottawa. Second, that one of the RCMP's undercover agents in Toronto (Pat Walsh) had reported in February 1940 that a Professor Herbert Norman, who had taught at McMaster University in Canada, was a member of the Communist

Party. (It was noted, however, that Norman had never been a member of the faculty at McMaster.)

The third piece of evidence, which would be cited again and again to demonstrate Norman's guilt, was Gouzenko's testimony to the Canadian Royal Commission back in 1946 about a man named Norman. In the full record of the testimony before the commission, which remained classified until 1982, Gouzenko had actually made two references to a "Norman," but in both cases he was talking about a man named Norman Freed, who lived in Toronto and was possibly working for the NKVD in 1944. Gouzenko recalled that the GRU in Moscow had asked Zabotin if he knew a man named Norman. Zabotin surmised that the person in question was Freed, who was running in municipal elections in Toronto and had been photographed for a Russian newspaper in Canada. Aware that Freed might be working for NKVD *rezident* Pavlov, Zabotin made inquiries. According to Gouzenko, Pavlov responded, "Don't touch Norman Freed. We work with him." Zabotin then sent a telegram to Moscow GRU headquarters saying, "The Norman about whom you ask we think is Norman Freed and Neighbors [NKVD] are busy with him."[36]

The RCMP report summarized Gouzenko's statements without making it clear that Pavlov and Zabotin were talking about Norman Freed. The RCMP concluded, "It would appear that NORMAN is the surname of a person in whom the Russian Intelligence Service had an interest." In a subsequent interview with the RCMP, Norman, who was unaware that Gouzenko's testimony had implicated him, openly admitted that he had known both Zabotin and Pavlov. They were all diplomats in Ottawa during the war and attended the same official gatherings and private parties, along with other dignitaries. Norman recalled getting into an argument with Pavlov concerning Russia's views of the two world wars. Asked about Norman many years later, Pavlov remembered him well, adding that Norman had even given him a copy of a paper he had written on Japanese Samurai. "But," Pavlov added, "I was not recruiting him, and as far as I know he had never been a Soviet agent."[37]

Incredibly, the flimsy and largely false evidence in the RCMP report – two address books containing Norman's name, a ten-year-old accusation that Norman (erroneously a "professor" at McMaster University) was a communist in 1936, and a misquoted piece of testimony from Gouzenko – resulted in Norman's immediate recall from Tokyo. Norman faced an awkward interview in Ottawa on October 24, 1950, with Norman Robertson and George Glazebrook, who informed him gravely that Halperin's notebook contained seven different entries with references to him. Norman assured them that he knew Halperin only as a former college friend. He also "categorically" denied that he had ever been a member of the Communist Party. His active interest in Marxism and his contacts with communists, he said, had been limited to the period of his years as an undergraduate student. When Glazebrook asked Norman why he had failed to inform the Department of External Affairs of his acquaintance with Halperin when the latter was publicly implicated in the Gouzenko spy case, Norman responded that he had worried about this problem a great deal, but decided that he himself should not raise the issue. Norman offered to resign from External Affairs, but he was placed on leave instead.[38]

On December 1, T.M. Guernsey of the RCMP sent a follow-up report to the FBI with the final conclusions of its "intensive investigation" of Norman, which included the interview with him.[39] It should have superseded the earlier RCMP report, because it was more thorough and based on a better understanding of the facts. And it exonerated Norman on several key points. Specifically, when Norman asked the FBI for the contents of Tsuru's library, he was not lying when he said he was representing the interests of the Canadian government: "It has been confirmed that NORMAN was, at the time, on special work for the Canadian Government which was of interest also to the United States authorities. The library of Tsuru's would have been a valuable asset for this specific task." Yes, as Norman admitted, his interest in the library was twofold, both for his diplomatic and his scholarly work. But the collection of books that interested him most was written in Japanese and mainly concerned with Japanese history, not Marxist propaganda.

As for Norman's name appearing in Halperin's address book, the RCMP went to great lengths to show that Norman had no idea that Halperin was a communist and was taken by surprise when he learned of Halperin's involvement in the espionage case. Norman and Halperin had few common interests, the report said, and were never close friends: "We feel satisfied that Norman was quite innocent of Halperin's covert political and espionage activity." The appearance of Norman's name in Frank Park's address book was also explained in Norman's favor. Questioned about Park, Norman claimed that he knew little about him and his political ideology. The RCMP believed him: "We are of the opinion that NORMAN is sincere in the explanation of his relationship with Park."

The RCMP was still of the view that the "Norman" Gouzenko had discussed in his Royal Commission testimony was Herbert Norman. But its considered opinion was that the Russians knew very little about him and had merely intended to cultivate him as a potential source of information rather than engage him in espionage. Finally, the allegation against Norman that had been made by an RCMP undercover agent in 1940 was now entirely discounted: "The information given is one of either mistaken identity or unfounded rumour by an unidentified sub-source. Of the numerous points supplied at the time, the majority have been absolutely determined to be in error. . . . The source does not recall the matter. We have therefore deleted the reference insofar as NORMAN is concerned."

In sum, the RCMP concluded, "Our investigation, while centered on the information previously supplied you, extended as it progressed. However, there has been no evidence uncovered which would indicate disloyalty on the part of NORMAN. The worst possible conclusion we can arrive at is the very apparent naïveté in his relationship with his fellow man." As a result, the RCMP was giving Norman a security clearance.

It is possible that the RCMP wrote this report reluctantly, following the advice of the Department of External Affairs. Nonetheless, it was passed on to FBI Ottawa liaison Glen Bethel who forwarded Hoover the five-page, top secret RCMP memorandum exonerating

Norman on December 7, 1950. In his covering letter, Bethel observed, "It will be noted that the RCMP have carefully examined all the information that is on record pertaining to Norman."[40] Significantly, Bethel also stressed to Hoover that the RCMP requested the FBI not disseminate the report outside the bureau, a stipulation that was apparently omitted on the earlier report.

But Hoover had already sent the first, highly damaging RCMP report to the U.S. Department of the Army. In early November, the report reached Intelligence Headquarters in the U.S. Far East Command in Japan, and Norman's nemesis, General Willoughby, soon got a hold of it. Willoughby used the report, along with FBI materials, to prepare a brief on Norman. He also took the RCMP report with him to Washington when he testified before SISS hearings on the IPR in August 1951 and handed it over to the subcommittee. Because the second RCMP report on Norman, which exonerated him, carried the caveat that it should not be distributed outside the FBI, Hoover never released it to the Department of the Army. Instead, he let the preliminary report stand.[41]

Hoover knew full well that the preliminary RCMP report on Norman would reach the hands of SISS investigators if he sent it to the Department of the Army. In the interests of setting the record straight, he could have requested permission from Canadian authorities to pass on the more accurate second report on Norman to the Department of the Army, so that it would also reach SISS. But he chose not to, apparently because he was not persuaded by the RCMP report that Norman was innocent. Hoover wanted to avoid any suspicion that his agency was involved in SISS investigations, so the FBI would not have passed on the RCMP report directly to SISS. But in fact the FBI and McCarran's subcommittee had established a secret liaison. According to McCarran's biographer: "The FBI would act as a kind of private detective agency for SISS, investigating suspects and furnishing leaks, while the committee would launder information for the bureau, publicly pillorying suspected subversives against whom a court case could not be made."[42]

Willoughby himself declined to comment on Norman when he testified to SISS, apparently because it would be a breach of diplomacy.

But some days later, a Professor Karl Wittfogel appeared before the subcommittee with new allegations. Wittfogel was a German-born professor and an expert on China, who joined the Communist Party in 1920 and fled Germany when the Nazis came to power. At Columbia University he continued his communist activities and reportedly taught young students who were part of an under-ground "cell." Wittfogel "saw the light," however, and when he renounced communism he became the darling of the anti-communists.[43]

Wittfogel testified that in 1938 Norman was a member of a communist study group organized by a graduate student at Columbia University named Moses Finkelstein. The testimony had obvious inaccuracies. Wittfogel recalled that Norman was studying at the time in the Japanese Department at Columbia University, when in fact Norman was finishing up a Harvard Ph.D. Second, and more important, both Norman and Finkelstein denied ever having met one another. But, as with other witnesses, once something was said in front of SISS, it stuck.[44]

Meanwhile, the FBI was vigorously pursuing its own investigation of Norman, which included an intensive search for a paper he had allegedly presented in 1937 at one of Tsuru's informal Harvard study groups. According to the voluminous FBI file on Herbert Norman, agents spent days at libraries during the latter part of 1950 and early 1951, fruitlessly trying to find a copy of "American Imperialism," by Herbert Norman.[45] Given the title, they reasoned, it would provide documentary evidence of Norman's subversive views. It seems they did not realize that Norman's paper would not reach libraries unless it was published.

~

Norman's name surfaced once more in the SISS hearings on the IPR. It appeared that in 1936, Norman had been on the provisional organization committee of the pro-communist Canadian Friends of the Chinese People. The RCMP, when it heard, was worried: "While Norman denied all the serious implications [sic] directed against him, it would seem there are far too many from various sources to entirely discount them all." The RCMP called him in for several interviews in early 1952. Asked if he had ever been a member of the Communist Party, Norman hedged: "In my Cambridge time I came close to it and if I had stayed there another year I might have." He also admitted that he had a "slight connection" with the League Against War and Fascism in 1936 and that he knew it was a communist organization. In a separate interview, Norman told George Glazebrook, who was responsible for security for External Affairs, that he could accurately have been described as a communist during his second year at Cambridge.[46]

Glazebrook and External Affairs chief Lester Pearson acknowledged that Norman had been vague when he was first questioned about his involvement with communism as a student, but they were not prepared to dismiss him from his foreign-service post simply because of this "blemish" on his past. Interestingly, they bolstered their argument by citing the British example. Glazebrook noted in a memorandum to the RCMP that the British "do not regard communism in a Cambridge undergraduate as necessarily a continuing risk." Despite the fact that Nunn May, Burgess, Maclean, and Philby had all been communists at Cambridge, neither the British nor the Canadians were prepared to assume that this was an automatic stepping stone to espionage. Shortly thereafter, Pearson told the RCMP that the Department of External Affairs had examined the evidence and reached the conclusion that, although Norman was a believer in the communist doctrine during his time at Cambridge, "he had later changed his opinion" and was "a loyal Canadian and an efficient and trustworthy member of the Department."[47]

Pearson, to his credit, had formed his own conclusion, based on the evidence available to him, that Norman was a devoted and talented Canadian diplomat, not a spy. But given the mood of Canada's southern neighbor, Pearson's simple decision was a courageous act. Indeed Pearson realized additional allegations against Norman could potentially emerge. The naming of names in Washington had become a frenzy, and Canadians, Pearson and Norman in particular, were on SISS's "hit list." In June 1953, a reluctant Pearson took the unusual step of appointing Herbert Norman as Canadian High

Commissioner to New Zealand, where he would be safely out of the way, but with his diplomatic skills vastly underutilized. For the next three years, things were relatively quiet as far as questions about Norman's loyalty were concerned – so quiet that Pearson felt comfortable moving Norman to a more prominent post.

In August 1956, Norman arrived in Cairo as Canadian ambassador to Egypt, just as the Suez crisis was heating up. He threw himself into his new responsibilities, working fourteen-hour days and sending "brilliant" analytical dispatches back to Canada. By October, the Egyptian blockade of the Suez Canal was threatening to boil over into war, with Britain, France, and Israel attacking Egypt. Lester Pearson resolved the crisis by getting all sides to agree to allow a UN peacekeeping force into the Sinai. Norman was a key player in this remarkable enterprise, managing to persuade President Nasser of Egypt to accept Canadians as part of the UN forces on Egyptian soil, despite their association with the British Commonwealth. The Canadian initiative marked the beginning of UN peacekeeping efforts for decades to come and earned Pearson the Nobel Peace Prize in 1957. In awarding him this honor, the Nobel Committee said he had "saved the world." Herbert Norman deserved much of the credit.[48]

Whatever Norman's accomplishments, SISS, still chaired by Senator Jenner with counsel Robert Morris running the show, had its own agenda. Senator McCarran had died in late 1954 (being replaced on SISS by Senator James Eastland) and McCarthy had been censured by the Senate. But the McCarthy era was not yet over. As Norman's biographer observed, "Success for peace in the Middle East meant nothing in Cold War Washington. Even as Norman was meeting with Nasser, Senate McCarthyites were reintroducing his name into SISS proceedings. They knew nothing of his efforts in Egypt, nor would they have cared if they had known. He was a one-dimensional man in Washington – he was a communist."[49]

On March 12, 1957, John Emmerson, the State Department official who had worked with Norman for several months in Japan after the war, was called to testify before SISS. Emmerson and his wife had recently spent an evening with the Normans in Beirut, where Emmerson was stationed. Ever since Emmerson and Norman had carried out General MacArthur's orders to free Japanese prisoners of war, arousing the ire of General Willoughby, Emmerson had been under a shadow, his career at the State Department threatened by accusations that he was Red. In 1952, he had been subjected to a State Department "Loyalty Board" hearing and, perhaps unaware of Norman's own troubles on the communist issue, had requested (and received) from Norman an affidavit in his support.[50]

Emmerson's testimony was favorable to Norman, in that he stated repeatedly that he saw no evidence that Norman was a communist. Although he had testified in executive session, which was secret, the subcommittee released his testimony to the press two days later. This might have been seen as an exoneration of Norman, except that SISS counsel Morris introduced into the testimony Karl Wittfogel's six-year-old allegations about Norman. More importantly, Morris included in the release the "security report" on Norman produced under Willoughby's direction some years back, which contained the RCMP allegations. The Canadians raised a storm of protests, pointing out that the allegations were based on old charges that had been refuted (which was true), but SISS was not to be dissuaded from its campaign against Norman.

Emmerson, who on March 12 had emphasized more than once that he had no doubt about Norman's loyalty, was criticized by a State Department security officer for being "less than forthcoming" in his testimony before the subcommittee.[51] With his career at the State Department on the line, Emmerson requested another appearance before the subcommittee to provide further details about Norman. At a second executive session, on March 21, Emmerson came up with something that SISS could use to inflict further damage. His statement was nuanced and subtle, but once again raised doubts about Norman's political convictions after he had become a diplomat:

> I can recall one conversation, which for some reason has stuck in my mind, which I had in the meantime forgotten. We were interviewing a Japanese, and – I cannot remember

his name – I believe he was a Socialist . . . he was giving us a history of the Japanese Socialist movement and its various factions and the personalities involved. And I recall at one point in the conversation that Mr. Norman made some statement which appeared to agree with the general thesis which this man was proposing . . . I know that it struck me, because it never occurred to me, in any interview with a member of any political party, to express any view whatsoever concerning what he was saying.[52]

SISS released Emmerson's testimony publicly on March 28, 1957. Norman apparently did not see either of Emmerson's statements before the committee. But he read enough in the press to know that what was said by his friend and former colleague, whom he himself had defended in 1952, did not bode well.

Making the situation even more difficult for Norman to endure was the fact that, on March 26–27 his old friend Shigeto Tsuru, at the time a visiting professor at Harvard, was called to testify before SISS. Although Tsuru swore he had never been a member of the Communist Party, he did confess to having associated with a large number of people with leftist tendencies during his student days in the United States. Among them was Herbert Norman. Tsuru told Senate investigators that Norman was part of a Marxist study group at Harvard that met several times in the spring of 1937. Tsuru's testimony received little attention in the United States, but it made the headlines in Japan and it is quite likely that Norman heard about it.[53]

The pressure became too intense for Norman. After being hounded for seven years about his youthful involvement with communism in the 1930s, and facing the prospect of more inquisitions, he finally gave up. On the warm and sunny morning of April 4, 1957, Norman got up early, said good-bye to his wife, and walked from his Cairo residence to a tall building down the street that looked over the Nile. He took the elevator to the top floor, then climbed the stairway to the roof terrace. After removing his coat, his glasses, and his watch, Norman flung himself off the terrace to his death.[54]

The public uproar in Canada following Norman's suicide was evidence of the deep gulf that now divided the Canadians and Americans on the issue of communist subversion. Cries of indignation erupted in the House of Commons and in the Canadian press over the slandering of Norman by the American witch-hunters. Students at the University of Toronto burned effigies of McCarthy, Eastland, and Morris, and Canada's ambassador to Washington handed the State Department a formal note of protest, stating that his government was reexamining its procedures for exchange of security data with the United States. But the red hunters in Washington were unrepentant. On April 11, senators Eastland and Jenner issued a statement saying they had cleared the subcommittee's release of information about Norman with the State Department and that the FBI had corroborated the accuracy of the release. Hoover, who always wanted the FBI to remain in the background, was unhappy: "This injection of the F.B.I. is most undesirable," he observed to his subordinates.[55]

Not all Canadians were outraged. Pat Walsh, the former RCMP undercover agent whose muddled and later discredited denunciation of Norman in 1940 had helped persuade the FBI that he was a spy, was one Canadian who approved of the American attacks on Norman. On April 6, he wrote a long congratulatory letter to Robert Morris, who, as it turned out, was a friend. Walsh was secretary-treasurer (and perhaps the only member) of a so-called Pan-Canadian Anti-Communist Secretariat. "Needless to say," Walsh stressed to Morris, "I was not swept away by the emotionalism and outbursts of indignation created by well-meaning but ill-informed persons in high places. I only too vividly recalled the parallel case of Harry Dexter White (an IPR friend of Norman's incidentally) and the almost unanimous defense of Alger Hiss in the early days. . . ." Walsh was wrong about White. He and Norman had never met. And much of the evidence against Norman that he went on to discuss was a distorted rehash of what had already come out publicly. But his words must have been reassuring to Morris nonetheless: "We believe that your subcommittee and the House Un-American Activities Committee has the right to denounce any Canadian Communist whose activities constitute a threat to the internal security of the USA. We are of the opinion that the Canadian public will eventually be grateful to the USA anti-subversive committee."[56]

Not surprisingly, SISS also received strong support from the right-wing press in America. In a nationwide radio broadcast on April 7, 1957, conservative journalist George Sokolsky linked Herbert Norman with State Department officials who were responsible for the "failed American policy" in the Far East, including the loss of the Korean War. Some of these same men, he alleged, were then transferred to the Middle East, where they were giving the government equally bad advice on Egypt. "Was it an accident that this transfer took place or are these men deliberately causing the West to lose in its struggle with Soviet Russia? I must regard the suicide of Herbert Norman, the Canadian Ambassador to Egypt, as a frightful act of conscience by one who was engaged in the Far East when permanent historic errors were made there and who was posted in Egypt when permanent historic errors were made there."[57]

Several weeks later, Robert Morris received a written message about the Norman case from his staff assistant, Bob McManus, who passed on his views as to why Norman had risen to such prominence in the Canadian diplomatic corps. Why, McManus wondered, was Norman protected when, like Soviet spies Guy Burgess and Donald Maclean, "he was doing such blatantly unethical things as he did at Cambridge [Massachusetts] when he tried to take possession of Tsuru's incriminating Communist documents . . . ?" In answer to his own question, McManus said it was because he was part of a team of bright young men – which included Norman Robertson, Lester Pearson, and others – who were "violently anti-American and violently pink."[58]

Although the FBI was doing its utmost to distance itself from the Norman affair, it closely followed the Canadian reaction to the case. Writing to Hoover, the FBI liaison in Ottawa, Glen Bethel, noted that most Canadians "are pleased to see Canada 'telling off' the

United States. Canada, with a population one tenth of the United States and a 3,500-mile common border, is affected by the United States in just about every phase of its life, whether it be economic, political, or cultural. Many Canadians, even though the majority are our friends, resent this influence, and this has been increasingly more apparent in recent years as Canada is developing as a more important country in international matters and as a spirit of nationalism and of national pride develops." Bethel went on to observe, however, that the Conservative Opposition, which would soon be challenging the Liberals in an election, would attack them for having retained Norman in a high position, given the serious charges raised against him.[59] In other words, despite the efforts of Pearson and his fellow Liberals, the Norman case and the issue of communism would become a political football in Canada, just as it was in the United States.

Lester Pearson had put himself in an awkward situation. His earlier public statements had suggested that Norman had not at any time been a communist, when in fact he had. Also, it soon emerged that much of the "slander" against Norman had emanated originally from the RCMP. Of course Pearson had no way of knowing that the RCMP had passed a report to the FBI, which had in turn disseminated it further. But all of this had occurred under the Liberal government's watch. As for Norman's past, Pearson was forced to respond to the information that was being cited from the RCMP report on Norman. He acknowledged in the House of Commons on April 12 that Norman had "associated with communists in his college years."[60]

But the charges against Norman in his student days were not, in Pearson's view, the real issue. His own department had already deemed that aspect of Norman's life to be irrelevant. In a letter to the *Globe and Mail*, Pearson pointed out that the Senate subcommittee's charges against Norman were not only about his former associations as a student, but also included claims that Norman remained a communist and was, as such, disloyal to his government. "This," Pearson wrote, "remains both the basic injustice in this case and an intolerable and public interference in our affairs by a legislative committee of a foreign country."[61] Pearson was of course correct, but the problem was he had not made this clear when he first defended Norman publicly in 1951. As the Montreal *Gazette* pointed out, Pearson's forthright words came too late: "The tragedy is that Mr. Pearson, by giving Dr. Norman this kind of defense in 1951, was not settling the matter; rather, he may have increased the probability that it would again be renewed."[62]

~

In notes written to his family and to the Department of External Affairs before he died, Norman did not say specifically why he decided to take his own life, but he did assert his innocence and express doubts that he would ever be exonerated. Norman had been terribly overworked and was suffering from depression, so there were doubtless several factors behind his suicide. But the timing suggests that, at the very least, the SISS publicity was the last straw.

SISS did not see it that way. An in-house memorandum, probably written by Robert Morris, read, "Just about everybody *except Norman* is holding us responsible for Norman's death. He never charged us with that. He did not say in his suicide notes, so far as we know, that the Internal Security Subcommittee had anything to do with his suicide. . . . Why should everyone jump to the conclusion that the Internal Security Subcommittee was responsible for the suicide? The Subcommittee has been charged with 'rehashing old charges.' Why would a man commit suicide over the rehashing of old charges with respect to which he had been cleared by his government six years earlier, and after the reaffirmation of that government's confidence in him?"[63]

The unremorseful and defensive tone of this note is hardly surprising. Five years earlier, Senator McCarran had learned of the suicide of Abraham Feller, general counsel at the UN, who was caught in the middle of an SISS campaign against communists in his organization. McCarran's response: "If Feller's conscience was clear, he had no reason to suffer from what he expected of our committee."[64]

But McCarran and his colleagues knew full well that a clear conscience could not put rumors to rest. Once allegations were in the public domain they took on a life of their own. Even Elizabeth

Bentley's blatantly false statements about Lester Pearson were repeated enough times that they gained some credibility. It may be true that if Pearson had been more forthcoming when the allegations about Norman began surfacing he would have quelled further accusations. It is hard to say what SISS would have done had the Canadian government said outright in 1951 that, yes, Norman had been a communist but was one no longer and that therefore the matter was closed. The committee members in the U.S. Senate would probably have been satisfied in that case with a ritual public recantation from Norman and asked him to name names, as several of his former associates did. However, this is doubtless a route Norman would have been highly reluctant to take.

In Pearson's defense, Norman did a lot of hedging on the extent of his communist associations during his student days. In fact, it never was clear whether Norman had a formal relationship with the Communist Party or was simply a student member of the pro-communist Socialist Society at Cambridge. For Pearson to have made a definitive statement about Norman in 1951, he would have needed an accurate picture of his involvement with communism, which Norman never gave.

Near the end of his life, Norman reportedly told a colleague that he thought Alger Hiss had been framed, and "that his only mistake had been that he said he didn't know Whittaker Chambers and he couldn't go back on that statement."[65] In fact, Hiss did go back on the statement in an indirect way, admitting before the Grand Jury in 1948 that he had known Chambers, but under a different name. Similarly, Norman retreated from his initial statements about his student days and, by the end of his interviews with the RCMP and External Affairs in 1952, had all but confessed that he was a communist at Cambridge. For both Hiss and Norman, their admissions came too late and too reluctantly.

Chapter 10

TRAITORS AND SPIES

Defect, v.: To desert a cause, country, etc., esp. in order to adopt another
Traitor, n.: A person who betrays his country by violating his allegiance
Spy, n.: A person employed by a government to obtain secret information on intelli-
gence about another country

Random House Dictionary of the English Language

Igor Gouzenko did not like being called a defector. It implied
that he was a traitor. Instead, he insisted, he should be called an
"escaper." As he saw it, someone who had run away from the
Soviets was not a traitor or a defector because the Soviet Union was
an evil state. A traitor was someone who betrayed trust or violated
an allegiance. How could one be accused of betraying a country
where there was no freedom and whose government did nothing but
lie to its citizens and make their lives miserable? He had a point.
Who would consider the generals who plotted to kill Hitler in 1943
traitors to their country? Without such people, how would democ-
racies ever defeat tyrannies?

Following this logic, when *Newsweek* magazine published an
article in February 1964 that referred to him as a defector, Gouzenko
went straight to a lawyer. As a journalist who was acquainted with
Gouzenko remarked, he felt that defector "was not a nice word. . . .
Mr. Gouzenko felt that from our side – our side being Canada, the
Allies, the United States – we should not be looking at him as a bad

man, as a traitor, which the Russians might want to look at him as, but in effect as a hero." Gouzenko also objected to *Newsweek*'s suggestion that defectors were psychologically troubled. He refused to settle when the magazine offered him one thousand dollars in damages and ended up getting nothing.[1]

Gouzenko was even more outraged when he was referred to as a spy. In March 1966, he appeared on a nationwide Canadian television show, *This Hour Has Seven Days*, with his trademark pillow-case over his head. The topic was Soviet spying techniques, an issue on which Gouzenko was a professed expert. He was anxious and defensive from the moment he appeared, objecting when he saw someone taking still photographs of him. Then, one of the hosts, Laurier LaPierre, asked in the course of the discussion, "Is that part of your experience as a spy?" Gouzenko bristled: "Don't use such horrible words. Don't forget, I exposed Soviet spy ring. Don't call me that."[2] After the taping of the program, Gouzenko threatened to sue the Canadian Broadcasting Corporation for libel. It was a good thing for him that he did not. As the person at the Soviet Embassy responsible for encoding GRU messages sent to Moscow, he had been a key participant in Soviet espionage operations. In other words, he had been a spy.

Gouzenko's lawsuit against *Newsweek* was one of a string of libel cases that he initiated over the years. Because of Canada's stringent libel laws, which favored the plaintiff, he was often successful. In Canada, it was, and still is, possible to be sued for writing anything that damages a person's reputation. It is not necessary for the plaintiff to demonstrate malicious intent, and the onus is on the defendant to prove that what he or she wrote is true.[3] Shortly after Gouzenko sued *Newsweek*, his lawyer filed a suit against *Maclean's* magazine for an article in which Gouzenko was discussed. Gouzenko was particularly offended by a passage that suggested he was no longer in danger of retaliation from the Soviets and was using the threat as a way of getting the Mounties to do household chores for him: "The Mounties soon noticed (or thought they did) that Gouzenko's fears for his own safety became particularly acute when it was time to put on the storm windows or the roof needed mending." After a lengthy and costly legal battle, *Maclean's* paid Gouzenko seventy-five hundred dollars in damages.[4]

Gouzenko also initiated litigation against several authors, including Frank Rasky, who wrote a 1958 book called *Gay Canadian Rogues*. The book (published before "gay" meant homosexual) contained eleven "true crime" stories. One featured the cipher clerk Gouzenko, who was depicted as a hero. Gouzenko nonetheless took offense at the lighthearted references to him and the implication that he was a rogue. He managed not only to get fifteen thousand dollars from the publishers, but also to have the book withdrawn from stores.[5]

Another successful libel suit was against David Martin, who wrote *Wilderness of Mirrors*, a book about the CIA and defectors, which appeared in 1980. Martin's skepticism toward defectors in general and Gouzenko in particular offended Gouzenko. Martin, echoing the *Newsweek* article, suggested that defectors tended to have psychological troubles and, using Gouzenko as an example, drinking problems. Martin also questioned Gouzenko's motives for defecting. As a result, Harper & Row, Martin's publishers, had to buy space in the *Globe and Mail* to apologize "for one short passage which Mr. Gouzenko has found objectionable." Gouzenko received ten thousand dollars in damages.[6]

Gouzenko later sued well-known author and journalist June Callwood over a book called *Portrait of Canada*, a social history, which contained only a couple of paragraphs about him. He didn't like it that Callwood referred to his behavior when he was seeking asylum as erratic and unstable. Callwood's publishers were forced to withhold the paperback edition of her book. Fortunately for Callwood, Gouzenko died before the case went to court. A dead person cannot be libeled, so the case was dropped.[7]

Journalist John Sawatsky was another target, for a book about the RCMP called *Men in the Shadows*, published in 1980 by Doubleday. The book, which included a chapter on the Gouzenko case, was selling well until Gouzenko registered his legal complaint: Sawatsky had defamed him. The planned paperback edition of Sawatsky's book was immediately canceled and Sawatsky, a freelancer, had to spend all his time on his defense. "Win or lose," Sawatsky said at the time, "any thought of having any semblance of economic viability to maintain myself as an author is out the window."[8]

In fairness to Gouzenko, impartial observers would likely conclude that what Sawatsky wrote about him was defamatory. He portrayed Gouzenko as a cold-blooded opportunist who sought celebrity status by exploiting people. And he included quotes like this one from a disgruntled Mountie: "'Gouzenko was not a true lover of liberty. He was a thoroughly ignorant Russian peasant who had no connection with the Russian Intelligence Service except as a cipher clerk. I have known him for some time and feel he is an unsavory character.'" Gouzenko had a good case, and if he had not died before it went to trial, he probably would have won.[9]

Sawatsky meanwhile, as part of his defense, set about interviewing everyone he could find who knew Gouzenko. As he delved deeper into the Gouzenko story, he began to realize that what the public knew about Gouzenko was more legend than fact. Sawatsky also came to understand that he had misjudged Gouzenko, that he had not sued for the money or publicity but because he wanted to maintain his standing in history. He wanted people to think of him as a hero. What emerged from Sawatsky's interviews with close to 150 people, published as an oral history, was that Gouzenko could not easily be summed up. He was a complex man, a blend of admirable qualities and deep faults, a person who was revered and scorned. He was both a victim of his fate and an engineer of his own demise. There were no easy answers to unravel the mystery of who he was.[10]

After Gouzenko's 1954 testimony before senators Jenner and McCarran, and his subsequent television interview with American journalist Drew Pearson, he had said virtually all he could say about Soviet espionage in the West. But Gouzenko managed to remain in the limelight: he became a best-selling author. Gouzenko's success as a novelist came as a surprise to everyone. His 1948 autobiography, a workman-like, uninspiring, and largely ghostwritten account of his life before his defection, had not sold well, although it ended up being profitable because it was made into a movie. Initially, Gouzenko had trouble finding an American publisher for his lengthy novel, *The Fall of a Titan*, which was translated from Russian by Mervyn Black. But after revisions and cuts, the manuscript was accepted by W.W. Norton and published in the spring of 1954. The book was a huge success and was translated into more than forty languages. It was a Book-of-the-Month Club selection and remained on the *New York Times* best-seller list for months. The *Toronto Daily Star* called *The Fall of a Titan* a "panoramic novel . . . Tolstoyan in its sweep," and it received the Governor General's Award in Canada for the best novel of 1954.[11]

The story centers around the figure of Mikhail Gorin, a famous Soviet writer who bears close resemblance to the real-life Maksim Gorky. Stalin and his men decide that Gorin has become a threat, and they engage the NKVD, though a professor at the University of Rostov, to bring about his downfall. Gouzenko's three-hundred-thousand-word epic, rich with engaging characters, plots, and counterplots, was a remarkable achievement. As Granville Hicks observed in the *New York Times*, the author was exceptionally skillful at handling a complicated narrative: "Involved as the story is, the reader never loses its thread, but goes on, always more and more absorbed, to the explosive climax."[12]

One might ask how a young man in his early thirties, with no experience at writing and little formal education in the arts, could have produced such a remarkable work. Some people even suggested that Gouzenko did not write the book himself. But according to the recollections of Gouzenko's American editor, George Brockway, this was clearly not the case. When Brockway met with Gouzenko to go over the final manuscript, Anna, "an extraordinarily pretty young woman," came along. She, it turns out, had been working alongside her husband, helping to transcribe the drafts. According to Brockway, Anna brought several suitcases that contained the manuscript in all its stages, "from germinal idea and several false starts, through several longhand drafts in Russian and two drafts of the English translation by Mervyn Black, to the final revised, corrected and re-corrected translation. It made a lot of manuscript – probably two million words from first to last – and the sheer physical labor of putting them down on paper is staggering. Mrs. Gouzenko remarked that she often had difficulty in getting to take time out to mow the lawn."[13]

In *The Fall of a Titan*, Gouzenko managed to portray for a Western audience the essence of the corrupt and immoral Soviet society in a literary form that was not only readable, but gripping. As Granville Hicks observed, "It is Mr. Gouzenko's ability to create this atmosphere – the anguish of the masses, the ruthlessness of the privileged few, the universal terror – that gives his book its over-whelming plausibility."[14] Where did this striking talent come from? In a subsequent article for the *Times*, Gouzenko explained that his creativity and his love of literature came from his grandmother, even though she could not read or write. As a young boy he listened to the poetry she composed aloud, and to the Russian folktales she narrated for him, "putting her whole soul into them." Gouzenko became an avid reader and devoured the Russian classics. "The public library became my favorite resort," he recalled. "I used to run there with palpitating heart and came away loaded with books." He learned to write by following the examples of his favorite authors, Tolstoy, Dostoevsky, Gogol, and Chekhov.[15]

Gouzenko's description of Soviet life under Stalin during the purges was so realistic that it almost seemed autobiographical. Yet he had been only in his teens at the time the story took place. His memory of this period and his ability to recreate it for the reader was nothing short of astonishing. As Brockway expressed it, "The most startling thing about [Gouzenko] is his youth. I was prepared with the knowledge that he was born in 1919, but still I was startled . . . his novel, all the action of which takes place in 1937 or earlier, has such exceptional 'presence' that one feels the author must have been a participant in the scene he describes, and so one expects him to be fifteen or twenty years older than he is."[16] In sum, *The Fall of a Titan* was the work of a young genius, a writer with great promise.

Shortly after the book appeared, Tania Long of the *New York Times* interviewed Gouzenko. Long was struck by "his intensity, and the restless energy which impels him to keep moving, even if only within the confines of a living room. . . . His face, his hands, his body are constantly in motion. . . . The question arises – how can a man of this type devote himself so painstakingly for four years to a book like 'The Fall of a Titan'? . . . Obviously beneath all this restlessness and nervous energy there is a drive as steady and unwavering as the powerful motors of a six-engine bomber."[17]

When Long asked him about his future plans, Gouzenko said that he wanted, above all, to be a good writer: "My immediate ambition you might say is to write my next book in half the time I took on my first. I think I have learned a lot, and what is most important is that I now have confidence in myself. Can you imagine how it was for four years, writing away day after day, with the feeling that maybe I was completely wrong and no one to encourage me?" Perhaps Gouzenko's self doubts during these four years were not just about his ability to write a great novel. He seems also to have been questioning his decision to abandon his homeland. That he was struggling with this issue is clear from the topic of his next book. Gouzenko told Long it would be about the impact of the West on a Soviet man who left his country, "his struggle with his conscience as he begins to break away from his beliefs, and the terrible choice he is faced with in the end – to flee to freedom and thus cause the death of a close relative held as a hostage in Russia or forever to submit to a regime he has learned to detest."[18]

Gouzenko and his wife had made exactly that terrible choice, and it was a decision they had to live with for the rest of their lives. It cannot have been easy. Anna recalled later that, when her husband first broached the idea of defecting, she asked him, "What would happen to all our relatives?" Gouzenko, who feared he was already in trouble with Soviet authorities, replied, "Have you got a guarantee that when we come back we will see our relatives? We could be sent right away to Siberia and . . . our relatives will [be] sent on the other side of Siberia and we would never meet." Anna attempted to convince herself that her family had escaped punishment because, as she said, her father was a valuable scientist, and he met Igor only twice: "His guilt is nil and his association with Igor is very short. He didn't marry me off, I did it all myself. So to Igor my father is . . . no relation."[19] But at some point she learned that the Soviet government thought otherwise.

Despite this cloud over their lives, Gouzenko was full of optimism about his writing career when Long interviewed him. He had already completed the first chapter of his new book, he told her, and perhaps he might get to the point where he could write one book each year. But his plans never came to fruition. He worked on *Ocean of Time* for over twenty years, producing enough pages, as Anna said, to fill three books. He would often get up to write in the middle of the night. Igor developed diabetes, started to go blind in the 1960s, and eventually he lost his sight completely. He then wrote on a braille typewriter or dictated the novel to Anna. Anna became increasingly frustrated. They were desperate for the money from his book. The manuscript was far too long and needed to be cut. Yet her husband just kept writing and writing. He never managed to finish.[20]

Anna put much store in Igor's next book. After all, reviewers of *The Fall of a Titan* had compared its author with Tolstoy. He was certainly similar to Tolstoy in temperament. Like Tolstoy, he had a tremendous ego, was driven by a sense of mission, and tormented by the need to find meaning in his life. Both were obsessed with an idea – Tolstoy with Christianity, and Gouzenko with the struggle against communism. Both gambled with their money and both, by all accounts, were difficult to live with. Their wives were long-suffering.

Although Igor adored Anna and she worshipped him, Anna's life with her husband – as attested to by her lengthy interview with John Sawatsky in 1984 – was a struggle. Gouzenko, who was at home most of the time, was volatile and authoritarian. He had frequent outbursts of violence, which began shortly after his defection. Sometimes he would lose his temper over something small and strike Anna. At least twice, Anna went to the RCMP with bruises on her body. She allowed that he did this a lot: "When he would get mad, he would slap me real well." But he would always feel guilty and apologize, and she would always forgive him. The only time

Anna considered divorce was when her husband had a fling with a young office worker, but she apparently put a stop to it.[21]

In addition to acting as her husband's secretary, copyist, and chauffeur, Anna gave birth to eight children, made all their clothes, ran the household (or tried to), and engaged in several entrepreneurial ventures, none of which, including the purchase of the farm and some butcher shops, proved profitable. Life in the Gouzenko home was chaotic. According to a former Mountie, at mealtime "everybody helped themselves. . . . If they opened a can of stuff they didn't like they would just leave it there. So you would see on the table several opened cans sitting around. There seemed to be no regular mealtime. There was an awful lot of waste. A great deal of stuff must have been thrown out that way. She did try. She did try. It got out of control as far as she was concerned."[22] Anna simply had too much going on in her life to maintain order in the household, let alone cut the grass, which was always too long. Overextended as she was, there was the occasional mishap. One occurred when Anna was out doing errands one day: "She had a pack of her kids in the car and left them in there while she went shopping. The kids released the brake and the car went rolling down the hill and banged into a couple of cars and finally came to a stop. Fortunately nobody was hurt."[23]

Money problems got worse and worse. The Gouzenkos continued their pattern of falling into debt and borrowing. In 1959, Igor and Anna went to see the Canadian editor of *The Fall of a Titan*. They were so broke, they said, that they could not even buy groceries. She gave them forty dollars, without asking what had happened to the approximately fifty thousand dollars he had received in royalties. (Much to his disappointment, his novel was not made into a movie.) The fifty thousand dollars had disappeared within just a few years. The Gouzenkos' car was repossessed on numerous occasions. They went into arrears on their mortgage and came close to losing their house. Not long after their twins were born, in 1961, they had no money for heating-oil or food. They had to go out borrowing again.[24]

Around this time the Gouzenkos got some help with their finances. A wealthy Toronto attorney named B.B. Osler offered to consolidate Gouzenko's debts, which amounted to over $150,000, and raised money to pay some of them off, particularly the smaller loans to people who badly needed repayment. The other creditors agreed to an indefinite postponement. Osler thought Gouzenko had done a service to Canada and deserved to be compensated, but after working (pro bono) with Gouzenko on his finances for a year and a half, he ended up being disgusted with the defector and refused to see him any more. He reached the conclusion that Gouzenko was an opportunist and a cheat. What really bothered Osler was how disingenuous Gouzenko was when he borrowed money: "He got a lot of his money . . . on the undertaking that within 30 days he would have money from our government to compensate him for what he'd done for the country . . . and because they felt he'd been useful to the country they'd advance, some of them, all they had to him. And he took it and he had no intention of paying it back."[25]

In 1962, the Canadian government awarded the Gouzenkos a pension of five hundred dollars a month, but this was not enough for the family to live on, even with the small annuity they had been receiving since 1947. A year or two later, a desperate Anna went to the House of Commons in tears and asked to see former Canadian prime minister John Diefenbaker, back in Opposition after his Conservative Party had lost the elections of 1963. They were starving on the pension, she told him, and they had to have more. Her husband was not able to provide for them and she was worried about the children. The Liberal government, she said, was not responsive to the problem.[26] It is not clear whether Diefenbaker helped the Gouzenkos or not. But sometime in the late 1960s Gouzenko started receiving annual increases in his pension, and the Canadian government hired an accountant to help straighten the family's finances out yet again. Gouzenko had said they were around $20,000 in debt, but it turned out to be close to $140,000. The government had to initiate the same process of negotiating with the creditors that B.B. Osler had gone through.[27]

Had Gouzenko invested wisely, or simply saved some of the money he had received, he would not have been in these dire straits. As more than one observer has pointed out, however, this was probably too much to expect of someone with no experience in a capitalist system. He had grown up in a society where there was little concept of earning a wage or being rewarded for hard work. The vast proletariat in the Soviet Union was essentially slave labor in the service of Stalin's all-powerful, greedy bureaucracy. Entrepreneurship did not exist. To improve one's lot economically one had to learn the way of bribes, payoffs, and cheating, some of which Gouzenko had witnessed at the Soviet Embassy in Ottawa.

For at least the first year after he defected, Gouzenko did not even handle money. All of his needs and those of his family were taken care of (albeit modestly) by the RCMP. Suddenly, with his 1947 article in *Cosmopolitan*, his first book, and the movie deal, Gouzenko struck it rich. The RCMP withdrew quickly, leaving him to his own devices, with the exception of the live-in guard. Gouzenko's instant fame brought him a sense of entitlement. He wanted to experience the good life and started taking people out to fancy Toronto restaurants, where he would often order the most expensive dish on the menu. According to Gouzenko's former trust officer at his bank, "If he took you out to lunch he made sure that you were well looked after. You didn't eat in greasy spoons. . . . He was very generous. Too generous. You've got to remember that somebody who is brought up in that particular culture who came to this culture – you're going from scrub boards to washing machines and I think he wanted to enjoy the best."[28] Anna, who some have said was the smarter of the two, or at least the more sensible, might have stepped in (as she did later in their marriage) and tried to prevent Igor from throwing away money and making careless investments, but she was burdened with small children and perhaps cowed by her husband's domineering ways.

Gouzenko took considerable interest in his children and was very proud of them. They were a close and devoted family. But the financial concerns, lawsuits, and feuds with the RCMP distracted both him and Anna. And then, of course, there was the strain of his false identity. The children were not told until each reached the age of sixteen that Krysac was not their real name and that their parents came from Russia, not Czechoslovakia. Evelyn Wilson recalled that she once became suspicious when she saw a man on television with a hood over his head and heard him talking. He sounded exactly like her father. She was nonetheless shocked when she learned the truth at sixteen: "When you are always cheering for the Czech hockey team over the Russian one and then you find out you are a Russian, you feel bad."[29]

Indeed, Evelyn was not only stunned, she was angry, as were her siblings when they learned the truth about their parents. "We rebelled," recalled Evelyn, "that's what happened. My poor parents, on top of all the troubles they had, there were these unruly teenagers, who in their state of mind wanted to distance themselves from this, so we took on some of the popular criticisms of our father." Evelyn recalls that she was particularly humiliated by the pillowcase her father wore when he appeared on television (her mother's idea). People said he looked like a member of the Ku Klux Klan. "For a long time," Evelyn says, "all I felt was embarrassment."[30]

One of Gouzenko's lawyers observed that "considering the circumstances of their upbringing, they were remarkably well-adjusted and personable young adults, which must be regarded as an enduring tribute to the character and example set by their parents."[31] But as their parents became obsessed with lawsuits and efforts to expose the sinister influence of the KGB, the job of raising eight children suffered. Evelyn, who was frequently saddled with taking care of her younger siblings in her parents' absence, escaped. She got married, and had her first child at the age of seventeen. Evelyn eventually returned to the fold and embraced her parents as heroes, as did her sisters. But there was ambivalence among the four sons. The sons were conspicuously absent at a ceremony held in September 2002 to honor their parents, and at two subsequent public ceremonies, where plaques dedicated to Gouzenko were unveiled. Evidently, they chose to preserve their identity as Krysacs rather than acknowledge that they were the sons of the famous defector Gouzenko.[32]

∽

Throughout his years in Canada, Gouzenko was obsessed with the idea that the KGB (as the Soviet secret police were called after 1954) wanted to kill him. When he was to meet someone, he never made an appointment beforehand. KGB assassins might be waiting for him. If he and Anna were driving someone to a Toronto restaurant, Anna would take a roundabout way to get there. Before long, Gouzenko decided that the RCMP, because it had been infiltrated by the KGB, was in on a plot against him. According to a journalist friend, "He was convinced his house was bugged by the Mounties. He said he in turn had put in a secret taping system that was voice-activated apparently. I have no idea where the tape was kept. I never pursued that with him because he was so paranoid that would have made him nervous. He said he taped his own house so that if anything should happen to him he or his family would have a record.[33]

On his way to Montebello to meet senators Jenner and McCarran in early 1954, Gouzenko became fixated with the idea that the RCMP was going to use the occasion to get rid of him. He thought they were planning to stage a car accident. When the Mounties circled around the town to make sure their two-car caravan was not being followed and suggested that Gouzenko ride separately from his lawyer, he became suspicious and upset.[34] A journalist who knew Gouzenko once observed, "I would assume, since I've known an awful lot of psychiatrists, they could spend 10 minutes with him and decide he was a paranoid personality. He did strike me that way . . . I had a feeling he was crazy but had good reasons for being that way."[35]

After several years of guarding Gouzenko from supposed Soviet assassins, the RCMP began to question whether their protection was really necessary. The simple fact that he had blown his cover on numerous occasions with no repercussions, and that journalists never seemed to have trouble finding him, made it doubtful that he was in danger of being murdered by the KGB. Frustrated by Gouzenko's carelessness and fed up with his demands, the RCMP gave up guarding him by the early 1960s.

But Gouzenko continued to insist he was a marked man. As one observer remarked, "Without this sense that there was some kind of physical danger attached to his existence a lot of the glamour surrounding him would have disappeared and he would have become like other defectors who, whether in art or science, were not as well known as Gouzenko and would live out fairly unremarkable lives."[36] Sometimes he even hinted to members of the media that an assassination attempt had been made against him. When asked for specifics, however, he would demur, claiming that what he had referred to was "character assassination." Gouzenko at some point convinced himself that before the Soviets killed him they would try to destroy his credibility. How would the KGB go about doing this? By using certain elements of the Canadian media that were controlled by communists. He once told an interviewer that one of the editors of the *Toronto Daily Star*, which Gouzenko sued more than once, was pro-Russian and followed the communist line. The same was true, in Gouzenko's view, of certain broadcasters at the Canadian Broadcasting Corporation. Protecting his reputation, then, was not only a personal matter, it was a fight against communists and the KGB.[37]

Gouzenko also developed the theory that the Canadian government had covered up many of the facts about his case, pointing out that the GRU documents he had produced were still not publicly available. He claimed that the documents contained the names of individuals receiving government protection. In a CBC television interview in the spring of 1981, Gouzenko stated flatly that the persons named were in high positions and that it would be embarrassing for the government to reveal them. Gouzenko added, "I have a feeling that if, say, I die, they would be published, you know, and the reason [is] it would be easy to clean them, to white wash and to purge them and nobody would be able to say they were [not] the same as before or the same number of them and so on. While I'm alive, I can say . . . 'just a moment, where is that document which I brought with me?' or 'just a moment, that document didn't read the way it used to be.'"[38]

Ironically, just a few months later, in October of 1981, the Canadian government declassified the testimony taken by the Royal Commission on Espionage (more than six thousand pages). Copies of the documents Gouzenko brought out, and also a substantial portion of the vast number of exhibits that were part of its inquiry, were declassified three years later. Although the RCMP and Canadian government files on the case remained closed, it could not be said that the commission had covered up evidence about spies that had cropped up in the course of its investigation. It is true that many names appeared in Israel Halperin's infectious address book, which the RCMP confiscated after his arrest and which to this day is still classified as secret. But these individuals, many of whom were not Canadians, were beyond the commission's purview. Besides, the RCMP had dutifully sent a copy of the address book to both the FBI and MI5.

Gouzenko's allegation that the Canadian government was shielding people who had been involved in spying was not true. Of all people, he should have known better. With his razor-sharp mind and his near-photographic memory, he knew by heart the details of all the documents he took from the Soviet Embassy and all that he said to his interrogators. Yes, several of those whose names had come up were suspected of involvement with the Russians and were never prosecuted. This had nothing to do with a cover-up. The evidence in those instances turned out to be too flimsy for Canadian authorities to even consider taking legal action.

Gouzenko's growing paranoia was partly the Canadian government's fault. Despite their initial efforts to cast him as a hero, Canadian authorities, particularly the RCMP, had never trusted his motives. (Indeed, the RCMP made this clear in giving Gouzenko his unflattering surname.) And they did not know what to do with him once the spy trials had ended. Instead of hiring him as a consultant to analyze unfolding events in the Soviet Union, or to develop a program of asylum for other defectors, they put Gouzenko out to pasture. He was not even thirty years old. As one of Gouzenko's many lawyers recalled, "Here is a superbly intelligent human being who really understands the Russian system, their mentality, their training, their approach. Why they wouldn't have made more use of him I'll never know. This really bothered him. I think he kind of hoped to be treated as an expert or a consultant. He felt they didn't get 10 per cent of what they could have out of him. . . . He might not have always had the answer but it would have been a very interesting sounding board because he was a very, very bright man."[39]

But the Canadian government, the RCMP in particular, had its reasons not to continue to seek Gouzenko's advice. Because

Gouzenko had come to the West at a young age and been out of touch with the Soviet Union ever since, it was thought he had little to offer. Also, while it is true that in the United States defectors from the Soviet Union were eventually used as contract advisers to the CIA, and some were considered quite valuable, when Gouzenko was offered asylum the Cold War was just beginning, and there were no policies or programs for dealing with defectors.[40]

Furthermore, Gouzenko, like many defectors, was convinced the Soviets had managed to put their spies everywhere, which prompted him to make questionable claims. Just after the Soviets launched Sputnik, the world's first artificial satellite, in October 1957, throwing Americans into a panic, he wrote a letter to U.S. president Eisenhower, reproduced in part in the *New York Times*. It read as follows: "The fact that the United States, with its advanced scientific and material resources, was not able to launch the first earth satellite should be the subject of serious thought and investigation. In my opinion, it indicates the work of well-organized spy rings in the United States missile production system. These rings on the one hand are pumping out of the United States valuable scientific and other information and on the other hand are sabotaging and delaying the United States missile effort under all kinds of seemingly logical excuses."[41]

Gouzenko was exaggerating. Had he been better informed, he would have understood that the Soviets had given their space program top priority and that their scientists in this area had made tremendous technological advances. Yes, the Soviets were spying, and they were after the secrets of America's military technology, but they had also poured tremendous resources into Sputnik. The Americans had simply fallen slightly behind in the race to launch a satellite.

A sympathetic Canadian journalist once observed of Gouzenko, "History in a way stopped with his defection. All the input was there. What carried him the rest of his life was the knowledge of the Soviet system and the KGB, which never changes and can't change."[42] Unfortunately, this was not the case. Gouzenko's knowledge of the Soviet system was limited to his brief years in the GRU, and things did change, especially after Stalin died. Gouzenko, with only Anna to bounce his ideas off of, was a world away from what was happening in Moscow. Posing as a Czech, he did not even associate with Russian émigrés.

∽

Blinded by Gouzenko's shortcomings, the Mounties, who had direct contact with the defector, failed to appreciate the almost impossible situation he was in. They were disgusted at what they saw as his sense of privilege. When he had trouble sticking to the couple of manual jobs they arranged for him, they put it down to laziness. They did not realize, or care, that these jobs were demeaning for Gouzenko, who understandably wanted more than anything to be of value in the struggle against communism.

Frustrated that his talents were being wasted, Gouzenko took on the battle against communism and the KGB single-handedly. The more he was ignored by the Canadian government, the more he was demeaned in the press, the greater was his need to open the eyes of the West to the evils of the Soviet Union. Convinced that the RCMP and the Canadian government were infiltrated by Soviet spies, Gouzenko felt that his own credibility depended on exposing them.

He was especially suspicious of the Liberals, who regained power in 1963 after a Conservative interval of six years. In 1968, he went so far as to distribute a pamphlet entitled "Trudeau, A Potential Canadian Castro" at the Liberal leadership convention in Ottawa. The pamphlet, which bore his signature, charged that both Lester Pearson and Pierre Trudeau were communists. Trudeau, he suggested, who was about to succeed Pearson as Liberal leader, might even be a spy. Gouzenko based his claims about Trudeau in part on Elizabeth Bentley's leaked 1951 testimony to SISS. But he got things mixed up. She had mentioned meeting in Washington with a wealthy young man from Montreal, who brought her tidbits of news from Lester Pearson, but she was referring to Hazen Sise, not Trudeau.[43]

Gouzenko's pamphleteering caught the attention of the *Toronto Daily Star*. The paper published an editorial, entitled "Hate Flows in Canada Too," in which it castigated Gouzenko for circulating inflammatory literature: "The poison flows from anti-Communist zealots who are attempting by innuendo and half truth to link Mr. Trudeau with a Communist conspiracy." Noting that Bentley's SISS testimony was unsupported, the editorial ridiculed Gouzenko's suggestion that "Communist sympathizer" Pearson was passing information to "Communist agent" Trudeau. Literature of the sort Gouzenko was circulating should be "stamped or exposed as vicious," the *Star* concluded.[44]

Not surprisingly, Gouzenko lashed out against his nemesis the *Star* yet again, accusing the paper of libel. This time no one settled; after a few years of haggling among the lawyers the case went to court. The author of the editorial, Val Sears, had been looking forward to the jury trial and his own opportunity, in his testimony as a defendant, to speak out against so-called hate literature. He was in for a rude shock. Instead of being asked to defend his editorial, he was questioned about Elizabeth Bentley. "The initial approach by Gouzenko's lawyer was devastating to me," he recalled, "because he said I had alleged in the editorial that Elizabeth Bentley's testimony was a lie and would I tell the courts what part of Elizabeth Bentley's testimony was a lie and what was the truth. I was stumped. I grew up with the idea that Elizabeth Bentley, viewed from a liberal perspective, was an inappropriate witness. But to go back to the late 40s and single out what parts of her testimony were accurate and what were not, I said I couldn't possibly do that."[45]

The judge suggested a recess to allow Sears time to consider his answer. Stunned, Sears went over to the hotel bar next door and had three Bloody Marys. He could not imagine how he was going to answer, until he remembered an old tactic from university days: stall your opponent by asking him to define his terms. "Bolstered by these Bloody Marys," Sears recalled, "I returned to the stand, and the lawyer said, 'I'll repeat the question about the lies of Elizabeth Bentley.' And I said, 'I'll have to tell you first off that I didn't say lies. I said half truths. Would you define what you mean by half truths? Because I have my own version of what a half truth is and I would be prepared to define that.' And I babbled on like this. And to my utter surprise and delight the lawyer said, 'Oh, never mind. I'm not going to pursue this line of questioning.' I stepped off the stand sweating profusely."[46]

Sears had hit upon an important point: in her numerous testimonies, Bentley invariably spoke in half truths. With her memories blurred by martinis and stimulated by what she read in the press, consistency was not one of her strong points, and by the time her allegations were repeated and passed on, the truth – if there ever was one – became even more mangled. In his response to Gouzenko's lawyer, Sears had demonstrated the Kafkaesque absurdity of having a court case center around Elizabeth Bentley's allegations. The jury found in favor of the defendant.

Gouzenko's last legal action, initiated in the spring of 1982, was once more against the *Toronto Star*. It related to an article entitled, ironically, "Libel: The Dark Cloud."[47] In discussing the growing trend of libel suits, the author, Daniel Stoffman, used Gouzenko as one example, citing his cases against John Sawatsky and June Callwood and noting generally that some individuals used libel suits as "a chance to cash in." This naturally infuriated Gouzenko, who went straight to his lawyer. His case was weak and it is unlikely he would have won, but as it was he died two months later.

Stoffman criticized Gouzenko for trying to prevent people from writing about him unfavorably by intimidating them with the possibility of legal action.[48] And he was of course right. Gouzenko had a vision of how he wanted to appear to others, and he did not want anyone to challenge that vision. (Yet he squandered the opportunity to tell the story himself. In 1974, he signed a contract with McGraw-Hill to publish his autobiography. Two years later, after collecting fifteen thousand dollars in advances, he had not produced a word.) The irony of Gouzenko's attempts to muzzle the press was that his tactics were similar to those used by the authorities in his former country, the Soviet Union. He claimed he was attracted to Canada because of its freedom and democracy, yet he attacked those same principles. As one Canadian writer observed, "In Russia they change history by destroying the evidence of what happened. I guess he didn't realize this. Allegedly he was attacking that vicious system which nurtured him and here he was playing the same role of book burner and record destroyer and perverter of the facts."[49]

But one acquaintance of Gouzenko had a less harsh and probably more fair explanation for Gouzenko's litigiousness: "He gave a great deal of thought to these cases. He had been left in a situation where he couldn't live in the open. It's like some great athlete who's living in the past and is obsessed by days gone by. To some extent, here's a man who had this incredible public exposure at one time and was a *cause célèbre* . . . he may have even put too much emphasis and importance on his own life, as we all do, but he had more reason than most of us. So I think you have a man who was obsessed with his place in history and how to protect it and enhance it, or at least establish the truth from his point of view."[50]

⌇

Gouzenko had a heart attack in June 1982 while he was sitting at the dining-room table pretending to conduct a symphony that was playing on the radio. He died instantly. The funeral was a quiet affair, attended only by the immediate family and a couple of acquaintances who knew his real identity. The minister who conducted the funeral referred to him as Mr. George Brown, a pseudonym he often used when he met people for the first time. It was as if Gouzenko, the famous defector, had never existed.[51]

Gouzenko's preoccupation with his place in history stemmed from the fateful decision he made in 1945 to escape from his native Russia and put his and Anna's lives in the hands of a Western democracy. Given the sacrifices they had made, it was crucial for him to affirm that his defection had a significant impact. As we know, Gouzenko's inspiration in making his fateful decision was Viktor Kravchenko.[52] Kravchenko, in his own words, chose "a precarious freedom against a comfortable enslavement," knowing of the possible "frightening consequences" of what he did.[53] Indeed, his decision to defect resulted in tragedy for those he left behind. Kravchenko's first wife, whom he had divorced before he left the Soviet Union, was shot. His son from that marriage, Valenin, was sent to a Soviet labor camp because he refused to denounce his father.

Twenty years after his defection, in 1964, Kravchenko took his own life.[54] His two decades of "precarious freedom" had come at a great cost.

Things had turned out much better for Gouzenko. He had Anna by his side throughout, and together they showed a remarkable resilience and resourcefulness in forging new lives in Canada. Their daughter Evelyn says that "even to the day they died, not once did they regret their choice."[55] But there must have been times when her parents wondered what would have happened had they chosen differently and returned, as ordered by the GRU, to the Soviet Union in the autumn of 1945. Gouzenko had been convinced he was in some sort of trouble with his bosses in Moscow. Indeed, though Gouzenko did not know it, Colonel Mil'shtein had given him a negative report when he returned from his trip to North America.

But if Gouzenko had been in serious trouble, the GRU would not have granted Zabotin's request to let him stay another year. Even with a black mark on his record, Gouzenko might not have fared too badly back in Moscow. Yes, the atmosphere was tense, fueled by the rivalry between the GRU and the NKVD, and by political intrigues in Stalin's Kremlin. But the purges of the late thirties and the war had depleted the ranks of the intelligence services. The GRU could ill afford to dispose of an intelligent and well-trained cipher clerk for some small malfeasance. Domestic life for the Gouzenkos back in Russia would have meant a crowded communal apartment (unless Anna's father had some pull with the housing bureaucrats) with just the bare necessities to survive on. They could not have supported more than two children. Nonetheless, if Gouzenko had worked hard and avoided trouble, there would have been more postings abroad and promotions. In the end, as the Soviet Union recovered from the devastation of the war, Igor and Anna might have lived reasonably comfortably – and, above all, they would not have sacrificed their family members to the grim retribution of Stalin's system.

But Gouzenko always said his choice was about more than physical comfort, or even freedom. He had hoped his defection, in exposing the evil intentions of the Soviet Union, would heighten the West's vigilance against spies and strengthen its resolve to stand up to the Soviet Union militarily. He had also imagined he would serve as an example for others to defect, thereby destabilizing Stalin's espionage apparatus and weakening the Soviet state. His case, and the ensuing spy scare in the West, most certainly provided the impetus for the United States, Canada, and Great Britain to strengthen their counterintelligence operations and heighten their vigilance. It also helped create the atmosphere that led to the U.S. military buildup and its determination to maintain nuclear superiority over the Soviet Union.

It would, however, take almost fifty years from the time Gouzenko defected for the Soviet Union to collapse. And, contrary to what Gouzenko had envisaged, it was not a weakened security and intelligence service that caused the demise of the Soviet Union. Rather, it was a corrupt and inefficient communist bureaucracy that ignored the country's problems until it was too late. Indeed, although there were continued defections throughout the years of the Cold War from both the GRU and the NKVD's successor organizations, these agencies became steadily stronger and more effective.[56]

Gouzenko's defection, we know, created a crisis at NKVD and GRU headquarters in Moscow.[57] The first reaction of the intelligence chiefs was to "cut and run." Spies were called back home and spying operations curtailed dramatically. Then, in 1947, came a complete reorganization of the intelligence services. At the instigation of Foreign Minister Molotov, the GRU was merged with what had earlier been the Foreign Intelligence Service of the NKVD into a single organization, called the Committee of Information (KI), under Molotov's chairmanship. The new arrangement worked out badly. According to Vitalii Pavlov, who was directly affected, "The amalgamation of the different services – political and military intelligence – turned out to be an impractical venture. The sharp differences in the style of work of the two different units soon led to ineffective intelligence operations. . . . During the time that the KI existed the level of precision in solving the problems of foreign intelligence declined."[58]

The experiment was short-lived. In 1948 military intelligence returned to the GRU, and by late 1951 the security services had reclaimed their foreign intelligence functions. Once Stalin and Beria were gone, the way was paved in 1954 for the new political leadership, led by Nikita Khrushchev, to introduce significant changes in the intelligence and security services and expand their operations. Khrushchev and his successors realized that their ambitious goals of extending Soviet power internationally and achieving military parity with the United States could not be accomplished without extensive foreign-intelligence operations. Beginning with Khrushchev, Soviet leaders pursued a policy of not only building up the strength of the services domestically and internationally, but also relying on them as a base of political support.

By 1982, the year Gouzenko died, the prestige and might of the KGB had risen to the point that one of its own, Iurii Andropov, became the Soviet leader. Andropov, since 1967, had been chief of the KGB, which incorporated both foreign intelligence and domestic counterintelligence. He was not a reformer in the Western sense of the word. As ambassador to Hungary, he had in 1956 presided over the Soviet invasion of that country. And in 1968, he urged the Politburo to move Soviet troops into Czechoslovakia. But he was sophisticated enough to understand that organizations must change with the times, and he managed to create a cadre of foreign-intelligence officers that in terms of training and professionalism was second to none. The high salaries, military ranks, and access to foreign currency offered by the KGB, as well as the opportunity to live abroad, attracted the best and the brightest from within the Soviet Union. The new breed of intelligence officer was well educated and fluent in several languages, with a broad knowledge of other cultures and a great deal of self-confidence.

The same was true of the GRU, Gouzenko's former agency, which expanded its operations abroad considerably in the late 1970s and 1980s, taking advantage of a more relaxed Western attitude toward Russians in the period of détente. The typical GRU officer at this time (and their numbers were constantly expanding) had all the scientific expertise and training necessary to supply the Soviet military with the vital intelligence. According to one source, the GRU was, "because of its overall scientific orientation, its bolder operational style, its increased collection opportunities that reflect a wider variety of technology-related cover positions overseas, and its clearer understanding of collection objectives," even more successful than the KGB.[59] This was a far cry from the days of Zabotin and his colleagues, who lacked the expertise to discern what was scientifically important and the incentive to devote themselves to their jobs.

The response of the allies to Gouzenko's revelations about Soviet espionage, particularly in the United States, where a new Central Intelligence Agency was established in 1947, gave additional incentive to the intelligence agencies in Moscow. (If we are to believe Pavlov, the creation of the KI in that year was a reaction to the establishment of the CIA.) A new kind of war had begun with the West, a war in which the soldiers were spies, and the Kremlin was determined to win. The stakes were high, because the Soviets also wanted to surpass the Americans in the arms race, and in order to do so they needed all the information they could get on Western military technology. It is no small wonder that, by the end of the 1980s, both the KGB and the GRU, with the aid of their colleagues in Soviet-controlled Eastern Europe, had developed into vast intelligence empires that played key roles in determining and implementing Soviet foreign policy.

What contributed to the Soviets' success in the intelligence wars of the 1970s and 1980s was the skill they acquired in recruiting and handling Western agents. Ideology could no longer be used to convert Westerners into spies, as it had been in the days of Philby and his Cambridge colleagues. Communism had lost its appeal, even among members of the Soviet elite, who used it mainly as window dressing for a regime that was based on coercion rather than consensus. But, as Gouzenko pointed out in his 1954 interview with SISS, money always held an allure. Three of the most important American spies – John Walker, who started spying for the KGB in 1967; Robert Hanssen, who offered his services to the GRU in 1979; and Aldrich Ames, recruited by the KGB in 1985 – all betrayed their country for money. All were eventually caught and prosecuted, but not without having inflicted significant damage on American national security. Walker, for example provided the KGB with U.S. cryptographic secrets that enabled them to decipher coded military messages for almost twenty years. Ames and Hanssen passed on information that resulted in the deaths of several Western agents in Russia.

For a while after the demise of the Soviet Union in 1991, it seemed that the Russian security and intelligence apparatus was doomed to extinction. The KGB was disbanded in disgrace, with its leaders implicated in the coup plot against Gorbachev. The KGB's empire in Eastern Europe was lost, along with its branches in the Soviet republics that were no longer part of the Soviet Union. There were cutbacks, dismissals, and defections from both the foreign and domestic sides of the security services. It did not take long, however, before the former KGB, reorganized under a new name, reestablished itself as a pillar of the Russian state. Russian president Vladimir Putin, himself a former KGB officer, can take a great deal of the credit for the fact that the security services have gained such prominence in Russian political life. But the process began under the presidency of Boris Yeltsin, who continued the Soviet habit of relying on the security services for his political support and designated Putin as his successor.

The history of both the KGB and the GRU is officially extolled in today's Russia. No one talks about the Gulag and the executions in Lubianka prison, but people are very vocal in expressing their pride in the achievements of Soviet intelligence during the Cold War. The surviving veterans of that war are revered. They live in the best apartments and enjoy generous pensions. Several, like Vitalii Pavlov, have written their memoirs, which sell well. Former spymasters like to get together to reminisce about old times and discuss past conquests. At one KGB reunion, President Putin showed up to join them.[60] Some of the old guard still call themselves communists, but for most communism is a relic of the past. In fact, for many of these veterans of the Cold War, it was never anything more than a convenient myth, a propaganda tool used to attract potential agents for their espionage effort. One wonders what they thought of Fred Rose, Sam Carr, Raymond Boyer, Gordon Lunan, and the others they recruited as agents and who consequently were sent to prison, the ones who were true believers.

CONCLUSION:

THE NAMING OF NAMES

When I took up my little sling and aimed at Communism, I also hit something else. What I hit was the forces of that great socialist revolution, which in the name of liberalism, spasmodically, incompletely, somewhat formlessly, but always in the same direction, has been inching its ice cap over the nation for two decades.

Whittaker Chambers, *Witness*

In 1972, when former MI5 and MI6 chief Sir Dick White was asked why the British services were still investigating old spy cases, he had the following reply: "One day it will be necessary to have a balance sheet on this subject. It ought not to take precedence over contemporary inquiries, yet we must know how at a particular moment in our history we were messed about and bewildered by all this."[1] White of course was referring to the fact that Philby and his friends had managed to deceive MI5 and MI6 for so many years before they were exposed. Like many of his colleagues, White had been charmed by Philby's wit and congeniality and never questioned his loyalty. Even Sir Roger Hollis, who developed an antagonism toward Philby, did not have the slightest suspicion that he was working for the Soviets. Hollis, who had little appetite for defectors, ignored Gouzenko's warning about a spy in British intelligence. Although "Elli" was probably not Philby, it should have alerted Hollis and his colleagues to the fact that there might be a mole in their midst.

The complacency of MI5 and MI6 can be attributed in large part to the fact that their services were dominated by an upper-class old-boy network that had a strong sense of cohesion and loyalty. As one British writer observed about MI6, "From 'C' the Chief, downwards, the Secret Intelligence Service acted on the cardinal principle that gentlemen were preferable to players in the underground world of espionage, because gentlemen could be trusted. This mystique of class superiority came as naturally to its members as breathing; that it might be a false mystique which had dangerously outlived its validity simply did not occur to anyone."[2]

But the FBI, a much more democratic organization than its British equivalent in terms of class origins, missed the boat as well. The FBI cooperated amicably with Philby from 1949 to 1951, when he was MI6 liaison in Washington, even sharing with him the Venona secrets. In *My Silent War*, Philby later scoffed at the FBI chief: "Hoover did not catch Maclean or Burgess; he did not catch Fuchs, and he would not have caught the rest if the British had not caught Fuchs and worked brilliantly on his tangled emotions . . . he did not even catch me. If ever there was a bubble reputation, it is Hoover's."[3] Philby of course ignores the fact that it was the FBI that tipped the British off about both Maclean and Fuchs, much to the embarrassment of MI5 and MI6. But it is true that Philby was operating, and meeting with his Soviet control in Washington, right under the noses of FBI agents.

A question that is just as important as why spies were overlooked is why so many innocent people were accused of spying: There are several answers, all having to do with the atmosphere of fear created by the espionage scare Igor Gouzenko's defection unleashed and the manipulation of that fear by those with a political agenda. As the Gouzenko affair demonstrates, the standards of proof required to label people as spies (as opposed to convicting them) was appallingly low. Hearsay evidence was widely accepted as fact. Gouzenko's rendition of what he heard from another code clerk back when he was in Moscow, for example, was taken as significant proof of Alger Hiss's guilt by the FBI and members of the U.S. Congress. And Elizabeth Bentley's allegations, even though she had never met Hiss and got his first name wrong, were enough for the FBI to obtain permission to conduct secret surveillance of him. In Canada, as the Royal Commission conducted its inquiry, much of the evidence, despite the documents from Gouzenko, was also hearsay, too flimsy to hold up in a court, but impressive enough to attach the label of spy to individuals who were completely innocent.

The principle of guilt by association became an accepted practice in building a case against people whose names came up as a result of the Gouzenko affair, in both Canada and the United States. (In fact, in Canada this principle had already been enshrined in the 1939 Official Secrets Act.) Friendships and acquaintanceships with left-wing intellectuals or, worse, communists were immediate grounds for suspicion, as were affiliations with groups and organizations that were considered ideologically dangerous, such as the Institute for Pacific Relations. Even having one's name listed in the address book of another suspected spy was tantamount to being guilty.

And finally, of course, adherence to the ideology of communism, or any expression of political beliefs that were close to that ideology, was the equivalent, in the eyes of the Royal Commissioners and men like Hoover, McCarthy, and McCarran, to espionage. It did not matter if the suspect had abandoned communism years before. The guilt could not be erased unless the individual came forward and renounced past beliefs, as Gouzenko, Bentley, and Chambers did. As Canadian scholar Reg Whitaker observed, to the anti-communist witch-hunters there was only one way to absolve oneself: "public renunciation of past sins and enlistment in the ranks of the inquisition, accompanied of course by the presentation of severed heads on a platter, or what is known in the trade as 'the naming of names.'"[4]

In Canada, once the Royal Commission had finished its investigation and the spy trials began, the standards of proof were much higher. This is why the prosecution was able to convict fewer than half of the defendants. Nonetheless, the process of justice was marred, several of those convicted having sealed their fate because, without access to lawyers and under extreme duress in the RCMP barracks, they had confessed to passing information to the GRU. With the exception of Fred Rose and Sam Carr, the convicted

Canadians never had the subversive intent of spies like Philby and his colleagues, who continued with their espionage well beyond World War II. The Russians were wartime allies of the West and the information they gave was intended to help them with the war effort. A broadcast journalist who interviewed several Canadians convicted of violating the Official Secrets Act makes this point well: "Almost all . . . who I met, and perhaps all of them, felt they had stumbled into something innocently and been hammered for it far more viciously than they could have ever imagined. It seemed to me that none of them ever expected that anything they were doing was going to lead them into any kind of trouble. And I got the impression [that] they wouldn't have done what they did had they thought there would be those kinds of consequences."[5]

However deplorably the Canadian authorities behaved in their treatment of the spy suspects in the Gouzenko case, Canada did not experience the prolonged inquisitions that took place in the United States in the late 1940s and 1950s. With the exception of a very few, like Alger Hiss, Americans who were suspected of spying never got their day in court. They were tried by congressional investigators, harassed by the FBI, and slandered by the press on the basis of evidence that would never have stood up to established judicial standards.

The academic community in America contributed to this process. The renowned American sociologist Robert Bellah, who had been a member of the American Communist Party in the late 1940s, recently described the enormous pressure exerted upon him as a graduate student at Harvard to "cooperate" with HUAC and the FBI. Bellah, who had left the party in 1949, was warned by Harvard dean McGeorge Bundy in 1954 that he would lose his Ph.D. fellowship if he did not agree to an interview with the FBI. A week later, Bellah was picked up off the street by the FBI and pressured to "name names," but he refused to do so. Bellah came close to having his dissertation funding cut off and had to refuse a faculty appointment at Harvard the next year because he would have to promise to answer questions posed by one of the committees in Washington. He later joined the Harvard faculty and taught there for many years, but he still has bitter memories about his experience as an ex-communist: "What all this amounts to is a record not of Harvard's being a bulwark against McCarthyism, but of abject cowardice. . . . What the committees and the FBI wanted was for people to name names, and Harvard willingly cooperated, using its power of appointment and renewal to pressure people to do so."[6]

Bellah's experience at Harvard sheds light on why Herbert Norman's friend and mentor Shigeto Tsuru agreed to testify about Norman at a SISS hearing shortly before Norman's suicide in 1957. As a visiting professor at Harvard and a non-American, Tsuru was probably threatened by the Harvard administration with immediate dismissal if he refused to appear before SISS. In fact, Harvard must already have been cooperating with the FBI in 1942, shortly after Tsuru was forced to leave the university and return to Japan because of the war. How would FBI agents have learned about Tsuru's library, with its collection of Marxist literature, and then have been allowed to confiscate it, if they had not had help from someone at Harvard?

American academia's discreet collaboration with the witch-hunters helped to damage the careers of many scholars, including Arthur Steinberg, just as it contributed to the demise of Herbert Norman. Why did authorities at Harvard, and many other highly reputable American educational institutions, acquiesce to the McCarthyites? To a certain extent they were intimidated into doing so. But many must also have accepted the underlying premise of the Red Scare – that communism was a terrible threat to Western democracy. Indeed, the common liberal view in the United States was that, although anti-communism was being taken too far, the danger of communism required firm action and justified many of the measures taken that impinged on civil liberties.

Anti-communism had been firmly entrenched in the FBI and the RCMP before Gouzenko's defection. Communists were considered dangerous subversives because of their radical ideology and their association with trade unions, which were seen as a threat to government stability. But it was the Gouzenko affair that forged the connection in many minds between domestic communism and Soviet espionage, a connection that would later be affirmed by Bentley, Chambers, and the defection of three of the Cambridge spies.

The problem with anti-communism was that it failed to distinguish between adherence to, or sympathy with, communism as an ideology and the concrete act of betraying one's country by spying for Stalin's secret police. Many of those suspected of spying had, like Herbert Norman, discarded communism altogether once World War II began. And most of those who continued to call themselves Marxists or communists were unwilling to spy for the Soviets. It may be true that Cambridge University, where Philby and his fellow spies studied, was "a hotbed of communism" in the 1930s, and that Harvard and Princeton harbored a lot of Marxists as well. But the mistake the red hunters in the United States and Canada made was to assume that all those who in the 1930s embraced Marxism, or even joined the Communist Party, were enlisted by the Soviets to be spies. Yes, Philby, Burgess, Maclean, Blunt, Alan Nunn May, and others did end up working for the Soviets. But most did not.

In the frenzy of the espionage scare, these considerations were discarded. Once a communist, always a Soviet spy. Indeed, the apparent reason why Hoover and McCarran had such disdain for Lester Pearson was that Pearson recognized the distinction between domestic communism and the ideology of the Soviet state, and between those who adhered to communism in the 1930s and those who acted as secret agents for the GRU and NKVD during and after the war. What Pearson and his colleagues tried to do in the Norman case was to look beyond his "youthful indiscretions" and consider Norman's career as a whole, his consistent record as a diplomat who discharged his duty to the interests of Canada and the West.

But this approach was far from the modus operandi of the McCarthyites in Washington. When SISS held its hearings in March 1957 in search of further evidence to label Norman a spy, its investigators paid no heed to the fact that he was at the time the Canadian ambassador to Egypt and that, as such, he had played a crucial role in resolving the Suez crisis. The automatic equation of communist leanings before the war years with active subversion of government policies during the war and after left no room for serious consideration of who the suspects were and what they had accomplished.

One of the most disturbing features of the Red Scare as it was played out after Gouzenko's defection was that separate pieces of inadequate evidence against those suspected of disloyalty were presented together in a composite picture that appeared more convincing. Unfortunately, historians of the Cold War over the past decade have adopted a similar practice in assessing spy cases. The Alger Hiss case is a good example.

A piece of evidence that is frequently cited by historians to show that Hiss was spying is a decrypted NKVD message from the Venona project, dated March 30, 1945.[7] The message discussed an employee of the State Department with the code name "Ales" who had been working with the GRU since 1935 and was given an award for his services by the Soviets. FBI agent Robert Lamphere, who was enlisted to help on the Venona project in 1948, tentatively identified "Ales" as Alger Hiss in May 1950, just as Hiss's appeal of the perjury conviction was being heard. But the identification was never verified, and it is easy to see why. The Soviets chose code names for their agents in order to conceal their identities. It is unlikely that they would have assigned Hiss a code name that so closely resembled his real name. Also, there is much syntactical ambiguity in this message, largely because of missing words and word endings.

The FBI frequently made tentative identifications of cover names in Venona messages, often changing them later as new information came to light. Indeed, an FBI memorandum warns: "The fragmentary nature of the messages themselves, the assumptions made by the cryptographers in breaking the messages, and the questionable interpretations and translations involved, plus the extensive use of cover names for persons and places, make the problem of positive identification extremely difficult."[8]

Venona was an invaluable tool in the effort to expose Soviet spies. Without Venona, neither Fuchs nor Maclean would have been uncovered, and the Americans and their allies would not have realized the extent of the Soviet espionage effort. Nonetheless, Venona must be treated with caution by historians. The decrypted messages that are available represent only a small portion of the NKVD and GRU traffic that passed back and forth between the United States and Moscow during the mid-1940s. Did that traffic include a message that might have exonerated Hiss? It is useful to recall the example of Arthur Steinberg, who, judging from a GRU message to Moscow produced by Gouzenko, appeared to have been a recruit for the GRU (he even had a code name). But as we have seen, another message from Gouzenko's documents, which apparently never left RCMP headquarters, showed that Steinberg was frightened by a Soviet attempt to recruit him and rejected the proposition outright.[9]

As we know, Gouzenko's stolen GRU documents were often difficult to interpret, especially since many were written in Russian. Although Gouzenko himself was able to provide most of the real names behind the code names, there were still a lot of ambiguities. In at least one case, the translator got the name wrong.[10] These documents were not sufficient in themselves as evidence for a prosecution. Similarly, the Venona telegram about "Ales" would never have held up in court as evidence against Alger Hiss. Yet historians over the past decade have almost unanimously declared it to be the definitive proof that Hiss was engaged in espionage for the Russians.[11]

The example of Gouzenko also illustrates the confusion that can arise out of verbal allegations from defectors, particularly after they have been interviewed repeatedly. Gouzenko's descriptions of the State Department spy, reported initially in 1945 as an assistant to an Assistant Secretary of State, changed markedly by the time he testified before senators Jenner and McCarran in 1954. Gouzenko also changed his testimony about "Elli." As one experienced RCMP counterintelligence officer observed, "Once you start interviewing and reinterviewing defectors their answers echo your questions. Passed from one person, or one agency to another, defectors glean information from their interrogators and start to incorporate it into their fund of knowledge."[12] This not only happened with Gouzenko, but also with Bentley and Chambers. Their stories changed after almost every interview they had with the FBI or with congressional committees. And yet the historical consensus today is that the thrust of their testimonies was reliable.

Another important lesson from the Gouzenko case is that when a name was mentioned in Soviet intelligence traffic it did not necessarily mean that the individual in question was a spy. Soviet intelligence officers passed on to Moscow names of persons they wanted to enlist, like Steinberg and Halperin, but were unsuccessful in doing so. It might be tempting to see a code name in a Soviet telegram and assume that person behind it was a full-fledged spy, but in many cases the "spy" was unsuspecting. Even in the case of Harry Dexter White, who is shown by Venona decryptions to have met with Soviet agents and passed information, there is no evidence that he was doing this with the intention of subverting American policies.[13]

GRU and NKVD officers also may have exaggerated the importance of what they received from their recruits. Indeed, it is difficult to know how useful the intelligence actually was to the Kremlin. The Soviet Union was a closed society, where all information, beyond what was disseminated in the official press, was secret. And what appeared in that press was a highly sanitized version of reality, excluding any news that reflected what was actually happening in the country. The public heard mainly about the birthday celebrations of Politburo members, milk production awards to kolkhozes, and, during the war, the valiant struggle against the Nazis. Imagine what Zabotin and his colleagues, having been raised in this environment, must have thought when they arrived in Canada and were allowed to tour military plants and talk with government employees about the war effort. To them, a glance at an open-source Canadian publication on the latest developments in arms-munitions research was the equivalent of being privy to one of the Kremlin's greatest secrets.

Soviet intelligence officers sent a great volume of material to Russia from the West. Their list of recruits, or potential recruits, was long enough to keep several officers at NKVD and GRU headquarters busy assigning, and reassigning, code names. But the content and value of the information is another question entirely. As British Cold War scholar Sheila Kerr reminds us, despite all new evidence, including the Venona decryptions, historians today do not have a clear picture of the significance of what the Soviets received from their spies. Referring specifically to Donald Maclean, Kerr observes that we know his potential for espionage, "but only Soviet sources can reveal the intelligence requirements Maclean was ordered to fulfill and exactly what intelligence he passed to his NKVD controller."[14]

The British, to their credit, did not indulge in inquisitions in the manner of the Canadians and Americans, and they avoided trampling on civil liberties in the wake of the spy scare. Although MI5 and MI6 went through terrible agonies about spies in their midst, in gentlemanly fashion they kept their investigations quiet, at least until journalist Chapman Pincher wrested the story from them and former MI6 officer Peter Wright wrote his exposé. But the British were not above reacting harshly to national security threats, as we know from the way they responded to the crisis in Northern Ireland in the 1970s. As for Canada, despite the lessons learned from the shameful disregard of civil liberties in the Gouzenko spy case, history briefly repeated itself in October 1970. In fear of terrorism by what turned out to be a small group of Quebec separatists, Trudeau's Liberal government declared a state of emergency and reinstated the draconian War Measures Act.

Today, in Canada, the United States, and Britain, there are again concerns about violations of civil liberties in the name of national security. It might be argued that analogies to the McCarthy era are inappropriate, because terrorism today is a much greater threat than that faced by the West during the Soviet espionage scare. But at the time, with visions of the atomic bomb exploding over Hiroshima and Nagasaki still fresh in people's minds, the thought that the Soviet Union could have this weapon at its disposal because of atomic espionage was no less frightening than the specter of terrorism is today. And once the fear took over, it was not difficult to convince people that the threat to national security justified infringements of individual rights and the rolling back of democratic principles of justice.

Although it was not Gouzenko's fault, his name became linked with the excesses of the spy scare in Canada and, indirectly, with the McCarthy era in the United States. This association explains why the Canadian government remained ambivalent about Gouzenko's place in Canadian history until the spring of 2004, when it grudgingly allowed a plaque to be erected in Ottawa honoring his memory.

That it was more than twenty years after Gouzenko's death suggests there was strong resistance to the idea of giving him back the hero status he first achieved in defecting. However grateful people were to Gouzenko for opening up their eyes to the dangers of Soviet espionage, many could not forget the price that was paid for that knowledge.

NOTES

INTRODUCTION

1. Hoover to Connelly, September 12, 1945, Harry S. Truman Library, President's Secretary's Files (Subject File), "FBI-Atomic Bomb," box 167.
2. Hoover to Lyon, September 18, 1945, U.S. National Archives [hereafter NARA], RG 59, 861.20242/9-1845. Hoover also sent another letter to the White House on that day, most of which is blacked out, but it probably contained the same information.
3. Hoover to Lyon, September 24, 1945, Central Intelligence Agency, Igor Gouzenko File.
4. The literature on the Alger Hiss case is vast. The best-known account is that of Allen Weinstein, *Perjury: The Hiss-Chambers Case* (New York: Random House, 1978). Revised edition, 1997. The office of Special Political Affairs was created at the State Department specifically for dealing with United Nations issues. After Hiss became the director of SPA in March 1945, he reported directly to Secretary of State Edward Stettinius.
5. Tom Bower, *The Perfect English Spy: Sir Dick White and the Secret War 1935–90* (London: Heinemann, 1995), p. 34.
6. For a thorough study of Krivitsky's life as a defector, see Gary Kern, *A Death in Washington: Walter C. Krivitsky and the Stalin Terror* (New York: Enigma Books, 2003). Kern leaves open the question as to whether Krivitsky killed himself or was murdered.
7. Richard J. Aldrich, *The Hidden Hand: Britain, America and Cold War Secret Intelligence* (London: John Murray, 2001), p. 96.
8. FBI Gouzenko file, 100-342972-37.

9. The two British services were formed in the early twentieth century out of sections five and six of British Military Intelligence (hence the MI designations). Their functions were not entirely separate, which caused some friction. MI5 was in charge of security and counterintelligence at home, but it also had similar responsibilities for British territory abroad. And MI6, while primarily concerned with intelligence gathering abroad, had its own counterintelligence department, section 5.

10. Bower, *The Perfect English Spy*, p. 66.

11. David Stafford, *Camp X* (Toronto: Lester & Orpen Dennys, 1986), p. 259.

12. As quoted in Roy Jenkins, *Churchill: A Biography* (New York: Farrar, Straus and Giroux, 2001), p. 781.

13. James Littleton, *Target Nation: Canada and the Western Intelligence Network* (Toronto: Lester & Orpen Dennys, 1982), p. 16; Bower, *The Perfect English Spy*, p. 78. Roger Hollis of MI5 counted at least eight "crypto communists" among Labour MPs.

14. Conrad Black, *Franklin Delano Roosevelt: Champion of Freedom* (New York: Public Affairs, 2004), p. 1096.

15. Vladislav Zubok and Constantine Pleshakov, *Inside the Kremlin's Cold War: From Stalin to Khrushchev* (Cambridge, MA: Harvard University Press, 1996), p. 45.

16. Fuchs had been recruited by the GRU in 1941 in London. By 1944, he was handed over from the GRU to the NKVD. See the Russian website www.agentura.ru/dosie/gru/imperia/atomspy, "atomnyi shpionazh," pp. 6-9. Also see David Holloway, *Stalin and the Bomb: The Soviet Union and Atomic Energy, 1939–1956* (New Haven: Yale University Press, 1994), chapter four.

17. The newly released files on the Gouzenko case from the National Archives in Britain are filled with reports to and from Philby. See the National Archives [hereafter TNA], KV 2/1419-KV 2/1424.

18. Soviet intelligence archives are not open to researchers, but many of their documents have been published in Russian, along with memoirs of former intelligence officers. Another important new source of materials on Gouzenko are the John Sawatsky Papers, recently donated to the University of Regina Library. The papers consist of interviews with people who knew Gouzenko personally. Although significant portions of these interviews were published as a book, John Sawatsky, *Gouzenko: The Untold Story* (Toronto: Macmillan of Canada, 1984), the unpublished portions provide fascinating new details about Gouzenko's life.

CHAPTER 1: THE DEFECTION

1. See Gouzenko's autobiography, *The Iron Curtain* (New York: E.P. Dutton, 1948); and Igor Gouzenko, "I Was Inside Stalin's Spy Ring," *Cosmopolitan*, February 1947.

2. Gouzenko's daughter Evelyn Wilson spoke about her parents at a conference in Ottawa, April 14, 2004.

3. Gouzenko, *The Iron Curtain*, pp. 50-69. Also see Gouzenko's testimony at the preliminary hearing for Fred Rose, March 22, 1946, pp. 1-26 in the Library and Archives Canada [hereafter LAC], MG 30, A 94, vol. 45, file 3155. The acronym GRU stands for *Glavnoye Razvedyvatel'noe Upravlenie*.

4. "Atomnyi shpionazh"; Gouzenko, *The Iron Curtain*, pp. 119-224; *The Report of the Royal Commission to Investigate the Facts Relating to and the Circumstances Surrounding the Communication, by Public Officials and Other Persons in Positions of Trust of Secret and Confidential Information to Agents of a Foreign Power, June 1946* [Hereafter *RC Report*] (Ottawa: Edmond Cloutier, 1946), pp. 11-18.

5. "The Canadian Case in Retrospect," MI5 report, TNA, KV 2/1424.

6. Merrily Weisbord, *The Strangest Dream: Canadian Communists, the Spy Trials and the Cold War* (Montreal: Véhicule Press, 1994), p. 119.

7. As told to this author by two former Canadian diplomats who were in Ottawa at the time.

8. Gouzenko, *The Iron Curtain*, p. 182.

9. Weisbord, *The Strangest Dream*, p. 134.

10. LAC, RG 33/62, volume 16, exhibits 576-578. The host of the Russians was Gerald Woods.

11. See TNA, KV 2/1424, "The Canadian Case in Retrospect."

12. Gordon Lunan, *The Making of a Spy: A Political Odyssey* (Montreal: Robert Davies, 1995), pp. 95-96.

13. Littleton, *Target Nation*, p. 20.

14. See his memoirs: Vitalii Pavlov, *Operatsiia "sneg," Polveka vo vneshnei razvedke KGB* (Moscow, 1996), pp. 44-55.

15. Ibid., pp. 66-87.

16. Gouzenko, *The Iron Curtain*, p. 205.

17. Ibid., p. 204.

18. Ibid., p. 188.

19. Ibid., p. 201; Gouzenko, "I Was Inside Stalin's Spy Ring," p. 85.

20. John Sawatsky Papers, University of Regina Archives, 84-38, box 1, file 8, interview with Bill McMurty, October 20, 1983.

21. Gouzenko, *The Iron Curtain*, p. 215.

22. Ibid., pp. 203-219.

23. Ibid.

24. Transcript of Gouzenko's testimony before the Royal Commission, LAC, RG 33/62, vol. 1, book one, February 13-22, 1946, pp. 370-371; 393-394; Also see TNA, KV 2/1419, report on Corby and a BSC (British Security Coordination) Report, dated September 1945, where it is stated that "without question, he [Gouzenko] was afraid of being liquidated." LAC, MG 26, J4, vol. 417.

25. Mikhail Mil'shtein, "Pobeg Guzenko," *Sovershenno sekretno*, no. 3, 1995, pp. 24-25.

26. Ibid.

27. In could be that Zabotin did not want either Romanov or Gouzenko going back early because they might "spill the beans" to headquarters about some of the things he did or said in unguarded moments.

28. Gouzenko, *The Iron Curtain*, pp. 218-219.

29. See Reg Whitaker and Gary Marcuse, *Cold War Canada: The Making of a National Insecurity State, 1945–1957* (Toronto: University of Toronto Press, 1994), pp. 43-46, for a discussion of Canadian and British participation in the Allied bomb project.

30. Gouzenko, *The Iron Curtain*, pp. 215; 222.

31. TNA, KV 2/1423, report from Major G.H. Leggett, Intelligence Bureau, Advance H.Q., Control Commission for Germany, June 17, 1946.

32. Ibid.

33. *RC Report*, p. 384.

34. Ibid., p. 135.

35. Ibid., p. 124.

36. Ibid., p. 145.

37. Ibid., pp. 142-143.

38. Ibid., pp. 135; 145-146.

39. Lunan, *The Making of a Spy*, p. 148.

40. Dmitrii Prokhorov, "Istoriia Allana Meia," February 26, 2001, www.agentura.ru/text/press/2001/mey.txt.

41. *Atomnyi shpionazh*, p. 15; Gouzenko, *The Iron Curtain*, p. 237. Gouzenko says that May handed over reports on atomic research several months before Hiroshima, but the GRU does not appear to have passed on his reports until July 1945. See *RC Report*, pp. 452-458.

42. Prokhorov, "Istoriia."

43. As quoted in www.agentura.ru/dosie/gru/imperia/atomspy.

44. *RC Report*, p. 452.

45. Sawatsky Papers, 85-26, box 1, Interview with Mrs. Gouzenko, March 17, 1984.

46. *RC Report*, p. 641; LAC, RG 33/32, Gouzenko testimony, pp. 120-121; February 13, p. 77, pp. 118.

47. Gouzenko, "I Was Inside Stalin's Spy Ring," p. 164.

48. The documents from Gouzenko were copied as exhibits for the Royal Commission on Espionage that investigated the Gouzenko case in 1946. For a list of the documents, see LAC, RG 33/62 Microfilm T-1368. Copies of the exhibits themselves are scattered throughout the Royal Commission records, but can be located in the index to the massive Royal Commission files.

49. LAC, MG 30 (Cohen Papers), series A94, vol. 45, file 3156; Author's interview with William Kelly, Ottawa, November 16, 2001.

50. The fact that Gouzenko had been recalled because he was in trouble was also covered up. In a signed statement to the RCMP, which was later published, Gouzenko said that he defected because he was attracted by Canada's democratic system of government and disgusted by the "double-faced politics of the Soviet government." *RC Report*, pp. 637-648. The statement was signed on October 10, 1945.

51. Sawatsky Papers, 84-38, box 2, Interview with Ken Parks, December 27, 1983.

52. Sawatsky, *Gouzenko*, pp. 21-25; Gouzenko statement of October 10, 1945, "account of steps taken on Sept. 5th, 6th, and 7th." CSIS files and microfilm C274152, LAC.

53. Sawatsky, *Gouzenko*, pp. 26-40; Gouzenko statement.

54. LAC, MG 26, J4, vol. 390, file 32; Testimony by Gouzenko and his neighbors, Mr. and Mrs. Harold Main and Mrs. Frances Elliott, before the Royal Commission on Espionage, LAC, RG 33/62, vol. 1, book 1, February 13-22, 1946, pp. 379-446.

55. Sawatsky Papers, 84-38, box 1, file 8, interview with Harold Main, March 8, 1984.

56. Sawatsky, *Gouzenko*, pp. 44-47.

57. "Preventative Medicine," *Time* magazine, January 7, 1946.

58. LAC, William MacKenzie King Diary [hereafter WMK Diary], Aug. 25, 1945.

59. WMK Diary, Sept. 6, 1945.

60. Ibid.

61. Ibid.

62. See the memoirs of the British High Commissioner to Canada: Malcolm MacDonald, *People & Places: Random Reminiscences of the Rt.*

Hon. Malcolm MacDonald (London: Collins, 1969), p. 188. Also see the memoirs of RCMP intelligence branch chief (and later commissioner) Charles Rivett-Carnac, *Pursuit in the Wilderness* (Boston: Little Brown, 1965), pp. 306-307; H. Montgomery Hyde, *The Quiet Canadian: The Secret Service Story of Sir William Stephenson* (London: Hamish Hamilton, 1962), pp. 229-232; and Stafford, *Camp X*, p. 258-259. The story that Stephenson was the mysterious intelligence officer in Ottawa that night is also repeated in William Stevenson, *Intrepid's Last Case* (New York: Random House, 1983), pp. 51-55.

63. Stafford, *Camp X*, p. 258. Hyde, *The Quiet Canadian*, pp. 229-232. According to Hyde, Stephenson "seldom left his New York headquarters, except to fly to Washington . . . or to cross the Atlantic to report progress to the prime minister and the various departments represented by the B.S.C." (p. 4)

64. Sawatsky Papers, 84-38, box 2, interview with George Glazebrook, February 29, 1984.

65. See John Bryden, *Best-Kept Secret: Canadian Secret Intelligence in the Second World War* (Toronto: Lester Publishing, 1993), pp. 267-275 and Mark Kristmanson, *Plateaus of Freedom: Nationality, Culture, and State Security in Canada, 1940–1960* (Toronto: Oxford University Press, 2003), pp. 143-173 for the speculation on Menzies.

66. TNA, KV 2/1425, telegram for Sir Alexander Cadogan from Malcolm MacDonald, dated September 10, 1945.

67. For Gouzenko's statement mentioning Mrs. Bourke, see LAC MG26, J4, vol. 390, file 32.

68. On the Elliotts, see Kristmanson, *Plateaus of Freedom*, pp. 168-170 and an interview with their former son-in-law: Sawatsky papers, 84-38, box 2, interview with M.J. Sumpton, undated. Sumpton said that his father-in-law, Mr. Elliott, was particularly angry that all the neighbors had to be quiet for the rest of their lives, when Gouzenko was allowed to write a book and magazine articles telling his version of events.

69. LAC, MG 26, J4, vol. 390, file 32. On this version, the person editing the statement earmarked this portion to be omitted.

70. See Athan Theoharis, *Chasing Spies: How the FBI Failed in Counterintelligence but Promoted the Politics of McCarthyism in the Cold War Years* (Chicago: Ivan R. Dee, 2002), pp. 50-53. In fact, the FBI seems to have backed out of this arrangement and left Kravchenko on his own after a series of interviews with him.

71. Interviews with William Kelly, Ottawa, November 16, 2001, and Dan Mulvenna (by telephone to Leesburg, Virginia), February 4, 2005.

Neither Kelly, who was eventually to become deputy commissioner of the RCMP, nor Mulvenna worked on the Gouzenko case until after the defection, however.

72. Transcript of interview with Lt-Gen. Vitalii Pavlov, conducted in Moscow on September 29, 2001, by Svetlana Chervonnaya and passed on to this author. Also see Pavlov, *Operatsiia "sneg,"* p. 75. Pavlov wrote: "I do not believe the widely spread myth that Gouzenko made the decision to defect independently."

73. Sawatsky Papers, 84-38, box 1, file 7, interview with John McCulloch, October 5, 1983.

74. WMK Diary, September 7, 1945.

75. "Soviet Espionage in Canada," Royal Canadian Mounted Police, Intelligence Branch, Ottawa, November 1945, p. 1.

76. LAC, RG 33/62, vol. 1, p. 526. Rivett-Carnac presented a totally different (and false) picture in his memoirs. According to Rivett-Carnac: "his [Gouzenko's] manner was composed as he took his place in the hard-bottomed chair. His eyes flickered to Leopold for a moment and then came back to mine. . . . He told us his story, how he'd left the Soviet Embassy two evenings before; that he knew that there were a number of spies operating against the interests of Canada. . . . It was breathtaking to hear him." Rivett-Carnac, *Pursuit in the Wilderness*, p. 311. He was clearly covering up Gouzenko's crazed state as part of an effort to protect the defector's image.

77. LAC, RG 13, A-2, vol. 2121, file 150262. The existence of this secret Order-in-Council, which was never acted upon, has never been acknowledged by the Canadian government.

CHAPTER 2: A MAN CALLED CORBY

1. Transcript of interviews by Svetlana Chervonnaya with Lt. Gen. Vitalii Pavlov, Moscow, Nov. 14 and 19, 1997; Sept. 29, 2001.

2. Mil'shtein, "Pobeg Guzenko."

3. LAC, RG 25, vol. 2620, file 50242-40, vol. 1.

4. Ibid.

5. J.L. Granatstein, *The Ottawa Men: The Civil Service Mandarins, 1935–1947* (Toronto: Oxford University Press, 1982), pp. 92-95. Also see J.L. Granatstein, *A Man of Influence: Norman A. Robertson and Canadian Statecraft, 1929–68* (Toronto: Deneau Publishers, 1981).

6. *The Guy Liddell Diaries, Volume I: 1939–1942*, ed. by Nigel West (London: Routledge, 2005), p. 268.

7. Granatstein, *A Man of Influence*, p. 174.

8. NAC, RG 13, series A2, vol. 2119, file 149685.

9. CSIS files, RCMP 45 D-1226–45 J-1226. The date of the RCMP's letters to the provincial departments and to Hoover was September 15, 1945.

10. I.A. Aggeeva, "Kanada i nachalo kholodnoi voiny: Delo Guzenko v sovetsko-kanadskikh otnosheniiakh," p. 8, citing Zarubin's secret diary: Dnevnik Zarubina G.N. Sekretno, AVP RF, fond 99, Opis 17, papka 7.

11. Venona decrypt, no. 46a, September 17, 1945, Moscow to London: www.nsa.gov/docs/venona.

12. Genrikh Borovik, *The Philby Files: The Secret Life of the Master Spy-KGB Archives Revealed* (New York: Little, Brown and Company: 1994), p. 239.

13. S.J. Hamrick, *Deceiving the Deceivers: Kim Philby, Donald Maclean and Guy Burgess* (New Haven and London: Yale University Press, 2004), p. 143.

14. Gordon Brook-Shepherd, *The Storm Birds: Soviet Post-War Defectors* (New York: Henry Holt, 1989), pp. 48-56.

15. Pavlov, *Operatsiia "sneg,"* p. 75. Zarubin had the same family name as Georgii Zarubin, Soviet ambassador to Canada, but they were not related.

16. Weisbord, *The Strangest Dream*, p. 141.

17. Lunan, *Making of a Spy*, p. 153.

18. Ibid., p. 155.

19. Sawatsky Papers, 85-26, box 1, interview with Mrs. Gouzenko, March 12, 1981.

20. Ibid.

21. Sawatsky, *Gouzenko*, pp. 50-57.

22. Steve Hewitt, "Royal Canadian Mounted Spy: The Secret Life of John Leopold/Jack Esselwein," *Intelligence and National Security*, vol. 15, no. 1, Spring 2000.

23. LAC, MG 26, vol. 329, file 3495, memorandum from W.J. Turnbull, July 6, 1942. According to Leopold's obituary in the *Ottawa Citizen*: "He regarded life with eternal good cheer except when communism was mentioned. On that he was deadly serious. It was a menace to which he dedicated his life." As cited in Hewitt, p. 159. When Leopold was promoted to head the intelligence branch of the RCMP Criminal Investigation Division, Rivett-Carnac was made chief of that division, still supervising the Gouzenko case.

24. Sawatsky, *Gouzenko*, pp. 52-62.

25. Stafford, *Camp X*, pp. 264-267; *British Security Coordination: The Secret History of British Intelligence in the Americas, 1940–1945*, Introduction by Nigel West (New York: Fromm International, 1999), pp. 423-425.

26. Sawatsky, *Gouzenko*, p. 60.

27. Ibid., p. 62.

28. CSIS (Canadian Security and Intelligence Service) Gouzenko file, 000116.

29. C.W. Harvison, *The Horsemen* (Toronto: McClelland & Stewart, 1967), p. 149.

30. Rivett-Carnac, *Pursuit in the Wilderness*, p. 307.

31. J.L. Granatstein and David Stafford, *Spy Wars: Espionage and Canada from Gouzenko to Glasnost* (Toronto: McClelland & Stewart, 1990), p. 58; Stafford, *Camp X*, p. 260. As MI5's Guy Liddell expressed it during a visit to Ottawa in 1942, "The RCMP are very well equipped to deal with Communism, but not very well equipped to deal with counter-espionage. They are essentially a police force employing police methods." *The Guy Liddell Diaries*, p. 267.

32. See LAC, MG 26, vol. 329, file 3495; FBI Gouzenko File (FOIPA no. 0944835-001), memorandum from Tamm to the Director, September 10, 1945; memorandum from Ladd to Tamm, September 10, 1945; Lamphere, *FBI–KGB War*, p. 67.

33. CSIS Gouzenko, 000067, letter dated September 13, 1945; FBI Gouzenko memorandum Ladd to Director, November 2, 1945.

34. Lamphere, *The FBI–KGB War*, p. 127; Kim Philby, *My Silent War* (New York: Grove Press, 1968), p. 160; and Kristmanson, *Plateaus of Freedom*, p. 101. Also see LAC, RG 32, acc. 85-86/096, box 39, Peter Michael Dwyer.

35. Stafford, *Camp X*, pp. 262-265; Peter Wright, *Spycatcher: The Candid Autobiography of a Senior Intelligence Officer* (London: Stoddart Publishing Co., 1987), p. 345. On MI5's concerns about messages going through SIS (MI6), see TNA, KV 2/1425, telegrams dated September 20 and 22, 1945. The FBI was also receiving at least some of the reports from New York.

36. The classic, but half fictional biography of Stephenson is: William Stevenson, *A Man Called Intrepid: The Secret War* (New York: Harcourt, Brace Jovanovich, 1976). More accurate is H. Montgomery Hyde, *The Quiet Canadian: The Secret Service Story of Sir William Stephenson* (London: Hamish Hamilton, 1962). Also see Timothy Naftali, "Intrepid's Last Deception: Documenting the Career of Sir William Stephenson," *Intelligence and National Security*, vol. 8, July 1993, 70-99; and http://william-stephenson.biography.ms.

37. *The Guy Liddell Diaries*, pp. 248-249.

38. Ibid; and TNA, KV 2/1419, letter from the director of British Government Code and Cipher School, dated September 21, 1945; Lamphere, *FBI–KGB War*, pp. 80-81.

39. Stafford, *Camp X*, pp. 262-265.

40. Bower, *The Perfect English Spy*, pp. 54-55.

41. Ibid.

42. Ibid., p. 80; TNA, KV 2/1425, telegram from Macdonald to Cadogan.

43. Brook-Shepherd, *The Stormbirds*, p. 30.

44. Bower, *The Perfect English Spy*, p. 80.

45. Granatstein and Stafford, *Spy Wars*, pp. 59-68. On Gouzenko's unhappiness over Hollis's reports, interview with Gouzenko's daughter, Evelyn Wilson, Toronto, December 12, 2002. On the suggestion of bringing Gouzenko to England, see TNA Gouzenko file, KV 2/1420, note accompanying first revision of report on Corby case. On his second meeting, KV 2/1423, telegram no. 762, dated May 23, 1946. No report is available on what happened at the meeting.

46. R. MacGregor Dawson, *William Lyon Mackenzie King: A Political Biography*, vol. 2 (Toronto: University of Toronto Press, 1963), p. 3.

47. "Preventative Medicine."

48. WMK Diary, September 23, 1945.

49. For a description of Menzies, see Kerns, *A Death in Washington*, p. 247.

50. FBI Gouzenko, 100-342972-27.

51. FBI Gouzenko, 100-342972-32, memorandum dated September 13, 1945, to Tamm, Ladd, and Tolson.

52. CSIS Gouzenko, C293177, September 23, 1945.

53. FBI Gouzenko, 100-342972-51, memorandum from Ladd to Hoover, October 29, 1945; 100-342972-130, Ladd to Hoover, May 27, 1947.

54. Harry S. Truman Library, Papers of Harry S. Truman. President's Secretary's files. "Soviet Espionage Activities," October 19, 1945.

55. FBI, FOIPA no. 0944835-001, the date and much of the report is blacked out.

56. Rivett-Carnac, *Pursuit in the Wilderness*, p. 315.

57. Harvison, *The Horsemen*, p. 150.

58. CSIS Gouzenko, 000132, letter dated October 11, 1945.

59. CSIS Gouzenko, 000332, letter dated November 11, 1945.

60. LAC, RG 25, vol. 2620, N-1, interview with Gusenko [*sic*], Memo I, n.d.

61. Ibid.

62. "Soviet Espionage in Canada," Royal Canadian Mounted Police, Intelligence Branch, November 1945.

63. CSIS Gouzenko, 000126, letter from McClellan, dated October 10, 1945.

64. CSIS Gouzenko, 000332, letter dated November 2, 1945; Sawatsky, *Gouzenko*, p. 64.

65. Rivett-Carnac, *Pursuit in the Wilderness*, p. 317. Rivett-Carnac notes that "my wife began to have serious doubts about my behavior. I could of course tell her nothing." In fact, his wife knew about the defector, passing the information on to her friend Ruth Fordyce, in the autumn of 1945. Interview with Ms. Fordyce, November 2001.

66. TNA KV 2/1420, "Note Accompanying First Revision of Report on Corby Case," September 25, 1945.

67. WMK Diary, private memorandum, September 10, 1945.

68. CSIS Gouzenko, 000068, letter from RCMP commissioner Wood, dated September 15, 1945. Sawatsky Papers, 84-38, box 1, file 5, interview with Cecil Bayfield, July 3, (no year given). Bayfield erroneously gives the date of the flight as October 6.

69. *RC Report*, pp. 453-454.

70. TNA, KV 2/1419, unsigned report (presumably from British intelligence), dated September 24, 1945.

71. TNA, KV 2/1421, telegram from Capt. G. Liddell.

72. WMK Diary, September 24, 1945.

73. WMK Diary, September 25 and 26, 1945.

74. CSIS Gouzenko, 000094, letter dated September 27, 1945.

CHAPTER 3: "PRIMROSE," MISS CORBY, AND THE POLITICS OF ESPIONAGE

1. WMK Diary, dictated on October 1, 1945.

2. Harry S. Truman Library, Papers of Harry S. Truman. President's Secretary's Files.

3. WMK Diary, October 1, 1945.

4. LAC, RG 25, 2620, Box 2620, N-1 (temp), letter from Pearson to Hume Wrong, dated October 1, 1945.

5. See John English, *Shadow of Heaven: The Life of Lester Pearson, Volume One: 1987–1948* (London: Vintage, 1990), p. 269.

6. See note 12 below.

7. English, *Shadow of Heaven*, pp. 282-283; David McCullough, *Truman* (New York: Touchstone, 1992), pp. 751-754.

8. Letter from Pearson to Wrong, October 1, 1945.

9. WMK Diary, October 1, 1945.

10. FBI Hiss file, 101-2668, sec. 02-284.

11. WMK Diary, October 1, 1945.

12. LAC, MG 26, J1, vol. 389, p. 349871.

13. WMK Diary, October 1, 1945.

14. English, *Shadow of Heaven*, p. 244; Gordon Robertson, *Memoirs of a Very Civil Servant: Mackenzie King to Pierre Trudeau* (Toronto: University of Toronto Press, 2000), p. 51.

15. TNA, KV 2/1425, telegram dated October 1, 1945.

16. TNA, KV 2/1425, telegram dated October 2, 1945.

17. See Whitaker and Marcuse, *Cold War Canada*, p. 41.

18. TNA, KV 2/1425, telegram dated October 6, 1945.

19. TNA, KV 2/1425, telegram, dated October 10, 1945; CSIS Gouzenko 000099, letter dated October 3, 1945; and CSIS Gouzenko 000110, telegram dated October 5, 1945. Hoover's response to Wood was that the FBI had no legal grounds for arrests of spy suspects in the United States either. CSIS Gouzenko 000122, telegram dated October 9, 1945.

20. TNA, KV 2/1425, telegram, dated October 1, 1945; WMK Diary entry for October 7, 1945.

21. TNA, KV 2/1425, telegram, October 7, 1945; Borovik, *The Philby Files*, p. 239.

22. WMK Diary, October 7, 1945.

23. WMK Diary, October 11, 1945; Also see, for "C"'s efforts to pressure Bevin and Attlee and Attlee's response, Kristmanson, *Plateaus of Freedom*, pp. 153-154.

24. TNA, KV 2/1425, letter to Prime Minister Attlee from Ernest Bevin, October 27, 1945.

25. WMK Diary, October 26, 1945.

26. TNA, KV 2/1425, telegram dated October 19, 1945.

27. Ibid.

28. Robert J. Lamphere and Tom Shachtman, *The FBI-KGB War: A Special Agent's Story* (New York: Random House, 1986), p. 35.

29. TNA, KV 2/1425, telegram to Hollis, dated October 31, 1945.

30. TNA, KV 2/1425, telegram from Hollis, dated November 2, 1945.

31. TNA, KV 2/1425, telegram dated November 7, 1945.

32. LAC, RG 25, box 2620, N-1 (temp), for a copy of the draft agreement.

33. Ibid.

34. CSIS Gouzenko file, no. 000122; list of reports, transcript 000008.

35. TNA, KV 2/1425, telegrams dated November 14–21, 1945; FBI Gouzenko file, 100-342972-86, memorandum from Hoover to Tolson, Ladd, Tamm, and Carson, November 30, 1945.

36. See Whitaker and Marcuse, *Cold War Canada*, p. 47; and Holloway, *Stalin and the Bomb*, p. 157.

37. Harry S. Truman, *Year of Decisions: 1945* (New York: Hodder and Stoughton, 1955), p. 477.

38. Harry S. Truman Library, Papers of Harry S. Truman. President's Secretary's Files.

39. Ibid.

40. FBI Bentley file, 134-435-174, letter to FBI Director from SAC, Los Angeles, dated July 28, 1955. There are two recent biographies of Bentley: Kathryn S. Olmstead, *Red Spy Queen: A Biography of Elizabeth Bentley* (Chapel Hill: University of North Carolina Press, 2002) and Lauren Kessler, *Clever Girl: Elizabeth Bentley: the Spy Who Ushered in the McCarthy Era* (New York: HarperCollins, 2003).

41. FBI Silvermaster, 65-56402-8. In checking Bentley's information out further, the FBI learned that Belfrage "had a very unsavoury reputation, that he was reputedly assigned the responsibility, while working for the British Security Coordination in New York City, of handling 'FBI and London reports.'" (Memorandum from Ladd to Hoover, November 26, 1945.) In late November the FBI furnished Stephenson with the additional information on Belfrage that it had collected.

42. For the text of Philby's message see Nigel West and Oleg Tsarev, *The Crown Jewels: The Secrets at the Heart of the KGB Archives* (New Haven: Yale University Press, 1998), pp. 238-239.

43. A telegram to MI6 sent via New York on November 19 gives details of the Bentley case, which Philby would have seen. See TNA, 2/1425. For the November 20 message, see Allen Weinstein and Alexander Vassiliev, *The Haunted Wood: Soviet Espionage in America – the Stalin Era* (New York: Random House, 1999), pp. 104-108. Weinstein and Vassiliev also say that the draft text of Mackenzie King's prepared statement to give publicly at the time of the arrests in Canada was given to Stalin himself from NKGB Chief Vsevold Merkulov. As I have written elsewhere, *The Haunted Wood* must be used with caution. It is based on summaries and translations by Vassiliev, a former KGB officer, of selected documents in the Russian Foreign Intelligence Archives in Moscow (as part of a financial agreement with the publisher). Because no photocopies of the original documents ever left the Russian archives, it has been impossible for anyone else to check their authenticity or the accuracy of the translations and summaries. Nonetheless, judging from the content, the messages about Philby that the authors cite seem credible.

44. FBI Silvermaster, 65-56402-581, vol. 24.

45. FBI Silvermaster, 65-56402, vol. 6-220.

46. Ibid.

47. FBI Silvermaster, 65-56402, 37, undated memorandum, mainly blacked out.

48. On Donald Hiss and Acheson, see McCullough, *Truman*, p. 179.

49. FBI Silvermaster, 65-56402-26.

50. FBI Silvermaster, 65-56402-94.

51. FBI Silvermaster, 65-56402-94.

52. Letter to FBI director Hoover, March 28, 1946, FBI Silvermaster 65-56402-31.

53. See Theoharis, *Chasing Spies*, pp. 42-43.

54. R. Bruce Craig, *Treasonable Doubt: The Harry Dexter White* Case (Lawrence, Kansas: The University of Kansas Press, 2004), p. 69.

55. Craig, *Treasonable Doubt*, p. 71.

56. FBI Silvermaster, 65-56402-306.

57. Weinstein and Vassiliev, *The Haunted Wood*, pp. 106-107; Pavlov, *Operatsiia "sneg,"* pp. 73-74.

58. FBI Gouzenko, 100-342972-86; LAC, RG 25, vol. 2620, N-1.

59. LAC, RG 25, vol. 2620, files 50242-40 and N-1.

60. LAC, RG 25, vol. 2620, King's plan also reached the FBI's representatives in Ottawa, prompting a telephone call to headquarters. FBI Gouzenko, memorandum to Tamm from Ladd, December 3, 1945.

61. TNA, 2/1425-120103, telegram dated December 2, 1945.

62. The diary was dictated by King and then later transcribed. When the volumes were assembled after King's death in 1950, the one for November 10–December 31, 1945, was missing. LAC, MG 26, J17, vol. 9.

63. LAC, RG 25, vol. 2629, N-1.

64. Whitaker and Marcuse, *Cold War Canada*, p. 53.

65. As quoted in Holloway, *Stalin and the Bomb*, p. 156. Groves was informed about Gouzenko's allegations against May around September 14, 1945. The British, not knowing what May had passed on to the Soviets, were worried that Groves would object to his being allowed to fly back to Britain. On September 14, Sir Alexander Cadogan, British undersecretary for foreign affairs, sent a telegram to Lord Halifax, his ambassador to the United States, saying: "Should he [GROVES] raise violent objection could not High Commissioner Canada . . . arrange for plane to be detained 24 hours pending further urgent consideration here?" TNA, KV 2/1425.

CHAPTER 4: RED STORM CLOUDS

1. Sawatsky, *Gouzenko*, pp. 65-66.
2. Sawatsky Papers, 84-38, box 1, file 8, interview with George Mackay, November 3, 1983.
3. LAC, RG 13, series a-2, vol. 2121, file 150262, E.K. Williams, "The Corby Case," December 7, 1945.
4. TNA, KV 2/1421, telegram from New York, dated December 15, 1945.
5. Prokhorov, "Istoriia Allana Meia"; Pavlov, *Operatsiia "sneg,"* pp. 73-74.
6. Mil'shtein, "Pobeg Guzenko"; "Atomnyi shpionazh," p. 19.
7. Ibid.
8. Ibid.
9. "Atomnyi shpionazh"; Vladimir Lota, "Khorosho, chto ne posmertno," *Sovershenno sekretno*, no. 6, 1999.
10. LAC, MG 26, J4, vol. 390, microfilm no. 1552, C272270; D. Prokhorov and O. Lemekhov, *Perebezhchiki: Zaochno rasstreliany* (Moscow, 2001) p. 132.
11. *Perebezhchiki*, p. 131-132; Interview with Evelyn Gouzenko (telephone), February 12, 2002. Interestingly, although Gouzenko says in his book that his father died in the Civil War, shortly after Gouzenko was born, his criminal file cited in *Perebezhchiki* says that his father, Sergei Davydovich Gouzenko, was living in Kiev before World War II.
12. Gouzenko, *The Iron Curtain*, p. 12.
13. FBI Gouzenko, 100-342972-113, 119. Both memorandums were in response to telephone calls, presumably with Canadian authorities.
14. WMK Diary, February 1, 1946.
15. Transcripts of Pearson's broadcasts about the Gouzenko affair are available in Personal Papers of Drew Pearson, Box G-182, 1, Lyndon B. Johnson Library.
16. The commission was officially called the Royal Commission to Investigate the Disclosures of Secret and Confidential Information to Unauthorized Persons, but it was referred to as the Royal Commission on Espionage.
17. WMK Diary, Tuesday, February 5, 1946, p. 107. Also see his entry for Feb. 4: "this business has become known to too many people. The President's office, the Secretary of State's office, the F.B.I., etc."
18. This was suggested in an internal FBI memorandum, citing a source (blacked out in the file) who claimed to have talked with Pearson about the leak. See FBI Gouzenko, 342972-125.
19. As quoted in Holloway, *Stalin and the Bomb*, p. 159; on Truman and Byrnes also see McCullough, *Truman*, pp. 278-280.

20. Lyndon B. Johnson Library, Personal Papers of Drew Pearson: folder Hoover, J. Edgar; Ellen Schrecker, *Many Are the Crimes: McCarthyism in America* (Princeton: Princeton University Press, 1998), p. 216.

21. TNA, KV 2/1015, no. 984 from New York, January 10, 1946. Sir William Stephenson actually took partial credit for the leak in a statement made some forty years later, claiming that he had consulted with Hoover and a White House official and that the three had agreed that Pearson should be told about the Corby case. As others have pointed out, however, Stephenson's claim (if accurately quoted) is questionable, mainly because he and Hoover did not get along. See Whitaker and Marcuse, *Cold War Canada*, p. 60.

22. FBI Gouzenko, 342972-139, memorandum from D.M. Ladd to Hoover, dated February 13, 1946.

23. Lamphere, *The FBI–KGB War*, p. 41.

24. LAC, RG 25, vol. 2620, file N1, note from Canadian intelligence attaché Tommy Stone.

25. TNA, KV 2/1423, letter to Hollis from J.A. Cimperman, dated October 9, 1946.

26. TNA, KV 2/1015, telegram no. 122 sent through the BSC in New York. Although the telegram was unsigned, as most were, it seems to have been sent by Dwyer.

27. *The Washington Post*, February 16, 1946.

28. See www.cia.gov/csi/books/venona/part1.htm; and FBI Silvermaster, 65-56403.

29. Craig, *Treasonable Doubt*, p. 246.

30. This telegram and the story behind it was unearthed in Canada's National Archives by Mark Kristmanson and described in his book *Plateaus of Freedom*, pp. 126-132, 264-266, citing LAC, RG 25, vol. 8561, file 50303-40, part 1.1. Kristmanson was not supposed to see these files because they are still top secret, but an archivist gave them to him by mistake.

31. Lamphere, *The FBI–KGB War*, p. 127.

32. Director to Tolson, Tamm, and Ladd, February 21, 1946, FBI, 65-56402-497.

33. *The Mackenzie King Records*, p. 134.

34. See, for example, James Barros, "Alger Hiss and Harry Dexter White: The Canadian Connection," *Orbis*, vol. 21, no. 3, 1977. Barros had obviously not seen the archival material that shows that the Canadians were getting the reports on "Lady Corby" or the originals of King's diary.

35. WMK Diary, February 15, 1945.
36. Ibid. Pavlov recalls this meeting in his memoirs, *Operatsiia "sneg,"* pp. 84-85, but he places it wrongly in the summer of 1946, shortly before he was recalled back to Moscow.
37. WMK Diary, February 20, 1946.
38. As reported in the *Ottawa Citizen*, February 21, 1946.
39. *Pravda*, February 24, 1946; Tass statement as reported by the Canadian Chargés d'Affaires, Moscow, March 3, 1946, LAC, MG 26, J4, vol. 390, no. 274734-274-735 (microfilm no. H1552).
40. WMK Diary, February 22, 1946.
41. See Whitaker and Marcuse, *Cold War Canada*, p. 58.
42. *RC Report*, p. 650.
43. One of the suspects, Fred Poland, had reportedly seen Vitalii Pavlov on several occasions after the defection, but Pavlov was from the NKVD and Poland was accused of spying for the GRU. Given that Pavlov socialized with many people in Ottawa, these meetings could have been innocent, especially since Pavlov was aware of the changed circumstances since Gouzenko departed and was on his guard.
44. TNA, KV 2/1421, telegram 165, February 19, 1946.
45. www.rcespionage.com: "The Royal Commission on Espionage."
46. Lunan, *The Making of a Spy*, p. 11.
47. Harvison, *The Horsemen*, p. 157.
48. Lunan, *The Making of a Spy*, pp. 21-29; 162-167; Weisbord, *The Strangest Dream*, p. 148.
49. Lunan, *The Making of a Spy*, pp. 140-148; author's interview with Lunan, Hawkesbury, Ontario, August 2, 2003.
50. Ibid.
51. Harvison, *The Horsemen*, p. 161.
52. TNA, KV 2/1421, top secret telegram no. 163, February 18, 1946.
53. TNA, KV 2/1421, top secret telegram no. 180, February 20, 1946; no. 186, February 21, 1946. These telegrams, all unsigned, were probably from Peter Dwyer.
54. *RC Report*, p. 671.
55. As quoted in Weisbord, *The Strangest Dream*, p. 149.
56. LAC, RG 25, box 2620, N-1, memorandum from Hume Wrong, dated February 17, 1946.
57. June Callwood, *Emma: A True Story of Treason* (New York: Beaufort Books, 1984), pp. 85-118.
58. *RC Report*, pp. 495-504.
59. Ibid., Callwood, *Emma*, pp. 85-118.

60. TNA, KV 2/1422, telegram no. 201 via New York, February 23, 1946.
61. LAC, MG 30, C421, Vol. 19/15, J. King Gordon Papers, Report of a Fact-finding Committee, Ottawa Civil Liberties Association, 1946.
62. Callwood, *Emma*, pp. 163-194.

CHAPTER 5: COLD WAR JUSTICE

1. TNA, KV 2/1422, telegram 324, March 8, 1946.
2. TNA, KV 2/1426, telegram no. 140, February 14, 1946.
3. TNA, KV 2/1427.
4. LAC, RG 33/62, Transcripts of the hearings of the Royal Commission, February 14, 1946, pp. 146-147.
5. Ibid.
6. TNA, KV 2/1421, telegram no. 181, February 18, 1946.
7. TNA, KV 2/1421, telegram no. 161 of February 18, 1946; telegram 178 of February 20, 1946.
8. *RC Report*, pp. 651-655.
9. LAC, RG 25, series A-12, vol. 2081, file, AR 13/13, pt. 1. Letter from Robertson to Pearson, October 29, 1946.
10. Granatstein, *A Man of Influence*, p. 174-175.
11. LAC, RG 33/62, Transcripts of the hearings of the Royal Commission, February 26, 1946.
12. *RC Report*, p. 254.
13. *RC Report*, pp. 227-260.
14. *RC Report*, p. 217, glossed over this stage of "Ernst's" employment, claiming that no proper translation could be made because the paper had been torn. But in his testimony before the commission (which was kept secret), Gouzenko made it clear that the words were all there and that this translation was accurate. See transcript of Royal Commission testimonies, Gouzenko, p. 143.
15. LAC, MG 30, J.L. Cohen papers, file 3155, "The King vs. Eric George Adams," pp. 20-29.
16. M.H. Fyfe, "Some Aspects of the Report of the Royal Commission on Espionage," *The Canadian Bar Review*, vol. XXIV, 1946, p. 778.
17. Report of a Fact-Finding Committee, 1946, LAC, MG 26, J4, vol. 329, file 3495.
18. Lunan, *The Making of a Spy*, p. 176.
19. Harvison, *The Horseman*, p. 162; Lunan, *The Making of a Spy*, p. 182. Harvison does not come right out and say that he was advising the commission, but he acknowledges that he was in contact with them and even lunched with the commission's counsel Williams.

20. Letter dated February 28, 1946, NARA, 861.20242/2-2846 citing the *Ottawa Journal*.
21. WMK Diary, February 27, 1946; *Globe and Mail*, February 27, 1946.
22. Ibid.
23. TNA, KV 2/1422, telegram dated March 2, 1946.
24. *RC Report*, pp. 693-696.
25. LAC, MG 26, N1, vol. 13.
26. Ibid.
27. LAC, MG 26, N1, vol. 13.
28. WMK Diary, March 3, 1946.
29. WMK Diary, March 5, 1946.
30. Ibid.
31. Jenkins, *Churchill*, pp. 812-813.
32. TNA, KV 2/1421, dated February 19, 1946.
33. LAC, RG 25, vol. 2620, file N-1.
34. TNA, KV 2/1426, report dated February 25, 1946.
35. TNA, KV 2/1422, memorandum dated March 1, 1946.
36. TNA, KV 2/1422, telegram no. 260, March 2, 1946.
37. TNA, KV 2/1411, telegram no. 502, March 3, 1946.
38. TNA, KV 2/1422, telegram 280, March 2, 1946.
39. The *New York Times* March 5, 1946; Weisbord, *The Strangest Dream*, p. 153.
40. TNA, KV 2/1422, telegram no. 321, March 8, 1946.
41. As cited in Dominique Clement, "The Royal Commission on Espionage, 1946–8: A Case Study in the Mobilization of the Post-WWII Civil Liberties Movement in Canada," p. 8, January 1, 2003, at www.circ.jmellon.com/history/gouzenko.
42. The *Toronto Daily Star*, March 8, 1946.
43. On CASCW and the RCMP, see Whitaker and Marcuse, *Cold War Canada*, pp. 84-91.
44. *RC Report*, p. 406.
45. *RC Report*, pp. 377-409 (quotations, p. 378, 406); TNA, KV 2/1422, telegram no. 196, February 22, 1946; no. 324, March 8, 1946.
46. TNA, KV 2/1422, telegrams 229 of February 27 and 240 of February 28, 1946; *RC Report*, pp. 319-353.
47. *Toronto Daily Star*, March 16, 1946.
48. Callwood, *Emma*, p. 168.
49. TNA, KV 2/1421, telegram no. 164, Feb. 18, 1946; KV 2/1422, telegram 306, March 5, 1946; *RC Report*, p. 701.
50. *RC Report*, p. 292.

51. TNA, KV 2/1422, telegram 242, February 28, 1946.

52. TNA, KV 2/1422, telegram no. 335, March 9, 1946.

53. TNA, KV 2/1422, telegram no. 338, March 11, 1946; *RC Report*, p. 702.

54. LAC, John Diefenbaker Papers, 1940–1956 Series, vol. 82. Letter from Shugar to Diefenbaker, dated July 21, 1946.

55. Callwood, *Emma*, p. 212.

56. Telephone interview with Dr. Shugar, May 2005, and e-mail correspondence.

57. TNA, KV 2/1422, draft of telegram no. 555, March 13, 1946. The telegram was drafted by the director of public prosecutions and sent to Philby for his perusal.

58. TNA, KV 2/1422, telegram no. 444, March 28, 1946, for Hollis from Cussen.

59. NARA, Record Group 59, 861.20241/52241.

60. Ibid.

61. LAC, RG 25, box 2620, N-1 (temporary).

62. LAC, RG 24, file 6265-94/6265-25, reel C 11672.

63. *The Guardian* (London), January 27, 2003.

CHAPTER 6: ANTI-COMMUNIST AGENDAS

1. *Toronto Daily Star*, March 15, 1946.

2. Ibid.

3. Ibid.

4. LAC, AH 2003/00019 (CSIS Fred Rose files), parts 9 and 10.

5. LAC, RG 25, A-12, vol. 2081, File AR/13/13, pt. 1. Reports from the press analysis section, the Canadian Embassy.

6. Ibid.

7. Ibid; Gregg Herken, *Brotherhood of the Bomb: The Tangled Lives and Loyalties of Robert Oppenheimer, Ernest Lawrence and Edward Teller* (New York: Henry Holt, 2002), p. 159.

8. Jessica Wang, *American Science in an Age of Anxiety: Scientists, Anticommunism and the Cold War* (Chapel Hill: University of North Carolina Press, 1999), p. 21.

9. Wang, *American Science*, p. 44.

10. LAC, RG 25, A-12, vol. 2081, File AR 13/13, pt. 1. Reports from press analysis section, the Canadian Embassy, special report no. 29, supplement no. 15.

11. Clement, "The Royal Commission on Espionage," p. 9.

12. TNA, KV 2/1015, RCMP report dated December 27, 1928.

13. TNA, KV 2/1015, Letter to the RCMP dated August 1, 1930, from the ship's interpreter.

14. Venona Decrypt, telegram no. 1328, New York to Moscow, August 12, 1943.

15. Whitaker and Marcuse, *Cold War Canada*, p. 209.

16. FBI Silvermaster, 65-56402-8, office memorandum on informant "Gregory."

17. Ibid. Bentley embellished her story about Rose and the Canadians over the years. In 1951, she told HUAC that in 1939 she was already acting as a "post office box for Canadians, such as Fred Rose." HUAC Hearings. House of Representatives. Eighty-Second Congress, First Session, October 11, 1951.

18. FBI Silvermaster, 65-564402-8.

19. www.agentura.ru/dosie/gru/imperia/atomspy, p. 12; Vladimir Lot, "Kliuch ot Ada," *Sovershenno sekretno*, August 1999.

20. Lamphere, *FBI–KGB War*, p. 22.

21. The *New York Journal*, December 3–5, 1945.

22. TNA, KV 2/1425, telegram dated December 4, 1945.

23. TNA, KV 2/1015, telegram dated March 21, 1946.

24. Ibid.

25. As cited in Lunan, *Making of a Spy*, p. 191.

26. Sawatsky, *Gouzenko*, pp. 92-93.

27. As quoted in Lunan, *Making of a Spy*, 192.

28. Callwood, *Emma*, p. 202.

29. LAC, MG 30, series A94, vol. 45, Rose preliminary hearing.

30. Ibid.

31. TNA, KV 2/1422, telegram dated March 22, 1946.

32. Sawatsky, *Gouzenko*, p. 95 citing Merrily Weisbord.

33. TNA, KV 2/1422, telegram dated March 22, 1946.

34. FBI Gouzenko, 100-342972-30, memorandum dated March 25, 1946.

35. LAC, RG 25, a-12, vol. 2081, file AR/3/13, pt. 1. Report from the press analysis section, the Canadian Embassy, March 26–28, 1946.

36. TNA, KV 2/1422, telegram to MI6 dated March 22, 1946.

37. FBI Gouzenko, 100-342972-354; 100-342972-355; memorandums dated March 28, 1946.

38. Report from press analysis section, March 26-28.

39. FBI Gouzenko, 100-342972-30, memorandum from Ladd to Hoover, March 29, 1946.

40. Ibid., memorandum from Ladd to Hoover, April 1, 1946.

41. Copy of a letter from Wood to the U.S. Secretary of State, June 12, 1946, NARA, HUAC files, folder on Gouzenko.
42. *Winnipeg Tribune*, March 19, 1946.
43. WMK Diary, March 18, 1946.
44. King's speech to House of Commons, March 18, 1946. *Hansard*, March 1946, p. 56.
45. WMK Diary, March 19, 1946.
46. WMK Diary, March 23, 1946.
47. AVP RF (Foreign Affairs Archives of the Russian Federation), Fond 012, Opis 7, delo no. 286. As cited in Aggeeva, "Kanada i nachalo kholodnoi voiny," p. 32.
48. LAC, MG26, J4, vol. 390, micr. no. 1552, C272270; C274500.
49. Venona decrypt, telegram no. 76, Moscow to Canberra (and elsewhere), April 7, 1946. The telegram was signed "Petrov," which the Americans assumed was Beria, but Beria had relinquished his post as head of the NKVD three months earlier.
50. TNA, KV 2/1421, telegrams dated February 2 and 4, 1946; KV 2/1422, telegram dated March 25, 1946; KV 2/1423, telegram dated March 29, 1946.
51. Venona decrypt, telegram no. 76.
52. See Amy Knight, *Beria: Stalin's First Lieutenant* (Princeton: Princeton University Press, 1993), pp. 132-140; 176-229.
53. WMK Diary, March 21, 1946.
54. As cited in Callwood, *Emma*, p. 174.
55. As cited in Paul Dufour, "'Eggheads' and Espionage: The Gouzenko Affair in Canada," *Journal of Canadian Studies*, vol. 16, nos. 3-4, Fall-Winter, 1981, p. 193.
56. TNA, KV 2/1421, telegram no. 163, 164, February 18, 1946; telegram 178 of February 20, 1946.
57. Sawatsky Papers, 84-38, box 1, file 7, interview with Wes Harvison, December 27, 1983.
58. As cited in Whitaker and Marcuse, *Cold War Canada*, pp. 70-71.
59. CSIS Gouzenko, 004589-004609; *RC Report*, pp. 153-160.
60. TNA, KV 2/1422, telegram dated March 1, 1946.
61. Callwood, *Emma*, p. 206.
62. *RC Report*, pp. 138-140.
63. *RC Report*, p. 143; CSIS Gouzenko, 000496 (from Gouzenko documents given as evidence).
64. Lunan, *Making of a Spy*, p. 145.

65. "The Princeton Mathematics Community in the 1930s," Transcript no. 18 (PMC 18), The Trustees of Princeton University, 1985.

66. LAC RG 33/62, transcripts of the Royal Commission Hearings, March 22, 27, and 28, 1946; TNA, KV 2/1423, telegram dated March 29, 1946.

67. Dufour "'Eggheads' and Espionage," pp. 190–191. Given the assumption of guilt by association that became widespread after the spy scare began, it is not surprising that the accusations against Halperin tainted others. The FBI cast a net of suspicion over those who had signed the petition in support of Halperin, requesting, in 1950, a copy for the use of the American Loyalty Review Board, which investigated federal employees. After getting permission from the Liberal government, the RCMP duly complied, with the admonition that the document be used with discretion. See Whitaker and Marcuse, *Cold War Canada*, pp. 104-105.

68. *RC Report*, addendum dated June 18, 1947.

69. Wang, *American Science*, pp. 96-98.

70. Whitaker and Marcuse, *Cold War Canada*, pp. 103-106; www.nyas.org/about/newsDetails.asp?newsID=122&year=1999.

71. Clement, "The Royal Commission on Espionage," pp. 14-15.

CHAPTER 7: THE RIGHT WING UNLEASHED

1. TNA, KV 2/1423, report on the trial by a witness from Britain's Special Branch.

2. Harvison, *The Horsemen*, pp. 164-165. Harvison was in the courtroom. The transcript of the Rose trial is unavailable.

3. LAC, AH 2003/00019 (CSIS Fred Rose files), vol. 4161, box 25, letter dated July 9, 1946.

4. Weisbord, *The Strangest Dream*, pp. 164-169.

5. Lunan, *Making of a Spy*, p. 191.

6. LAC, MG 30, series A94, vol. 45, file 3156.

7. Sawatsky Papers, 84-38, box 2, interview with Vera Rosenbluth, April 17, 1984.

8. Judith A. Alexander, "Agatha Chapman (1907–1963)," www.yorku.ca/cwen/chapman.htm.

9. Sidney Shallet, "How the Russians Spied on Their Allies," The *Saturday Evening Post*, January 23, 1947.

10. TNA, KV 2/1423, unsigned memorandum, "Appendix I."

11. WMK Diary, July 12, 1946; LAC, MG 26, J4, vol. 390, Microfilm H-1552, C 274505.

12. Ibid.

13. Pavlov, *Operatsiia "sneg,"* pp. 84-85. Pavlov says he attended the July 1946 meeting with King, but he apparently confused this meeting with the one he and Belokhvostikov had with King in February 1946.

14. *Montreal Star*, July 23, 1946.

15. Pavlov, *Operatsiia "sneg,"* p. 86.

16. Ibid., p. 88.

17. Ibid., pp. 91-93. The chief of Foreign Intelligence, now part of the MGB, was Pavel Fitin.

18. *Pravda*, August 3, 1946. English translation in TNA, KV 2/1423.

19. Zubok and Pleshakov, *Inside the Kremlin's Cold War*, p. 40.

20. WMK Diary, August 14, 1946.

21. Newton, *The Cambridge Spies*, pp. 95-96; Bower, *The Perfect English Spy*, pp. 94-95.

22. NARA, U.S. Congress Joint Committee on Atomic Energy, S.3437. Fuchs Case, 882012-359-383; Bower, Ibid; Lamphere, *The KGB–FBI War*, pp. 133-136.

23. West, *Mortal Crimes*, p. 133.

24. *RC Report*, pp, 97-105.

25. "Atomnyi shpionazh," p. 15.

26. FBI Gouzenko, 100-342972-1664, memorandum to Hoover, January 26, 1949; 100-342972-1748, memorandum from Whitson, February 28, 1949.

27. FBI Gouzenko, 100-342972-1164, memorandum to the Director from Ladd, January 16, 1949; 1666, memorandum to Ladd, January 31, 1949; 1668, from the Attorney General to Hoover, January 28, 1949; 1733, memorandum to Ladd, March 1, 1949; 100-342972-1689.

28. Harry S. Truman Library, RG 118, Grand Jury Testimony in Alger Hiss case, February 1, 1949.

29. Ibid.

30. FBI Gouzenko, 100-342972-1808.

31. Royal Canadian Mounted Police, "Soviet Espionage in Canada," p. 43.

32. *RC Report*, pp. 481-493.

33. Ibid; Littleton, *Target Nation*, p. 21; Montreal *Gazette*, April 12, 1949.

34. Papers of Arthur Steinberg, American Philosophical Society, Philadelphia, PA, response to questionnaire of a loyalty review board, 1964.

35. *RC Report*, pp. 396-397.

36. Telephone interview with Dr. Steinberg, January 30, 2002; also see exhibit 182 of the Royal Commission investigation, a letter from Steinberg to "Nicholls," dated July 17, 1944, and apparently found by the RCMP in one of the offices at McGill. See LAC, RG 33/62, Microfilm no. 3425.

37. *RC Report*, p. 491.

38. Original transcript of commission hearings: RG 33/62, vol. 1, book 1, pp. 314-316; *RC Report*, pp. 491-492.

39. CSIS Fred Rose, AH 2003/00014, vol. 4162, box 123.

40. As reproduced by the Senate Internal Security Subcommittee, December 1, 1953, NARA, RG 46, Name file, Arthur Steinberg.

41. "Soviet Espionage in Canada," RCMP, November 1945, p. 44.

42. Papers of Arthur Steinberg.

43. *RC Report*, p. 493.

44. Papers of Arthur Steinberg, letter to Dr. S. Farber, December 1953. Unfortunately, Steinberg's FBI file is unavailable. The FBI messages on Steinberg cited here are from the Gouzenko file.

45. NARA, RG 46, Arthur Steinberg file; papers of Arthur Steinberg.

46. Papers of Arthur Steinberg, letter from Dave Rife, dated April 21, 1948.

47. Telephone interview with Dr. Steinberg, January 30, 2002.

48. NARA, RG 46, SISS name file, Arthur Steinberg.

49. HUAC Investigative Name Files, Arthur Steinberg, memo dated July 12, 1950, from Owens to Russell.

50. Ibid.

51. See Mike Marqusee, "Patriot Acts," *The Nation*, December 13, 2004; and a recent biography of McCarran: Michael J. Ybarra, *Washington Gone Crazy: Senator Pat McCarran and the Great American Communist Hunt* (Hanover, NH: Steerforth Press, 2004).

52. NARA, RG 46, Records of the U.S. Senate Internal Security Subcommittee, Arthur Steinberg name file; Transcript of the interview: NARA, RG 46, Records of the U.S. Senate Internal Security Subcommittee, vol. 32.

53. Steinberg Personal Papers, letter to Dr. Farber, December 11, 1953; U.S. National Archives, RG 46, Arthur Steinberg name file.

54. Steinberg Personal Papers, letter to Dr. Mayo; letter from Mayo to Steinberg; letter to Ephraim Martin.

55. Wang, *American Science in an Age of Anxiety*, pp. 280-281.

56. Steinberg Personal Papers, draft of letter, undated, to Mrs. Hobby.

57. Ibid., draft of letter, undated, but apparently sent in April 1954.

58. LAC, MG 26, N1, vol. 33, Gouzenko I, 1953-54, pt. 1, #D1-35A, Department of Justice, Transcript of the Proceedings of a meeting held on January 4, 1954.

59. Interview with Dr. Steinberg, January 30, 2002.

CHAPTER 8: THE SOUTH AGAINST THE NORTH

1. Whitaker and Marcuse, *Cold War Canada*, pp. 161-206; Sawatsky, *Men in the Shadows*, pp. 116-125.

2. Whitaker and Marcuse, *Cold War Canada*, p. 197.

3. David McCullough, *Truman*, pp. 552-553.

4. See Craig, *Treasonable Doubt*, pp. 68-79; Theoharis, *Chasing Spies*, pp. 114-120.

5. Ibid.

6. Craig, *Treasonable Doubt*, pp. 43-58.

7. See letters to the FBI Director from the New York office, dated May 14, 1942 and March 26, 1946 (available on the website www.algerhiss. com). The 1946 letter observes that Chambers "recalled that after 1937 he was of course no longer actively associated with the Communist Party . . . and had lost all contact with Alger Hiss and the only information that he has concerning him is that which has appeared in various newspapers."

8. FBI Hiss, 101-2668, sec. 02-52.

9. Belmont to Ladd, November 23, 1953, FBI Hiss, 100-342972-2022.

10. LAC, RG 2, vol. 54, file 1-40-3; MG 26, N-1, vol. 33, file Gouzenko, I 1953-54, pt. 2 #D 1-35a.

11. Royal Canadian Mounted Police Supplement "J." Corby case – Testimony Before United States Senate Subcommittee.

12. LAC, MG 26, N-1, vol. 33, file Gouzenko I, 1953-54, pt. 2 #D 1-35a.

13. *Toronto Daily Star*, October 27, 1953; Sawatsky, *Gouzenko*, pp. 124-129.

14. LAC, MG 26, N-1, vol. 33, file Gouzenko I, 1953-54, pt, 2 #D 1-35a. Pearson statement before the House of Commons, November 17, 1953; memorandum for Pearson, November 25, 1953. Also see Sawatsky, *Gouzenko*, pp. 125-126.

15. Ibid., memorandum for Pearson, November 28, 1953.

16. *Toronto Telegram*, November 22, 1953.

17. FBI Pearson, 65-60356-35.

18. FBI Pearson, 65-60356-25.

19. Sawatsky Papers, 84-38, box 1, file 8, interview with Robert Morris, February 22, 1984.

20. FBI Elizabeth Bentley, 134-435-69; Kessler, *Clever Girl*; and Olmstead, *Red Spy Queen*.

21. Transcript of Hearings before the Subcommittee to Investigate the Administration of the Internal Security Act and Other Internal Security Laws of the Committee on the Judiciary United States Senate, Washington, D.C., August 14, 1951, vol. 96, reproduced in James Barros, *No Sense of Evil: Espionage, the Case of Herbert Norman* (Toronto: Deneau, 1986), pp. 185-192.

22. FBI Pearson, 65-60356-14.

23. FBI Pearson, 65-60356-11; 65-60356-14.

24. FBI Pearson, 65-60356-35.

25. See a message from the Canadian ambassador to the United States, Heeney, to Pearson, dated November 17, 1953, LAC, MG 26, N1, vol. 33, Gouzenko, I, 1953-54, part 2, #D1-35A.

26. LAC, MG 26, N1, vol. 33, Gouzenko I 1953-54, part 1, #D1-35A, Press Conference-L.B. Pearson-November 21, 1953.

27. The information on Bentley's charges and the Grand Jury request is in the FBI's file on Sise: 100-364301-S. Letter from Sise to Pearson, September 13, 1948. LAC, MG 30, D187, vol. 7, file 27 (Hazen Sise). Sise by this time had left the public service.

28. LAC, MG 26, N-1, vol. 33, file Gouzenko I, 1953-54, pr. 2 #D 1-35a, message from Heeney to Pearson, dated November 19, 1953. In the meantime, the FBI and the U.S. Attorney General, as part of an attack on former president Truman for being soft on communism, dredged up the Harry Dexter White case and mentioned publicly Canada's alleged warning about White to the FBI. Much to the annoyance of J. Edgar Hoover, Pearson told the Canadian Parliament that no member of the Canadian government ever warned the FBI about White.

29. LAC, MG 26-N1, vol. 33, Gouzenko, I 1953-54, part 2 #D 1-35A.

30. *Times-Herald*, November 25, 1953.

31. *Counterattack: Facts to Combat Communism*, November 27, 1953, vol. 7, no. 48.

32. See Kessler, *Clever Girl*, pp. 276-78.

33. WMK Diary, July 16, 1946.

34. Sawatsky, *Gouzenko*, pp. 99-107; Archives of Ontario, F1322, MV7494, Joseph Sedgwick Fonds, Transcript of the Investigation for Discovery of Igor Gouzenko.

35. The Montreal *Gazette*, April 1, 1947.

36. TNA, KV 2/1419, Letter from Wood to Sillitoe, December 13, 1946.

37. Pat MacAdam, "The Cipher Clerk Who Knew Too Much," *Ottawa Citizen*, February 13, 2000.

38. LAC, MG 26L, vol. 99, file E-14-G, letters dated May 1 and May 7, 1951.

39. Transcript of the Investigation for Discovery of Igor Gouzenko, pp. 35-36.

40. Gouzenko's daughter Evelyn was unaware of what Krysac meant until after her mother died. Interview with Evelyn Wilson, Toronto, December 12, 2002.

41. LAC, RG 2, vol. 54, file 1-40-3, Letter from Wood to Ilsley, January 20, 1948, referring also to an earlier letter.

42. Ibid.

43. Ibid.

44. Sawatsky, *Gouzenko*, pp. 112-113.

45. Ibid., p. 118; interview with Evelyn Wilson, December 12, 2002.

46. Transcript of the Investigation for Discovery, p. 22.

47. The *Toronto Daily Star*, October 30, 1953; Sawatsky, *Gouzenko*, pp.121-123.

48. Transcript of Gouzenko testimony, January 1954, LAC, MG 26, N1, vol. 33, Gouzenko I, 1953-54, pt. 1, #D 1-35A, p. 10.

49. Ibid., p. 67.

50. Ibid., pp. 74-78.

51. Drew Pearson, *Diaries, 1949–59*, ed. by Tyler Abell (New York: Holt, Rinehart and Winston, 1974), p. 296.

52. Lyndon B. Johnson Library and Museum, Personal Papers of Drew Pearson, "Television Interviews from 1954," interview with Gouzenko.

53. The *Washington Post*, January 7, 1954; *Toronto Daily Star*, January 4, 1946; *New York Times*, January 6, 1954; April 14, 1954.

CHAPTER 9: "ELLI," PHILBY, AND THE DEATH OF A DIPLOMAT

1. Intelligence Department of the Red Army in Ottawa, p. 30

2. Peter Wright, *Spycatcher: The Candid Autobiography of a Senior Intelligence Officer* (New York: Viking, 1987), p. 345.

3. TNA, KV 2/1425, telegram to RCMP from Captain Liddell, September 23, 1945.

4. CSIS Gouzenko, transcript 000009, interview 2, October 29, 1945.

5. In fact, a message reprinted from Russian archival files shows that Philby reported to the NKVD in the mid-1940s that the local MI6 representative in the Soviet Union had a source in Moscow who was code-named

"Temny." See West, *The Crown Jewels*, p. 315. If it were not for the fact that Gouzenko's "Elli" was a GRU agent with a Russian background, this piece of information would point us straight to Philby as the Elli suspect.

6. Genrikh Borovik, author of *The Philby Files* mistakenly assumes that Gouzenko was referring to Philby but this is because Borovik thought Gouzenko mentioned an NKVD agent in British Intelligence, rather than someone from the GRU.

7. Transcript of 1954 Gouzenko interview, pp. 63-64. In the copy of the transcript the name of the organization to which the individual belonged is blackened out, but it is clear from the context that Gouzenko is talking about "Elli." In fact, Gouzenko said nothing to the Royal Commission beyond that there was an agent named Elli in Britain, but the commission probably had access to his statements made in earlier interviews. See LAC, RG 33/62, vol. 1, book 1, p. 230.

8. Transcript of 1954 interview, pp. 62-63.

9. Bower, *The Perfect English Spy*, pp. 296-329; Wright, *Spycatcher*, pp. 344-346.

10. Ibid., Wright claims that Gouzenko talked about a spy in MI5 from the very beginning, in 1945, but that was not the case.

11. Wright, Ibid.

12. Kristmanson, *Plateaus of Freedom*, pp. 123-124.

13. Bower, *The Perfect English Spy*, p. 354.

14. Lamphere, *The FBI–KGB War*, p. 244.

15. Sawatsky, *Gouzenko*, pp. 217-223.

16. "KGB Connections," CBC, June 8, 1981; Sawatsky, *Gouzenko*, pp. 217-223. Gouzenko apparently met Chapman Pincher, author of the explosive and largely discredited book *Too Secret Too Long* (1984) on more than one occasion. Pincher was a strong proponent of the theory that Hollis was a mole, and he probably had little trouble persuading Gouzenko to agree with him.

17. Lamphere, *The FBI–KGB War*, pp. 132-137.

18. Ibid., p. 238.

19. Borovik, *The Philby Files*, p. 266.

20. NARA, s. 3437, Fuchs Case, 882012-379.

21. Whitaker and Marcuse, *Cold War Canada*, pp. 413-414; also, p. 487, n 24.

22. For an illuminating and informative study of Norman's life and career, see Roger Bowen, *Innocence Is Not Enough:The Life and Death of Herbert Norman* (Vancouver/Toronto: Douglas & McIntyre, 1986). Also see Reg Whitaker, "Return to the Crucible," *The Canadian Forum*, November 1986, pp. 11-28.

23. See Bowen, *Innocence Is Not Enough*, pp. 55-65, for a discussion of Norman's time at Cambridge, based on interviews and a careful examination of all the sources. For a dissenting view, see Barros, *No Sense of Evil*, pp. 6-11. When questioned by the RCMP in 1952 as to whether he had ever been a member of the Communist Party, Norman replied "No, I considered myself very close to it for about a year, but I didn't accept any posts or responsibilities." CSIS Norman file.

24. Bowen, *Innocence Is Not Enough*, pp. 65-78.

25. See The *Washington Post*, April 19, 1957, for the full story on Walsh.

26. Bowen, *Innocence Is Not Enough*, pp. 80-81.

27. Ibid.; Schrecker, *Many Are the Crimes*, pp. 244-245.

28. Bowen, *Innocence Is Not Enough*, pp. 172-200.

29. CSIS Norman, RCMP report, dated October 17, 1950.

30. Bowen, *Innocence Is Not Enough*, pp. 148-168.

31. See FBI reports, dated October 16, 1946, and March 11, 1947, from Boston. In FBI Norman.

32. See Bowen, *Innocence Is Not Enough*, pp. 206-208.

33. Ibid., p. 208.

34. CSIS Norman, undated secret RCMP report: "The Norman Case: Some Factors and Considerations."

35. CSIS Norman.

36. LAC, RG 33/62, vol. 2, book 10, p. 5063, April 26, 1946. When mentioning this episode in an earlier testimony before the Royal Commission (February 16, 1945), Gouzenko had been less specific, but he nonetheless made it clear that he thought that the Norman in question was Norman Freed. Interestingly, only the February testimony has been cited by historians, who apparently have not realized that Gouzenko had more to say about "Norman" when he appeared before the Royal Commission again in April.

37. CSIS Norman, "E.H. Norman: Summary of the Case," top secret, 23 pages, undated; interview with Lt.-Gen. Vitalii Pavlov, Moscow, Sept. 29, 2001.

38. Secret memorandum, dated October 24, 1950, CSIS Norman.

39. The report is in CSIS Norman.

40. FBI Norman, 100-346993-24.

41. See FBI Norman, memorandum from Boardman to Belmont, April 12, 1957; memorandum, Belmont to Roach, April 16, 1957; memorandum to the Attorney General, to the Director, April 26, 1957.

42. Ybarra, *Washington Gone Crazy*, p. 547. Also see Theoharis, *Chasing Spies*, pp. 210-223. The Norman case illustrated this point. On

August 7, 1951, someone from the McCarran Committee called the FBI with a request for background information on Norman. FBI Norman, memorandum from Laughlin to Ladd, August 7, 1951.

43. In a March 12, 1957, SISS hearing, for example, SISS counsel Robert Morris stressed that Wittfogel was "a distinguished professor" and referred to his academic career as if to say that his scholarship enhanced his credibility as a witness. No such reverence for scholarly accomplishments was shown toward Norman.

44. FBI Norman, file, memorandum from Laughlin to Ladd, August 23, 1951. Laughlin reports that "no information was found in Bureau files indicating that Norman had ever attended Columbia University."

45. FBI Norman, 100-346993.

46. CSIS Norman, "Egerton Herbert Norman: Brief of Information and Investigation," undated; "E.H. Norman: Summary of Case."

47. CSIS Norman, "Summary of the Case," undated.

48. "The Suez Crisis," *Canada World View*, issue 6, Winter 1999, www.dfait-maeci.gc.ca/CanadaMagazine; Bowen, *Innocence Is Not Enough*, pp. 273-289.

49. Bowen, *Innocence Is Not Enough*, p. 289.

50. Ibid., p. 174; 387, note 3.

51. Barros, *No Sense of Evil*, pp. 108-110.

52. FBI Norman, mimeographed copy of Emmerson testimony before SISS, March 21, 1957.

53. FBI Norman, memorandum from Roach to Belmont, April 11, 1957.

54. Bowen, *No Sense of Evil*, pp. 318-319.

55. FBI Norman, 346993-98; 346993-107; *Ottawa Citizen*, April 11, 1957; Bowen, *Innocence Is Not Enough*, pp. 324-327.

56. Ibid., RG 46, E.H. Norman file, Box 235.

57. FBI Norman, 100-346993.

58. NARA, RG 46, Country Files-Canada, Canada 1951–1967. Note dated April 18, 1957.

59. FBI Norman, memorandum from Legat, Ottawa to Director, April 12, 1957.

60. Pearson's comments are in the CSIS Norman file.

61. *Globe and Mail*, April 20, 1957.

62. Montreal *Gazette*, April 15, 1957.

63. NARA, RG 46, E.H. Norman file, Box 235.

64. As cited in Ybarra, *Washington Gone Crazy*, p. 656.

65. RCMP files, Kilgour to Leger, April 10, 1957, as cited in Bowen, *Innocence Is Not Enough*, p. 305.

CHAPTER 10: TRAITORS AND SPIES

1. Sawatsky Papers, 84-38, box 1, file 7, interview with Lloyd Tararyn, April 19, 1984.
2. CBC Archives (www.cbc.ca), program dated March 11, 1966.
3. As one observer of the Canadian legal scene expressed it: "Stringent libel laws may have made sense five hundred years ago, when British royalty wanted to stop the nobility from duelling by giving them a legal remedy against character slurs. But we don't live in the time of Henry VII any longer." Jeffrey Shallit, "It's Time to Reform Canadian Libel Law," http://www.cs.uwaterloo.ca/~shallit/libel3.html.
4. Archives of Ontario, Joseph Sedgwick Fonds, Transcript of Investigation for Discovery, Frazer, p. 45.
5. Sawatsky Papers, 84-38, box 2, interviews with Lloyd Tataryn and Frank Rasky.
6. Ibid., interview with Tataryn; Sawatsky, *Gouzenko*, pp. 245-251. The apology appeared on April 26, 1982.
7. Sawatsky Papers, interview with June Callwood, February 26, 1984.
8. The *Toronto Star*, April 11, 1982.
9. On the Sawatsky libel case, see the observations of Gouzenko's attorney: John D. Holding, Q.C., "Reflections on Igor Gouzenko," *The Advocates Society Journal*, October 1985, p. 7.
10. The oral history, cited earlier, is Sawatsky's *Gouzenko: The Untold Story*. Sawatsky donated the complete set of interviews, used here, to the University of Regina Archives.
11. The *Toronto Daily Star*, June 25, 1954.
12. The *New York Times*, July 18, 1954.
13. George Broadway, "My Interview With Igor Gouzenko," LAC, MG 26, N1, vol. 33, Gouzenko I, 1953–54, part 1, D1-35A.
14. The *New York Times*, July 18, 1954.
15. Igor Gouzenko, "The Writers in My Life and Work," The *New York Times*, December 12, 1954.
16. Broadway, "My Interview with Igor Gouzenko."
17. The *New York Times*, July 18, 1954.
18. Ibid.
19. Sawatsky Papers, 84-38, box 1, file 4, interview with Anna Gouzenko, March 17, 1984.
20. Ibid., interview with Anna Gouzenko, March 16, 1984.
21. Ibid., interview with Anna Gouzenko, March 17, 1984.
22. Sawatsky Papers, 84-38, box 1, file 6, interview with Don Fast, November 4, 1983.

23. Ibid.
24. Sawatsky Papers, 84-38, box 1, file 5, interview with Peggy Blackstock, February 22, 1984.
25. Sawatsky Papers, 84-38, box 1, file 8, interview with Osler, February 11, 1984.
26. Sawatsky, *Gouzenko*, pp. 186-187.
27. Sawatsky Papers, 84-38, box 1, file 8, interview with Del Maulsby.
28. Sawatsky Papers, 84-38, box 1, file 8, interview with George Burnett, January 11, 1984.
29. Author's interview with Evelyn Wilson, Toronto, December 12, 2002.
30. The *Globe and Mail*, September 14, 2002, p. F3.
31. John D. Holding, Q.C., "Reflections on Igor Gouzenko," *The Advocates Society Journal*, October 1985, p. 7.
32. The *Globe and Mail*, September 14, 2002; author's interview with Evelyn Wilson, Toronto, December 12, 2002. The city of Ottawa erected a plaque honoring Gouzenko in June 2003 and the government of Canada in April 2004.
33. Sawatsky Papers, 84-38, box 2, interview with John Picton, January 9, 1984.
34. Sawatsky, *Gouzenko*, pp. 124-137.
35. Sawatsky Papers, 84-38, box 1, file 6, interview with Robert Glasgow, February 16, 1984.
36. Sawatsky Papers, 84-38, box 1, file 8, interview with Gary Marcuse, December 5, 1983.
37. "Recent Interview of J.K. Thomas, Editor of the New World Illustrated, with Igor Gouzenko," April 1947, NARA, RG 59, 861.20242/4-1447.
38. Sawatsky Papers, 85-26, box 2, interview with Igor Gouzenko by James Dubro, April 4, 1981.
39. Sawatsky Papers, 84-38, box 1, file 8, interview with Bill McMurty, October 20, 1983.
40. Author's telephone interview with Dan Mulvenna, February 4, 2005.
41. The *New York Times*, October 7, 1957.
42. Sawatsky Papers, box 2, interview with Peter Worthington, October 19, 1983.
43. Similar to Gouzenko was Anatolii Golitsyn, who defected to the United States in 1961. According to one source: "His paranoia that the KGB had penetrated every nook and cranny of the Western intelligence edifice was so intense that he suspected any CIA or MI6 official who

spoke his own language to be working for his own service." Brooks-Shepard, *The Stormbirds*, p. 204.

44. The *Toronto Daily Star*, June 7, 1968.

45. Sawatsky Papers, box 2, interview with Val Sears, February 22, 1984.

46. Ibid.

47. The *Toronto Star*, April 11, 1982.

48. Interview with Daniel Stoffman, March 6, 1984, Sawatsky Papers, 84-38, box 2.

49. Sawatsky Papers, interview with Frank Rasky, October 15, 1983.

50. Sawatsky Papers, interview with Bill McMurty.

51. Sawatsky, *Gouzenko*, pp. 254-266.

52. Anna affirmed this, noting that the news of his defection was in all the newspapers and was the talk of the Soviet Embassy: "his example was one of the decisive points for us, that it's possible to do." Sawatsky Papers, 84-38, box 1, file 4, interview with Anna Gouzenko, March 12, 1984.

53. Kravchenko, *I Chose Freedom*, p. 474.

54. Gary Kern, "First Son of Kravchenko," Johnson's Russia List (www.cdi.org/Russia.Johnson), August 13, 2001.

55. Evelyn Gouzenko, speaking at the National Library of Canada, April 16, 2004.

56. For detailed accounts of the history of both the GRU and the KGB, see the Russian website: www.agentura.ru. Also see Amy Knight, *The KGB: Police and Politics in the Soviet Union* (Boston: Allen & Unwin, 1988).

57. The dramatic defection in 1954 of Soviet Foreign Intelligence officers Vladimir and Evgenia Petrov in Australia contributed further to the crisis atmosphere.

58. Pavlov, *Operatsiia "sneg,"* pp. 96-97. Also see A.I. Kolpakidi and D.L. Prokhorov, *Imperiia GRU: Ocherki istorii Rossiiskoi voennoi razvedki* (Moscow, "OLMA," 1999).

59. As cited in Knight, *The KGB: Police and Politics in the Soviet Union*, p. 283.

60. Nigel West, "Treason Still Shadows J.R. Oppenheimer," *Insight Magazine*, October 9, 2002, www.insightmag.com/news.

CONCLUSION: THE NAMING OF NAMES

1. Bower, *A Perfect English Spy*, p. 370.

2. Andrew Boyle, *The Climate of Treason: Five Who Spied for Russia* (London: Hutchinson, 1979), p. 218. As cited in Kerns, *A Death in Washington*, p. 267.

3. Philby, *My Silent War*, p. 174.

4. Reg Whitaker, "Return to the Crucible," p. 16.

5. Sawatsky Papers, 84-38, box 1, file 7, interview with Jim Littleton, April 4, 1984.

6. "McCarthyism at Harvard," *The New York Review of Books*, February 10, 2005, pp. 42-43, letter to the editor from Robert N. Bellah.

7. Venona No. 1822, March 30, 1945. Another supposedly major source of new evidence against Alger Hiss that appeared in the 1990s was *The Haunted Wood* by Allen Weinstein and Alexander Vassiliev. The authors reproduce parts of messages that were sent back and forth between the United States and Moscow by the Russian Foreign Intelligence agency in the prewar and war period. In certain messages Hiss is supposedly discussed in a way that incriminates him. But Hiss's name appears in brackets. According to a Russian press officer who was involved with the book deal: "if you want to be correct, don't rely much on *The Haunted Wood*. . . . When they put this or that name in Venona documents in square brackets, it's the mere guess of the co-authors. Whether they are right or not, we do not comment. And it concerns all the cases of square brackets in this book. . . . Mr. Vassiliev worked in our press service just here in Moscow, but, if he's honest, he will surely tell you that he never met the name of Alger Hiss in the context of some cooperation with some special services of the Soviet Union." As cited in John Lowenthal, "Venona and Alger Hiss," *Intelligence and National Security*, vol. 15, no. 3, autumn 2000, p. 116.

8. FBI memorandum from Belmont to Boardman, February 1, 1956, as cited in Lowenthal, "Venona and Alger Hiss," p. 112. Also see a memorandum from Ladd to Belmont, May 15, 1950, FBI Venona file, which discusses the difficulties of identifying the persons behind the code names. John Lowenthal in "Venona and Alger Hiss" does a good job of casting doubt on the theory that "Ales" was Alger Hiss. For an opposing view, and there are many, see Eduard Mark, "Who Was 'Venona's Ales'?" *Intelligence and National Security*, vol. 18, no. 3, autumn 2003, pp. 45-72.

9. In fact, the Venona messages that have been released include one cable with an open reference to Hiss, a cable sent by the head of GRU operations in North America, Pavel Mikhailov ("Molière"): Venona no. 1579, September 28, 1943. Mikhailov, it will be recalled, was dispatched hastily back to Moscow after the Gouzenko defection. In this cable Mikhailov refers in passing to someone "from the State

Department by the name of Hiss." It appears from the reference that Hiss was unknown to Mikhailov and was not a GRU spy because otherwise he would have had a cover name. This message has been conveniently ignored, or explained as a fluke, by the historians who have decided that Hiss is guilty.

10. The name Ferris, for example, was transliterated from Russian as Ferns, resulting in the mistaken identity of an unfortunate Canadian civil servant named Henry Ferns as a possible spy, while the reference was to a scientist named Ferris. See Whitaker and Marcuse, *Cold War Canada*, pp. 107-109.

11. See, for example, Thomas Powers, "The Plot Thickens," *The New York Review of Books*, May 11, 2000. Powers opines that the Venona documents and those from the Russian archives have "illuminated and sometimes even definitively settled many old controversies about the guilt or innocence of people accused during the 1950s of having spied for the Soviet Union."

12. Interview with Dan Mulvenna, February 4, 2005.

13. This is convincingly demonstrated in Craig, *Treasonable Doubt*.

14. Sheila Kerr, "Investigating Soviet Espionage and Subversion: The Case of Donald Maclean," *Intelligence and National Security*, vol. 17, no. 1, spring 2002, p. 112.

ACKNOWLEDGMENTS

Above all, I owe thanks to my husband, Malcolm, both for inspiring me to write this book and for reading and commenting on the draft manuscript. Without his wisdom, insight, and encouragement this book might not have been written. I am also grateful to Reg Whitaker and Bruce Craig for reviewing the manuscript and offering valuable criticism, and to my daughter Molly for her excellent suggestions and support.

My editor at McClelland & Stewart, Alex Schultz, has been wonderful to work with and deserves much of the credit for this book. He gave me indispensable advice and edited my manuscript with a thoroughness and precision that is an author's dream. Thanks also to Jenny Bradshaw for her superb copyediting.

I also am indebted to my research assistant, Andrew Cameron, who worked long hours in Library and Archives Canada on my behalf and was there for me when I needed to track down documents from across the ocean.

I appreciate the help and encouragement from colleagues in my field: Wesley Wark at the University of Toronto; Martin Rudner and Larry Black at Carleton University; Christopher Andrew at Cambridge University; Mark Kramer at Harvard University; and John Fox, historian at the FBI. I also want to thank Dan Mulvenna, Roger Bowen, Kurt Jensen, John Sawatsky, Svetlana Chervonnaya, Irina Aggeeva, Gordon Lunan, Arthur Menzies, Paul Broda, Evy Wilson, Tony Hiss, Jeff Kisseloff, and Dan Bjarnason for their help.

This book would not have been possible without the assistance and expertise of the staff at archives and libraries: Normand Sirois,

Nicole Jalbert, and Roger Chartrand at the Canadian Security and Intelligence Service; Sophie Teller, Boniface Kadore, Dave Smith, Sarah Gawman, Jean Matheson, and many others at Library and Archives Canada; Edward Schamel and Jessica Kratz at the Center for Legislative Archives in Washington, D.C.; Michael Hussy and John Taylor at the National Archives and Records Administration in Maryland; Paul McIlroy at the Archives of Ontario; Mona Davis, Charlotte Bell, Carol Kelley, and Laura Corbman at the FBI; Megan Sheils at the Ralph J. Bunch Library, U.S. Department of State; Margaret Harman at the Lyndon B. Johnson Library; Dennis Bilger at the Harry S. Truman Library; Rob Cox and Charles Greifenstein at the American Philosophical Society; George Brandak at the University of British Columbia Library, Rare Books and Special Collections; Mark Vajcner and Elizabeth Seitz at the University of Regina Archives; and Howard Davies and Hugh Alexander at the National Archives in Britain.

INDEX